THEORETICAL BOUNDARIES OF ARMED CONFLICT AND HUMAN RIGHTS

In the last two decades, human rights law has played an expanding role in the legal regulation of wartime conduct. In the process, human rights law and international humanitarian law have developed a complicated sibling relationship. For some, this relationship is viewed as a mutually reinforcing effort between like-minded regimes designed to civilize human behavior. For others, the relationship is a more complicated sibling rivalry. In this book, an unparalleled collection of legal theorists examine the relationship between these two bodies of law. Each chapter skilfully maps the possibilities of harmonization while, at the same time, raising cautionary flags about the limits of that project. The authors not only chart the existing state of the law, but also debate the normative implications of the continuing influence of human rights norms on current practices including torture, targeted killings, the conduct of non-international armed conflicts, and post-war state building.

Jens David Ohlin is Professor of Law and Associate Dean for Academic Affairs at Cornell Law School. He specializes in international law and all aspects of criminal law, including domestic, comparative, and international criminal law.

The purpose of the ASIL Studies in International Legal Theory series is to clarify and improve the theoretical foundations of international law. Too often the progressive development and implementation of international law has foundered on confusion about first principles. This series raises the level of public and scholarly discussion about the structure and purposes of the world legal order and how best to achieve global justice through law.

This series grows out of the International Legal Theory project of the American Society of International Law. The ASIL Studies in International Legal Theory series deepens this conversation by publishing scholarly monographs and edited volumes of essays considering subjects in international legal theory.

Volumes in the Series:

International Criminal Law and Philosophy
edited by Larry May and Zachary Hoskins

Customary International Law: A New Theory with Practical Applications
by Brian D. Lepard

The New Global Law by Rafael Domingo

The Role of Ethics in International Law
edited by Donald Earl Childress III

Global Justice and International Economic Law: Opportunities and Prospects
edited by Chios Carmody, Frank J. Garcia, and John Linarelli

Parochialism, Cosmopolitanism, and the Foundations of International Law
edited by Mortimer Sellers

Morality, Jus Post Bellum, and International Law
edited by Larry May and Andrew T. Forcehimes

The Future of International Law: Global Governance
by Joel P. Trachtman

Normative Pluralism and International Law: Exploring Global Governance
by Jan Klabbers and Touko Piiparinen

Jus Post Bellum and Transitional Justice
by Larry May and Elizabeth Edenberg

Negotiating State and Non-State Law: The Challenge of Global and Local Legal Pluralism
edited by Michael A. Helfand

The Theory of Self-Determination
edited by Fernando R. Tesón

Theoretical Boundaries of Armed Conflict and Human Rights

Edited by

JENS DAVID OHLIN

CAMBRIDGE
UNIVERSITY PRESS

CAMBRIDGE
UNIVERSITY PRESS

One Liberty Plaza, 20th Floor, New York NY 10006, USA

Cambridge University Press is part of the University of Cambridge.

It furthers the University's mission by disseminating knowledge in the pursuit of education, learning, and research at the highest international levels of excellence.

www.cambridge.org
Information on this title: www.cambridge.org/9781107137936

First published 2016

A catalog record for this publication is available from the British Library.

Library of Congress Cataloging in Publication Data
Names: Ohlin, Jens David, editor.
Title: Theoretical boundaries of armed conflict and human rights / edited by Jens David Ohlin.
Description: New York : Cambridge University Press, 2016. | Series: Asil studies in international legal theory | Includes bibliographical references and index.
Identifiers: LCCN 2015042016 | ISBN 9781107137936 (Hardback)
Subjects: LCSH: War (International law) | Human rights. | BISAC: POLITICAL SCIENCE / Political Freedom & Security / Human Rights.
Classification: LCC KZ6355 .T44 2016 | DDC 341.4/8–dc23 LC record available at http://lccn.loc.gov/2015042016

ISBN 978-1-107-13793-6 Hardback

For my family

-JDO

Contents

Contributors

John C. Dehn is Assistant Professor at Loyola University Chicago School of Law where he is Co-Director of the National Security and Civil Rights Program. Professor Dehn served over fifteen years as an Army judge advocate in positions ranging from detainee abuse prosecutor to faculty member at West Point where he taught courses in international, constitutional and military law, coordinated international law training for all academy programs, and coached the Jean-Pictet International Humanitarian Law Competition team.

Janina Dill is an Assistant Professor in Normative International Theory at the Department of International Relations at the London School of Economics and Political Science and a Research Fellow of the Oxford Institute for Ethics, Law and Armed Conflict (ELAC) at the University of Oxford. Her first monograph, Legitimate Targets? Social Construction, International Law and US Bombing, was published by Cambridge University Press in October 2014.

Adil Ahmad Haque is Professor of Law and Judge Jon O. Newman Scholar at Rutgers Law School. His scholarship focuses on the law of armed conflict, international criminal law, and criminal law theory. He is currently writing a book on the moral foundations of the law of armed conflict for Oxford University Press.

Kevin Jon Heller is Professor of Criminal Law, SOAS, University of London. He is the author of *The Nuremberg Military Tribunals and the Origins of International Criminal Law* (OUP, 2011) and the co-editor (with Gerry Simpson) of *The Hidden Histories of War Crimes Trials* (OUP, 2013).

Jonathan Horowitz is a Legal Officer at the Open Society Justice Initiative, where he focuses on issues relating to human rights, national security and counterterrorism, and international humanitarian law. Prior, Mr. Horowitz worked at the U.S. Embassy in Kabul, Afghanistan, on detainee affairs; documented and reported on detainee and "night-raid" abuses in Afghanistan; and was an investigator for habeas lawyers representing Guantanamo Bay detainees.

David Luban is University Professor and Professor of Law and Philosophy at Georgetown University, as well as Class of 1984 Distinguished Chair in Ethics at the Stockdale Center for Ethical Leadership, U.S. Naval Academy. His more than 150 articles cover international criminal law, moral and legal philosophy, professional ethics, law and literature, just war theory, and the U.S. "war on terrorism."

Marko Milanovic is Associate Professor at the University of Nottingham School of Law. He is Vice-President, European Society of International Law, an Associate of the Belgrade Centre for Human Rights, and Co-Editor of EJIL: Talk, as well as a member of the EJIL's Editorial Board.

Naz K. Modirzadeh is Director of the Harvard Law School Program on International Law and Armed Conflict. Modirzadeh teaches, writes about, and engages in academic and policy initiatives concerning international law related to armed conflict.

Jens David Ohlin is Professor of Law at Cornell Law School. His published books include *The Assault on International Law* (2015); *Defending Humanity: When Force is Justified and Why*, with G.P. Fletcher (2008); *Targeted Killings: Law and Morality in an Asymmetrical World*, edited with C. Finkelstein & A. Altman (2012); and *Cyberwar: Law & Ethics for Virtual Conflicts*, edited with C. Finkelstein & K. Govern (2015).

Brian Orend is the Director of International Studies, and a Professor of Philosophy, at the University of Waterloo in Canada. He has taught at Columbia, Waterloo, and the University of Lund in Sweden (where he was recently Distinguished Visiting Professor of Human Rights). His research concentrates on three areas: the ethics of war and peace (especially post-war reconstruction); human rights; and happiness.

Acknowledgments

This book began with a conference in Washington, D.C. on November 8, 2013, co-sponsored by the Legal Theory Interest Group of the American Society of International Law (ASIL) and the Berger Program International Fund of Cornell Law School. Several staff members at ASIL worked diligently to ensure the conference's success.

Associate Dean Laura Spitz and Prof. Jack Barcelo, both of Cornell Law School, were instrumental in securing the necessary funding for the conference.

Prof. Mortimer Sellers of the University of Baltimore School of Law offered his time and expertise in guiding the assembled papers toward ultimate publication in this volume. The papers from the conference workshops were revised and then supplemented by additional chapters from leading scholars in the field.

Chapter 6 is an abridged version of Naz K. Modirzadeh, *Folk International Law: 9/11 Lawyering and the Transformation of the Law of Armed Conflict to Human Rights Policy and Human Rights Law to War Governance*, 5 HARV. NAT. SEC. J. 225–304 (2014) and is published with the permission of the journal.

Introduction

The Inescapable Collision

JENS DAVID OHLIN

1 Introduction

The interplay between International Human Rights Law (IHRL) and International Humanitarian Law (IHL) is complex, contested, and evolving. While IHRL constrains government conduct, IHL both regulates and licenses government conduct during an armed conflict. While IHRL has expanded rapidly in codification and application since the end of World War II, IHL has a far older history in the laws and customs of warfare and, before that, ancient traditions of chivalry and honor in battle.[1] The origins of these two fields of law could not be more difficult and they intersect – indeed collide – at the commencement of armed conflict. One would think that understanding their exact interplay and developing a decision procedure for resolving conflicting norms would be a top priority for public international law, and one that should have been completed generations ago. Why was the ambiguity and uncertainty allowed to fester for so long?

For many years the issue was unaddressed because human rights had not achieved enough salience for anyone to consider that they would apply in wartime. Now that human rights – both in discourse and practice – are more fully entrenched, the question remains as to why their interplay with IHL has not yet been resolved. The answer is that two legal doctrines constrain the application of IHRL, thus substantially limiting the instances when IHL and IHRL might collide. First, states

[1] For historical accounts of the laws of war, see John Fabian Witt, Lincoln's Code: The Laws of War in American History (2013); Stephen C. Neff, War and the Law of Nations: A General History (2005); Alexander Gillespie, A History of the Laws of War: The Customs and Laws of War with Regards to Civilians in Times of Conflict (2011).

can derogate from some of their human rights obligations during cases of armed conflict, though *jus cogens* rights are, by definition, non-derogable.[2] Second, some states, most notably the United States, do not recognize the extraterritorial application of the International Covenant on Civil and Political Rights (ICCPR).[3] Both of these doctrines may limit the frequency and severity of the conflict between IHRL and IHL. If the underlying human rights can be derogated from during armed conflict, then the conflict – and the need to create a decision procedure to resolve it – disappears. Similarly, if the ICCPR does not apply extraterritorially, then there will be no conflict between IHL and IHRL during extraterritorial military actions (with the exception of *jus cogens* obligations). IHRL will largely vanish from the scene, leaving only IHL to regulate government behavior.

In the current climate, however, both of these strategies for limiting the application of IHRL are increasingly implausible. As Marko Milanovic explains, states rarely use explicit derogations for their extraterritorial conduct, though for Milanovic it might be preferable if they did.[4] From the perspective of the human rights lawyer, it might constitute a net improvement on the situation if states conceded that the ICCPR (or ECHR) applied extra territorially, but then announced their intention to derogate from it.[5] This would give the state what it wants – some relief from international legal scrutiny in the immediate situation – but, in the long run, advance the interests of IHRL in the broadest possible sense. It would, in other words, support the universal scope of the ICCPR and IHRL in general. Human rights activists and supporters of a broadly construed ICCPR ironically might have reason to support the use of state

[2] For a discussion of derogation, see Marko Milanovic, *Extraterritorial Derogations from Human Rights Treaties in Armed Conflict*, *in* Collected Courses of the Academy of European Law (Nehal Bhuta ed., forthcoming).

[3] For a discussion, see Michael Dennis, *Application of Human Rights Treaties Extraterritorially During Times of Armed Conflict and Military Occupation*, 100 Am. Soc'y Int'l L. Proc. 86, 88 (2006).

[4] *See* Milanovic, *supra* note 2, at 2 ("And the wider the geographical scope of human rights treaties, the more relevant the question of extraterritorial derogations becomes. Such derogations might start looking increasingly appealing to states, especially those who have initially miscalculated in arguing that the treaties do not apply at all, and avoided derogating in the fear that doing so would count as an admission that the treaties do apply. Derogations have the potential of bringing both clarity and flexibility to the applicable legal framework, especially in situations of armed conflict and with regard to possible interactions between human rights and international humanitarian law (IHL).").

[5] *Id.*

derogations – a surprising result but one whose logic is unassailable.[6] This would be analogous to states joining the Rome Statute but then exempting themselves from the court's jurisdiction over the crime of aggression – a carrot designed to encourage states to joint the Rome Statute.[7] In the short run, such moves increase state impunity but in the long run they contribute, in a circular way, to the anti-impunity project to which the ICC is a central player. So too derogations, packaged within a claim regarding the extraterritorial application of the ICCPR, might advance the long-term agenda of human rights lawyers.

As to the second legal mechanism – the U.S. argument that the ICCPR does not apply extra territorially – the winds may be shifting on that front. Although the issue is a complex question of treaty interpretation, the United States has long held the view that the ICCPR only constrains governmental conduct over individuals within their jurisdiction and territory. However, that position has been the focus not just of international controversy but also internal controversy within the U.S. government. During his tenure at the State Department, Legal Advisor Harold Koh signed a memorandum recommending that the U.S. government change its longstanding interpretation of the ICCPR, an interpretation that he viewed as unsupportable given the text, negotiating history, and policy behind the treaty.[8] Consequently, it is unclear how long the current U.S. position will hold. At the very least, it is a wavering position, subject to differing interpretations among the individuals and agencies within the U.S. government. The weight of scholarly authority is also on the side of extraterritorial application, though the issue is by no means settled.[9]

[6] *Id.*

[7] *See, e.g.*, ICC Statute, art. 15bis(4) ("The Court may, in accordance with article 12, exercise jurisdiction over a crime of aggression, arising from an act of aggression committed by a State Party, unless that State Party has previously declared that it does not accept such jurisdiction by lodging a declaration with the Registrar. The withdrawal of such a declaration may be effected at any time and shall be considered by the State Party within three years.").

[8] *See* Harold Hongju Koh, Legal Advisor, U.S. Department of State, *Memorandum Opinion on the Geographic Scope of the International Covenant on Civil and Political Rights* (Oct. 19, 2010) [hereinafter Koh Memo].

[9] *See, e.g.*, Marko Milanovic, Extraterritorial Application of Human Rights Treaties (2011). *See also* Aldo S. Zilli, Note, *Approaching the Extraterritoriality Debate: The Human Rights Committee, the U.S. and the ICCPR*, 9 Santa Clara J. Int'l L. 399 (2011); K. da Costa, The Extraterritorial Application of Selected Human Rights Treaties (2012).

The point here is that the two biggest avenues for avoiding a collision between IHL and IHRL – derogations and a strictly territorial reading of the ICCPR – are increasingly nonviable avenues for states to avoid human rights obligations during armed conflicts.[10] These doctrines are safety valves keeping IHL and IHRL apart, relieving pressure that might otherwise cause a legal explosion. With these valves no longer in operation, the day will soon come when public international law will be forced to adopt a clear understanding of how IHL and IHRL interact with each other – a situation that has been deferred for too long.

This book is an intervention in this debate – an attempt to grapple with this inescapable collision and conceptualize the relationship between the two bodies of law. Of course, this is a big topic and one that cannot be exhausted in a single monograph or edited volume.[11] However, the enclosed chapters both define the outer contours of the debate and also fill in the structure of new and unconventional arguments, testing out potential decision procedures to resolve the conflict or new ways of understanding the role of human rights in armed conflicts.

Part 2 of this introduction will analyze in greater detail the various arguments for the extraterritorial application of the ICCPR, as well as the importance of the Koh memorandum as a harbinger of things to come: the recognition by all governments that the ICCPR applies extraterritorially. Then, Part 3 will outline the chapters in this volume to situate this volume's intervention in the larger debate. Although the volume does not offer definitive or knockdown solutions to the dilemma, it does provide the reader with the full scope of normative, ethical, and legal positions at stake in the current debate. It also includes a number of innovative solutions that have not appeared in print elsewhere.

2 Extraterritorial Application of Human Rights Treaties

Generally speaking, it has become common for human rights experts to argue that IHRL always applies, i.e., that it is a universally applicable legal

[10] On derogations, see also Stuart J. Macdonald, *Derogations under Article 15 of the European Convention on Human Rights*, 36 COLUM. J. TRANSNAT'L L. 225 (1997).

[11] For other interventions in this debate, see generally INTERNATIONAL HUMANITARIAN LAW AND INTERNATIONAL HUMAN RIGHTS LAW (Orna Ben-Naftali ed., 2011). *See also* DEREK JINKS, *International Human Rights Law in Time of Armed Conflict*, *in* THE OXFORD HANDBOOK OF INTERNATIONAL LAW IN ARMED CONFLICT 656, 659 (Andrew Clapham & Paola Gaeta eds., 2014) (concluding that "the very notion of competing legal frameworks is incompatible with the text, structure, and history of the Geneva Conventions").

framework, even when a state is acting extraterritorially (and perhaps even when a state is involved in an armed conflict). There is much to recommend this approach, especially since human rights attach to individual human beings (or to persons), and it is difficult to comprehend how objects of moral concern could ever lose, sacrifice, or forfeit these rights, especially due to the contingent fact of their extraterritorial location.[12] However, the United States has repeatedly denied that the ICCPR applies to its extraterritorial conduct.[13] Although the language and specific content of these claims has shifted slightly over the last fifteen years, the general parameters of the claim remained stable until Harold Koh's recent intervention in the debate.

In the Second and Third Periodic Reports to the Human Rights Committee, submitted in 2005, the United States argued that the ICCPR did not apply extraterritorially *at all*, and indeed argued that this interpretation was mandated by the Vienna Convention on the Law of Treaties.[14] Rather, the United States concluded that the key provision in the ICCPR limiting its jurisdiction is Article 2(1): "[e]ach State Party to the present Covenant undertakes to respect and to ensure to all individuals *within its territory and subject to its jurisdiction* the rights recognized in the present Covenant, without distinction of any kind."[15] The key element here is the conjunctive "and" in between "territory" and "subject to its jurisdiction." Under the official U.S. reading of the treaty as of 1995, both territory and jurisdiction need to be established in order for the ICCPR to apply.[16] Under this view of the *travaux preparatoires*, the

[12] See Jens David Ohlin, *Is the Concept of the Person Necessary for Human Rights?*, 105 Colum. L. Rev. 209 (2005).

[13] *See* Statement of State Department Legal Advisor Conrad Harper, U.N. Hum. Rts. Comm., 53rd Sess., 1405th mtg., U.N. Doc. CCPR/C/SR 1405 (April 24, 1995) (expressing the view that the ICCPR has no extraterritorial application) [hereafter Harper Statement].

[14] U.N. Human Rights Comm., *Third Periodic Reports of States Parties Due in 2003: United States of America*, U.N. Doc. CCPR/C/USA/3 (Nov. 28, 2005).

[15] International Covenant on Civil and Political Rights, Dec. 16, 1966, 999 U.N.T.S. 171 [hereinafter ICCPR].

[16] In making this argument, the U.S. government has relied on Legal Advisor Harper's statement: "Mr. Klein had asked whether the United States took the view that the Covenant did not apply to government actions outside the United States. The Covenant was not regarded as having extraterritorial application. In general, where the scope of application of a treaty was not specified, it was presumed to apply only within a Party's territory. Article 2 of the Covenant expressly stated that each State Party undertook to respect and ensure the rights recognized 'to all individuals within its territory and subject to its jurisdiction'. That dual requirement restricted the scope of the Covenant to persons under United States jurisdiction and within United States territory. During the

phrase "in their territory" was the result of negotiators desiring a limiting principle to constrain the extraterritorial application of the ICCPR. Efforts to delete "in their territory" from the draft of Article 2 of the ICCPR were ultimately defeated.[17]

The uncertainty with regard to Article 2 of the ICCPR stems from the ambiguity of the range over which the "and" operates. The provision can be read in one of two ways. In the first reading, the "and" operates over the entire obligation, which is composed of two smaller sub-obligations: "each party undertakes to respect and ensure the human rights of all individuals within its territory" and "each party undertakes to respect and ensure the human rights of all individuals subject to its jurisdiction." In this way, the "and" functions to combine two related obligations, one with regard to territorial subjects and one with regard to jurisdictional subjects. On the second reading, the "and" functions to unite two separate limiting principles with regard to the ICCPR's applications, both of which must be satisfied in order for the Covenant to apply: "The individual must be both on the territory and under the jurisdiction of the state party for the enumerated rights of the Convention to apply." The first interpretation involves a wider range for the conjunctive operator while the second interpretation involves a much narrower one. The choice between them must be made with reference to the intentions of the negotiators and the object and purpose of the ICCPR and its human rights framework.[18]

In its Fourth Periodic Report, the U.S. position shifted slightly from its prior reports; the United States dropped the unequivocal language about the inapplicability of the ICCPR to extraterritorial conduct.[19]

negotiating history, the words 'within its territory' had been debated and were added by vote, with the clear understanding that such wording would limit the obligations to within a Party's territory." Harper Statement, *supra* note 13, at 7, 20.

[17] France argued that the phrase should be removed from the draft covenant while the United States insisted that it remain. *See* US Third Periodic Report, at appendix.

[18] The subsequent practice of states might be relevant to the treaty's interpretation, but only insofar as the state practice is made in *application* of the treaty, rather than mere supererogatory practice. *See* Draft Conclusion 5, Annual Report of the International Law Commission, Sixty-fifth session (6 May–7 June and 8 July–9 August 2013), Supplement No. 10 (A/68/10), at 41–42. For a discussion of this broader issue of interpretation, see Sean D. Murphy, *The Relevance of Subsequent Agreements and Practice for Treaty Law to Date and in the Future, in* Treaties and Subsequent Practice (Georg Nolte ed., 2013).

[19] U.N. Human Rights Committee, Consideration of reports submitted by States parties under Article 40 of the Covenant, Fourth Periodic Report, United States of America (Dec, 30, 2011). For more commentary on this issue, see Beth Van Schaack, *United States*

Although the United States did not completely disclaim this argument, it stated that it was "mindful" that the Human Rights Committee and even the ICJ had concluded that human rights obligations apply extraterritorially.[20] However, it should be noted that the ICJ statement in question comes from the *Wall* opinion, which dealt with the law of occupation.[21] This is not very much in doubt, so it is unclear how much the United States was actually conceding by making this statement. When a sovereign power is engaged in an occupation of foreign territory, it by definition has control and jurisdiction over the territory, making it the de facto sovereign (if not necessarily the de jure sovereign, depending on the situation). It would seem less controversial to apply IHRL in that context, though it is true that applying IHRL during occupation raises similar issues of whether the law of occupation should be considered *lex specialis* to IHRL.[22]

On October 9, 2010, Harold Koh signed a memorandum regarding the geographic scope of the ICCPR under his authority as Legal Advisor to the U.S. Department of State.[23] Ostensibly, the document calls on the U.S. government to abandon or revise its long-held view that the ICCPR has no extraterritorial effect. However, the learned memo is more than just a piece of governmental advice: it also laid out, clearly and effectively, an academic argument regarding the proper interpretation of the treaty.

Koh's argument regarding extraterritoriality boiled down to three essential ingredients: (1) a close reading of the treaty's language; (2) the object and purpose of the ICCPR; and (3) the *travaux preparatoires* leading up to the crafting of the ICCPR language on "jurisdiction." An analysis of all three elements follows.

First, as to the treaty language, Koh starts with the premise that the language is fundamentally ambiguous, thus paving the way for the relevance of the second and third elements of the argument (under

Report to the UN Human Rights Committee: Lex Specialis and Extraterritoriality, Just Security (Oct. 16, 2013), available at http://justsecurity.org/2013/10/16/united-states-5th-periodic-review/.

20 Fourth Periodic Report at para. 505.

21 *See Legal Consequences of the Construction of a Wall in the Occupied Palestinian Territory*, Advisory Opinion, 2004 I.C.J. 136, 178 (July 9) (describing IHL as *lex specialis* during armed conflict).

22 *Id.*

23 *See* Koh Memo, *supra* note 8, at 56. For a discussion of the memorandum on the occasion of its release, see Charlie Savage, *U.S. Seems Unlikely to Accept That Rights Treaty Applies to Its Actions Abroad*, N.Y. Times (March 6, 2014).

the regular rules of treaty interpretation in the Vienna Convention).[24] The language is ambiguous for the reason already noted earlier, and also that the constraint regarding territoriality and jurisdiction could range over all of the obligations in Article 2 of the ICCPR or it could range simply over the obligation to "ensure" the rights in the Convention, leaving the obligation to "respect" the rights in the Convention completely unbounded.[25] One way of putting the ambiguity is that the "and" between the phrases "within its territory" and "subject to its jurisdiction" could be read conjunctively or disjunctively. In other words, a signatory might only have obligations to ensure rights if both constraints exist (territory and jurisdiction), or the signatory might have obligations to ensure if either constraint applies. Intuitively, it might seem that "and" should always be read conjunctively since it is, after all, *a conjunction*, but there are many applications of statutory interpretation that recognize the so-called disjunctive nature of some uses of the word "and."[26]

More importantly, Koh argues that the traditional U.S. interpretation produces grammatical irregularities.[27] While it is grammatically natural to speak of a requirement that states "ensure to all individuals within its territory," it makes no sense to speak of a requirement "to respect to all individuals within its territory. . ."[28] This suggests, according to Koh, that the obligation to respect is unbounded and that the territorial and jurisdictional constraints apply only to the obligation to ensure the rights

[24] *See* Koh Memo, *supra* note 8, at 3 (discussing contradictory evidence), 7 (calling the relevant provisions "far from being unambiguous").

[25] *Id.* at 8.

[26] For example, New York guidelines on statutory interpretation recognizes the disjunctive reading of "and" as applicable in some circumstances. *See* 1 McKinney's Consolidated Laws of New York § 365 (West 1971) ("Generally, the words 'or' and 'and' in a statute may be construed as interchangeable when necessary to effectuate legislative intent"). The commentary for section 365 notes that "the popular use of 'or' and 'and' is notoriously loose and inaccurate, and this use is reflected in the wording of statutes." *Id.* However, it is notable that the commentary refers to this as a "common mistake made by the drafters" of a statute, i.e., the use of a conjunction to express a disjunction. These uses are *mistakes*, albeit common ones. The commentary concludes that when "it is apparent that the Legislature has erroneously used the wrong word, the courts will make the necessary change in the statute in order that it shall conform to the legislative intent." *Id.* As a matter of statutory interpretation, shifting "and" to "or" is only permissible "to carry out the legislative intent" and "courts will never indulge in such library with the words of a statute where the effect of the change will be to thwart the legislative purpose." *Id.* Of course, the entire question in this case is determining the purpose of the drafters.

[27] *See* Koh Memo, *supra* note 8, at 10 (calling the 1995 interpretation "grammatically problematic").

[28] *Id.* at 10–11 (also noting same grammatical problem in French version of the provision).

enumerated in the ICCPR.[29] While this argument makes sense, it is not entirely persuasive. Assume for the sake of argument that the standard U.S. interpretation of the language is correct. How would the drafters have codified this intuition in a manner consistent with the standard grammatical usage identified by Koh? Presumably the phrase would come out in the following way:

> Each State Party to the present Covenant undertakes to respect the rights recognized in the present Covenant with regard to all individuals within its territory and subject to its jurisdiction, without distinction of any kind, such as race, colour, sex, language, religion, political or other opinion, national or social origin, property, birth or other status, and to ensure to all individuals within its territory and subject to its jurisdiction the rights recognized in the present Covenant, without distinction of any kind, such as race, colour, sex, language, religion, political or other opinion, national or social origin, property, birth or other status.

This, I suggest, is an epic mouthful, and basic cannons of linguistic and judicial economy counsel against it, thus suggesting that the crisper formulation was naturally selected, although it had the unfortunate consequence that an inexact preposition was logically appended to the word "respect." As if this exercise in hypothetical statutory reconstruction is not difficult enough, the other alternative for reaching the same result is the use of some commas:

> Each State Party to the present Covenant undertakes to respect, and to ensure to, all individuals within its territory and subject to its jurisdiction, the rights recognized in the present Covenant, without distinction of any kind, such as race, colour, sex, language, religion, political or other opinion, national or social origin, property, birth or other status.

This would also arguably produce an unambiguous formulation according to the U.S. interpretation. Should readers assume that the correct interpretation of Article 2 hinges on the absence of two commas? While that is certainly possible, it may also be the case that the drafting committee simply did not like commas very much.

Finally, Koh offers a more convincing argument about the grammatical structure of the provision: under the U.S. interpretation, the territorial restriction is superfluous or redundant.[30] Article 12 includes a territorial constraint regarding the "right to liberty of movement and freedom to choose his residence." If the *entire* convention is territorially

[29] *Id.* at 11. [30] *Id.* at 11.

limited by Article 2, why would the drafters feel compelled to introduce, a second time, a more specific territorial constraint for Article 12, which arguably would already be covered by the more general putative territorial constraint announced in Article 2.[31]

Turning now to the object and purpose of the treaty, Koh concludes that the ICCPR was – and is – designed to implement and advance basic human rights protections that are articulated in the U.N. Charter and the Universal Declaration of Human Rights.[32] The underlying impulse here is "universal protection for human rights" – a goal that would be hampered by a "rigidly territorial construction" of the treaty.[33] Furthermore, a rigidly territorial construction of the treaty would appear to conflict with the impulse behind Article 5 of the Convention, which specifically disclaims "any right to engage in any activity or perform any act aimed at the destruction of any of the rights and freedoms recognized therein."[34] For Koh, a territorially constrained concept of "respect" would appear to violate Article 5, since it would imply that a state could violate the rights enumerated in the ICCPR outside of its territory. This argument, while clever, is arguably teleological, in the sense that it assumes what it seeks to prove. In other words, one cannot assume that the state is violating any specific ICCPR right when it acts extraterritorially because the whole point of the U.S. interpretation is that ICCPR rights, and their associated state obligations to respect and ensure them, do not apply extraterritorially. There is something suspicious about an argument with this basic structure: states do not have the right to violate the rights in the ICCPR, therefore the rights must be understood in a particular (expansive) way, rather than in a limited fashion. The second does not follow from the first, because if the extraterritorial right does not exist in the first place, then a state acting extraterritorially would not have violated the Article 5 prohibition against "destruction" of those rights. That being said, it is true that Koh's reading of Article 5, while dispositive of the question of interpretation by itself, may be one element within a larger argument about the correct reading of Article 2 of the Covenant.

As a final point regarding object and purpose, Koh makes one macro-argument and one micro-argument. The macro-argument simply appeals to the absurdity of saying that a state must respect and ensure ICCPR rights internally but can do whatever it wants externally.[35] While that

[31] *Id.* [32] *Id.* at 12. [33] *Id.* at 12. [34] ICCPR, art. 5.

[35] *See* Koh Memo, *supra* note 8, at 13 (rejecting as unreasonable and absurd any interpretation that "would yield the bizarre result that a state that was obligated to protect citizens

sounds right, no one asserts that governmental conduct outside of the country is unbounded. Indeed, during armed conflict IHL unquestionably applies extraterritorially, and even outside of armed conflict some aspects of *customary* human rights law might apply extraterritorially; this takes the sharp edge off the absurdity quite considerably.[36] As for the micro-point, Koh rightly points out that some rights are meaningless unless applied extraterritorially, such as the right to enter a country under Article 12(4), a right that by definition must apply to those outside of the country or not at all.[37] However, the ensuring and respecting of that right happens internally, on behalf of the government here, so it is a stretch to claim that the right must have extraterritorial application to have some meaning. The location of the entry point is internal, not external, which seems enough to give the codified protection a geographical home within the state.

The last element of Koh's argument appealed to the negotiating history of the ICCPR.[38] Standard U.S. accounts have generally cited Eleanor Roosevelt's role in the negotiations as supporting the U.S. view. Under the standard U.S. story, Roosevelt introduced the territoriality constraint because the United States did not want the ICCPR to apply to situations such as the post–World War II occupations in Germany or Japan, or even their aftermath where U.S. participation fell short of the technical definition of occupation. Although the former locations were clearly governed by the law of occupation, to suggest that the United States would be responsible for the full menu of ICCPR obligations in these areas would be to place too high a burden on the United States and other states similarly situated. Under this view, then, Roosevelt suggested – and received – a territorial constraint on the operation of the ICCPR, thus making clear that the treaty would have no extraterritorial effect.

Koh takes this argument and by identifying a more *specific* impulse from Roosevelt and the United States, effectively turns the argument on its head and uses it as evidence *against* the U.S. interpretation of the ICCPR. He does this by looking at Roosevelt's statements, many of them focused on a desire to avoid an affirmative obligation on the part of the

within its borders could act against those same citizens with impunity under the Covenant, the moment they stepped outside the state's borders").

36 However, one might argue that customary human rights law does not apply extraterritorially, although in that case the conclusion would stem not from an interpretation of the text of the ICCPR but rather from the U.S. position as a persistent objector.

37 *Id.* 38 *Id.* at 15.

United States to pass legislation ensuring the protection of all Covenant rights in occupied territory.[39] This is a specific anxiety that arguably applies to the "ensure" prong of Article 2 but not the "respect" prong. Consequently, the U.S. anxiety over its obligations in occupied territories supports the bifurcated reading of Article 2 whereby only the "ensure" prong is territorially constrained and the "respect" prong is not similarly constrained.

One consequence of this new argument is that it throws into sharp relief how this new reading of Article 2 of the Covenant incorporates one positive obligation and one negative obligation in the very same provision. This interpretation cuts across the perhaps simplistic and conventional interpretation that the ICCPR codified negative obligations while the International Covenant on Economic, Social and Cultural Rights (ICESCR) codified positive obligations.[40] This is no small matter. In the early days of the negotiations, work began on a single convention. However, the United States and U.S.S.R. quickly arrived at loggerheads over the type of rights that should be codified: the United States preferred political and legal rights that were best described as negative rights, i.e., freedom from government abuse.[41] In contrast, the U.S.S.R., a country not terribly interested in political and civil rights, could not agree to a convention that would force them to extend widespread civil rights to their population. Furthermore, the U.S.S.R. supported economic and social rights best described as positive rights, i.e., the necessary conditions required to exercise freedom in a meaningful way, including food, shelter, and other categories of care.[42] These are precisely the type of rights guaranteed, at least in theory, in socialist and communist systems. From this split, the ICCPR and ICESCR – as separate conventions – were born.

[39] *Id.* at 16–17.

[40] *See, e.g.*, Eric A. Posner & A.O. Sykes, Economic Foundations of International Law 201 (2013); Anthony J. Langlois, *International Covenant on Economic, Social, and Cultural Rights (ICESCR), in* Martin Griffiths (ed.), Encyclopedia of International Relations and Global Politics 419 (2005). *But see* Beth A. Simmons, Mobilizing for Human Rights: International Law in Domestic Politics 162 (2009) (concluding that the ICCPR codifies positive rights as well); Christian Tomuschat, *International Covenant on Civil and Political Rights (1966), in* Max Planck Encyclopedia of Public International Law (2014) ("Although the text of the ICCPR emphasizes the negative character of the rights enunciated in Arts 6 to 27, some social elements can also be discerned").

[41] Posner & Sykes, *supra* note 40, at 201.

[42] *See* Makau Mutua, Human Rights: A Political and Cultural Critique 178 n.45 (2002).

In a sense, they produced one Convention for the East and one for the West.

The reading of so-called positive rights into the ICCPR may already be mainstream thinking in IHRL, though if this is the case it is a decidedly European phenomenon. In the United States, by contrast, civil and political rights enshrined in the U.S. Constitution are generally thought not to *require* the government to enact certain legislation to operationalize those rights, except in the rarest of circumstances. More common is the notion that such provisions *enable* or *authorize* the government to pass legislation.[43] As an illustration, consider the famous case *M.C. v. Bulgaria*, in which the European Court of Human Rights concluded that Bulgaria was under a positive obligation to conform its substantive criminal law on rape to standards embodied in the European Convention.[44] A decision like this would be unheard of from an American court, where civil rights are generally regarded simply as constraints on governmental action. Although this hypersensitivity to "positive rights" does not carry over to other western European states, it is important not to underestimate the American hostility toward positive rights.[45]

The new Koh interpretation of the ICCPR throws into doubt the conventional (albeit over simplistic) account of the Covenant as enshrining negative rights. Instead of the ICCPR codifying negative rights and the ICESCR codifying positive rights, Article 2 of the ICCPR now internalizes both negative obligations (respect) and positive obligations (ensure). While the rights are not economic or social in nature, this new interpretation of Article 2 of the ICCPR does cast a more "positive" shadow onto the rest of the Convention, not simply telling governments what they cannot do but also telling governments what they must do in order to "ensure" that the rights in the Convention are brought to fruition. This recasts the ICCPR in a new light. It is respectively submitted that this new interpretation of Article 2 is therefore fundamental, and

43 An example would be section five of the Fourteenth Amendment, which states "Congress shall have power to enforce, by appropriate legislation, the provisions of this article."

44 *See* M.C. v. Bulgaria, Eur. Ct. H.R., 39272/98 (2003) (holding that Bulgaria violated the European Convention by requiring proof of physical force before convicting assailant of rape).

45 The point should not be overstated. There are, of course, positive rights enshrined in the U.S. legal system; the point is simply that they are the exception that proves the rule. It is also true that some rights claims defy classification and can be considered as either negative or positive rights. *See* David Robertson, *Thick Constitutional Readings: When Classic Distinctions are Irrelevant*, 36 G. J. INT'L & COMP. L. 277, 282–83 (2007).

that any consideration of the *travaux preparatoires* must interrogate not just the Roosevelt statements regarding territoriality but also the larger discussions of negative and positive obligations that took place between the negotiators and also privately among future state parties.

Stepping back from the veracity of each element of Koh's arguments, the larger picture is more important. The standard U.S. position, in place at least since 1995, is facing both external and internal pressure. So the day may soon come when even the United States concedes that the ICCPR has extraterritorial effect.[46] When that day comes, territoriality will no longer be the safety value that keeps IHL and IHRL apart; they will come in direct conflict. At that point, the United States will be forced to come to a more coherent assessment of the relationship between these two bodies of law. (Indeed perhaps that day has already arrived for countries that recognize the extraterritorial application of the ICCPR). International law will need more than a slogan – *lex specialis* – to define their interaction; it will require a philosophically nuanced theory to explain the relationship between two bodies of law, each with its own tradition, lexigraphy, and constituency.[47]

With that horizon in mind, this volume aims to map out the conceptual contours of that present and coming debate. The volume as a unifying work offers no clear answer, no unitary prescription for how to harmonize two bodies of law that, at first glance, appear inconsistent and bipolar. The result is a conversation between different perspectives regarding the nature of legal regulation of armed conflict in the twenty-first century.

3 This Volume's Intervention in the Debate

The first group of chapters in the volume address the moral foundation for regulating armed conflict. The first and most pressing question is whether basic principles of human rights – which prohibit violence against legally protected persons – are logically consistent with the laws of war, which by their very nature define wide-scale killing as lawful as

[46] *See* Beth Van Schaack, *The United States' Position on the Extraterritorial Application of Human Rights Obligations: Now is the Time for Change*, 90 Int'l L. Stud. 20 (2014).

[47] *Cf.* David Luban, *Military Necessity and the Cultures of Military Law*, 26 Leiden J. Int'l L. 315 (2013) (noting the difference between military lawyers steeped in the language of military necessity and humanitarian lawyers steeped in the language of human rights and human dignity).

long as those killings are performed in compliance with the basic pillars of the law of armed conflict: distinction, proportionality, humanity, and necessity.[48] The opening chapters explicitly address possibilities for convergence of human rights norms and specific rules of IHL.

In this light, Adil Haque starts the volume with a unique philosophical framework.[49] Instead of adopting a balancing approach whereby the point of IHL is to balance military and humanitarian considerations (a frequent refrain in the IHL literature, so much so that one might even describe it as orthodoxy), Haque instead defends the view that the point of IHL is to prohibit morally unjustified killing.[50] In this sense, the aim of IHL is consistent with, and protects, basic human rights. His argument combines multiple elements. First, Haque notes that the regular rules of IHL prohibit the intentional killing of civilians, killings that are clearly unjustified.[51] Second, as to the *unintentional* killing of civilians as collateral damage, some theorists worry that IHL permits the *unjust* side of the conflict to perform such killings (assuming they satisfy the principle of proportionality).[52] Haque concedes that these killings might be viewed as unjustified but correctly notes that *jus ad bellum* – and its codification in the U.N. Charter – prohibits such behavior.[53] The result is a "division of labor" between the bodies of law, such that if "both bodies of law are functioning properly, compliance with each body of law will be individually necessary and jointly sufficient for moral justification."[54]

[48] For a description of these principles, see generally GARY D. SOLIS, THE LAW OF ARMED CONFLICT: INTERNATIONAL HUMANITARIAN LAW IN WAR (2010).

[49] *See* ADIL HAQUE, *Laws For War*, Chapter 1, this volume.

[50] For examples of the traditional view, see M.N. SCHMITT, *The Conduct of Hostilities During Operation Iraqi Freedom: An International Humanitarian Law Assessment, in* YEARBOOK OF INTERNATIONAL HUMANITARIAN LAW 73, 102 (2003) ("IHL seeks balance between humanitarian concerns and military necessity"); MARY ELLEN O'CONNELL, *Historical Development and Legal Basis, in* Dieter Fleck (ed.), THE HANDBOOK OF INTERNATIONAL HUMANITARIAN LAW 1, 37 (2013) ("The existence of these rules shows that consideration of military necessity have already been taken into account in framing the rules of humanitarian law, which are intended to achieve a balance between military necessity and the requirements of humanity.").

[51] *See* HAQUE, *supra* note 49, at 46.

[52] This anxiety is particularly acute among revisionist Just War Theorists, many of whom argue that soldiers participating in an unjust war are morally culpable for the killings they perform, even though these battlefield killings are not violations of IHL. *See, e.g.*, JEFF MCMAHAN, KILLING IN WAR 15–20 (2009) (asking whether unjust combatants can satisfy the moral requirements of jus in bello).

[53] *See* HAQUE, *supra* note 49, at 46–47.

[54] *Id.*

Consequently, Haque believes that the impetus behind IHL is to help soldiers conform to their moral obligations and avoid morally impermissible killings.[55]

David Luban's chapter, "Human Rights Thinking and the Laws of War," asks whether IHL and IHRL share the same "essence," i.e., whether they are both animated by a cardinal respect for the inherent moral dignity of the person.[56] As a historical and genealogical matter, Luban's answer is no; IHL and IHRL flow from different sources and historical particularities. However, as to the present and future of international law, Luban's answer is an emphatic yes: human rights thinking has migrated and influenced, in ways both subtle and profound, the understanding and application of IHL. Luban's task is then how to explain this rich and complex migration – a process that involved decisions from international tribunals generally and international criminal law tribunals specifically, international reaction to the U.S. conduct of the armed conflict against al-Qaeda, and the need for more constraining rules regarding military occupations (over and above the very limited obligations imposed by the international law of occupation).[57] Luban's view of these developments is not just descriptive but normative; he criticizes attempts to blindly harmonize IHL and IHRL with insufficient attention to their fundamental differences. However, Luban emphatically supports a more limited form of harmonization, one that uses human rights thinking to prioritize the concerns and realities of civilians on the ground who are most affected by war's horror.[58] The result is a new form of IHL that, under the influence of human rights, concerns itself with the fate of civilians on the ground just as much as military commanders and their political leaders who use armed conflict to pursue their Clausewitzian objectives. This transformation, long underway for several decades, is by no means complete.

Marko Milanovic rethinks the relationship between IHL and IHRL by providing an in-depth examination – a genealogy if you will – of the principle of *lex specialis*, the idea that IHL rules operate as more specific exceptions that trump the general background rules of IHRL.[59] Milanovic's investigation stems from an anxiety that the genesis of the *lex*

[55] *Id.* at 56–57.
[56] David Luban, *Human Rights Thinking and the Laws of War*, Chapter 2, this volume.
[57] *Id.* at 87, 100. [58] *Id.* at 111.
[59] Marko Milanovic, *The Lost Origins of Lex Specialis: Rethinking the Relationship between Human Rights and International Humanitarian Law*, Chapter 3, this volume.

specialis rule (that norms of IHL prevail over inconsistent rules of IHRL) seemed to come out of nowhere. This insight provided the occasion for an empirical investigation of the birth of the doctrine, and the results confirm the hypothesis: the supposedly ancient rule dates only as far back as the ICJ opinion on nuclear weapons in 1996.[60] Of course, the recent vintage of the principle does not, by itself, entail its invalidity. However, as Milanovic notes, getting its historical origins correct is a necessary prolegomenon to the substantive debate; the *lex specialis* principle deserves none of the presumption of validity one usually associates with equitable maxims. In that sense, Milanovic's chapter constitutes an urgently needed corrective to the existing literature and its occasionally uncritical acceptance of *lex specialis* and its alleged provenance.[61]

My own contribution to the volume attempts to provide some of that underlying normative argument by deploying first-order legal theory to the question. The chapter posits that IHL and IHRL regulate two fundamentally different modes of governmental action.[62] IHL regulates a government when it is acting as a belligerent in the course of an armed conflict, while IHRL constrains a government when it is acting as a sovereign in regulating its subjects. The former mode (acting as a belligerent) involves two, formally co-equal collectives who meet each other in battle; the latter mode (acting as a sovereign) involves an asymmetrical relationship wherein the state exercises power or control over the individual.[63] The remainder of the chapter is devoted to cashing out the concept of control through a critical reevaluation of the European Court of Human Rights' jurisprudence regarding the extraterritorial application of the European Convention on Human Rights.[64] I demonstrate that the

[60] *Id.* at 123.

[61] *But see* William A. Schabas, *Lex Specialis - Belt and Suspenders - The Parallel Operation of Human Rights Law and the Law of Armed Conflict, and the Conundrum of Jus Ad Bellum*, 40 Isr. L. Rev. 592 (2007); Nancy Prud'homme, *Lex Specialis: Oversimplifying a More Complex and Multifaceted Relationship*, 40 Isr. L. Rev. 356 (2007); Jinks, *supra* note 11, at 665 (rejecting the notion that IHL is more "narrowly tailored to the exigencies of armed conflict").

[62] Jens David Ohlin, *Acting as a Sovereign versus Acting as a Belligerent*, Chapter 4, this volume.

[63] *Id.* This argument was also briefly discussed in Jens David Ohlin, *The Duty to Capture*, 97 Minn. L. Rev. 1268, 1324–1341 (2013).

[64] *See, e.g.*, Bankovic and Others v. Belgium and Others (App. No. 52207/99), ECHR Grand Chamber (Dec. 12, 2001); Al-Saadoon and Mufdhi v. United Kingdom (App. No. 61498/08), ECHR (July 3, 2009); Al-Skeini and Others v. United Kingdom (App. No. 55721/07), ECHR Grand Chamber (July 7, 2011).

two competing theories applied by the ECHR, territorial control versus personal control, collapse into each other and therefore are not wholly distinct frameworks.

Part II of the volume offers powerful and at times searing criticisms of the U.S. legal framework for counter-terrorism operations and trenchant criticisms of its application of law of war and human rights principles. In particular, all three chapters identify and decry a profound ad hockery in U.S. legal positions, which often involve mixing and matching between legal standards and legal frameworks in new and perhaps illegitimate ways.

Specifically, Jonathan Horowitz's chapter focuses on ending the "Global War" – the armed conflict against al-Qaeda and other terrorist groups that has lingered since 9/11 and spanned not just Afghanistan and Pakistan, but other countries where al-Qaeda or affiliated terrorists were located.[65] Horowitz's concern is the unbounded geographical nature of this non-international armed conflict (NIAC); unlike typical civil wars, which are usually limited to the territory of a single state, the NIAC against al-Qaeda allegedly extends beyond the state to wherever the combatants are located.[66] The chapter criticizes this development from the perspective of IHRL. Specifically, a government could impermissibly give consent to a foreign military to engage in conduct (such as killing its citizens) that the government could not do by itself because of its human rights obligations.[67] For Horowitz, this outsourcing of human rights violations – a frequent occurrence in the new "global war" – contravenes the larger structure of international law to which both IHL and IHRL belong.[68]

In her contribution, Naz Modirzadeh has coined a new term, "folk international law," which is sure to have a long life.[69] The idea is far more than a pithy phrase; it encapsulates an entire methodology that Modirzadeh diagnoses in the current academic and political landscape: the mixing and matching of different legal concepts and doctrines, often in

[65] Jonathan Horowitz, *Ending the Global War: The Power of Human Rights in a Time of Unrestrained Armed Conflict*, Chapter 5, this volume.

[66] For an extensive discussion of the geography of IHL, see Jennifer C. Daskal, *The Geography of the Battlefield: A Framework for Detention and Targeting Outside the "Hot" Conflict Zone*, 161 Univ. Penn. L. Rev. 1165 (2013).

[67] The basic structure of this problem is also discussed in Ashley S. Deeks, *Consent to the Use of Force and International Law Supremacy*, 54 Harv. Int'l L.J. 1 (2013).

[68] *See* Horowitz, *supra* note 65, at 241.

[69] Naz K. Modirzadeh, *Folk International Law: 9/11 Lawyering and the Transformation of the Law of Armed Conflict to Human Rights Policy and Human Rights Law to War Governance*, Chapter 6, this volume.

incoherent ways, in order to justify (and provide some meaningful constraint over) U.S. military power in the armed conflict against al-Qaeda and other terrorist organizations. Modirzadeh's diagnosis of this process picks up on a phenomenon also explored by Kevin Jon Heller, who complains that American administration offers pick and choose (selectively and strategically) when and how they want to apply principles from International Armed Conflict (IAC) to the non-international armed conflict against al-Qaeda. Modirzadeh's chapter catalogues the critical legal doctrines applied to battlefield conduct, including criteria for lawful targeting, and shows how they involved a convergence of IHL and IHRL in unpredictable and often confusing ways.[70] The result was a lack of "sharpness" in the law governing these military engagements.

Kevin Jon Heller's chapter resides in the same critical space, analyzing the arguments used by proponents of strong military action against al-Qaeda and other terrorist organizations.[71] In particular, Heller diagnoses a selective borrowing of IAC rules to be applied in non-international conflicts against al-Qaeda. For Heller, this process is performed inconsistently and often without legal justification, so as to expansively apply the permissive rules of targeting, detention, and *jus ad bellum* principles that apply in the IAC context. At least part of the inspiration for this selective analogizing from IAC to NIAC is to avoid the conclusion that more restrictive rules of international law, whether from more classical interpretations of the law governing NIAC or even human rights law, apply to U.S. military action against al-Qaeda operatives.[72] The situation is therefore one of ulterior motivation: the desire to switch frameworks or analogize between them in order to apply the least-restrictive legal rule to governmental conduct.

The third and final part of the volume offers new legal approaches for regulating armed conflict generally and counter-terrorism operations specifically. Janina Dill starts the conversation under the rubric of "forcible alternatives to war."[73] By that phrase, Dill means to interrogate the moral permissibility of war and examine its constitutive elements.[74]

[70] *Id.* at 292–93.

[71] *See* Kevin Jon Heller, *The Use and Abuse of Analogy in IHL*, Chapter 7, this volume.

[72] *Id.* at 352–53. [73] Janina Dill, *Forcible Alternatives to War*, Chapter 8, this volume.

[74] Her previous work in this area includes Janina Dill & Henry Shue, *Limiting the Killing in War: Military Necessity and the St. Petersburg Assumption*, 26 Ethics & Int'l Aff. 311 (2012).

Dill tackles IHL's central concession toward legitimate state violence – its sanctioning of killing enemy soldiers – head on. The question is whether one could imagine a system of international law that is better than IHL in limiting the number of civilians who are killed – the guiding impulse behind human rights law. However, Dill is well aware of the risk of employing a more restrictive human rights framework during armed conflict: it may produce the opposite result and increase the number of moral violations. In a highly novel conclusion, Dill asks whether "de-collectivizing" conduct might produce a path forward as a way of safeguarding individual human rights.[75] The result would be an asymmetrical alternative to warfare, one that pits state violence not against another state but against the offending individual as a single target. However, Dill does not deploy the argument as a simple justification for U.S.-style targeted killings, but rather a broader legal regime involving international arrest warrants, targeted abduction, enforcement via Special Forces, and killing only as a last resort, i.e., a true forcible alternative to war. The resulting argument moves briskly from reorienting our abstract normative framework to specific details of institutional design.

John Dehn develops and expands upon the innovative idea of an international "martial law" that would apply in spaces where no other sovereign has effective control.[76] The upshot of this concept is that it would apply a legal framework for evaluating the use of force in counter-terrorism operations. It should be noted, however, that Dehn's understanding of the lack of control that triggers international martial law is de facto, not simply de jure. In other words, in situations where a state continues to exist as a legal person but does not have sufficient control to adequately respond to a terrorist threat emanating from its territory, the principles of international martial law would be triggered and would provide a set of standards against which the counter-terrorism force could be evaluated. Dehn describes the framework as a "hybrid" of IHL and IHRL and is "not intended to evoke images of harsh military rule and perfunctory punishment, but rather of militarized law enforcement operations rendered necessary by the nature, gravity, and location of a threat."[77] As a hybrid regime, the martial law framework would permit targeting and detention of security threats but would reject IHL's permissive rules regarding civilian collateral damage, which is permitted

[75] Dill, *supra* note 73, at 463.
[76] John Dehn, *Whither International Martial Law?*, Chapter 9, this volume.
[77] *Id.* at 474.

under IHL as long as the civilian casualties are not disproportionate to the value of the military advantage gained from the attack.

In the final chapter, Brian Orend continues the normative theme by proposing a new Geneva-style Convention that would codify the responsibilities of belligerents at the conclusion of an armed conflict.[78] The problem with the existing regulations of *jus post bellum* (justice after war) is that most of the legal obligations are explicitly tied to a state's status as a belligerent occupier. For states that finish an armed conflict but do not occupy enemy territory, the law of occupation as traditionally defined does not apply. Enter Orend to offer a set of normative principles that would constrain the post-war conduct of belligerents and impose on them affirmative obligations to mitigate and alleviate the negative consequences of the armed conflict suffered by the civilian population.[79] For Orend, the *content* of these obligations is provided by human rights values, thus demonstrating the conceptual affinity between human rights generally and *jus post bellum* in particular.[80] These obligations would certainly be triggered by U.S. counter-terrorism operations in foreign locations.

4 Conclusion

What emerges from this conversation is a portrait of international law in a state of evolution and perhaps fragmentation. These are trite, over-used phrases. But the sentiment gestures toward a deeper point, i.e., that the boundaries and scope of different international legal regimes is radically under-theorized and under-conceptualized. Indeed, there is not even agreement on whether the regimes, in this case IHL and IHRL, are complementary or competing. But such questions cannot be answered by reference to the positive law alone without reference to a deeper account of the grounding for each field of law. Only by interrogating the tropes of international law – dignity, humanity, balancing, humanitarianism, necessity, *lex specialis*, etc. – will we gain any traction on this seemingly intractable problem. The essays in this volume are important contributions in this dialogical endeavor.

That being said, this volume is not confined to abstract analysis. Each and every contribution, not just those in Part II, engage with both theory

[78] Brian Orend, *The Next Geneva Convention: Filling a Law-of-War Gap with Human Rights Values*, Chapter 10, this volume.
[79] *Id.* at 539. [80] *Id.* at 540.

and practice, interrogating both doctrinal inconsistencies and current military practices that run afoul of these legal paradigms. The result is a conversation that is at once theoretical and practical, carefully navigating both philosophical and legal terrain. Theoretical commitments are followed through and explored to their logical consequence on the ground in terms of legal and military practice. Like the best forms of reflective equilibrium, this provokes an on-going conversation between abstract principles and the reality on the ground during armed conflict, with the hope that the legal regulation of armed conflict will move toward greater clarity and effectiveness. One animating impulse behind this entire academic endeavor is the assumption that lack of clarity regarding fundamental principles is a major obstacle toward effectiveness on the ground. This work is therefore a necessary prolegomenon to the important work of humanitarian workers seeking to alleviate the suffering imposed by armed conflict. Without clarity regarding the scope and aim of these legal regimes, complete compliance and effectiveness remain a distant dream.

PART I

Convergence & Divergence of Human Rights and Laws of War

1

Laws for War

ADIL AHMAD HAQUE

Introduction

I will assume that international human rights law (IHRL) aims in part to prohibit violations of basic moral rights that all human beings enjoy simply in virtue of their humanity. Of these rights, the most fundamental is the right not to be killed. The most important legal recognition of this right is found in Article 6 of the International Covenant on Civil and Political Rights (ICCPR), which states that "Every human being has the inherent right to life. This right shall be protected by law. No one shall be arbitrarily deprived of his life."[1]

Of course, such gentle words confront a harsh reality. Each year, thousands of women, men, girls, and boys are killed by military operations. Some of these military operations conform to international humanitarian law (IHL). This obvious fact raises a troubling question: Might some killings that conform to IHL nevertheless violate human rights?

There are at least three contexts in which this question might be posed. First, a state engaged in an internal armed conflict with an organized armed group needs to know if IHRL constrains its military operations. Second, a state engaged in a noninternational armed conflict with an organized armed group operating from the territory of another state needs to know if the territorial state can consent to military operations on its territory without violating its own human rights obligations. Finally, a state's legal duty to respect human rights may apply extraterritorially, in which case even a state engaged in an international armed conflict with another state needs to know if its military operations are constrained by IHRL.

Earlier versions of this chapter were presented at the American Society of International Law, the Stockholm Centre for the Ethics of War and Peace, and Osgoode Hall Law School. Special thanks to Seth Lazar, Helen Frowe, Victor Tadros, Jonathan Parry, and Janina Dill for their comments and suggestions.

[1] International Covenant on Civil and Political Rights, Dec. 16, 1966, 999 U.N.T.S. 171, art. 6(1).

There are four ways in which we might resolve apparent conflicts between IHL and IHRL. The first is to define the problem away by maintaining that killings that conform to IHL are *ipso facto* not "arbitrary" within the meaning of the ICCPR and therefore cannot violate IHRL. The second is to maintain that IHL displaces or prevails over IHRL such that killings that conform to IHL are lawful even if they violate IHRL. The third is to maintain that IHRL prevails over IHL such that killings that violate IHRL are unlawful even if they conform to IHL. The last is to maintain that neither IHL nor IHRL prevails over the other, such that some killings are both lawful (under IHL) and unlawful (under IHRL).

The first, comforting reply that a lawful act cannot be arbitrary is belied by Article 17 of the ICCPR, which states that "No one shall be subjected to *arbitrary or unlawful* interference with his privacy, family, home or correspondence, nor to *unlawful* attacks on his honour and reputation."[2] Assuming, as we must, that legal terms are not redundant but instead carry distinct meanings, it follows that an action can be lawful but still arbitrary. More precisely, an action can be arbitrary within the meaning of the ICCPR even if it conforms to some other legal norm.

Of course, one could simply assert that while some acts can be both lawful and arbitrary, acts that are lawful under IHL are necessarily not arbitrary. But such a definitional fiat renders the idea of arbitrary killing morally unintelligible. After all, IHL and IHRL developed along parallel but separate tracks and were informed by different interests and constituencies. The resulting legal norms were crafted by human beings and therefore could have been quite different than they are. For example, it is hard to accept that the 1977 Additional Protocols did nothing to make IHL more respectful of human rights or to limit arbitrary killing in war. Similarly, it is hard to accept that if Protocol I had omitted important provisions then this would not have affected its human rights credentials. It can hardly be an *a priori* or conceptual truth that IHL, *whatever its content*, prohibits arbitrary killing. If IHL prohibits even most arbitrary killing in armed conflict, then this is a contingent and reversible human achievement.

The better view seems to be that, in principle, IHL and IHRL can conflict, the former permitting what the latter forbids. One task, then, is to interpret specific norms in a way that avoids or reduces potential conflict between them. Another task is to revise existing norms and design additional norms to narrow the gap between the two legal regimes. Ideally,

[2] *Id.* art. 17(1).

legal conflicts between IHL and IHRL would be resolved by reference to a shared moral aim. For example, if both IHL and IHRL aim to prohibit morally unjustified killing then conflicts can be avoided by interpreting their respective norms in light of this shared aim; residual conflicts can be resolved by privileging the specific norm that best achieves this shared aim in the context of armed conflict; and new norms can be developed to realize this shared aim. This is the approach I shall pursue.

We have seen that lawfulness alone does not necessarily negate arbitrariness. What might? Moral justification. Moral rights are infringed but not violated if their infringement is morally justified. Since human rights are moral rights that human beings enjoy in virtue of their humanity, human rights are violated only if they are infringed without moral justification. In particular, morally justified deprivations of life may infringe but do not violate the human right not to be killed. Since IHRL declares that "arbitrary" killings violate the human right not to be killed, it follows that morally justified killings cannot be "arbitrary" within the meaning of IHRL.

What does this mean for the relationship between IHRL and IHL? It means that killings that are lawful under IHL are lawful under IHRL to the extent that they are morally justified. In other words, IHL and IHRL are consistent to the extent that IHL prohibits morally unjustified killing in armed conflict. The right way to reconcile IHL and IHRL is not by definitional fiat or by privileging one over the other, but by enhancing the moral credentials of IHL.

On my view, IHL should aim to prohibit morally unjustified killing and thereby protect human rights.[3] However, many insist that IHL should instead aim to balance military and humanitarian considerations, permitting types of killing that generally are necessary for military victory and prohibiting types of killing that generally are not. In this way, IHL will reduce killing in armed conflict to the greatest extent practically possible. On this view, IHRL and IHL have very different aims, the former to *respect* human rights and *prohibit* their violation and the latter to *promote* human rights and *minimize* their violation. Conflicts between these two aims will prove impossible to avoid and possible to resolve only by privileging one aim over the other. Toward the end of this chapter, I argue that we should reject this familiar but flawed view.

[3] I pursue this project in greater depth in LAW AND MORALITY AT WAR (OUP, forthcoming 2016).

IHL and *Jus ad Bellum*

Before evaluating the moral credentials of specific IHL norms, we must first address a threshold objection to the view that IHL aims to prohibit morally unjustified killing. By design, IHL applies symmetrically to all sides of a conflict, independently of the *jus ad bellum* morality and legality of their resort to military force. As a result, it is no violation of IHL for combatants fighting for an unjust cause (say, territorial conquest) to kill combatants fighting for a just cause (say, national self-defense). Yet it seems morally impermissible to kill combatants fighting for a just cause, since such combatants have done nothing to forfeit their moral right not to be killed.[4]

More worrisome still, it is not necessarily a violation of IHL for combatants fighting for an unjust cause to unintentionally, but foreseeably kill civilians as a side-effect of their military operations. According to IHL, all sides of a conflict are capable of satisfying *jus in bello* proportionality. Yet it seems morally impermissible to kill civilians, even unintentionally, in pursuit of an unjust cause.

At one level, it seems undeniable that the moral status of killing in armed conflict depends in part on the aims of the opposing parties. If one party's aims are unjust, then the pursuit of those aims cannot justify initiating or continuing armed conflict. Ideally, that party should instead seek an immediate ceasefire and offer restitution for any wrongful harm already inflicted. Now, if the opposing party continues to use military force, either in retaliation or to extract unjust concessions, then the first party might acquire, for the first time, a moral justification to use military force in self-defense. But if the opposing party would accept a just peace then the attacking force may not simply continue to fight and kill.

We should therefore concede that IHL alone cannot prohibit all morally unjustified killing in armed conflict. The achievement of this aim also requires that international law prohibit the morally unjustified resort to military force, for example through Articles 2(4) and 51 of the United Nations Charter as well as through customary international law. The legal prohibition of morally unjustified killing is the shared aim of the law governing the resort to force and IHL, and requires a division

[4] Elsewhere I argue that it can be objectively permissible to kill just combatants in order to protect civilians from unintended and proportionate harms to which they are not morally liable. See Adil Ahmad Haque, *Rights and Liabilities at War*, in Criminal Law Conversations 395 (Paul H. Robinson, Stephen Garvey & Kimberly Ferzan eds., 2009).

of labor between the two. The former prohibits all killing pursuant to a morally unjustified resort to force, while the latter prohibits killing that is morally unjustified even pursuant to a morally justified resort to force. If both bodies of law are functioning properly, compliance with each body of law will be individually necessary and jointly sufficient for moral justification.

More precisely, IHL has two aims. IHL aims to prohibit morally unjustified killing pursuant to a morally justified resort to force and to prohibit the morally worst killings pursuant to a morally unjustified resort to force. IHL claims that, by complying with its demands, combatants who fight for a just cause will avoid morally unjustified killing. As we have seen, IHL cannot make the same claim regarding combatants who fight without a just cause. However, IHL can claim that combatants fighting without a just cause will act *less wrongfully* if they follow IHL than if they violate IHL. In other words, IHL can claim that killings pursuant to a morally unjustified resort to force are *morally worse* if they also violate IHL than if they conform to IHL.

For example, targeting civilians is morally worse than targeting combatants even when neither have done anything to forfeit their moral rights not to be killed. Combatants often pose or directly contribute to threats to civilians who retain their moral rights as well as threats to combatants who may forfeit their rights not to be killed or injured but who nevertheless do not deserve death or injury. In addition, combatants are more likely than civilians to place themselves in harm's way; are better equipped than civilians to defend themselves; and often become combatants precisely to draw fire away from the civilian population.[5]

Similarly, it is morally worse to kill civilians as a side-effect of preventing less or no harm to others than to kill civilians as a side-effect of preventing substantially greater harm to others. There is always some moral reason to protect civilians, so an act that prevents substantially more harm to civilians than it inflicts is always partially morally justified. Of course, collateral harm inflicted in pursuit of an unjust cause can never be fully morally justified. However, ordinary combatants fighting for an unjust cause generally lack the ability to end the conflict as a whole and instead must choose between killing just combatants and foreign civilians or allowing just combatants to kill their fellow soldiers and their own civilians. By respecting *jus in bello* proportionality, these combatants

[5] See Seth Lazar, Sparing Civilians (OUP 2015).

can at least ensure that their own actions prevent substantially greater harm to their own forces and civilians than they inflict on the civilians of the opposing party.[6]

It follows that IHL gives combatants on all sides of an armed conflict decisive moral reasons to respect rather than ignore both civilian immunity and proportionality. Ideally, all IHL norms will do the same.

Objective Moral Justification

There are three primary senses in which an act can be morally justified. An act is objectively justified only if the act is supported by undefeated moral reasons. In these cases, there is no decisive moral reason not to perform the act. Generally, the fact that an action infringes a moral right is a decisive reason against its performance. However, individuals can forfeit some of their moral rights through their own voluntary actions; in such cases, the reasons ordinarily generated by their rights are cancelled or suspended. In other cases, the reason generated by a right may be outweighed or overridden by competing reasons; these rights are infringed but not violated.

Many scholars maintain that, outside of armed conflict, IHRL only permits killing individuals who pose an imminent threat to the lives of others. This position is probably too strong, since many legal systems permit killing that is immediately necessary to prevent an individual from carrying out a nonimminent threat to the lives of others, as well as to prevent greater harm to others (in so-called "choice of evils" cases).[7]

Still, there is no question that the scope of lawful killing is broader in war than in peace. Under IHL, individuals who pose no serious threat nevertheless voluntarily forfeit their legal right not to be killed by directly participating in hostilities, by assuming a continuous combat function within an armed group, or by joining the armed forces of a state. Roughly, taking direct part in hostilities means threatening to directly harm the armed forces or civilians of one party to a conflict on behalf of the opposing party; assuming a continuous combat function means making it one's job to take direct part in hostilities; and joining an armed

[6] See Adil Ahmad Haque, *A Theory of Jus in Bello Proportionality*, in Weighing Lives: Combatants & Civilians in War (Jens David Ohlin, Larry May, Claire Finkelstein eds., forthcoming 2016).

[7] See, e.g., American Law Institute, Model Penal Code and Commentaries §3.02 & §3.04 (1985).

force involves, among other things, making it one's job to take direct part in hostilities if ordered to do so.[8] However, under IHL, direct participation in hostilities need not involve "the infliction of death, injury, or destruction on military personnel and objects, but [encompasses] essentially any consequence adversely affecting the military operations or military capacity of a party to the conflict."[9] Even "clearing mines placed by the adversary" constitutes direct participation in hostilities under IHL.

To be clear, the problem is not that IHRL does not permit the peacetime killing of direct participants in hostilities who pose no imminent threat. After all, in peacetime, there are no hostilities in which one can participate. It is only in wartime that opposing parties deploy their respective armed forces to achieve their political objectives through organized violence. Individuals fighting within or alongside these armed forces are killed not (necessarily) to repel the threat they individually pose but (also) to defeat the armed force for whom they fight. The relevant question, then, is whether it is morally justifiable to kill individuals who fight on behalf of an armed force as a means of defeating that armed force.

There are two main possibilities. The first possibility is that all combatants, or at least all unjust combatants, forfeit their moral right not to be killed. The second possibility is that combatants only forfeit their moral right not to be killed when they participate in lethal military operations.[10] At the same time, support personnel – including cooks, mechanics, and lawyers – attenuate their moral rights in a variety of ways, most notably by placing themselves in harm's way and by preparing to fight if so ordered. The distinction between civilians and combatants is therefore preserved, albeit in modified form. On this second view, it is morally permissible to kill support personnel only if their rights are overridden, but their attenuated rights are also more readily overridden than the unattenuated rights of civilians. Intentionally killing support personnel might be permissible to prevent much greater harm to others, while unintentionally killing support personnel might be permissible to prevent comparable harm to others.

[8] See ICRC, Interpretive Guidance on the Notion of Direct Participation in Hostilities Under International Humanitarian Law 16 (Nils Melzer ed., 2009).

[9] *Id.* at 47.

[10] On "low threshold" views, even small causal contributions to an unjust threat are sufficient to forfeit one's moral right not to be killed. See Jeff McMahan, Killing in War (2009). On "high threshold" views, forfeiture requires either large causal contribution to an unjust threat or high culpability. See Seth Lazar, *Responsibility, Risk, and Killing in Self-Defense*, 119 Ethics 699 (2009).

If the first view is correct then IHL requires no modification: just combatants are morally justified in killing unjust combatants and, as we have seen, unjust combatants act less wrongfully when they kill just combatants than when they kill civilians. In contrast, if the second view is correct then IHL may require modification: since killing support personnel seldom prevents much greater harm to others, it seems that IHL should prohibit intentionally killing *known* support personnel.[11] Such a prohibition would allow the attacking force freedom of action when combat and support personnel cannot be easily distinguished and imposes no new precautionary obligations. Nevertheless, even a subjective, knowledge-based standard could prevent at least some morally unjustified killing.

In addition, under IHL the legal right of civilians not to be killed may be overridden if their deaths are a necessary and proportionate side-effect of pursuing an otherwise legitimate military advantage. Much as before, the problem is not that IHRL does not permit peacetime killing in pursuit of military advantage, since in peacetime there is no opposing armed force against which military advantage might be sought. The relevant problem is that *jus in bello* proportionality calls for a comparison between apparently incommensurable values, namely civilian losses and military advantage.[12]

Some revisionist scholars argue that the moral value of a military advantage lies in its contribution to the achievement of a just cause.[13] There are many problems with this view. First, the value of a just cause (such as collective self-determination) also may be incommensurable with the value of civilian losses. In addition, it is often impossible to even roughly quantify the contribution of a particular military advantage to the achievement of a just cause. Finally, on this view combatants who fight without a just cause cannot satisfy *jus in bello* proportionality and therefore have no reason to try.

[11] Adil Ahmad Haque, *Criminal Law and Morality at War*, in Philosophical Foundations of Criminal Law 481 (R.A. Duff & Stuart P. Green eds., 2011).

[12] See, e.g., Michael N. Schmitt, *The Principle of Discrimination in 21st Century Warfare*, 2 Yale Hum. Rts. & Dev. L.J. 143, 151 (1999) ("Optimally, balancing tests compare like values. However, proportionality calculations are heterogeneous, because dissimilar value genres–military and humanitarian–are being weighed against each other. How, for example, does one objectively calculate the relative weight of an aircraft, tank, ship, or vantage point in terms of human casualties?")

[13] See McMahan, Killing in War; Thomas Hurka, *Proportionality in the Morality of War*, 33 Philosophy & Public Affairs 34 (2005).

Instead, I argue elsewhere that the value of a military advantage lies in the losses to combatants and civilians that achieving that advantage will prevent or avoid over the remainder of the conflict.[14] Since doing harm is substantially morally worse than allowing harm, inflicting civilian losses in pursuit of a military advantage is proportionate only if achieving that military advantage will prevent or avoid substantially greater losses over the remainder of the conflict. If other norms of *jus ad bellum* and *jus in bello* are respected, the rights of civilians killed by a proportionate attack are overridden and therefore justifiably infringed rather than arbitrarily violated. Indeed, as we have seen, even unjust combatants would act less wrongfully by complying with *jus in bello* proportionality.

Epistemic Moral Justification

Clearly, not all acts that conform to IHL are objectively permissible. For example, IHL requires soldiers to "do everything feasible to verify" that their targets are combatants or military objectives.[15] However, even soldiers who satisfy this requirement will sometimes make mistakes, erroneously attacking civilians and civilian objects, and thereby act objectively impermissibly. Similarly, IHL requires soldiers to refrain from launching attacks if the *expected* harm to civilians is excessive in relation to the military advantage *anticipated*.[16] Unfortunately, soldiers often overestimate the likelihood or magnitude of potential military advantages and underestimate the likelihood or magnitude of potential harm to civilians. As a result, soldiers often launch attacks that inflict disproportionate harm on civilians and are therefore objectively impermissible.

Such cases bring us to the second sense of moral justification. An act is *epistemically* justified only if the actor reasonably believes that the act is objectively justified. More precisely, epistemically permissible acts are based on reasonable beliefs that, if true, would render the acts objectively permissible. In these cases, the actor has no decisive *epistemic* reason to believe that there is decisive *moral* reason not to perform

[14] Haque, *A Theory of Jus in Bello Proportionality*.

[15] Protocol Additional to the Geneva Conventions of 12 August 1949, and Relating to the Protection of Victims of International Armed Conflicts (Protocol I) art. 57(2)(a)(i), June 8, 1977, 1125 U.N.T.S. 3 (entered into force Dec. 7, 1978) [hereinafter Protocol I].

[16] Protocol I art. 51(5) & art. 57(2)(a)(iii).

the act. For example, a soldier who kills a civilian whom the soldier reasonably believes is a combatant is objectively unjustified but may be epistemically justified.[17]

Now, since human rights exist in virtue of facts about putative rights-holders (namely their humanity and their voluntary conduct), there is one important sense in which all objectively unjustified killings violate human rights. In this sense, a killing that is epistemically justified but objectively unjustified also violates human rights. On the other hand, a killing violates the ICCPR only if it is *arbitrary*, and an epistemically justified actor does not act arbitrarily. Epistemically justified actors are appropriately guided by moral considerations, and such guidance is the antithesis of arbitrariness. An epistemically justified soldier does not deprive others of life arbitrarily (even if some turn out to be civilians) any more than an epistemically justified judge deprives criminal defendants of liberty arbitrarily (even if some turn out to be innocent). So to the extent that IHL permits only epistemically justified killings, soldiers who conform to IHL will conform to IHRL as well.

To ensure that soldiers act with epistemic justification, IHL should be interpreted so that an attack is lawful only if the attacking force *reasonably believes* that the object of attack is a lawful target and *reasonably believes* that the military advantage they will gain will outweigh the civilian losses (if any) they will inflict. On this interpretation, soldiers should launch attacks only if the object of their attack is *probably* a combatant or military objective and only if they will *probably* prevent substantially greater harm than they will unintentionally inflict on nearby civilians. So interpreted, IHL would prohibit many wartime killings that are morally arbitrary because they are epistemically unjustified.

Some moral philosophers hold that reasonable belief is both necessary and sufficient for epistemic justification.[18] However, this view ignores the fact that often the moral risks of action and inaction are asymmetrical.[19] Indeed, other things equal, intentionally doing harm to the innocent is

[17] Derek Parfit writes that an act may be permissible or impermissible in the "fact-relative sense," the "evidence-relative" sense, or the "belief-relative" sense. DEREK PARFIT, 1 ON WHAT MATTERS, 150–51. In my terminology, an act is epistemically justified if it is permissible in both the evidence-relative sense and the belief-relative sense. My understanding of epistemic justification coheres nicely with the legal standard that reasonable belief in objective justification relieves one of criminal liability.

[18] See, e.g., *id.* at 151.

[19] Adil Ahmad Haque, *Killing in the Fog of War*, 86 SOUTHERN CALIFORNIA LAW REVIEW 63 (2012).

substantially worse than unintentionally allowing harm to the innocent. It follows that it is epistemically permissible to intentionally kill an individual only if you have (i) undefeated reason to believe that individual poses a threat to many others or (ii) very strong reason to believe that individual poses a threat to one other person. In addition, other things equal, intentionally doing harm to the innocent is much worse than unintentionally allowing harm to the innocent. It follows that it is epistemically permissible to kill one individual only if you have either (i) undefeated reason to believe that individual poses a threat to a much greater number of others or (ii) much stronger reason to believe that individual poses a threat to one other person than to believe that individual poses no threat to anyone.

It follows that soldiers often must have undefeated, decisive, or, in some cases, conclusive reason to believe that an individual is a combatant before using lethal force. For example, a targeted killing operation directed at a suspected low-level insurgent who poses no immediate threat generally is morally permissible only if the operator has conclusive reason to believe that the individual is in fact a combatant and not a civilian. Since killing low-level insurgents hardly ever prevents substantially greater harm to others, it would be epistemically impermissible to take a substantial risk of mistakenly targeting a civilian. If IHL is interpreted to impose parallel epistemic requirements, then IHL will prohibit this form of epistemically unjustified killing.

Morally Justified Legal Justification

Let us now turn to the third form of moral justification: individuals are often morally justified in following morally justified laws. Often, a law is morally justified directly, by tracking the content of objective or epistemic moral permissibility. In such cases, law simply alerts individuals to the moral reasons they have prior to and independently of law. But sometimes a law is morally justified indirectly, by helping individuals better conform to their moral obligations. When individuals would better conform to their moral obligations by following the law than by trying to follow prelegal morality the law gives individuals new reasons for action.

In following morally justified laws, individuals may sometimes perform objectively unjustified acts, but they will perform fewer or less serious objectively unjustified acts than they would by relying in their own moral judgments. In such cases, we might say that individuals have decisive reason *to do* what is objectively morally required but they also have decisive reason not *to try* to do what is objectively morally required. If they try they are likely to fail, but if they follow the law they are likely to succeed.

In general, soldiers only have decisive reasons to follow IHL if doing so will help them fulfill their moral obligations. If soldiers would make morally better decisions by ignoring IHL and relying on their own moral judgment then they would have decisive reason to do just that. As Joseph Raz famously argues, the practical authority of law rests on the service it provides to those subject to the law.[20] Soldiers should follow the law only if, by doing so, they would better conform to the other reasons that apply to them than if they tried to act directly on those reasons.[21]

To see the potential significance of this form of justification, suppose that revisionist just war theorists like Jeff McMahan are correct that some civilians forfeit their moral right not to be killed by contributing to the war effort of a party fighting for an unjust cause. On this view, IHL prohibits what is sometimes objectively justifiable: the intentional killing of civilians not directly participating in hostilities. Moreover, there may be rare cases in which intentionally killing morally liable civilians will prevent harm to others who retain their full moral rights. Nevertheless, if relatively few civilians forfeit their moral rights, and if these civilians are very difficult to distinguish from the majority of civilians who retain their moral rights, and if killing liable civilians is seldom necessary to prevent harm to others, then generally soldiers will best conform to their moral obligations by following the law rather than trying to identify liable civilians.

Now suppose that scholars like Janina Dill and Henry Shue are correct that even some combatants retain their moral right not to be killed, for example, those who act under duress or ignorance or who pose no threat and contribute little to the threats posed by their comrades. On this view, IHL permits what is sometimes objectively impermissible: the intentional killing of combatants. Nevertheless, if relatively few combatants retain their moral rights, and if these combatants are very difficult to distinguish from the majority of combatants who forfeit their moral rights, and if killing opposing combatants is often necessary to prevent harm to others who retain their full moral rights, then generally soldiers will best conform to their moral obligations by following the law rather than trying to identify non-liable combatants.

20 Joseph Raz, The Morality of Freedom (1986).

21 Adil Ahmad Haque, *Law and Morality at War*, 8 Criminal Law & Philosophy 79 (2014).

In both cases, soldiers are forced either to risk killing the morally immune or to risk allowing the morally liable to kill or help kill individuals the soldiers have a duty to protect. In these contexts, conformity to IHL is morally justified if soldiers are less likely to commit serious moral wrongs by following IHL rather than their own moral judgment. If soldiers try to distinguish morally liable combatants from morally immune combatants then they are much more likely to hesitate to use objectively justified force and allow their fellow soldiers or civilians to be harmed than to refrain from objectively unjustified force. Conversely, if soldiers try to distinguish morally liable civilians from morally immune civilians then they are much more likely to use objectively unjustified force than to refrain from objectively justified force and allow their fellow soldiers to be harmed. In such circumstances, soldiers would better conform to their moral obligations by following IHL rather than their own moral judgment.

Since doing harm generally is morally worse than allowing harm, it may seem that the legal permission to kill opposing combatants is in some ways harder to justify than the legal prohibition on killing civilians. Recall, however, that generally it is easier to justify killing nonliable combatants than to justify killing nonliable civilians since the former place themselves in harm's way, are better able to defend themselves, and choose to draw fire away from civilians. These same considerations make the legal permission to kill opposing combatants somewhat easier to justify.

In addition, the scope of the legal permission requires qualification. If it becomes apparent that an opposing combatant performs a noncombat function and is unlikely to directly participate in hostilities, then soldiers would best conform to their moral obligations by sparing that combatant. As Raz recognizes, in such clear cases, the law provides no service to its subjects and instead only leads them astray.[22] I argued earlier that IHL should adopt a new rule prohibiting the intentional killing of combatants whom one knows do not perform combat functions and are not directly participating in hostilities. As the law stands, the legal permission to kill opposing combatants carries moral force only in unclear cases. Naturally, it is in unclear cases that sparing combatants is most likely to result in allowing harm to one's own forces or civilians. So understood, the legal permission to kill opposing combatants seems morally justified.

It might appear that on these issues IHL simply requires epistemic permissibility. If most civilians are not morally liable then perhaps it is

[22] Raz, The Morality of Freedom, at 62.

presumptively reasonable to believe that each particular civilian is not morally liable. Similarly, if most unjust combatants are morally liable then perhaps it is presumptively reasonable to believe that each particular combatant is morally liable. However, things are not as they appear. On the revisionist account, moral liability to attack is a function of (a) the degree of an individual's contribution to a threat, (b) the degree of her moral responsibility, and (c) the degree of her moral justification. On such an account, the fact that an individual is a civilian or a combatant is at best very weak evidence that the individual is morally liable to attack. It cannot be epistemically permissible to kill another human being based on such weak evidence. The point of relying on IHL is to allow soldiers to bypass individualized assessments of liability when the moral stakes are high but the available evidence is weak. Moreover, soldiers should not trust the reasonableness of their beliefs regarding the moral liability of civilians, which are susceptible to distortion by nonrational factors. Soldiers would better avoid killing morally immune civilians by following IHL than by following their own judgment. This is the service IHL should aim to provide soldiers.

Limiting Killing in War

I have proposed that the guiding aim of IHL should be to help soldiers avoid morally impermissible killing. To the extent that IHL fulfills this aim it will be substantively compatible with IHRL, irrespective of their formal relationship.

Admittedly, mine is a heterodox account of IHL. According to the orthodox account, the guiding aim of IHL should be to prohibit militarily unnecessary killing. For example, on this view IHL rightly prohibits targeting civilians because generally it is unnecessary for armed forces to target civilians in order to defeat opposing armed forces. This view is sometimes expressed in terms of striking a balance between military and humanitarian considerations.[23] Unfortunately, the rhetoric of balancing often proves empty. When military and humanitarian considerations

[23] See, e.g., Declaration Renouncing the Use, in Time of War, of Explosive Projectiles Under 400 Grammes Weight pmbl., Nov. 29, 1868, 18 Martens Nouveau Recueil (ser. 1) 474 (provisions "fixed the technical limits at which the necessities of war ought to yield to the requirements of humanity").

directly and broadly conflict, military considerations always prevail.[24] On the orthodox view, IHL should only prohibit killings that are always militarily unnecessary or hardly ever militarily necessary.

Recently, Janina Dill and Henry Shue have offered a vigorous philosophical defense of the orthodox account. On their view, the aim of IHL should be "to limit *all* killing [in armed conflict] as much as possible."[25] It is not possible to limit killing in ways that make winning impossible, because parties determined to win will simply ignore such limitations. However, it is possible to limit killing in ways that make winning more difficult. Dill and Shue reason that the law is right to categorically prohibit targeting civilians because this prohibition limits the killing of a large category of individuals and generally it is possible to win without targeting civilians. In some cases, it may be *easier* to win by targeting civilians, but this is an option that the law can foreclose without being systematically ignored. The law is also right not to prohibit targeting combatants because generally it is not possible to win without targeting combatants. According to Dill and Shue, "the rules for the conduct of war cannot in general restrict the killing of combatants" or they will be ignored.[26] Since all individuals are either civilians or combatants, it follows that the legal prohibition on intentionally killing civilians limits lawful killing in armed conflict as much as possible.[27]

Importantly, Dill and Shue argue that most combatants do not forfeit their moral right not to be killed. It seems to follow that, on this view, IHL and IHRL conflict sharply, since intentionally killing individuals who retain their moral right not to be killed (almost always) violates IHRL. Moreover, since IHL and IHRL have different guiding aims,

[24] See, e.g., Convention Respecting the Laws and Customs of War on Land, pmbl. para. 5, Oct. 18, 1907, 36 Stat. 2277, 207 Consol. T.S. 277 (Hague Convention IV "inspired by the desire to diminish the evils of war, as far as military requirements permit"); Michael N. Schmitt, *Military Necessity and Humanity in International Humanitarian Law: Preserving the Delicate Balance*, 50 Virginia Journal of International Law 796 (2010).

[25] Janina Dill & Henry Shue, *Limiting the Killing in War: Military Necessity and the St. Petersburg Assumption*, 26 Ethics & International Affairs 311, 319 (2012).

[26] *Id.* at 323.

[27] Interestingly, Dill and Shue write that "proportionality . . . prohibits conduct that, even though it might be necessary, can be expected to cause unintended but foreseeable civilian damage that is excessive." Dill & Shue, at 320. Presumably they believe that attacks that are tactically necessary to achieve concrete and direct military advantages are seldom strategically necessary to defeat opposing armed forces. Otherwise, on their assumptions, *jus in bello* proportionality would fail to constrain the conduct of parties determined to win.

conflicts between them can be resolved only by subordinating one aim to the other. For example, Dill and Shue argue that, by limiting lawful killing as much as possible, IHL indirectly minimizes human rights violations as much as possible.[28] Thus, while IHRL aims to *prohibit* human rights violations, IHL aims to *minimize* human rights violations in part by *permitting* some human rights violations. If IHL displaces IHRL then international law simply privileges the aggregative aim of IHL over the individualistic aim of IHRL.

As Dill and Shue observe, "even if we all agree on noncombatant immunity, it matters what underlies the application of discrimination."[29] As it happens, Dill and Shue provide the wrong explanation for the right result. Dill and Shue recognize that, if many soldiers retain their moral rights then in some cases soldiers may violate fewer rights by targeting civilians than by targeting combatants. In these cases, by limiting *lawful* killing in war IHL may increase *actual* killing. When means subvert ends in this way, rule-consequentialism seems like rule-fetishism. It is not clear why combatants who internalize the aim of reducing overall suffering in war will follow the legal rule prohibiting attacks on civilians if attacking civilians will in fact reduce overall suffering. While the orthodox view aims to reduce overall suffering in war, IHL in fact concentrates suffering in war on one category of individuals and away from another category of individuals.

The deeper problem with the orthodox view is that the utility of targeting civilians is an empirical, contingent matter. It may turn out that sharp wars are brief, that wars are less frequent if they are more terrible, and that fewer restraints will mean less overall suffering. To take an extreme example, suppose that a legal rule permitting the intentional killing of young children will in fact reduce overall suffering in war. Such a rule might deter states from initiating armed conflict and encourage belligerents to surrender more quickly when victory is in doubt. On the orthodox view, this seems like a strong reason for IHL to adopt this legal rule and permit the intentional killing of young children. If that implication seems hard to accept then civilian immunity likely does not rest on empirical contingencies as the orthodox view suggests. On the contrary, it is intrinsically wrong to intentionally kill civilians and a legal permission to do so would lack legitimate authority because it would not help combatants conform to their moral obligations.

[28] Dill & Shue, at 329. [29] Dill & Shue, at 330.

Similarly, there is only an empirically contingent connection between the voluntary conduct of combatants and the utility of killing them, but there is a morally necessary connection between the voluntary conduct of combatants and the morality of killing them. There are moral considerations that systematically favor legal rules that permit targeting combatants and prohibit targeting civilians. Suppose that individuals who fight on behalf of an armed force pursuing an unjust cause do not forfeit their moral right not to be killed as a means of defeating that armed force. It remains the case that many combatants pose unjust threats to others (either individually or jointly) or intentionally make direct and substantial contributions to the unjust threats posed by others. This contrasts sharply with the indirect and marginal contributions of almost all civilians. In addition, even conscripts have some opportunity to avoid becoming or remaining combatants, while civilians have no opportunity to avoid becoming or remaining civilians (other than becoming combatants, of course). Finally, combatants are less vulnerable and defenseless than civilians because they are trained and equipped to protect themselves and each other.[30] It follows that killing civilians is, at a minimum, intrinsically morally worse than killing combatants. Accordingly, IHL should not aim to limit all killing as much as possible and distribute lawful killing accordingly. Instead, IHL should skew the distribution of actual killings by strictly limiting the morally worst killings (of civilians) while broadly permitting comparatively less morally regrettable killings (of combatants).

There is a subtler problem with Dill and Shue's account. It is not clear why individual soldiers would follow rules justified solely on such grounds rather than follow their own moral judgment. After all, Dill and Shue do not argue that soldiers will violate fewer people's right to life by following IHL than by violating IHL, or even that a smaller proportion of their killings will violate human rights if they follow IHL than if they violate IHL. They argue only that soldiers who follow IHL will only violate the human rights of one category of people but not another category of people. It is hard to see why a rational, moral soldier would abstain from militarily efficacious actions on such grounds.

Soldiers are not computers, and legal norms are not software programs. Soldiers are human beings with moral obligations and capable of moral judgment, and the law of armed conflict must address them as such. Soldiers need a reason to obey the law, and the most obvious reason

[30] Lazar, Sparing Civilians.

to do so is that they will better fulfill their moral obligations by following the law than by following their independent moral judgment. As Lazar nicely observes, rule-consequentialism is a third-personal view of moral justification, while soldiers need a first-personal view that addresses them as moral agents.[31] While the orthodox account may provide a causal explanation of why states accept IHL it does not provide a moral account of why soldiers should follow IHL.

Interpretation

I have argued that IHL should aim to prohibit morally unjustified killing in armed conflict, and that IHL's success in pursuing that aim will determine the compatibility of IHL and IHRL. With this aim in mind, I have offered novel interpretations of several IHL norms, at times drawing on unfamiliar concepts and novel moral claims. In offering these interpretations, I have implicitly assumed that it is legitimate to interpret a body of laws in its morally best light, in accordance with the aim it morally should have rather than the aim its creators might have had.

The problem begins with the drafters of Protocol I, who deployed imprecise terms such as "feasible," "excessive," "expected," and "anticipated" without defining them. It is futile to interpret these terms "in good faith," "in accordance with the[ir] ordinary meaning," and "in their context."[32] Such a narrow approach inevitably "[l]eaves the meaning" of these terms "ambiguous or obscure," and this legal indeterminacy cannot be resolved through "recourse . . . to supplementary means of interpretation" such as preparatory materials and concluding commentary.[33] The only hope seems to lie in recourse to the "object and purpose" of Protocol I, the Geneva Conventions and Protocols as a group, and perhaps the law of armed conflict as a whole.

Now suppose that the orthodox view is descriptively sound even if it is normatively unsound. Suppose, that is, that the conscious object and purpose of the drafters of Protocol I was not to prohibit morally unjustified killing but to limit all killing in armed conflict to the greatest extent that most states would accept. We could then interpret vague and ambiguous terms in Protocol I in light of this aim. On this view, interpretation of IHL would have a peculiar predictive dimension: a "feasible" precaution would

[31] See SETH LAZAR, *The Morality and Law of War*, in ROUTLEDGE COMPANION TO PHILOSOPHY OF LAW (Andrei Marmor ed. 2012).

[32] Vienna Convention, art. 31. [33] *Id.* art. 32.

be the most demanding precaution that most states would accept; harm to civilians would be "excessive" only if most states would be willing to forego the anticipated military advantage under similar circumstances. No doubt it will prove difficult to reliably predict the behavior of most states. Moreover, such predictions will presumably depend on the actual motivations of most states, which may be morally defective. This is not an attractive view. Importantly, were we to try to salvage this view by instead asking whether most states could *reasonably* reject a possible interpretation of IHL we would presumably reduce the orthodox account to my heterodox account. After all, no state could reasonably reject an interpretation of IHL that prohibits morally unjustified killing.

Perhaps the orthodox account yields a different interpretive principle. Suppose that the aim of IHL is simply to limit all killing in armed conflict, subject to the constraint that it cannot limit killing more than most states would accept. On this view, once the existence of an IHL norm has been accepted by most states its content should be interpreted solely in light of the aim of limiting all killing. On this view, interpretation of IHL would have a consequentialist character: a "feasible" precaution would be one whose expected benefits outweigh its expected costs; expected harm to civilians would be "excessive" in relation to anticipated military advantage if an attack's expected costs outweigh its expected benefits. This view ignores both the moral asymmetry between doing and allowing harm and the reasonable belief requirement of epistemic permissibility. This, too, is not an attractive view.

What we need is an argument to the effect that, when the content of a legal norm cannot be fixed solely by reference to positive legal materials, it is not only morally desirable but also legally legitimate to resolve any residual legal indeterminacy in the most morally attractive way possible. A full presentation of such an argument would require a deeper engagement with jurisprudential questions than I can offer here. What follows is a sketch of what such an argument might look like.

The constitutive aim of all law is to guide human conduct through positive normative standards. The positive nature of law distinguishes law from morality while the normative nature of law distinguishes law from mere incentives. For law to succeed in its constitutive aim, it must provide those subject to the law with decisive reasons to accept its guidance. The basic task of legal interpretation is to help law achieve its constitutive aim by casting positive legal materials in their morally best light, that is, in the light that most clearly reveals the reasons the law provides. Of course, some laws are clear, unambiguous, and morally indefensible. In such cases, positive legal materials make a morally attractive interpretation unsustainable. The failure of such laws to achieve their constitutive aim is so complete that the failure cannot be cured through interpretation alone. But if a particular law is unclear and ambiguous then interpretation can serve the constitutive aim of all law without directly contradicting the specific aim of the law in question. Put another way, where the specific aim of the drafters of a law is indeterminate it is appropriate to revert to the constitutive aim that the drafters implicitly adopted as their own general aim when they chose to pursue their specific aims through law.

To close on a conciliatory note, observe that, in a sense, my heterodox view also balances military and humanitarian considerations. On my view, the military considerations favoring a permissive interpretation of IHL are just the moral reasons supporting a legally questionable attack, such as the losses the attack might prevent to the attacking force or its civilian population. The humanitarian considerations favoring a restrictive interpretation of IHL are just the moral reasons opposing the attack, such as the losses the attack might inflict on the civilian population of the opposing party. The morally appropriate balance between these competing considerations is struck through moral principles that permit an attack only when the moral reasons in favor of the attack are at least as strong as the moral reasons against the attack, rendering the attack morally justifiable. In this sense, the heterodox approach to interpreting IHL is itself a morally attractive interpretation of the orthodox approach to interpreting IHL.

Conclusion

As we have seen, there is no *a priori* guarantee that IHL respects human rights, prohibits arbitrary killing, or converges with IHRL. Such convergence remains a contingent, incomplete, and fragile human project. Certainly, IHL cannot prevent all objectively impermissible killing or undeserved suffering in armed conflict. At its best, war is never more than the lesser of two grave evils. However, IHL can prohibit objectively and epistemically impermissible killing and serve soldiers well by indirectly helping them avoid objectively impermissible killing. If IHL achieves this goal then a soldier who follows IHL – as well as a morally sound law governing the resort to military force – will avoid morally arbitrary killing and thereby respect human rights. This limited yet still ambitious goal should be the guiding aim of IHL.

2

Human Rights Thinking and the Laws of War

DAVID LUBAN*

In a significant early case, the ICTY found a Croatian military commander named Anto Furundzija guilty as an aider and abettor of rapes committed by his troops. In the course of its judgment, the Trial Chamber of the ICTY commented:

> The essence of the whole corpus of international humanitarian law as well as human rights law lies in the protection of the human dignity of every person.... The general principle of respect for human dignity is ... the very *raison d'être* of international humanitarian law and human rights law; indeed in modern times it has become of such paramount importance as to permeate the whole body of international law.[1]

Is it true that international humanitarian law (IHL) and international human rights law share the same "essence," and that essence is the general principle of respect for human dignity? Is it true that, in the words of Charles Beitz, humanitarian law is "perhaps better described as the law of 'human rights in armed conflicts'"?[2] To answer yes, I will argue, amounts to a reinterpretation of IHL that drifts far from its history. In its origins, IHL was not designed to protect human dignity, but to reduce human suffering. The ICTY Trial Chamber instead viewed IHL through a human rights lens that assimilates the two motivations, as does Beitz and the authors he quotes.

* University Professor in Law and Philosophy, Georgetown University Law Center; Class of 1984 Distinguished Visitor in Ethics, Stockdale Center for Ethical Leadership, United States Naval Academy. This paper owes an obvious debt to Theodore Meron, *The Humanization of Humanitarian Law*, 94 AJIL 239 (2000) and Gabriella Blum, *The Individualization of War: From War to Policing in the Regulation of Armed Conflicts*, LAW AND WAR 48 (AUSTIN SARAT ET AL. EDS., 2014), available on SSRN at http://ssrn.com/abstract=2231168. The argument and analysis are, however, different from both Meron and Blum.

1 Prosecutor v. Furundzija, Judgment, Case No. IT-95-17/1-T, T.Ch. II, 10 Dec. 1998, 183.

2 CHARLES R. BEITZ, THE IDEA OF HUMAN RIGHTS 14 (2009) (quoting Sean MacBride, as quoted in Geoffrey Best, *Justice, International Relations and Human Rights*, 71 INT'L AFFAIRS (1995), at 780).

This is not a criticism of the *Furundzija* dictum. Law changes. In every field of law, latter-day authorities – paradigmatically, but not solely, courts and tribunals – retroactively reinterpret the law. Their reinterpretation takes on a self-fulfilling, performative role: the court's saying it is so helps make it so. This is the path of the law; it is one way law evolves. Perhaps the nature of IHL has evolved over time in the direction of human rights thinking, and should evolve that way.

That, in fact, is the view I will defend – with some qualifications – in the final sections of this essay. First, though, I want to explore the very different genealogies of IHL and human rights law, and explain how human rights thinking migrated into IHL. (To briefly foreshadow my argument, I attribute the migration to international criminal law, military occupations, and the U.S. war on terrorism.) In the final sections, I explore two ways human rights thinking can be pursued in wars. One of them, I will argue, overplays and overestimates what human rights thinking can accomplish. It does so by, in effect, willing away fundamental differences between war and peace. The other is an approach that I have defended for more than three decades. It consists, at bottom, of taking a civilian's-eye view of the disasters of war and reading the law accordingly – recognizing, one might say, that Mother Courage and her children matter just as much to the law of war as Henry V and his band of brothers.

Human Rights Thinking and Human Dignity

Human rights law gives pride of place to what *Furundzija* calls "the general principle of respect for human dignity." Most of the central international human rights instruments, including the U.N. Charter, the UDHR, the two major human rights covenants, the Helsinki Accords, the African Charter of Human and Peoples' Rights, the American Convention on Human Rights, and the European Charter of Human Rights, link human rights with human dignity. Some of these documents declare that human dignity is the basis of human rights.

Does that make human dignity the "essence" of human rights law, as the *Furundzija* dictum says? Set to one side the question of whether human rights law *has* an essence, an issue about which philosophers disagree.[3] Set aside as well the question of what human dignity is,

[3] This is one of the major themes of BEITZ's book, *supra* note 2. See also John Tasioulas, *Human Rights, Universality and the Values of Personhood: Retracing Griffin's Steps*, 10

exactly – for of course the concept of human dignity lacks anything remotely like a consensus definition. A worked-out theory of human rights would have to answer these questions. Here I am asking something different: whether, pretheoretically and intuitively, there is a connection between human dignity and human rights. I think the answer is yes.

Whatever one's theory of human rights, ascribing moral importance to them involves at least two fundamental commitments: that every individual human being should count as a worthy object of concern, and that no one should have to beg for their rights. Rights fulfillment is not charity on the part of the powerful toward the less fortunate. The former commitment *is* a commitment to human dignity, at the very least because viewing individuals as worthy objects of concern confers dignity on them. The latter is a commitment to treat human rights as rights. It is hard to see how someone who rejects the commitment to valuing humans as individuals could believe in human dignity under any conceivable definition. Nor could someone who rejects the commitment to viewing concern for the individual as an entitlement rather than a gratuity believe that human rights are, in fact, *rights*. Someone who shares these individual-value and entitlement commitments will engage in what I call *human rights thinking*, and will incline to bring it into the interpretation of law, including humanitarian law. Notice also that these commitments imply the kind of universalism characteristic of international human rights: everyone has human dignity and human rights, regardless of nationality.

Let me reiterate that human rights thinking is not the same thing as human rights theory or human rights law. The individual-value and entitlement commitments are pretheoretical and prelegal. As bare normative attitudes, they are too general and too thin to generate a theory of human dignity or human rights on their own. A full-fledged theory will need additional premises to get off the ground.

To illustrate: some religious people will ground human dignity in the divine creation of an immortal human soul, or in humanity's divinely ordained superiority to the rest of nature. Secularists might ground human dignity in rationality, or in autonomy, or in agency – or, as I think, in the reciprocal recognition of the dignity of others: the relation

EUROPEAN J. PHIL. 79, 88–94 (2002). Compare Beitz's anti-essentialist view with JAMES GRIFFIN, ON HUMAN RIGHTS (2008) (arguing that human rights are protections of human beings' normative agency).

between the dignifier and the dignified.[4] Provided the believer and the secularist share a commitment to honoring individual human worth as an entitlement, both engage in human rights thinking, and both may wind up approaching concrete practical issues of implementation the same way even though their theories of human dignity are radically inconsistent.

What about the entitlement commitment? As Joel Feinberg explains,

> Rights are not mere gifts or favors, motivated by love or pity, for which gratitude is the sole fitting response. A right is something that can be demanded or insisted upon without embarrassment or shame.... A world with claim-rights is one in which all persons, as actual or potential claimants, are dignified objects of respect, both in their own eyes and in the view of others.[5]

If Feinberg is right (as I think he is), the entitlement commitment seamlessly meshes with the commitment to viewing others as, in his words, dignified objects of respect. But that commitment could come from many possible religious or secular doctrines – or, for that matter, from no doctrine at all.

Human Rights Thinking and Humanitarianism: No Necessary Connection

The next question is whether everyone who participates in the project of furthering humanitarian law shares the twin commitments of human rights thinking. The answer is no; they may, but they don't have to. An anti-individualist who believes that individuals take on value only within and through collectivities, or even a cynic who doesn't think individuals matter much, can still favor regulating war to minimize suffering and destruction; and a commitment to eliminate unnecessary suffering and destruction does not imply that humane treatment is a right.

I don't mean this purely as a theoretician's point. Everyone working in this area has met tough-minded humanitarians with years of field experience who are allergic to human rights pieties and skeptical that their job has to do with enhancing human dignity rather than stanching the flow of blood in catastrophes. Some of these workers nonetheless put their lives on the line repeatedly in the world's most dangerous conflict zones,

[4] David Luban, Torture, Power, and Law 141–42 (2014).
[5] Joel Feinberg, Social Philosophy 58–59 (1973).

perhaps feeling more affinity with the combat soldiers than with the human rights NGOs. For that matter, operational military lawyers and advisors may be whole-heartedly committed to humanitarian law, but view it as a matter of military honor rather than human rights. Of course, other humanitarian workers and lawyers do share the individual-value and entitlement commitments, and believe that their humanitarian efforts are part of a larger human rights project. As a factual matter, then, human rights thinking is optional, not mandatory, for humanitarians. There is no intrinsic connection between the humanitarian project and the human rights project.

As the papers in this volume illustrate, it is a difficult and contested legal question whether international human rights law (hereafter "IHRL") takes priority over IHL, or the other way around, or neither, in armed conflicts. This can be treated as a lawyer's technical question. As such, it quickly leads down the rabbit hole into a Wonderland of dueling dicta, fragmented legal authorities, conflicting proportionality tests, and numbing intricacy. The International Court of Justice and the U.N. Human Rights Committee tell us that human rights law applies at all times, but they add that in wartime it must be interpreted through the *lex specialis* of IHL.[6] The European Court of Human Rights finds that the European Charter does not apply in active combat when NATO is bombing a Belgrade television station, but it does apply when Turkish troops cross the border and murder shepherds in Iraq.[7] The U.S. government and the U.N. Human Rights Committee offer conflicting interpretations of the grammatically ambiguous jurisdiction clause in the ICCPR, with one finding human rights obligations only within a state's own territory and jurisdiction while the other finds them everywhere – both readings that the clause can support[8] – and so on.

But the legalisms are pretty clearly a stand-in for a broader debate about the very nature of war and peace and the laws that regulate them, and that debate is not technical at all. Is IHRL fundamentally law for peacetime, because it assumes a set of peacetime institutions to give it effect? Must it, therefore, give way in armed conflicts to the law of war? Or is IHRL a universal law governing war as well as peace? How we

6 ICJ Nuclear Weapons Advisory Opinion, I.C.J. Reports 1996, p. 226; Human Rights Committee General Comment 31, §11.

7 Banković and Others v. Belgium, [2001] ECHR 890, Issa and Others v. Turkey, [2004] ECHR 629.

8 General Comment 31, §§3, 10.

answer that question will very likely turn on whether we share the commitments of human rights thinking. Whatever one's answer to legal questions about the scope and meaning of treaties, the current state of customary international law, or the doctrine of *lex specialis*, texts like the *Furundzija* dictum vividly illustrate something far less legalistic: human rights thinking at work in IHL. Even if the legal authorities are ambiguous and opaque, yielding no obvious answer to questions about the reach of human rights law during armed conflict, the urge to export human rights *thinking* to IHL is evident, and in some cases it affects legal outcomes.[9]

A Genealogy of Humanitarian Law

To understand how far human rights thinking departs from the original spirit of IHL, we would do well to revisit the "creation myths" of IHL and IHRL. As every student of the subject knows, modern IHL began when the Swiss businessman Henri Dunant visited the battlefield of Solferino shortly after the battle; the horrible suffering of thousands of wounded and dying men moaning for surcease moved Dunant to found the Red Cross. The Red Cross's purpose was relief of suffering in the horrors of war, and that was the motivation for the founding treaties of modern IHL. In philosophical terms, we could say that IHL was Benthamite in spirit – although I will use the lower-case "benthamite" to decouple the point I am making from the historical Bentham. A benthamite focuses on aggregate pleasure and pain as the measure of good and bad, and its moral imperatives are to maximize pleasure and minimize pain.[10] Philosophers refer to the pain-minimization component as "negative utilitarianism," and humanitarianism in war is plainly a form of negative benthamism.[11]

[9] This phenomenon might be regarded as an instance of the emergence of "humanity law," Ruti Teitel's term for a kind of unified-field theory of protections of human interests running across IHL, IHRL, and ICL. Ruti Teitel, Humanity's Law (2011). I think of human rights thinking as a more discrete and particular phenomenon; and in any case, as I show below, "humanity" is ambiguous. It can be interpreted in an aggregative way that excludes human rights thinking from IHL, or in the individuating, human dignity oriented way of the individual-worth and entitlement commitments. See the following discussion of the genealogy of humanitarian law.

[10] So much, at any rate, corresponds with the thought of the historical Bentham, as the opening paragraphs of *The Principles of Morals and Legislation* makes clear.

[11] John Fabian Witt argues that in the 19th century there was also an alternative conceptualization of wartime suffering as an ennobling byproduct of the hard work of

Notoriously, utilitarianism in both its negative benthamite form (focusing on pain minimization) and other forms is an anti-individualist doctrine. What matters is the aggregate of utility within some population of sentient beings. In the words of H.L.A. Hart,

> utilitarianism is not, as it is sometimes said to be, an individualistic and egalitarian doctrine, although in a sense it treats people as equals, or of equal worth. For it does this only by in effect treating individual persons as of *no* worth; since not persons . . . but the experiences of pleasure or satisfaction or happiness which persons have are the sole items of worth or elements of value.[12]

Each counts for one because none counts for anything. In the familiar language of Rawls, Nozick, and Hart, utilitarianism disregards the separateness of persons.

Within humanitarian law, there is no clearer example than the doctrine of *in bello* proportionality, which forbids attacks in which "incidental" civilian damage is anticipated to exceed concrete and direct military advantage. The "incidental" civilian damage is *aggregate* damage from the attack. It follows that individual civilians can lose protection from attack merely because they have the bad luck to be near an important target and surrounded by too few other civilians. Their human rights play no role in the proportionality assessment, which aggregates damage to civilian persons, and indeed aggregates damage to persons with damage to inanimate objects. Perhaps the decision to label unintended civilian

accomplishing just ends in the world. John Fabian Witt, *Two Conceptions of Suffering in War*, *in* Knowing the Suffering of Others 129 (Austin Sarat ed., 2014). Such a view, which Witt finds in the outlook of Dunant's contemporary Francis Lieber – the drafter of the first modern code of IHL – of course has a hard time making sense of the suffering of innocent civilians. Indeed, Lieber's thinking is quite antithetical to negative benthamism, and thus to the tradition of IHL I am describing. Famously, Lieber was among those who believed that ferocious wars that inflict a great deal of suffering will be shorter, and therefore save more lives in the long run. As Witt shows in his magnificent historical study Lincoln's Code: The Laws of War in American History (2012), U.S. delegates to the Hague conferences trotted out Lieber's "short, sharp wars" thesis to ward off humanitarian rules they disliked. *Id.* at 350–52. Thus, the tradition of IHL I am describing is not at all Lieber's view; however, it does represent the international view embodied in the St. Petersburg Declaration and the Hague Conventions.

Of course, what is remarkable about Lieber's "short, sharp wars" thesis is its total lack of any empirical basis. Obviously, there is no way to test whether more or fewer lives would have been lost if a war had been fought differently under different rules. There is nothing "realist" about an argument couched in the idiom of alternate-reality fiction.

12 H.L.A. Hart, *Between Utility and Rights*, 79 Columb. L. Rev. 828, 830 (1979).

damage "incidental" is already a tip-off that human dignity does not play a starring role in the proportionality rule.

One might object that the proportionality rule is simply one feature of the broader principle of distinction, and that principle should be understood as a recognition of the human dignity of noncombatants. That is possible, and understanding it this way represents human rights thinking in IHL. But the principle of distinction can just as readily be interpreted along benthamite lines as an effort to minimize unnecessary suffering in war, given the axiom that targeting civilians is militarily unnecessary.

That is exactly how the founding documents of IHL reasoned. Consider the preamble to the 1868 St. Petersburg Declaration, one of the earliest documents in modern IHL:

> Considering that the progress of civilization should have the effect of alleviating as much as possible the calamities of war:
>
> That the only legitimate object which States should endeavour to accomplish during war is to weaken the military forces of the enemy;
>
> That for this purpose it is sufficient to disable the greatest possible number of men. . . .[13]

The first clause sets out a benthamite rationale for IHL (alleviating the calamities of war), while the third asserts the (debatable but henceforth axiomatic) military proposition that disabling combatants is by itself sufficient to win wars. Although the operative portions of the St. Petersburg Declaration do not include the principle of distinction, the principle follows naturally from the reasoning in this preamble. If disabling combatants suffices to win wars, targeting civilians is unnecessary, so it is not (in the words of the second clause) a "legitimate object" for states. The reasoning, grounding IHL in the benthamite concern to alleviate the calamities of war rather than respect for human dignity, seems the more plausible origin of the principle of distinction.

This is not to say that originally there were no human dignity concepts in the historical law of war. Quite the contrary: from the time of *The Iliad* to the chivalric period to modern times, the laws of war placed heavy emphasis on the dignity of the warriors. When two Homeric princes set about the grim business of trying to slaughter each other, recognizing the enemy as a doughty warrior like oneself is the form respecting human dignity takes. In the *Mahabharata*, the *dharmayuddha* ("righteous war")

[13] Declaration of St. Petersburg, Nov. 29, 1868, available at http://avalon.law.yale.edu/19th_century/decpeter.asp.

emphasizes chivalry and symmetrical response: chariots must fight other chariots, and it would be dishonorable, contrary to the *dharma*, for a charioteer to fight a mere foot-soldier.[14] Parallel examples of dignity understood as warrior's honor can be found in texts as disparate as Chinese chronicles of the Duke of Sung and the medieval English poem *The Battle of Maldon*, both of which portray commanders for whom losing honorably is better than winning dishonorably.[15] Warriors' honor was and remains the central concept of military ethics as militaries understand it. The dignity of the warrior may be the prototypical conception of human dignity in warfare. Warriors had agency; civilians would be treated mercifully as a matter of policy or compassion, but that would be the warrior's prerogative, a matter of warrior's virtue and not of the dignity and rights of civilians.

To be sure, the Martens Clause of the 1899 Hague Convention places civilians under the protection of the "laws of humanity, and the requirements of public conscience," but it does not specify the content of those laws or explain what public conscience requires. The preamble speaks of a "desire to diminish the evils of war so far as military necessities permit," but this is just as consistent with negative benthamism as it is with human rights thinking. Historical evidence suggests that the drafters had in mind the persecution of Christians in the Ottoman Empire, which were denounced as offenses against the laws of humanity.[16] We could call this human rights thinking; if so, however, the emphasis is on the collective right of a religious minority, and not individual human rights more generally. The only place civilian rights are mentioned as such in the Hague Convention is in Article 46 of the Annex to Hague II. Article 46

14 In recent times, an Indian general blamed the *dharmayuddha* tradition for the bad decision to deploy Indian tanks solely against enemy tanks in the 1965 India–Pakistan war. Kaushik Roy, Hinduism and the Ethics of Warfare in South Asia: From Antiquity to the Present 245 (2012).

15 5 The Chinese Classics 183 (James Legge ed. and trans., 1893), quoted in Michael Walzer, Just and Unjust Wars: A Moral Argument with Historical Illustrations 225 (1978). The Battle of Maldon (Douglas B. Killings trans. 1991), at www.english.ox.ac.uk/oecoursepack/maldon_resources/Translations/Killingsfull.htm.

16 On this point see the fascinating article by Peter Holquist, "Crimes Against Humanity": Genealogy of a Concept (unpublished manuscript 2012), at 15–16. Holquist traces the concept back to the energetic activism of progressive Russian jurists in czarist Russia. For a skeptical reading of the Martens Clause, see Antonio Cassese, *The Martens Clause: Half a Loaf or Simply Pie in the Sky?*, 11 Eur. J. Intl. L. 187 (2000). Cassese argued that the great powers inserted the Martens Clause in order to forestall more specific protections of occupied countries favored by smaller states.

protects "[f]amily honor and rights, individual lives and private property, as well as religious convictions and liberty," but only in the context of military occupation – a point that we shall see is extremely important in modern debates about IHL and human rights law.[17] "Family honor and rights" refers obliquely to the rights of families not to have their wives and daughters raped; the individual right of the wives and daughters not to be raped is subsumed into family honor. So, while the Martens Clause and Article 46 can be regarded as proto-human-rights doctrines for countries under military occupation, both are limited in scope and radically defective by modern standards. And neither so much as mentions individual human rights as a moral or legal category.

Humanitarianism and Disaster Relief

Sometimes newcomers find the label "humanitarian law" applied to the law of armed conflict startling – almost a joke, and not an especially funny one. War is the least humanitarian of activities. The incongruity dissolves, of course, once we understand that the label doesn't refer to war-fighting, but to the effort to mitigate the suffering it inflicts.

In this respect, humanitarianism in the face of war is like humanitarianism in the face of earthquakes, floods, plagues, or famines: it aims at disaster relief. When the disasters are natural, we do not think of the victims' sufferings as human rights violations. Mother Nature has not violated the victims' human rights by causing an earthquake.[18]

From the point of view of common people through most of history, wars were like natural disasters. The Second Horseman of the Apocalypse, "given power to take peace from the earth and to make men slay each other" (Revelations 6:3–4), rides side by side with Famine, Pestilence, and Death, representing natural disasters.[19] Wars were launched by distant princes for inscrutable reasons; warriors descended on the countryside like a force of nature; common people suffered and died, as

[17] Article 46, Annex.

[18] This is not to deny that states may violate their human rights *ex ante* by neglecting earthquake-safety measures and *ex post* by doing too little to respond to the catastrophe.

[19] Today, thanks to Amartya Sen, we know that famines are generally man-made disasters, not natural disasters. Amartya Sen, Poverty and Famines: An Essay on Entitlement and Deprivation (1983) (arguing that famines result from lack of money, not lack of food). It would be anachronistic to think the authors of the Book of Revelations held this view.

in a plague. Those were the facts of life. The humanitarian mission, when it existed, was to ease the pain – not because the rights of the suffering had been violated, but because human compassion and simple decency demanded it.

Of course, we don't have to see things this way: we can recognize that war-fighters are not impersonal violent forces; they have agency and responsibility. International criminal law insists that we view them that way – and, I will suggest below, international criminal law was one of the forces that brought human rights thinking into humanitarian law. My point here is that in its original motivation, humanitarian law is more like disaster relief than the vindication of rights.

Disaster relief seldom if ever makes the victims of a large-scale disaster whole; that is nearly impossible. This is another signal that humanitarianism has little to do with the rights of the victims. There is an illuminating parallel in the law of torts. When an individual suffers a tort, she has a right to compensation, typically if fancifully described as "making her whole." In mass torts with thousands of victims, make-whole compensation seldom happens; it would cost too much, and the threat of defendant bankruptcy that would further deplete the settlement fund keeps awards relatively small. The settlement fund pays victims a few cents on the dollar; it offers help but not full compensation. As thoughtful commentators have noticed, that makes the settlements in mass tort more like disaster relief than make-whole compensation – and to just that extent, they have faint connection to the victims' rights, only to their needs, and even there only up to a point.[20]

And, of course, "disaster relief" as I have described it, is another name for negative benthamism in the face of catastrophes.

A Genealogy of International Human Rights Law

The creation story of the UDHR is also well known. It has been elegantly told in the books by Mary Ann Glendon and Johannes Morsink. Only slightly less well-known is the diplomacy that went into the U.N. Charter's embrace of human rights (although on the latter issue there

[20] John C. P. Goldberg, *Misconduct, Misfortune, and Just Compensation: Weinstein on Torts*, 97 Colum. L. Rev. 2034 (1997) (analyzing the thinking of Judge Jack Weinstein, one of the major figures in both the theory and practice of U.S. mass tort litigation, to show that Weinstein models mass tort settlement on disaster relief).

is historical controversy over whether the prime movers were diplomats or NGOs).[21] Notable in the UDHR story are

(i) the focus on individual rights – in which the individualist emphasis, championed by the Lebanese diplomat-philosopher Charles Malik, ultimately prevailed over Soviet objections;[22]

(ii) the decision to ground individual rights in "human dignity" (a phrase originally inserted in the drafts by René Cassin, to echo the U.N. Charter's invocation of "the dignity and worth of the human person"); and

(iii) the inclusion in the Preamble of the important claim that human beings "are endowed with reason and conscience and should act towards one another in a spirit of brotherhood."

As Glendon tells the story, the latter idea was a true East-West product. When he submitted his draft of the UDHR, Cassin explained that "the concept of solidarity and fraternity among men" was one of its two leading ideas (the other was "that every human being has a right to be treated like every other human being").[23] Cassin's idea was endorsed by the influential Chinese delegate P.C. Chang, who emphasized a Confucian concept similar to Cassin's "solidarity and fraternity": "two-man mindedness" (*ren*, 仁, typically translated as "sympathy" or "benevolence").[24] Eventually, the drafters chose to call this capacity "conscience" – perhaps not the best word, but etymologically suggestive ('con-science', 'knowing-with', suggests two-man mindedness).

The idea was clear even if the word-choice was not: reason alone, unaccompanied by conscience, fraternity, sympathy, *ren* (call it what you will) cannot motivate us to care about the rights of distant strangers

[21] Mary Ann Glendon, A World Made New: Eleanor Roosevelt and the Universal Declaration of Human Rights (2002); Johannes Morsink, The Universal Declaration of Human Rights: Origins, Drafting, and Intent (2000). On the human rights language in the Charter and the controversy surrounding it, see James Loeffler, *"The Conscience of America": Human Rights, Jewish Politics, and American Foreign Policy at the 1945 United Nations San Francisco Conference*, 100 J. Amer. Hist. 401 (2013) and the sources cited in that article, at 402 n. 2, 3.

[22] Glendon, at 39–42.

[23] Glendon, at 67.

[24] *Id.* The *Analects* of Confucius offers two characterizations of *ren*: "Now the *ren* man, wishing himself to be established, sees that others are established, and, wishing himself to be successful, sees that others are successful." Analects 6:30. "When you are out in the world, act as if meeting an important guest. . . . What you don't want done to yourself, don't do to others" (the so-called negative Golden Rule), Analects 12:2.

in distant lands.[25] The important point for present purposes is that benevolence and sympathy are emphatically *not* the moral sentiments at work in armed conflict. On the battlefield, the prevailing moral sentiments are hate, rage, fear, and one-sided loyalty, occasionally tempered with compassion. There can hardly be a clearer indication that the drafters of the UDHR were not thinking about standards of conduct in war.

Indeed, the opening paragraphs of the UDHR's preamble focus entirely on peace, arguing that human rights are the precondition of peace; and of course the U.N. Charter's preamble begins with the determination "to save succeeding generations from the scourge of war, which twice in our lifetime has brought untold sorrow to mankind." The contrast drawn in both documents is between a world of human rights and peace, and a world bereft of human rights, and as a consequence doomed to the untold sorrow of war. The idea of human rights as standards of conduct in war was simply not in the same conceptual universe as the Charter and the UDHR – not because of substantive disagreement, but because the Charter and the UDHR projects are to offer a roadmap out of war, not a roadmap for how war must be waged.

For the framers of human rights law, the main point was to get states to honor the human rights of their own people. Eventually, the project expanded to include the notion that the international community should provide backup for the human rights of people in other states whose own governments would not or could not honor them. The thought exemplified by the *Furundzija* dictum – that states should honor the human rights of a military adversary's people during armed conflict – was not yet on the horizon.

As further evidence consider the subsequent development of human rights doctrine into the current U.N. formula "respect, protect, fulfill": "By becoming parties to international treaties, States assume obligations and duties under international law to respect, to protect and to fulfill human rights."[26] The philosophical source of this mantra is Henry Shue's powerful argument that the very structure of rights implies social

[25] The inadequacy of reason alone is a philosophically debated proposition, but this is not the place to debate it. The debate goes back at least as far as Adam Smith, Hume, and Kant, with the latter insisting that reason alone suffices to derive and motivate human rights, while Smith and Hume believed that moral motivation comes from a faculty of sympathy that is distinct from reason.

[26] Office of the High Commissioner for Human Rights, *International Human Rights Law*, available at www.ohchr.org/en/professionalinterest/pages/internationallaw.aspx.

guarantees that people can actually enjoy the substance of rights.[27] Shue argued that social guarantees imply the three-level obligation in the formula: social guarantees include steps taken not only to avoid infringing rights, but to protect against infringement by others and to ensure to the extent possible that the rights are fulfilled and do not remain mere words on paper.[28] Shue began by working on the right to adequate food; official bodies subsequently expanded his rights analysis to include, for example, the right to housing and to a livable environment – all of which, it was argued, must be respected, protected, and fulfilled by states.[29]

Obviously, "respect, protect, fulfill" is a thick and demanding set of obligations, far thicker than the requirement that states merely respect rights by not violating them. If "respect, protect, fulfill" indeed represents the structure of human rights in the best thinking of the human rights community, it becomes clear that human rights is a peacetime project. A state at war can hardly be expected to provide social guarantees to fulfill a panoply of human rights for the population of its adversary. I note that Shue himself is skeptical that IHL has much to do with human rights.[30]

The Natural State of Humankind

Deeply woven into the two modes of thinking that I have been describing is the question of whether war or peace represents the baseline state of

[27] Henry Shue, Basic Rights: Subsistence, Affluence, and U.S. Foreign Policy 13 (1980).

[28] *Id.* at 52, 60. UN official Asbjørn Eide introduced the current terminology in Asbjørn Eide, *The International Human Rights System, in* Food as a Human Right 154 (Asbjørn Eide, Wenche Barth Eide, Susantha Goonatilake, Joan Gussow, and Omawale eds., 1984). Eide explicitly credits Shue with this conception of human rights *(Id.);* Eide's duty to "respect" rights corresponds with Shue's duty "to avoid depriving" people of the rights, while his duty to "fulfill" the rights corresponds with Shue's "duty to aid" (dropping, however, Shue's argument that the duty to aid is grounded in reparation for earlier deprivation).

[29] On "respect, protect, fulfill" in connection with the right to food, see Committee on Economic, Social and Cultural Rights, General Comment 12, Right to adequate food (20th session, 1999), U.N. Doc. E/C.12/1999/5 (1999), §15. On the right to housing and a safe environment, see the African Commission on Human Rights's decision in SERAC v. Nigeria, Comm. No. 155/96 (2001), §§44–47. In *SERAC* the African Commission expands "respect, protect, fulfill" even further to "respect, protect, promote, fulfill."

[30] Henry Shue, *Laws of War, in* The Philosophy of International Law 511–16 (Samantha Besson & John Tasioulas eds., 2010). In war, Shue remarks, "shit happens," and the best we can demand is to constrain the shit.

human existence. Of course Hobbes placed this question at the heart of his political theory: the state of nature is the state of war; and he believed that the realm of international relations, where no sovereign reigns over states, exemplifies the state of nature. He does not deny that states are sometimes at peace. Rather, he argues that even if "there had never been any time, wherein particular men were in a condition of warre one against another; yet in all times, Kings, and Persons of Soveraign authority, . . . are in continuall jealousies, and in the state and posture of Gladiators."[31] This is an ancient view. Plato, who argued that only just wars can legitimately be waged, also held that Greeks and barbarians are "enemies by nature."[32] And anthropological evidence suggests that our evolutionary ancestors, the hunter-gatherers whose way of life constitutes 99.5 percent of *homo sapiens*' timeline, were extremely violent.[33]

Of course we know the countervailing arguments that belligerence is not the baseline condition of humankind. Our evolutionary potential for violence can be tamed, depending on social institutions and context; the violence of hunter-gatherers tells us very little about violence today. Hobbes's great critic Pufendorf pointed out that even without a sovereign, states can and do enter into friendship and alliances; so Hobbes's "inexcusable" view is "a contradiction evident to the common sense of mankind."[34] For Pufendorf, "nature has established a kind of kinship among men."[35] Though admittedly "kinship usually has a rather weak force among those who live in natural liberty with each other,"[36] it suffices to make "common sociality" possible.[37]

Such debates are irresolvable, and it is not my purpose to delve into them any further. The important point is that those who see peace as the normal condition of human life will regard respect for peacetime human rights as a baseline, and the normative requirements in war as an aberration. And, of course, vice-versa: those who regard war as regrettable but not aberrational will grant equal normative rank to the laws of war, and won't be inclined to interpret them through human rights thinking. Precisely because the arguments about the natural baseline of human

31 Hobbes, Leviathan 90 (Richard Tuck ed., 1991).

32 Plato, Republic, 470e. The argument that only just wars may legitimately be waged comes from Plato, Alcibiades I, 109d.

33 Azar Gat, War in Human Civilization 11–36 (2006).

34 Samuel Pufendorf, The Law of Nature and of Nations, II.2.8.

35 Pufendorf, On the Duty of Man and Citizen 64 (James Tully ed. 1991), I.8.1; also *Id.* at 119, II.1.11.

36 *Id.* at 119, II.1.11.

37 *Id.* at 64, I.8.1.

existence are impossible to resolve, this clash of normative commitments will be as well.

The Great Transformation

It is an interesting historical question when human rights thinking first began to enter IHL. Theodore Meron dates the "humanization of humanitarian law" to the 1968 Tehran conference and a pair of 1970 UN Secretary General reports.[38] But we can see glimmerings already in the Geneva Conventions of 1929 and 1949. The 1929 Convention states that prisoners of war "are entitled to respect for their persons and honor" (Article 3) – a dignity-based right – and then spells out the detailed obligations of captors to POWs. And common Article 3 of the 1949 Conventions, prohibiting various kinds of mistreatment of captives, is clearly a mini-human-rights treaty within the broader protections of the Conventions. It seems overwhelmingly likely that the 1949 Conventions were inspired by the same revulsion against the mass human rights violations of World War II that gave birth to the nearly contemporaneous UDHR.

An even clearer example of human rights thinking in IHL is the prohibition on reprisals against civilians in Additional Protocol I to the Geneva Conventions (1977).[39] For the first time, it became a rule of warfare that the traditional method of policing enemy misconduct in wartime – self-help by taking reprisals – could never include targeting civilians, even if the enemy misconduct itself targets civilians.

Conspicuously, though, the Geneva Conventions do not use the language of human rights.[40] By 1977 the preamble to AP I explains its goal as "protecting the victims of armed conflicts," which sounds more like rights protection than the mitigation of suffering. But even the Additional Protocols make no explicit mention of human rights as a category, and certainly there is no reference to the international human rights conventions. Thus, if human rights thinking motivated the GCs and their

[38] Meron, *supra* note *, at 247.

[39] Additional Protocol I, art. 51(6). On the point that this represents human rights thinking, see Gabriella Blum, *The Fog of Victory*, 24 EJIL 391, 403 (2013).

[40] William Hitchcock argues that the omission was deliberate; Great Britain quashed the suggestion to incorporate human rights, possibly in anticipation of colonial wars. William I. Hitchock, *Human Rights and the Laws of War: The Geneva Conventions of 1949*, *in* The Human Rights Revolution: An International History 93 (Akira Iriye & Petra Goede eds., 2012).

Protocols, it did so rather furtively – it was the moral commitment that dare not speak its name.

Given their different DNA, what brought human rights thinking into humanitarian law? Almost all observers agree that visual images of dead and wounded civilians, shown in near-real time on television or spread through social media, have a great deal to do with it. What about developments within the law? Here, I suggest, three are decisively important. The first is the rebirth of international criminal law, particularly the creation of the ICTY in response to the Balkan Wars. The second is the increasing salience of the law of belligerent occupation. And the third is the U.S. war on terrorism.

International criminal law. For our purposes, the most important fact about the Balkan Wars is that what began as a war of secession – a fight by the Federal Republic of Yugoslavia to stop its components from breaking away – morphed into a war of ethnic cleansing and annihilation, in which attacks on civilian populations became, in actual fact, the dominant war aim for at least some of the contesting forces. As a result, when the Security Council created the ICTY and the modern era of international criminal law began, the crimes at the top of its agenda were attacks on civilians and civilian targets. Add to this that Yugoslavia had been at peace for forty-five years, successfully managing its ethnic tensions, so the horrific ethnic violence had no fig-leaf of inevitability to it. Third, it was a European war, that is, a war in the region of the world that most firmly embraced the linkage of human rights with peace. Taken together, these facts overwhelmingly suggested that the war crimes and crimes against humanity in former Yugoslavia should be conceptualized as violations of the human rights of innocent, peaceful civilians.

Against such a background, the human rights thinking of the *Furundzija* dictum comes naturally. Yugoslavia and its component regions could have remained part of the realm of rights, in which civilians would enjoy lives of human dignity as they had for decades. Instead, the conflict entrepreneurs seceded from the realm of rights and blew it to smithereens, not as a side-effect of some conceivably legitimate war aim, but as a central effort to deprive civilians of their rights. The jurisprudential focus becomes the rights of civilians.

Quite apart from the particularities of the Yugoslav tribunal, criminal law lends itself naturally to human rights thinking. Crimes with human victims are easily conceived as violations of their victims' rights, as well as of the public order.[41] This changes the emphasis of IHL from prophylactically regulating the discipline of military forces – the main purpose of the GCs and their additional protocols – to vindicating victims' rights. Gabriella Blum has noted that international criminal law individualizes agency in war crimes, because it charges individual defendants, rather than holding the entire collectivity responsible for intercommunal violence – even though the latter might be a more truthful way to look at matters.[42] I agree with Blum, but my present point is that ICL also individualizes victims. The indictment will charge that perpetrator P killed victims A, B, and C, and raped victims D, E, and F, and that these were grave breaches and crimes against humanity. The fatal encounter involves a rights-violator with a name and the named victim whose rights are violated. Under the retributive and expressive rationales for criminal punishment, the justice meted out by the tribunals aims to vindicate the dignity of individualized victims. This is human rights thinking, even if ICL is by no means identical with human rights law. The vindication of human dignity, not (or not only) the reduction of aggregate suffering, lies at the core of international criminal law.

Occupation. As we saw earlier, the only hint of protection of the rights of civilians in the Hague Conventions was in military occupations. That makes sense. When an army occupies foreign territory, IHL requires that it take over governance responsibilities in that territory. The occupier is the surrogate of the occupied state, and it assumes its obligations, except to the extent that the fighting is still going on and security requires martial measures. In a world that takes IHRL seriously, governance implies that occupation law must be constrained by human rights standards. They blend together. In occupations, human rights thinking in IHL seems natural and inevitable.

41 Of course not all war crimes cause direct harm to human victims. In the Rome Statute of the ICC, causing disproportionate damage to the natural environment, transferring civilians into occupied territory, intentionally targeting historic monuments, declaring that no quarter will be given (regardless of subsequent conduct), and employing banned weapons (even if they cause no harm) are war crimes: art. 8(b) (iv), (viii), (ix), (xii), (xx). None of these directly or necessarily violates the human rights of any determinate human victim.

42 Blum, *The Individualization of War*, at 67–69. Martti Koskenniemi makes a similar point in *Between Impunity and Show Trials*, 6 Max Planck Yrbk. Int'l. L. 1, 11–16 (2002) (arguing that it falsifies history to focus on individual rather than collective guilt in large-scale criminal enterprises).

In recent decades, the two most important armed conflicts for the development of IHL have been the Israeli-Palestinian conflict and the Iraq war. Both have generated landmark legal developments, intense media coverage, and political reflection. And, of course, both involve military occupations. Unsurprisingly, they are conduits of human rights thinking into humanitarian law.

During this period, the concept of an occupation has expanded beyond what the 1907 Hague Convention Annex envisaged. According to the Annex, "Territory is considered occupied when it is actually placed under the authority of the hostile army. The occupation applies only to the territory where such authority is established, and can be asserted."[43] Military occupation meant physical takeover. This, we might say, is the original heartland of occupation law. Under this conception, developments in occupation law would hardly carry over to *in bello* rules of armed conflict on the hot battlefield.

Inevitably and unsurprisingly, however, occupation law eventually expanded beyond the heartland, as lawyers argued about what actually placing territory under an army's authority means. The legal test that developed is "effective control." But in an age of long-distance technology, effective control can sometimes be exercised from afar. In *Banković*, the ECHR case about NATO's bombing of the Belgrade television station, the plaintiffs argued that once NATO knocked out Serbia's air defenses, it had effective control over the rights of potential civilian targets. Although the Court rejected the argument, it made a certain amount of sense.

This issue became especially important after the 2005 Israeli disengagement from Gaza. Even though it evacuated its settlers and troops, Israel's tight grip over the borders, air space, and sea access of Gaza left it in at least partial control of the material conditions of Gazans' daily life. Was this "effective control"? If so, Israel was occupying Gaza, with concomitant human rights obligations, notwithstanding the absence of Israeli troops.[44] A parallel question arose in Iraq, when, long after the formal occupation ended, Coalition forces continued to control everyday life in many areas of

[43] Hague Convention II Annex, art. 42.

[44] For a recent discussion, see the ICC Prosecutor's report on Israel's conduct in the flotilla incident: Office of the Prosecutor, *Situation on Registered Vehicles of Comoros, Greece and Cambodia, Article 53(1) Report*, Nov. 6, 2014, available at www.icc-cpi.int/iccdocs/otp/OTP-COM-Article_53(1)-Report-06Nov2014Eng.pdf, §§23–29 (concluding in §27 that "the prevalent view in the international community is that Israel remains an occupying power in Gaza despite the 2005 disengagement").

the country. The question of whether Israel had effective control over Gaza led to weirdly metaphysical debates among international lawyers (is a potential reoccupation an actual occupation? etc.[45]), fittingly described by Aeyal Gross as "transcendental nonsense" – Felix Cohen's famous label for debates conducted entirely in the Heaven of Legal Concepts.[46]

> Some of my international law colleagues argued that these territories are no longer occupied, while others disagreed. Listening to this debate, I began to think that "occupation" should be included in the category Cohen calls "magic solving words" – words that are actually incapable of solving anything if we remain within the binary on/off framework of the traditional international law of occupation.[47]

Gross proposes a functional approach, in which we unbundle the various responsibilities of an occupier to examine which of them is actually within the power of the occupier to address.

This approach is a form of human rights thinking, because Gross believes as an ethical matter that "*the responsibility of an occupier is as great as its power.*"[48] If the "occupier" can effectively exercise governance functions, and no conflicting sovereign can do so, it must – and governance functions fall within the province of human rights.

The same idea appears in Judge Giovanni Bonello's eloquent concurring opinion to the European Court's *Al-Skeini* decision. *Al-Skeini* asked whether the European Convention on Human Rights applied within the British occupation zone in Iraq, and concluded that it did. Judge Bonello ridiculed the British government's complaint that the Court was indulging in human rights imperialism: "It ill behooves a State that imposed its military imperialism over another sovereign State... to resent the charge of having exported human rights imperialism to the vanquished enemy."[49] He added that his fondest dream would be to be regarded as a human rights imperialist.[50]

[45] *Id.* at §§24, 28.

[46] Aeyal Gross, *Rethinking Occupation: The Functional Approach*, Opinio Juris weblog, Apr. 4, 2012; the phrase comes from Felix Cohen's classic article *Transcendental Nonsense and the Functional Approach*, 35 Colum. L. Rev. 809 (1935). As some might say: can implies ought.

[47] *Id.* [48] *Id.*

[49] Al-Skeini and Others v. United Kingdom, Application no. 55721/07, Council of Europe: European Court of Human Rights, 7 July 2011, available at: www.refworld.org/docid/4e2545502.html [accessed Sept. 30, 2014], separate opinion of Judge Bonello, ¶37.

[50] "At my age, it may no longer be elegant to have dreams. But that of being branded in perpetuity a human rights imperialist, I acknowledge sounds to me particularly seductive." ¶39.

Judge Bonello proposes a "functional" test of jurisdiction that resembles Gross's: when a European state has "authority and control" to perform any of the enforcement functions for securing human rights in occupied territory, the jurisdiction of the European Convention includes that territory, and the state must perform the function in accordance with European human rights law.[51]

This is not the occasion to discuss the merits of Gross's and Bonello's legal proposals to unbundle human rights obligations and define military occupation functionally as the power to fulfill some parts of the bundle. Here, my point is to emphasize how they bring human rights thinking to bear on one special area of IHL – occupation law – and then expand that area beyond its original heartland. On the surface, this represents a minor expansion of human rights thinking into IHL. Judge Bonello's proposal still pertains solely to occupation. But I want to suggest that it carries far more dramatic implications.

That is because the "functional" approach to occupation law bases human rights responsibilities on a state's power to make a practical difference to human rights within a foreign territory, during armed conflict. Under this test, it no longer matters whether we use legal labels like "occupation" or "effective control." Take these magic solving words away and what remains? Just one thing: the basic fact of asymmetric military power in a conflict. Whenever the stronger force in a deeply asymmetric conflict can respect, protect, or fulfill the human rights of the enemy's civilians in an armed conflict, it has at least an imperfect obligation to do so, because functionally speaking it is an occupier.

This is not official legal doctrine; rather, it is moral imagination. The law of occupation becomes a moral template for interpreting IHL in *all* asymmetric conflicts, a template according to which the human rights of civilians play a central role. What began as the law of belligerent occupation grows into the law of asymmetric armed conflicts.

An illustration of this phenomenon is the capture-rather-than-kill controversy in the ICRC's *Interpretive Guidance on Direct Participation in Hostilities*. In its 2006 opinion on targeted killings, the Israeli Supreme Court required that if a targeted individual can be captured rather than killed without jeopardizing the mission or the captor's safety, he must be.[52] Citing this opinion as legal authority, and appealing to the principle of avoiding unnecessary civilian harm, the

[51] *Id.* at ¶¶10–13, 16.

[52] HCJ 769/02 Pub. Comm. against Torture in Israel v. Gov't of Israel [2005] IsrSC 57(6) 285, reprinted in 46 I.L.M. 375 (Isr. 2007)[henceforth, PCATI v. Israel], ¶40.

ICRC proposed a capture-not-kill requirement whenever a state military goes after a civilian who directly participates in hostilities.

Some military lawyers angrily rejected the capture-not-kill requirement as an inappropriate intrusion of human rights requirements where they don't belong, which puts undue risk on soldiers.[53] They argued that IHL has never prohibited killing an enemy who is not disabled and hasn't surrendered. Hayes Parks, pre-eminent among U.S. law of war experts, dismissed the Israeli requirement as purely domestic law with no international significance.[54] That's a tendentious conclusion, because as one of the world's most active war-fighting states (and the only one whose courts review military decisions in real time), Israel's jurisprudence automatically has international significance.[55] But Parks is right in one respect: the Israeli court put a great deal of weight on the fact that some of its targeted killings take place in occupied territory, where its human rights obligations are at a maximum.[56] The ICRC generalized a doctrine growing out of occupation law to encompass *all* IHL. This is a perfect illustration of how the template of occupation law can export human rights thinking to IHL in all asymmetric conflicts.[57]

[53] W. Hayes Parks, *Part IX of the ICRC "Direct Participation in Hostilities" Study: No Mandate, No Expertise, and Legally Incorrect*, 42 NYU J. Int'l. L. & Politics 769–832 (2010). The subtitle accurately conveys the rancor of the author's response to the ICRC study. To show the undue risk, the author goes into some grisly medical details about how long someone shot in the chest can continue to fight back. *Id.* at 810–12.

[54] *Id.* at 792–93.

[55] Furthermore, Parks misreads the Israeli opinion. The portion he quotes says that "a civilian taking a direct part in hostilities cannot be attacked at such time as he is doing so, if a less harmful means can be employed. *In our domestic law*, that rule is called for by the principle of proportionality." PCATI v. Israel, ¶40, Parks's emphasis added. He reads the quoted language to say that only Israeli domestic law calls for the use of less harmful means. In fact, Justice Barak's opinion does not say that the requirement can be derived only from the domestic law principle and exists only within Israeli domestic law. Read in context, he first sets out an interpretation of international law and then, because that interpretation "has not yet crystalized" in "the 'gray' cases" of customary international law, he finds a domestic law source as well.

[56] PCATI v. Israel, ¶¶2, 40, 41, 60, which emphasize that capture is especially feasible in border areas proximate to Israel, or within Israeli territory, or under the conditions of belligerent occupation.

[57] The ICRC study does acknowledge that capturing rather than killing is most likely to be feasible in military occupations and police actions, not "classic large-scale confrontations between well-equipped and organized armed forces." But it doesn't rule out the capture-don't-kill requirement even in the latter. Nils Melzer, *Interpretive Guidance on the Notion of Direct Participation in Hostilities* (ICRC 2009), available at www.icrc.org/eng/assets/files/other/icrc-002-0990.pdf, at 80–81.

The war on terrorism. The U.S. war on terrorism, in which any geographical locale harboring al Qaeda and its (unnamed) associated forces is a potential battle space, regardless of whether the state regards itself as at peace or at war with the United States, lends special urgency to human rights thinking. As I argued soon after 9/11, an unending armed conflict of indeterminate and potentially unlimited geographical scope threatens to depress peacetime human rights to the more limited rights protected by IHL.[58]

Why "more limited"? Consider that under IHL, enemy combatants can be targeted based on status alone, regardless of their level of personal involvement or actual behavior; standards of evidence and due process for killing or detaining suspected enemies are relaxed far below those of peacetime civilian life; civilians and their property can lawfully be exposed to higher risk of collateral damage than peacetime life would ever tolerate. Faced with the prospect of long-term displacement of human rights to the lower level of wartime protections, it seems quite proper to push back by trying to inject human rights thinking into the laws of war. Otherwise, the entire project of international human rights is as good as gone – placed in perpetual derogation by an endless war on terrorism. Once the U.S. government declares that in principle all the world could be a battlefield, then the demand for human rights even on the battlefield becomes entirely justifiable.

Overextending Human Rights Thinking

It is entirely possible for human rights advocates to push back too hard and too far – to deny that armed conflict is different, in fact decisively different, from peacetime. The most common form of this denial is insisting that contemporary state conflicts with terrorist groups are always law enforcement matters governed by human rights standards of due process in targeting, arresting, detaining, and trying terrorism suspects. I agree that sometimes insisting on law enforcement standards is absolutely right. For example, when the U.S. government arrested suspected terrorist Jose Padilla in 2002, it declared him an enemy combatant in the armed conflict with al Qaeda.[59] This allowed the government to hold

[58] David Luban, *The War on Terrorism and the End of Human Rights*, 22 PHIL. & PUB. POL'Y Q. 9 (Summer 2002), available at http://scholarship.law.georgetown.edu/facpub/892. Reprinted in multiple sources, most recently as chapter 1 of TORTURE, POWER, AND LAW.

[59] Padilla v. Bush, 233 F. Supp. 2d 564, 606–08 (S.D.N.Y. 2002)

Padilla as a military prisoner for years, and he was not charged with any crime until 2005. But Padilla was arrested by civilian law enforcement in Chicago, not captured by the military on the battlefield. He was and is a U.S. citizen with the full panoply of constitutional rights. The only basis for finding that Padilla was an enemy combatant was an affidavit by a civilian official in Washington, with no supporting evidence. Instead of offering evidence, the government asserted that U.S. courts must defer to the commander in chief in "military" matters (the reason for the scare-quotes should be obvious). The judge pointed out that he was fully competent to evaluate evidence about Padilla's legal status, and indeed that this is the heart of a court's institutional competence. But he concluded that he must defer to the commander in chief.[60]

Padilla's capture and imprisonment were factually indistinguishable in every way from a criminal arrest. The sole reason the government classified him as a wartime captive was to interrogate him without a lawyer, or indeed any human contact – and to expand the president's power as commander in chief. This was outrageous.[61] It is obvious that civilian law enforcement standards should have protected Padilla, and that the government grossly abused its power in order to advance the frightening proposition that the president has near-absolute authority to strip legal protections away from whomever the president wants, simply by declaring the person an enemy combatant.

But in other cases, denying the existence of an armed conflict and insisting on peacetime due process standards flies in the face of reality. Human rights groups have reflexively described drone strikes as extra-judicial assassinations without due process of law.[62] They can be under some circumstances. But they needn't be. A drone is nothing more than a platform for long-distance weapons delivery, no different in principle from a bomber or for that matter a cannon. It is clearly permissible to use long-distance weapons in an armed conflict. Indeed, in an armed conflict a targeted killing is not only different from an illegal assassination, it is the *only* legally permitted form of killing: the opposite of a targeted attack

[60] *Id.* at 607–08.

[61] So I've argued at length, in David Luban, *On the Commander-in-Chief Power*, 81 S. Cal. L. Rev. 477 (2008).

[62] E.g., Report of the Special Rapporteur, Asma Jahangir, U.N. Doc. E/CN.4/2003/3 (Jan. 13, 2003), §39, describing a 2002 U.S. drone strike in Yemen on an al Qaeda planner that also killed five passengers in his car as "a clear case of extrajudicial killing." Subsequent UN Special Rapporteurs have been more circumspect about whether or not drone strikes are properly described as extrajudicial killings.

is an untargeted and therefore indiscriminate attack. The argument that conflicts with terrorist groups can never, as a matter of human rights principle, count as armed conflicts, only as law enforcement problems, seems dogmatic and wrong in a world where law enforcement against terrorists is spotty and often nonexistent or even impossible. The argument overextends the proper reach of human rights thinking, declaring that the rule of law prevails everywhere – presumably, in the hope that declaring it so will make it so.

Another overextension of human rights thinking arises in some of the revisionist just war theory that occupies a prominent place in contemporary philosophical discussions of war. Some revisionists operate from within a framework set by three premises.[63] First, the human rights against killing and other aggravated violence are of fundamental moral importance. Second, individuals lose those rights only by their own conduct that menaces the basic rights of other people – paradigmatically, violently assaulting the innocent or causing others to do so. Third, the conditions under which individuals lose those rights are the narrow conditions for self- and other defense in domestic society. (The third premise is not always obvious in revisionist theory, but it is implicit in the characteristic and striking way that revisionists argue from moral intuitions about self-defense in hypothetical situations of one-on-one murderous assault.) From these premises, important and controversial conclusions follow. To cite just one example: the conditions of targetability under a theory of individual self-defense do not map comfortably onto IHL's status-based distinction between combatants and noncombatants, so revisionism may reject both sides of the principle of distinction: civilian immunity and military targetability.

The first premise of revisionism – the central role of human rights against violence – is unproblematic. No form of human rights thinking could reject it; I am tempted to say that no respectable moral code could reject it, even if the code does not use the vocabulary of human rights. The other two premises, however, lean too heavily on the conditions of peacetime society; as Michael Walzer pointedly quipped, revisionist theory is a perfect ethics of warfare if war were a peacetime activity.[64]

[63] I am thinking particularly of path-breaking work such as JEFF MCMAHAN'S KILLING IN WAR and DAVID RODIN'S WAR AND SELF-DEFENSE, as well as their numerous papers. I don't mean, however, that they explicitly set out and endorse the premises I am attributing to them here.

[64] Michael Walzer, *Response to McMahan's Paper*, 34 PHILOSOPHIA. 43 (2006).

Human rights thinking simply cannot will away the dramatic differences between war and peace. The peacetime use of lethal violence in self-defense can be narrowly constrained because in domestic society the need for self-help is an exception. Leviathan is a few blocks away in a police cruiser, and even on mean streets, most of the time you can flee or dial 911, rather than pulling out a gun and blazing away. In peacetime society, trigger-happy defenders can be more dangerous than murderers; hence the narrow conditions of personal self-defense in domestic law. That's a poor model of self-defense in wartime.

As for the wartime use of lethal violence, it cannot always be narrowly focused on all and only those individuals who actually pose a threat, because in the fog of war we seldom know which is which. Individual liability is far too granular a criterion for violence in armed conflict, where action is at a distance and armed enemies operate in groups. The domestic analogy of war to peacetime conflict risks losing sight of the terrifying disanalogies, and I think revisionists would do well to abandon their domestic hypotheticals and show a bit more skepticism about moral intuitions honed in peacetime society.

Human Rights Thinking and the Civilian Point of View

What, then, is the proper place for human rights thinking in armed conflict? We have seen it several times in the course of this argument: it consists in a heightened solicitude toward the civilians caught in a battle space whose basic rights are affected by the war.

This heightened solicitude can manifest itself in many specific ways. As someone who has written about various aspects of just war from the standpoint of human rights thinking, I will risk self-indulgence and draw from my own work to illustrate. I don't mean to suggest that the positions on the issues that follow are the only ones that human rights thinking permits, or even that they harmonize perfectly with human rights thinking. They don't. They merely represent one line of thought that brings human rights thinking to bear on the theory of just war and IHL.

Jus ad bellum. Start with Kofi Annan's famous address to the General Assembly in 1999:

> State sovereignty, in its most basic sense, is being redefined by the forces of globalization and international cooperation. The State is now widely understood to be the servant of its people, and not vice versa. At the same

> time, individual sovereignty – and by this I mean the human rights and fundamental freedoms of each and every individual as enshrined in our Charter – has been enhanced by a renewed consciousness of the right of every individual to control his or her own destiny.[65]

On Annan's conception, state sovereignty exists to protect the human rights of the state's people, not (as in the classic *Island of Palmas* doctrine) to protect foreigners' interests within the state, and certainly not to protect a massive human rights violator from outside intervention. Sovereignty loses its normative force when the state violates basic human rights.[66] In that case, we should reinterpret just cause of war in terms of defending people's basic rights rather than defending states' sovereignty. The Article 2(4)–Article 51 framework of the U.N. Charter must accordingly be reinterpreted. In 1980, I argued that the formula should be this:

(1) A just war is a war in defense of basic human rights, or (alternatively) a war of self-defense against an unjust war.
(2) An unjust war, on the other hand, is a war subversive of human rights that is not a war in defense of basic human rights.[67]

Clause (1) brings human rights thinking to Article 51 self-defense, while clause (2) brings human rights thinking to the concept of aggression.

Notice that on this reconceptualization of just cause, humanitarian military interventions to stop widespread violations of human rights can be justifiable – and not only when the human rights violations are core international crimes, as under the Responsibility to Protect doctrine, but also in cases where other basic rights are threatened, such as famines where only outside military forces are capable of rescuing the endangered population.[68] It likewise follows from human rights thinking that

[65] Secretary-General Presents His Annual Report to General Assembly, UN Press Release SG/SM7136, GA 9596 (Sept. 20, 1999), available at www.un.org/News/Press/docs/1999/19990920.sgsm7136.html.

[66] The term "basic rights" can be understood intuitively as the most fundamental human rights; but I prefer Shue's definition of basic rights as those human rights (like the right to physical security against violence and to minimum subsistence) the fulfillment of which is necessary to enjoying any other human rights.

[67] David Luban, *Just War and Human Rights*, 9 Phil. & Public Affairs 160 (1980), corrected and reprinted in International Ethics: A Philosophy & Public Affairs Reader (Charles Beitz et al. eds., 1985).

[68] See Margaret M. DeGuzman, *When Are International Crimes a Just Cause of War?*, Va. J. Int'l. L. (forthcoming) (arguing that it is a mistake to link the R2P doctrine to international crimes, and that R2P can rightly be expanded to cover other situations that

punishing an enemy's bad behavior through military violence cannot constitute just cause of war, because using violence against an adversary state inevitably amounts to collective punishment of its civilians.[69]

Risk. On the other hand, preventive war necessary to forestall a massive attack on basic rights can, under some circumstances, be morally permissible under human rights thinking, provided of course that it satisfies *ad bellum* proportionality as well as other relevant criteria.[70] It can readily be subsumed under Shue's conception of a social guarantee that a state provides against a standard threat to the basic rights of its inhabitants – in other words, the "protect" part of human rights under the "respect, protect, fulfill" model. Recall that under Shue's thick conception of human rights obligations, it is not enough for a state to protect its citizens from ongoing attacks on their basic rights. It is also supposed to guarantee its inhabitants' rights against standard threats, and an armed attack under preparation by an enemy is a standard threat. It follows that human rights thinking about war encompasses risk management as well as ongoing military defense. It may sound counterintuitive that human rights thinking could countenance preventive war rather than forbidding it, but the phrase "anticipatory self-defense" is not simply a newspeak name for aggression (notwithstanding its abuse by the United States in Iraq), and it is an aspect of the defense of basic rights.

One might object that by weighing the magnitude of a nascent attack on basic rights against the magnitude of an armed preventive response, the preventive war argument departs from human rights thinking by aggregating rather than individuating rights infringements. According to this objection, genuinely human rights–based thinking would focus instead on the fact that a preventive war will inevitably damage innocent civilians in violation of their own basic rights. Because the war is

jeopardize a population). I discuss the permissibility conditions of humanitarian intervention in David Luban, *Intervention and Civilization: Some Unhappy Lessons of the Kosovo War, in* Global Justice and Transnational Politics: Essays on the Moral and Political Challenges of Globalization 79 (Pablo de Greiff & Ciaran Cronin, eds., 2002).

[69] David Luban, *War as Punishment*, 39 Phil. & Public Affairs 299 (2011).

[70] The circumstances, I have argued, are tailored narrowly to an adversary whose ideology and past history of violence, combined with current hostile intentions and weapons programs, make it likely that it plans to launch an attack when it acquires the capacity. Furthermore, it has to be an attack with a weapon one use of which is likely to cause mass casualties. David Luban, *Preventive War*, 32 Phil. & Public Affairs 207, 229–32 (2004); *Preventive War and Human Rights, in* Preemption: Military Action and Moral Justification 171 (Henry Shue & David Rodin, eds., 2007).

preventive, neither they nor their state has actually done anything yet that would justify an attack on their rights.[71]

Without offering a detailed reply to this objection (which I have done elsewhere[72]), I want to acknowledge something importantly correct in it. In wartime, human rights will be violated on all sides, and comparing the violations by aggregating them is a "utilitarianism of rights," which some philosophers reject as a mistake about the very nature of rights.[73] These objectors find something fundamentally inconsistent between body-counts and the commitment to individual human dignity.[74] This is not a trivial or mistaken concern, but I think the utilitarianism of rights is inescapable in human rights thinking about war. It is still human rights thinking because the weighing and trade-offs take place between rights and rights: basic rights cannot be traded off for interests less significant than basic rights. To be sure, allowing a right to be traded off for anything, even another right, offends against the entitlement commitment inherent in human rights thinking. But when entitlements conflict with each other, something has to give, and human rights thinking cannot ignore conflicts among rights or argue them away.[75]

The argument about preventive war adds an additional wrinkle to the aggregation of rights: it allows states to take military action against massive threats to its inhabitants' basic rights that are not sure things but only highly probable, in the strong sense that not only is the likelihood very high, but one thing that makes it high is the adversary's belligerent intentions, demonstrated through ongoing action, past track record, and ideology. Not just any remote threat to basic rights is a just cause for preventive war, only one that crosses a high-risk threshold

[71] See, e.g., David Rodin, *The Problem with Prevention*, in Shue & Rodin, *supra* note 70.

[72] Luban, *Preventive War and Human Rights, supra* note 70.

[73] Robert Nozick coined the term; see Anarchy, State, and Utopia 28–30 (1973); he contrasts it unfavorably with the view of rights as side-constraints on action, under which minimizing rights violations cannot be a goal of action.

[74] The classic statement of this view is John M. Taurek, *Should the Numbers Count?*, 6 Phil. & Public Affairs 293 (1977). Taurek's answer to his title question is a resounding no, and he believes that if you have a choice between saving one life and saving five, you should flip a coin, because that gives each of the six an equal chance of surviving. *Id.* at 303. Several philosophers, including Francies Kamm, Gregory Kavka, Rahul Kumar, and T. M. Scanlon have responded with nonconsequentialist arguments that the numbers count. For a survey essay showing that those responses confront knotty problems, see David T. Wasserman & Alan Strudler, *Can a Nonconsequentialist Count Lives?*, 31 Phil. & Public Affairs 71 (2003).

[75] On this point, see Griffin, *supra* note 3, chapter 3.

because the adversary is deliberately pushing toward the brink. My claim here is that warding off high-likelihood massive threats to rights, even though they are not certain, is required by the "protect" obligation in the "respect, protect, fulfill" trio.

Jus ex bello. Parallel reasoning about risk to basic human rights can be used to address the question of *jus ex bello*, the morality of when one must terminate a just war. Can states keep fighting a just war until they have so decisively beaten their adversary that the risk the adversary poses to basic rights is effectively reduced to zero? To say yes means that the state can keep pounding away until the adversary's military capability is not merely defeated but completely pulverized. Cast in the language of risk, that means the state could continue to transfer risks from its own population to the population of the enemy even when its marginal gains in safety are slight and the marginal damage to the enemy's population are large. This, under human rights thinking, is immoral. The world is an intrinsically risky place, with an irreducible "cosmic background radiation" of risks to basic rights posed by enemies. States are never justified in continuing a war that shifts risks onto others once they have reduced their own to the background level.[76]

This matters enormously in the so-called war on terror. Recall that President George W. Bush proclaimed that the war "will not end until every terrorist group of global reach has been found, stopped and defeated."[77] As recently as 2013, the *Washington Post* editorialized that "like all wars, this one will end only if one party is defeated or both agree to lay down their weapons."[78] President Bush and the *Post* editorialist voice the demand for zero risk, even as the U.S. campaign continues to impose grave risks on others. Under human rights thinking, such an approach to the *jus ex bello* is unacceptable.

Jus in bello. These *ad bellum* and *ex bello* questions of basic human rights and risk transfer have *in bello* counterparts. One much-discussed issue is whether a state's soldiers must take on additional risk to themselves in order to minimize civilian casualties among the enemy's civilians. IHL gives no clear answer. It requires fighters to take "constant

[76] So Gabriella Blum and I argue in *Unsatisfying Wars: Degrees of Risk and the Jus ex Bello*, 125 Ethics 751 (2015).

[77] "Transcript of President Bush's address," Sep. 20, 2001. *Available at* http://georgewbush-whitehouse.archives.gov/news/releases/2001/09/20010920-8.html.

[78] Washington Post Editorial Board, *Wishful Thinking in the War on Terror*, Wash. Post, Aug. 5, 2013, available at www.washingtonpost.com/opinions/wishful-thinking-on-the-war-on-terror/2013/08/05/3485e982-fde3-11e2-9711-3708310f6f4d_story.html.

care" to reduce civilian casualties, and to do everything "feasible" to that end, but there is no agreement about how much risk-taking on the part of soldiers is feasible, nor what "constant care" means in practice. In a well-known article, Asa Kasher and Amos Yadlin argued that although state soldiers must place the protection of their own civilians above their own protection, they can place self-protection above the protection of the enemy's civilians.[79] Avishai Margalit and Michael Walzer responded that a civilian is a civilian regardless of nationality, and soldiers must take exactly the same risks on behalf of enemy noncombatants as they would if the civilians were their own people.[80]

There are really two issues here, one about the relative worth of soldiers and civilians, the other about "our" civilians versus "theirs." I believe that human rights thinking gives a clear answer: all lives, soldiers' lives and civilians', our civilians and theirs, have the same worth.[81] Therefore soldiers must take on the same minimum levels of risk to spare "enemy" civilians as they would to spare their own civilians. (Of course, they can choose to take additional heroic risks, and it would not be wrong to do so selectively on behalf of their own civilians.)

Does this argument also mean that soldiers can transfer risks to civilians at a one-to-one exchange rate? If all else were equal, human rights thinking answers yes: the individual-worth commitment is egalitarian. The complication is that all else is not equal, because in many cases the soldiers are the ones creating the risk to civilians, and common sense morality suggests that the larger burden of risk falls on risk-causers than innocent bystanders. In the words of the old tort chestnut *Rylands v. Fletcher*, "When one person, in managing his own affairs, causes, however innocently, damage to another, it is obviously only just that he should be the party to suffer."[82] Here, as in other instances of human rights thinking, examining the problem

[79] Asa Kasher and Amos Yadlin, *Assassination and Preventive Killing*, 25 SAIS Review 41, 49–51 (Winter-Spring 2005).

[80] Avishai Margalit and Michael Walzer, *Israel: Civilians and Combatants*, New York Review of Books, May 14, 2009; Asa Kasher and Major General Amos Yadlin, with a reply by Margalit and Walzer, *Israel & the Rules of War: An Exchange*, New York Review of Books, June 11, 2009.

[81] David Luban, *Risk Taking and Force Protection*, in Reading Walzer 277 (Itzhak Benbaji & Naomi Sussmann, eds., 2014). For another example of human rights thinking about this issue, see Eyal Benvenisti, *Human Dignity in Combat: The Duty to Spare Enemy Civilians*, 39 Isr. L. Rev. 81 (2006).

[82] Rylands v. Fletcher, L.R. 3 H.L. 330 (1868) (Cranswell, L.).

from the standpoint of the innocent civilian helps us disentangle a knotty problem. Although the morality of war cannot ask soldiers to take suicidal risks to save civilians, their vocation requires them to take on *some* additional risk to spare the basic rights of civilians, because the soldiers are the ones whose attacks create the risk to civilians.

Military necessity. As a final example, I believe that human rights thinking requires us to reconceptualize the concept of military necessity. Military necessity has always been the counterargument to the claims of humanitarianism, and until very recently it was a decisive counterargument: *Kriegsraison* trumps *Kriegsmanier*, as the Prussian military maxim would have it. The Lieber Code of 1863 was the first explicit statement that military necessity cannot justify war crimes; even so, historian John Fabian Witt argues that the Code contains so many inconsistencies on this point that Lieber could not have really meant it.[83] Only in the post–World War II *Hostages* case did anything like settled law emerge that prohibits war crimes even in cases of military necessity.

However, the *Hostages* formula remains distinctly forgiving to militaries under the guise of necessity:

> Military necessity permits a belligerent, subject to the laws of war, to apply any amount and kind of force to compel the complete submission of the enemy with the least possible expenditure of time, life, and money.[84]

So, provided that a military force avoids overt LOAC violations, it can describe all advantageous actions as military necessities, regardless of how much suffering they inflict on civilians and how trivial the advantage. Furthermore, this expansive conception of military necessity comes close to eviscerating the LOAC requirement to take all "feasible" precautions to protect innocent civilians: the military necessity of not taking a precaution makes it infeasible. From the standpoint of human rights thinking, these consequences are intolerable. Human rights thinking demands a different conception of necessity, according to which military advantage must be weighed against civilian damage. If the marginal military advantage is slight,

[83] Lieber Code, art. 14. See generally John Fabian Witt, Lincoln's Code, chapter 8, and Witt, *A Response to David Luban*, JustSecurity weblog, Oct. 3, 2013, available at http://justsecurity.org/1615/witt-response-david-luban/.

[84] US v. List (American Military Tribunal, Nuremberg, 1948), 11 NMT 1230, at 1253.

but the marginal civilian damage is not, the claim of military necessity must be rejected.[85] In other words, the concept of military necessity contains a proportionality requirement within it that requires taking civilian harm into account.

The important difference between this marginal conception of necessity and the *Hostages* formula is that the latter simply ignores the rights of civilians, where the marginal conception demands that necessity assessments take full account of them.

No doubt objections could be raised against all the arguments and conclusions I have canvassed here. My aim here is not to defend them, but to propose them as examples of the kind of human rights thinking that rightfully belongs in IHL – human rights thinking that does not downplay the difference between war and peace, but that insists on the basic human rights of civilians as well as warriors as the moral heart of just war theory properly conceived – in the language of *Furundzija* with which I began this essay, "the essence of the whole corpus of international humanitarian law as well as human rights law."

[85] David Luban, *Military Necessity and the Cultures of Military Law*, 26 Leiden J. Int'l. L. 315, 341–47 (2013).

3

The Lost Origins of *Lex Specialis*

Rethinking the Relationship between Human Rights and International Humanitarian Law

MARKO MILANOVIC*

1. The State of the Debate

In this paper, I try to outline the current state of the debate on the relationship or interaction between international human rights law (IHRL) and international humanitarian law/law of armed conflict (IHL). The topic is well-worn and I will not recapitulate the basics. I will rather try to set out as clearly as possible the extant points of controversy, their driving factors, and the logical order in which they should be addressed in order to advance the debate further. After providing a broad overview of the debate, I will look at one of its key concepts – the *lex specialis* principle. I will show that, despite the Latin veneer of antiquity, scholars have generally started using *lex specialis* to describe the relationship between IHL and IHRL only after the ICJ's 1996 *Nuclear Weapons* advisory opinion. Rather than being some kind of unassailable orthodoxy, *lex specialis* is a principle whose effects and utility need to be critically re-examined, and it is only after having done so that the debate can move forward.

In the broadest of strokes, the debate is waged between two camps, comprised on both sides of academics, judges, government and military lawyers, various types of activists, etc. The first are the human rights enthusiasts, who generally believe that human rights law can and does substantively apply in situations of armed conflict, and that human rights enforcement mechanisms can have an important role to play in such

* Associate Professor, University of Nottingham School of Law; Vice-President, European Society of International Law. Much of the research for this paper was done while I was visiting professor at the University of Michigan Law School in Fall 2013, and I am most grateful to Seth Quidachay-Swan, Betty Lim, and the staff of the University of Michigan Law Library for their invaluable research assistance. I am also grateful to Francoise Hampson, Robert Kolb, Dino Kritsiotis, Marty Lederman, and Jens Ohlin for their suggestions and comments.

situations. The second are the human rights skeptics, who for a variety of reasons resist the encroachment of human rights onto areas best left to IHL, pure and simple. The enthusiasts and the skeptics obviously vary in the intensity and in the particulars of their enthusiasm or skepticism.[1] There is also a level of professional variety (e.g., academics are generally more prone to enthusiasm, government and military lawyers to skepticism) and some geographical variety (e.g., U.S. lawyers of all stripes are less likely to be enthusiasts than their European counterparts, again painting with the broadest of brushes).

Both camps frequently deploy Koskenniemian apology/utopia critiques[2] in order to discredit the positions of the other. Thus, the enthusiasts accuse the skeptics of being morally inconsistent apologists for state power who only wish to facilitate the exercise of that power by making wholly arbitrary distinctions with regard to who is protected by human rights and who is not. The skeptics, on the other hand, accuse the enthusiasts of being a utopian, dovish bunch of fluffy, mushy-wushy do-gooders, who know nothing about the realities on the ground in wartime and who risk compromising both human rights and IHL with their relentless and illegitimate activism.

Similarly, both camps are prepared to use all of the tools in the lawyerly toolbox to advance their broader agenda, be it formalism/positivism/textualism, teleological interpretation, pragmatism, or various moral, value, and policy judgments. I think it fair to say that while some of these tools might be used a bit more by one camp than by the other, there is really no methodological consistency in that regard – the same person can be a textualist by day (e.g., in rejecting the extraterritorial application of the ICCPR) and a pragmatist by night (e.g., by using the nebulous *lex specialis* principle to disregard the clear text of human rights treaties). I also think it fair to say that, as a general matter, the positivist interpretative positions of the members of either camp align perfectly with their individual policy preferences. I, at least, have not met anyone who thinks that *de lege lata* human rights apply everywhere and all the time, including in armed conflict, but that this is a bad thing which is unfortunately unavoidable, nor conversely anyone who thinks that it would be just fantastic to apply human rights as broadly as possible, but that the current legal framework simply does not at all allow it.

The split between the two camps is exacerbated by the complexity of the applicable legal framework. The relationship between IHRL and IHL can be

[1] For the avoidance of doubt, I would label myself as a moderate enthusiast, if that is not overly oxymoronic.

[2] *See generally* Martti Koskenniemi, From Apology to Utopia: The Structure of International Legal Argument (2006).

analyzed at either a very general level, as was largely the case until relatively recently in the evolution of the debate, or at the level of specific problems regulated by specific norms. These specific norms may either be complementary and go in the same general direction (which is most often the case), or they may at least apparently conflict (e.g., with regard to targeting and detention). This set of issues, about the relationship between specific norms emanating from the separate IHL and IHRL regimes, is interwoven with two further questions – that of the extraterritorial application of human rights treaties and that of the possibility and utility of derogations from human rights treaties, particularly in extraterritorial situations (e.g., regarding UK forces in Iraq or Afghanistan) and situations of armed conflict. The issue of extraterritorial application is both broader and qualitatively different from that of the relationship between IHL and IHRL, but the apology/utopia dynamics are similar and will drive the enthusiast and skeptic camps along their existing policy preferences.[3] Thus, I again have not met anyone who is in favor of a broad intermingling of IHL and IHRL but narrowly interprets the territorial scope of IHRL treaties, or vice versa.

All this complexity is further exacerbated by the (frequently underappreciated) fact that there are significant textual differences between the various human rights treaties. Compare, for example, (1) the jurisdiction clauses, (2) the derogation clauses, and (3) the substantive provisions on the right to life and the liberty of person in the International Covenant on Civil and Political Rights (ICCPR), the American Convention on Human Rights (ACHR), and the European Convention on Human Rights (ECHR).[4] Article 2(1) ICCPR explicitly mentions territory, whereas Article 1 ECHR and Article 1 ACHR do not. Article 4(1) ICCPR does not explicitly mention "war" as a situation allowing for a derogation, whereas Article 15(1) ECHR and Article 27 ACHR do. While Article 4(2) ICCPR and Article 27(2) ACHR prohibit derogations from the right to life, Article 15(2) ECHR allows them with respect to "deaths resulting from lawful acts of war." Finally, while the drafters of the ICCPR and the ACHR opted to use a relatively loose and open standard of *arbitrariness* in defining the right to life and the liberty of person, in Articles 6 and 9 ICCPR and

[3] *See generally* Marko Milanovic, Extraterritorial Application of Human Rights Treaties: Law, Principles, and Policy (2011).

[4] International Covenant on Civil and Political Rights, G.A. res. 2200A (XXI), 21 U.N. GAOR Supp. (No. 16) at 52, U.N. Doc. A/6316 (1966), 999 U.N.T.S. 171, entered into force March 23, 1976; [European] Convention for the Protection of Human Rights and Fundamental Freedoms, 213 U.N.T.S. 222, entered into force September 3, 1953; American Convention on Human Rights, O.A.S. Treaty Series No. 36, 1144 U.N.T.S. 123, entered into force July 18, 1978.

Articles 4 and 7 ACHR, the drafters of Articles 2 and 5 ECHR used closed lists and stricter standards, such as absolute necessity. These differences are particularly important when we try to understand the exact nature and ambit of the *lex specialis* maxim – is it simply an interpretative tool that allows us to read IHL rules into vague human rights standards such as an "arbitrary" deprivation of life, or is it a rule of hierarchy that allows us to disregard one conflicting rule in favor of the other?

The final nail in the complexity coffin, as it were, is the frequent introduction of *jus ad bellum* questions and/or domestic law questions into the mix (e.g., with regard to the so-called "naked self-defence" rationale for targeted killings),[5] or other tangential questions of IHL or other parts of international law that carry their own uncertainties (e.g., the classification of armed conflicts, or the attribution of conduct in multinational military operations).[6] Not only does the complexity now become simply unbearable, but the opportunities for the derailment of any discussion or plain misunderstanding multiply exponentially. Anyone who has ever participated in an academic symposium on the difficulties raised by the interaction between IHL and IHRL will know just how quickly the discussion can veer off-topic and lose focus.[7]

So how to move forward? There have been enthusiasts and skeptics even since the issue of the relationship between IHL and IHRL has arisen, and that is a good and natural thing. I do not propose to somehow fully reconcile these two camps, although I would submit that the differences between them are not as stark as is sometimes thought. But the main prerequisite for the debate to move forward is that we speak a common language and have conceptual clarity, and advancing this clarity is precisely the purpose of this paper. In doing so, I will take a deeper look at *lex specialis*, (supposedly) the main tool in our conceptual apparatus for dealing with normative conflicts between IHL and IHRL. I will first try to establish its intellectual roots, and

[5] *See more* Kenneth Anderson, *Targeted Killing and Drone Warfare: How We Came to Debate Whether There Is a "Legal Geography of War,"* Hoover Institution (2011), at http://media.hoover.org/sites/default/files/documents/FutureChallenges_Anderson.pdf; Geoffrey S. Corn, *Self-Defense Targeting: Blurring the Line between the* Jus ad Bellum *and the* Jus in Bello, 88 International Law Studies 57 (2012).

[6] On which *see generally* the contributions in International Law and the Classification of Conflicts (Elizabeth Wilmshurst ed., 2012), as well as Marko Milanovic and Vidan Hadzi-Vidanovic, *A Taxonomy of Armed Conflict*, *in* Research Handbook on International Conflict and Security Law 256 (Nigel White & Christian Henderson eds., 2013).

[7] The ASIL symposium which produced this book is an obvious exception!

then explain that we are dealing not with one, but with three distinct versions of the principle. I will then conclude by making some suggestions on how the debate should actually move forward.

2. The Genesis of *Lex Specialis*

A. *Defining the Question*

The *lex specialis* principle is frequently taken for granted, as if it has somehow always been there, carved in stone. But what is its actual genesis? By "genesis" I do not mean its ancient history. Yes, it was in the Digest of Justinian. But we honestly have little or no idea of what exactly the lawyers of the Roman and Byzantine empires meant by the expression and how they applied it in practice, and, as I will show in the next section, there are several different ways of conceptualizing *lex specialis.*

My question is rather this: when did *we*, the community of international lawyers, start using this language to describe the relationship between IHL and IHRL? The timeframe for answering that question is necessarily more limited and easier to manage, since IHRL did not become a part of public international law until after the Second World War. I am obviously too young to have direct experience of this, but my impression has been that during the first fifty years or so of their co-existence comparatively little thought was given to how IHL and IHRL would interact, especially to how any conflict between the norms of the two regimes would be resolved, and when the issue was discussed it was generally *not* framed in terms of *lex specialis.* My hypothesis is thus that the term entered common parlance among the international lawyers who have dealt with the issue only after the end of the Cold War, and specifically only after the ICJ's 1996 *Nuclear Weapons* advisory opinion, when the Court itself first used the term:

> In principle, the right not arbitrarily to be deprived of one's life applies also in hostilities. The test of what is an arbitrary deprivation of life, however, then falls to be determined by the applicable *lex specialis*, namely, the law applicable in armed conflict which is designed to regulate the conduct of hostilities. Thus whether a particular loss of life, through the use of a certain weapon in warfare, is to be considered an arbitrary deprivation of life contrary to Article 6 of the Covenant, can only be decided by reference to the law applicable in armed conflict and not deduced from the terms of the Covenant itself.[8]

[8] *Legality of the Threat or Use of Nuclear Weapons,* Advisory Opinion, 1996 ICJ Rep. 226 (hereinafter *Nuclear Weapons*), para. 25.

To prove or disprove this hypothesis I need to do two things. First, I need to establish how the Court itself got the idea to use the *lex specialis* terminology to describe the relationship between the rules of IHL and IHRL. Was it innovation on its part? Did it come from the pleadings of some of the participants in the advisory proceedings? Or did it come from generally accepted scholarship on the issue? Second, I need to look at the scholarship itself, specifically those works that examined the issue *before* the *Nuclear Weapons* opinion.

B. *The Two ICJ Cases*

The first prong of this inquiry is more feasible, and I can at least try to provide a comprehensive answer. Recall that the *Nuclear Weapons* advisory proceedings took place simultaneously with those following the request of the World Health Organization to pose a question on the legality of nuclear weapons to the Court, a request that the Court ultimately dismissed for being outside the WHO's competence.[9] The WHO's request[10] came two years before the U.N. General Assembly's,[11] and so the written proceedings in the two cases did not entirely overlap. The Court, however, decided to hear the oral proceedings in the two cases at the same time, and rendered its two opinions on the same day.[12] I will hence look (1) at the written pleadings in the WHO case; (2) the written pleadings in the *Nuclear Weapons* case; and (3) the combined oral pleadings in the two cases, in order to establish which (if any) of the participants looked at the question of interaction between IHL and IHRL, and relied on the *lex specialis* principle in its analysis, i.e., whether they used the Latin terminology or in some other words described the

[9] *Legality of the Use by a State of Nuclear Weapons in Armed Conflict*, Advisory Opinion, 1996 ICJ Rep. 6.

[10] The question posed in the WHO's request was as follows: "In view of the health and environmental effects, would the use of nuclear weapons by a State in war or other armed conflict be a breach of its obligations under international law including the WHO Constitution?" See Request for an advisory opinion transmitted to the Court under a World Health Assembly resolution of May 14, 1993, available at www.icj-cij.org/docket/files/93/7648.pdf.

[11] The question posed in the General Assembly's request was as follows: "Is the threat or use of nuclear weapons in any circumstance permitted under international law?" See Request for an advisory opinion transmitted to the Court under the United Nations General Assembly resolution 49/75 K of December 15, 1994, available at www.icj-cij.org/docket/files/95/7646.pdf.

[12] For a comprehensive account of the two cases see INTERNATIONAL LAW, THE INTERNATIONAL COURT OF JUSTICE AND NUCLEAR WEAPONS (Laurence Boisson de Chazournes and Philippe Sands eds., 1999).

relationship between IHRL and IHL as one of general law to special law, in which the special law takes some kind of precedence.

A total of thirty-five states submitted written statements in the first written round of the WHO case.[13] Most of the written statements were brief and conclusory. Only five mentioned human rights law generally or the right to life specifically in the context of the use of nuclear weapons in armed conflict, with all but one arguing that the use of nuclear weapons would violate the right to life as protected by IHRL.[14] None, however, made any mention of *lex specialis*.

The second round of the WHO case coincided with the first written round in the *Nuclear Weapons* case; eight states, all of whom participated in the first round, submitted written comments.[15] Of these eight, only one – India – made no arguments regarding human rights law.[16] Nauru and Malaysia made an identical submission in which they remarked that: "[a]pparently no statement submitted to the Court has challenged the relevance to the question before the Court of the right to life and health, as embodied in the International Covenant on Civil and Political Rights and other international law instruments."[17] Costa Rica now submitted an extensive argument that nuclear weapons would violate the right to life,[18] while

[13] Rwanda, North Korea, Ukraine, Lithuania, Netherlands, Russia, Philippines, Kazakhstan, Papua New Guinea, Italy, Moldova, Mexico, United States, Norway, France, Saudi Arabia, Solomon Islands, Costa Rica, New Zealand, Samoa, Germany, United Kingdom, Ireland, Australia, India, Sweden, Colombia, Japan, Finland, Sri Lanka, Malaysia, Uganda, Iran, Nauru, and Azerbaijan.

All written submissions available at www.icj-cij.org/docket/index.php?p1=3&p2=4&k=09&case=93&code=anw&p3=1.

[14] Written Statement of the Netherlands, June 6, 1994, para. 34 (arguing that the right to life is not absolute, that Article 6 ICCPR prohibits only arbitrary deprivations of life, and that deaths resulting from lawful acts of war – by reference to the *travaux* of the ICCPR and Art. 15(2) ECHR – should not be considered arbitrary in the sense of Article 6); Written Statement of Mexico, June 9, 1994, paras. 30–34 (arguing that the use of nuclear weapons would per se violate the right to life and the right to health); Written Statement of Solomon Islands, September 9, 1994, paras. 4.24–4.32 (arguing that the use of nuclear weapons would violate a number of human rights and environmental law instruments), and 4.33–4.46 (arguing that these instruments would continue to apply during armed conflict); Written Statement of Malaysia, September 20, 1994, at 12–13 (arguing that the use of nuclear weapons would violate the right to life); Written Statement of Nauru, September 20, 1994, at 48–51 (same).

[15] Nauru, United Kingdom, Russia, Malaysia, Solomon Islands, India, United States, and Costa Rica.

[16] Written Comments of India, June 20, 1995.

[17] Written Comments of Nauru, June 15, 1995, at 28; Written Comment of Malaysia, June 19, 1995, at 29.

[18] Written Comments of Costa Rica, July 4, 1995, at 5–7.

the Solomon Islands similarly reiterated their previous position in that regard.[19] None of these states made any mention of *lex specialis.*

On the other hand, Russia argued that "the use of nuclear weapons in self-defence does not constitute a violation of the right to life,"[20] as did the United States:

> None of these [human rights] instruments prohibits, directly or indirectly, the taking of life for legitimate purposes, including in the exercise of the right to self-defense. That inherent right has long been understood and intended to comprehend the right to use lethal force, and it is inconceivable that the various human rights instruments cited could have been intended to abridge that right so long as the rules of armed conflict and the limitations of the U.N. Charter are observed. Thus, the prohibition in the International Covenant on Civil and Political Rights against arbitrarily depriving someone of his or her life was clearly understood by its drafters to exclude the lawful taking of human life.[21]

Neither Russia nor the United States made any mention of *lex specialis.* Their argument was essentially that a killing that complied with IHL *and* with the U.N. Charter was not an "arbitrary" deprivation of life in the sense of Article 6 ICCPR.[22] The closest the United States came to articulating the principle was when it concluded that:

> Accordingly, the citation of human rights instruments adds nothing to the analysis of the question whether the use of nuclear weapons is consistent with existing international law. The answer to that question is determined, as it must be, not by reference to human rights instruments but by application of the principles of international law governing the use of force and the conduct of armed conflict.[23]

Note the echo of this wording in the ICJ's holding in *Nuclear Weapons* that "whether a particular loss of life, through the use of a certain weapon in warfare, is to be considered an arbitrary deprivation of life contrary to Article 6

[19] Written Comments of the Solomon Islands, June 19, 1995, paras. 4.85–4.87 (responding inter alia to the written statement of the Netherlands by arguing that the "Netherlands implicitly accepts the relevance and applicability of human rights instruments to the use of nuclear weapons. Second, Netherlands appears to accept that death from an unlawful use of nuclear weapons would violate Article 6. Solomon Islands agrees with both these conclusions, and considers further that since it is inconceivable that any use of nuclear weapons would be lawful it follows that any use of nuclear weapons would also violate Article 6 and, in the words of the Human Rights Committee, constitute a 'crime against humanity'.")

[20] Written Comments of Russia, June 19, 1995, at 9–10.

[21] Written Comments of the United States, June 20, 1995, at 20.

[22] *Id.*, at 21: "we know of no significant opposition to the proposition that the deprivation of life as a 'lawful act of war' would not be violative of the protected right to life."

[23] *Id.*, at 22–23.

of the Covenant, can only be decided by reference to the law applicable in armed conflict and not deduced from the terms of the Covenant itself."

So did *lex specialis* even make an appearance? Why yes it did, albeit very briefly, in the submissions of a single state – the United Kingdom. In the first round of the WHO case the UK did not even discuss the human rights issue. When it came to the second round of written pleadings, which were due at the same time as the first round of pleadings for the General Assembly *Nuclear Weapons* case, the UK decided to give its comments on the submissions in the WHO case in its written statement in *Nuclear Weapons*, i.e., that single document was both the second submission in the WHO case and the first in *Nuclear Weapons*.[24] The UK now did extensively discuss human rights and environmental law,[25] arguing that the issue was not the compatibility of nuclear weapons with these legal regimes *in abstracto*, but "whether any of the rules of the law of human rights or the law on environmental protection can be construed, in accordance with the general principles stated above, as prohibiting the use or threat of use of nuclear weapons *when carried out by way of legitimate self-defence.*"[26]

In that regard, the UK noted that Article 15(2) ECHR explicitly referred to derogations from the right to life for deaths resulting from lawful acts of war, and argued that:

> Although the International Covenant on Civil and Political Rights contains no provision equivalent to Article 15(2) of the European Convention, Article 6(1) prohibits only the 'arbitrary' deprivation of life. If the Covenant is applicable at all to the taking of life in the context of an armed conflict, it is necessary to determine what the term 'arbitrary' means in that context. Since the taking of life is an inescapable feature of the conduct of armed conflict and since it has never seriously been suggested that the Covenant outlaws the use of force by way of national self-defence, the reference to 'arbitrary' deprivation of life must contain the means for distinguishing between those acts of taking life in armed conflict which are compatible with Article 6 of the Covenant and those which are not. The only sensible construction which can be placed on the term 'arbitrary' in this context is that it refers to whether or not the deliberate taking of life is unlawful under that part of international law which was specifically designed to regulate the conduct of hostilities, that is the laws of armed conflict. On that basis, the use of a weapon to take life in armed conflict could only amount to an arbitrary deprivation of life, for the purposes of Article 6 of the Covenant, if it was contrary to the laws of armed conflict but not otherwise.[27]

[24] See Letter dated June 16, 1995 from the Legal Adviser to the Foreign and Commonwealth Office of the United Kingdom of Great Britain and Northern Ireland.

[25] Written Statement of the United Kingdom, June 16, 1995, paras. 3.84 ff.

[26] *Id.*, para. 3.98 (emphasis in original).

[27] *Id.*, para. 3.101.

After briefly looking at the *travaux* of the Covenant and the work of the Human Rights Committee, the UK concluded its submissions on human rights as follows:

> The protection given by the law of human rights does not, therefore, lead to a different conclusion regarding the legality of the use of nuclear weapons from that provided by the law of armed conflict. Since the law of human rights is concerned primarily with the protection of human rights in peacetime, whereas the law of armed conflict is a *lex specialis* designed to regulate the conduct of hostilities, it is entirely appropriate that the human rights agreements should, in effect, refer to the law of armed conflict in order to determine whether or not any particular instance of the deprivation of life in wartime is arbitrary. The same principle applies, *a fortiori*, in respect of the protection of other human rights.[28]

This, then, was the very first appearance of *lex specialis* in the written pleadings, and indeed the *only* such appearance in the UK's written statement. Notably, neither of the paragraphs I have just quoted in full provide any references or citations to authority of any kind. The UK's counsel nonetheless did their job well, since the language of the UK's submissions is clearly reflected in paragraph 25 of the Court's *Nuclear Weapons* opinion. This is, to my mind, undoubtedly the intellectual genesis of the Court's holding.

But lest I be accused of jumping the gun, let us look at the other written pleadings in the *Nuclear Weapons* case as well. Twenty-nine states filed written statements in the first round.[29] The cast of characters was very similar to those of the WHO case (and the WHO submissions frequently got regurgitated), but with a few new arrivals. Only two states, Egypt and the Solomon Islands, further decided to submit written comments in the second round of *Nuclear Weapons*. Of all of these states, eleven made arguments about human rights law.[30] And again, no state

[28] *Id.*, para. 3.108.

[29] North Korea, Finland, Japan, Samoa, Nauru, Ireland, Netherlands, Bosnia and Herzegovina, United Kingdom, San Marino, Iran, Mexico, Malaysia, Solomon Islands, Italy, Russia, Burundi, Egypt, India, Sweden, United States, France, Germany, Lesotho, New Zealand, Qatar, Ecuador, Marshall Islands, Costa Rica. Written pleadings available at www.icj-cij.org/docket/index.php?p1=3&p2=4&k=e1&case=95&code=unan&p3=1.

[30] Written Statement of Nauru, June 15, 1995, at 20–22; Written Statement of the Netherlands, June 16, 1995, para. 27; Written Statement of San Marino, June 16, 1995; Written Statement of the United Kingdom, June 16, 1995, paras. 3.84–3.108; Written Statement of Iran, June 19, 1995, at 5–6; Written Statement of Malaysia, June 19, 1995, at 13–14; Written Statement of Solomon Islands, June 19, 1995, paras. 4.32–4.49; Written Statement of Russia, June 19, 1995, at 9–10 (same document as the written comments in the WHO case); Written Statement of Egypt, June 20, 1995, paras. 26–28; Written Statement

but the United Kingdom made any reference to *lex specialis*, including Russia and the United States, as well as France, which now made its first submissions regarding human rights.[31]

Let us move now to the combined oral round in the two cases, in which other states would have had the opportunity to react to the UK's reference to *lex specialis*. Twenty-one states participated in the oral hearings,[32] and twelve of them made submissions on human rights law.[33] And how many of these states mentioned *lex specialis*? Precisely zero. Not even the United Kingdom did so, although it did argue that:

> [Human rights] treaties were never intended to regulate the conduct of hostilities in wartime. The practice of States who are parties to human rights conventions is, unambiguously, to test the legality of acts of warfare by reference to the laws of war, not by reference to treaties safeguarding human rights in time of peace. Moreover, the right to life is not absolute. The prohibition – to draw on the International Covenant on Civil and Political Rights – is in respect of the *arbitrary* deprivation of life. In so far as this applies in armed conflict at all, it can only mean deprivation of life which is contrary to the laws of war. The reference to human rights treaties thus adds nothing, for the legality of a use of nuclear weapons continues to turn on the laws of war.[34]

What are the lessons we can draw from the two advisory proceedings? First, we can observe that human rights were a relatively marginal argument,

of the United States, June 20, 1995, at 42–46; Written Statement of France, June 20, 1995, at 37–38. See also Written Comments of Egypt, September 1995, paras. 63–65; Written Comments of Solomon Islands, September 20, 1995, paras. 31–32.

[31] Written Statement of France, June 20, 1995, at 38: "Aucune prohibition d'emploi des armes nucléaires ne peut être déduite des principes relatifs aux droits de l'homme, et en particulier du droit à la vie. La situation de conflit armé entraîne nécessairement des atteintes à la vie, et les textes conventionnels qui consacrent le droit à la vie ne lui reconnaissent pas un caractère absolu. On mentionnera, à cet égard, le paragraphe 2 de l'article 15 de la convention européenne des droits de l'homme, du 4 novembre 1950, qui apporte, pour les actes licites de guerre, une exception explicite au principe du droit à la vie posé par l'article 2 de la convention. Ainsi que le montrent les travaux préparatoires, l'article 6 du Pacte des Nations Unies relatif aux droits civils et politiques doit être interprété dans le même sens."

[32] Australia, Egypt, France, Germany, Indonesia, Iran, Italy, Mexico, Japan, Malaysia, Marshall Islands, New Zealand, Philippines, Qatar, Russia, Samoa, San Marino, Solomon Islands, United Kingdom, United States, Zimbabwe. The WHO also made oral submissions.

[33] Australia – CR 1995/22, at 45, para. 27; France – CR 1995/24, at 20, para. 44; Indonesia – CR 1995/25, at 30–31, paras. 50–52; Mexico – CR 1995/25, at 56; Malaysia – CR 1995/27, at 55–56, paras. 8-10; Qatar – CR 1995/29, at 33, para. 30; Russia – CR 1995/29, at 44; San Marino – CR 1995/31, at 20; Solomon Islands – CR 1995/32, at 52–57; Costa Rica CR 1995/33, at 23 & 27; United Kingdom – CR 1995/34, at 43–44; United States – CR 1995/34, at 66.

[34] CR 1995/34, at 43–44 (emphasis in original).

initially advanced in a coordinated fashion by the Solomon Islands, Malaysia, and Nauru in the first written round of the WHO case. Second, that argument progressively gained traction and attracted responses from the pronuclear weapons states. Third, the only state to refer to *lex specialis* during the pleadings was the United Kingdom, and it did so only once. Fourth, among the states that did address the human rights issue there was actually a significant degree of agreement on the basic approach, regardless of whether they were pro or antinuclear weapons. They all essentially agreed that the right to life was not absolute, that the interpretation of the arbitrariness standard in Article 6 ICCPR should take into account both *jus in bello* and the *jus ad bellum* (the latter having somehow dropped from the Court's radar in paragraph 25 of its *Nuclear Weapons* opinion as a condition for nonarbitrariness), and pointed to the Article 15(2) ECHR reference to deaths resulting from lawful acts of war and similar references in the ICCPR's preparatory work.[35] Where they fundamentally disagreed was in the substantive application of this approach, with the pronuclear weapons states

[35] See, e.g., France – CR 1995/24, at 20, para. 44: "Or, les instruments relatifs aux droits de l'homme ne reconnaissent pas un caractère absolu au droit à la vie. Ils n'établissent pas, en particulier, de garantie contre les atteintes à la vie du fait d'actes licites de guerre"; United States – CR 1995/34, at 66: "It has been suggested that the use of nuclear weapons would violate the right to life that is recognized in international instruments such as the Universal Declaration of Human Rights, the International Covenant on Civil and Political Rights, and the European Convention on Human Rights. These instruments do not, by their terms, prohibit the use of nuclear weapons, or any other weapons for that matter. Nor, more broadly, do they prohibit the taking of life for otherwise lawful purposes, either directly or by implication. One such lawful purpose is, of course, the right of self-defence, which has long been understood to encompass the right to use lethal force. These human rights instruments cannot and should not be construed as undermining fundamental provisions of the law of war. In fact, the European Convention on Human Rights specifically recognizes that persons may lose their lives through lawful acts of war. As discussed in our submission, a similar understanding guided the negotiation of the International Covenant on Civil and Political Rights. Were this not the case – were the Court to give the right to life unwarrantedly broad effect – international humanitarian law would, as a consequence, be rendered meaningless and irrelevant, as the right to life would then be construed to prohibit the loss of life in all forms of armed conflict, without reference to self-defence, necessity, proportionality, or any of the other relevant legal standards"; Solomon Islands – CR 1995/32, at 57, paras. 14–15: "[I]t is said by some that the right to life is not absolute and derogations may be permitted in times of war. Solomon Islands does not disagree. But we must be clear: these derogations apply only to 'lawful acts of war'. No derogations are possible for unlawful acts of war, acts of war which violate *jus in bello* or *jus ad bellum*, or the rules of neutrality prohibiting transboundary consequences. . . . At the very least an unlawful use of nuclear weapons would *also* and additionally violate the right to life of victims. Since the effect of any use of a nuclear weapon would violate, in Solomon Islands' view, any or all of the rules of international humanitarian law, it is also our view that any use of a nuclear weapon must necessarily also violate the right to life of those persons situated in the target State."

arguing that in the absence of the illegality of nuclear weapons as such under the *jus ad bellum* and the *jus in bello* it would be "against both the tenets of treaty interpretation and the underlying principle of good faith to read an indirect prohibition of nuclear weapons into general treaties which deal neither with weapons nor with warfare."[36]

But the bottom line is this: despite the Latin veneer of antiquity, and whatever its exact conception or the merits thereof, *lex specialis* was *not* part of mainstream thinking on the relationship between IHL and IHRL before the 1996 *Nuclear Weapons* opinion (assuming there was *any* mainstream thinking on this issue in the first place). If it was, one would have expected to find more than a single, isolated, and conclusory reference to the term in the hundreds of pages of written and oral pleadings before the ICJ. This conclusion is confirmed by my examination of the pre-1996 scholarship on the issue.

C. *In pre-1996 Scholarship*

While I could aim for comprehensiveness in my analysis of the ICJ pleadings, I can claim no such thing with regard to scholarship. The potential scope of study is vast, while the time I had was limited. So are my languages, and so are the resources themselves even though I had the invaluable help of the University of Michigan Law Library, whose staff searched through several electronic research databases. In particular, fewer non-English works are digitized and readily available. I have thus confined myself to works in English and French, and even so the analysis inevitably has an Anglophone bias. But while the bias is there, it is (I think) not fatal, since extensive discussions in other languages of the *lex specialis* principle in the IHL/IHRL context would inevitably have migrated to the English or French literature.

We can divide this body of scholarship into two groups. First, those works whose main or predominant subject of inquiry is the relationship between IHL and IHRL, or that otherwise discussed the issue extensively. They have been the predominant focus of my inquiry, since it is in these works that most thought was given to the issue and where one would expect *lex specialis* to figure prominently, if it was widely acknowledged as relevant.[37] Second, those works where there is a tangential or fleeting reference to the relationship between IHL and IHRL, usually in no more than a

[36] United Kingdom – CR 1995/34, at 53.

[37] A helpful bibliography compiled by Robert Kolb and the ICRC can be found at www.icrc.org/eng/resources/documents/misc/57jpgs.htm.

couple of pages or paragraphs. It is obviously far harder to provide a comprehensive overview of this category, and I have not attempted to do so.

With regard to the first category, I have identified twenty-five works primarily dealing with the relationship between IHL and IHRL that were written in English,[38] and ten works written in

[38] In chronological order, with brief summaries of relevant arguments only: various short papers or verbatim statements in the PROCEEDINGS OF THE INTERNATIONAL CONFERENCE ON HUMANITARIAN LAW (Grassi: Istituto Editoriale Ticinese, 1970), a record of the founding conference of the San Remo Institute the topic of which was human rights as the basis of international humanitarian law; Sean McBride, *Human Rights in Armed Conflict: The Inter-relationship between the Humanitarian Laws and the Law of Human Rights*, 9 REVUE DE DROIT PÉNAL MILITAIRE ET DE DROIT DE LA GUERRE 373, 383 (1970) (arguing that human rights treaties apply in armed conflict, subject to their provisions on derogation, and that "when a Government wishes to avoid its obligations under the normal provisions of the Law of Human Rights, it will have to take formally the stand that there exists 'a public state of emergency threatening the life of the nation'"); G.I.A.D. Draper, *The Relationship between the Human Rights Regime and the Law of Armed Conflict*, 1 ISRAEL YEARBOOK ON HUMAN RIGHTS 191, 198, 206 (1970) (arguing that the law of war is not "an alternative to the law of peace, the old and classic positioning, but . . . an exceptional and derogating regime from that of human rights, contained, controlled and fashioned by the latter at every point possible' and that while IHL is essentially a part of IHRL, it is 'a derogation from the normal regime of human rights'"); Gerhard von Glahn, *The Protection of Human Rights in Times of Armed Conflicts*, 1 ISR. YB HUM. RTS 208 (1970), at 213–214 (arguing that human rights continue to apply in armed conflict, but not fully); Morris Greenspan, *The Protection of Human Rights in Times of Warfare*, 1 ISR. YB HUM. RTS 228 (1970) (arguing for the continued application of human rights in wartime, and discussing the limitation and derogation clauses of human rights treaties); Frits Kalshoven, *Human Rights, the Law of Armed Conflicts and Reprisals*, 11 IRRC 183 (1971); Keith D. Suter, *An Enquiry into the Meaning of the Phrase "Human Rights in Armed Conflicts,"* 15 REVUE DE DROIT PÉNAL MILITAIRE ET DE DROIT DE LA GUERRE 393 (1976) (highly critical of the relevance of human rights in armed conflict, while accepting in principle that human rights treaties could apply; arguing that the ICCPR would not apply to the conduct of a state against the nationals of other states, at least in the absence of control over the latter's territory (at 404)); G.I.A.D. Draper, *Humanitarian Law and Human Rights*, ACTA JURIDICA (1979) 193, 204–205 (backtracking from his 1971 article, arguing that the two bodies of law are diametrically opposed and that IHRL would not apply to the relations between a detaining power and POWs, or between combatants engaging in military operations against one another, because there is "no society and government-governed relationship in such cases"); Robert Quentin-Baxter, *Human Rights and Humanitarian Law – Confluence or Conflict?*, 9 AUST. YBIL 94, 103 (1980) (noting the derogability of human rights and arguing that IHL "is the exceptional regime which then springs into action to safeguard the most fundamental of human values"); Dietrich Schindler, *Human Rights and Humanitarian Law: Interrelationships of the Law*, 31 AM. U. L. REV. 935, 938–939, 941–942 (1982) (noting that most human rights are derogable in armed conflict, and arguing that the ICCPR is territorially restricted; arguing that the classical division between the law of war and the law of peace is no longer tenable; the same issue of the journal contains several brief pieces commenting on Schindler's article, which do not contest the co-applicability of IHL and IHRL); Theodor Meron, *On the Inadequate Reach of Humanitarian and Human Rights Law and the Need for a New Instrument*, 77 AJIL 589 (1983); YORAM DINSTEIN,

French.[39] They mostly deal with the question of the relationship between IHL and IHRL at a very high level of generality and abstraction, e.g., by examining the history and philosophical foundations of the two regimes. They also tend to deal with a whole variety of other, more or less related

Human Rights in Armed Conflict: International Humanitarian Law, in HUMAN RIGHTS IN INTERNATIONAL LAW: LEGAL AND POLICY ISSUES (Theodor Meron ed., 1984) 345, 351 (IHRL and IHL should not be confused, but they are part of the same overarching regime; most human rights can be suspended in wartime, yet the suspension is not automatic, but is left to state discretion via derogation); ASBJORN EIDE, *The Law of War and Human Rights – Differences and Convergences*, in STUDIES AND ESSAYS ON INTERNATIONAL HUMANITARIAN LAW AND RED CROSS PRINCIPLES IN HONOUR OF JEAN PICTET 675, 680–681, 686, 690 (Christophe Swinarski ed., 1984) (human rights normally apply in peacetime, but also in wartime, discussing derogation; also discusses the right to life, but not the conflict between the norms of IHL and IHRL); ARTHUR ROBERTSON, *Humanitarian Law and Human Rights, in* Swinarski, *ibid.*, 793, 797 (noting that "human rights law is the genus of which humanitarian law is a species," that IHRL protects all human beings everywhere, at all times, and discussing derogations); David Weissbrodt and Beth Andrus, *The Right to Life During Armed Conflict: Disabled Peoples International v. United States*, 29 HARV. INT'L L.J. 59 (1988) (arguing that the right to life in the American Declaration on Human Rights should be interpreted by taking into account customary IHL); HERNÁN SALINAS BURGOS, *The Application of International Humanitarian Law as Compared to Human Rights Law in Situations Qualified as Internal Armed Conflict, Internal Disturbances and Tensions, or Public Emergency, with Special Reference to War Crimes and Political Crimes*, in IMPLEMENTATION OF INTERNATIONAL HUMANITARIAN LAW 1 (Frits Kalshoven and Yvez Sandoz eds., 1989) (extensively discussing derogations); CHRISTINA CERNA, *Human Rights in Armed Conflict: Implementation of International Humanitarian Law Norms by Regional Intergovernmental Human Rights Bodies*, in Kalshoven and Sandoz, *ibid.*, 31 (arguing for the direct application of IHL by human rights bodies, and extensively discussing derogations); Jovica Patrnogic, *Human Rights and International Humanitarian Law*, 91 BULLETIN OF HUMAN RIGHTS 1 (1992); Hector Gros Espiell, *Human Rights and International Humanitarian Law*, 91 BULLETIN OF HUMAN RIGHTS 13 (1992); Bosko Jakovljevic, *Human Rights Accorded by International Humanitarian Law*, 91 BULLETIN OF HUMAN RIGHTS 25 (1992); Theodor Meron, *The Protection of the Human Person under Human Rights Law and Humanitarian Law*, 91 BULLETIN OF HUMAN RIGHTS 33 (1992); Francoise Hampson, *Human Rights Law and International Humanitarian Law: Two Coins or Two Sides of the Same Coin?*, 91 BULLETIN OF HUMAN RIGHTS 46 (1992); Cornelio Sommaruga, *Human Rights and International Humanitarian Law*, 91 BULLETIN OF HUMAN RIGHTS 55 (1992); Francoise Hampson, *Using International Human Rights Machinery to Enforce the International Law of Armed Conflict*, 31 MILITARY LAW AND LAW OF WAR REVIEW 117 (1992); Louise Doswald-Beck and Sylvain Vité, *International Humanitarian Law and Human Rights Law*, 33 IRRC 94 (1993), 106–107 (discussing derogation and the vague and general nature of human rights provisions, which allows for more restrictive interpretations in armed conflict).

[39] Claude Pilloud, *La Déclaration universelle des droits de l'homme et les Conventions internationales protégeant les victimes de la guerre*, 31 (364) IRRC 252, 258 (1949) (mainly dealing with the legal nature of the UDHR and its interplay with the 1949 Conventions, concluding that "nous voudrions souligner que leur coexistence ne présente aucun inconvenient. Au contraire, il est certain qu'il en résultera un renforcement des Conventions humanitaires puisque de nombreux principes qu'elles contiennent sont déclarés

issues, such as the classifications of conflicts, the regulation of NIACs in particular, guerrilla warfare, wars of national liberation, and reprisals.

Both the generality and the eclecticism of this body of work stemmed from its context. Virtually all of it was written in response to major initiatives in the late 1960s and the 1970s by NGOs such as the International Commission of Jurists and within the U.N.[40] In 1968 the International Conference on Human Rights in Tehran, convened on the occasion of the twentieth anniversary of the UDHR, adopted a resolution on "human rights in armed conflicts,"[41] whereby it inter alia invited the Secretary-General (in a call endorsed by the U.N. General Assembly) to produce reports on this topic, in particular on the need for drafting and adopting further IHL instruments. He produced two such reports.[42] They were noted by appreciation by the General Assembly in 1970, which expressed its view that "[f]undamental human rights, as accepted in international law and laid down in international instruments, continue to apply fully in situations of armed conflict."[43]

This was all part of the process that ultimately led to the negotiation and adoption of the 1977 additional protocols, and to the widespread rebranding of the law of war as international humanitarian law. The

valables en tout temps et en tout lieu."); Henri Meyrowitz, *Le droit de la guerre et les droits de l'homme*, 88 REVUE DU DROIT PUBLIC ET DE LA SCIENCE POLITIQUE EN FRANCE ET À L'ÉTRANGER 1059 (1972); Alessandro Migliazza, *L'évolution de la réglementation de la guerre à la lumière de la sauvegarde des droits de l'homme*, 137 RECUEIL DES COURS 142 (1972-III); Dietrich Schindler, *Le Comité international de la Croix-Rouge et les droits de l'homme*, 61 IRRC 3, 10–11 (1979) (discussing derogations, noting the convergence of IHL and IHRL and the insufficiency of IHRL when it came to the right to life and liberty of persons in armed conflict, essentially seeing IHL and as an elaboration of IHRL); ARISTIDIS CALOGEROPOULOS-STRATIS, DROIT HUMANITAIRE ET DROITS DE L'HOMME: LA PROTECTION DE LA PERSONNE EN PÉRIODE DE CONFLIT ARMÉ (1980); Sylvie Junod, *Les droits de l'homme et le Protocole II*, 65 IRRC 254 (1983); IQBAL AL-FALLOUJI, *Pour une thèse plus humaniste de "tous les droits de l'homme,"* in Swinarski, *supra* note 38, at 625; ARISTIDIS CALOGEROPOULOS-STRATIS, *Droit humanitaire – Droits de l'homme et victimes des conflits armés*, in Swinarski, *ibid.*, at 655 (brief summary of the key arguments in his earlier monograph); Jacques Meurant, *Droit humanitaire et droits de l'homme: spécificités et convergences*, 75 IRRC 93 (1993); ÉRIC DAVID, PRINCIPES DE DROIT DES CONFLITS ARMES 73–84 (1994).

40 But see, as a notable exception, the article by Pilloud, *supra* note 39. Katharine Fortin has also identified a couple of earlier (if brief) references to the continued application of human rights in wartime – see Katharine Fortin, *Complementarity between the ICRC and the United Nations and International Humanitarian Law and International Human Rights Law*, 1948–1968, 94 IRRC 1433 (2012), at 1446–1448.

41 Human Rights in Armed Conflicts, Resolution XXIII adopted by the International Conference on Human Rights, Teheran, May 12, 1968.

42 Respect for Human Rights in Armed Conflicts, U.N. Doc. A/7720, 20 November 1969; Respect for Human Rights in Armed Conflicts, U.N. Doc. A/8052, September 18, 1970.

43 General Assembly resolution 2675 (XXV) of December 9, 1970, op. para. 1.

support for this process among a number of states stemmed in no small part from their desire to enhance the condemnation of Israel for its conduct in the then Israeli-Arab conflict, and the project was thus perceived as heavily politicized among many specialists in the law of armed conflict.[44] This is not to say that the absence of extensive scholarship before 1968 was due to some entrenched, well-established narrative that IHRL simply did not apply in wartime. Rather, the applicability of IHRL to armed conflict was already raised during the drafting of the derogation clauses of the human rights treaties, and as persuasively shown by Katharine Fortin it simply took time for the appreciation of the issue to build up before it came on the academic radar.[45]

The Secretary-General's two reports also dealt with a variety of issues, mostly focusing on improving compliance with and further reforms of IHL. But they also touched on the issue we are directly concerned with here, the co-application of IHRL and IHL in armed conflict and the possible norm conflict between them. In his first, preliminary report, the Secretary-General emphasized that "the human rights provisions of the Charter make no distinction in regard to their application as between times of peace on the one hand and times of war on the other."[46] Neither did the UDHR, although its general limitations clause meant that an "emergency consisting of a State being involved in an armed conflict might justify therefore certain temporary limitations on the exercise of some of the human rights proclaimed in the Declaration."[47] The same went for the ICESCR.[48]

When it came to the ICCPR, the Secretary-General noted that the absence of an express reference to war in its Article 4 derogation clause was due to the drafters' desire to avoid, even by implication, endorsing the possibility of future wars.[49] Nonetheless, the concept of a public emergency in Article 4 ICCPR included armed conflict, enabling states to take derogation measures to the extent strictly required by the exigencies of the situation.[50] Crucially for our purposes, the Secretary-General then briefly looked at the central question of the taking of life during armed conflict, and noted the defeat of the UK proposal during the drafting to introduce into Article 4 ICCPR language similar to that found in Article 15(2) ECHR, i.e., derogation from the right to life in respect of

[44] For some of the strongest critiques in that regard see Meyrowitz, *supra* note 39; Suter, *supra* note 38.

[45] See more Fortin, *supra* note 40.

[46] UN Doc. A/7720, para. 23.

[47] *Id.*, para. 24.

[48] *Id.*, para. 25.

[49] *Id.*, para. 26.

[50] *Id.*, para. 29.

deaths resulting from lawful acts of war. He however refused to take a position on the issue in the first report.[51]

The first report also included communications from many governments, at various levels of generality. Neither the report nor any state made any mention of the *lex specialis* principle. For example, the United States remarked that it fully endorsed the need for the Secretary-General's study, in part because of "a strongly held conviction that steps are urgently needed to secure better application of existing humanitarian international conventions to armed conflicts. *This is a matter involving fundamental human rights* and one which should be of major concern to the United Nations."[52]

The Secretary-General's second report affirmed the first, while noting that it was generally agreed by the experts he consulted that "the international instruments on human rights adopted under the auspices of the United Nations afford a measure of protection of certain important rights of all persons involved in all armed conflicts which complements and strengthens and to some extent even exceeds, the protection derived from the rules of the Geneva Conventions and other humanitarian instruments which were expressly designed to apply solely to situations of armed conflict."[53] He also noted that an advantage of human rights protections was that they did not depend on the classification of the conflict and the status of any given individual in that conflict.[54]

A detailed study on the interaction between IHL and IHRL was attached as Annex I to the report. And it is in that study that we find the most meaningful appreciation of the norm conflict problem to date, specifically with regard to the right to life.[55] The study extensively analysed the derogation clauses of human rights treaties and the *travaux* of the ICCPR, and concluded that taking of life in wartime would not be considered as "arbitrary" in the sense of Article 6 ICCPR if it complied with the rules of IHL:

[51] *Id.*, paras. 28–29.

[52] *Id.*, at 91, para. 2 (emphasis mine). Speaking of prisoners of war in particular, the U.S. also noted that POWs "are helpless human beings and have no means of defending themselves. The humanitarian provisions of the Geneva Convention constitute more than simple statements of legal obligation. They are based upon a recognition of the dignity and worth of the human person as proclaimed in the United Nations Charter. They embody expressions of fundamental humane precepts which should characterize the conduct of any Government in dealings with another, whether friend or enemy."

[53] UN Doc. A/8052, para. 20. [54] *Id.*, paras. 24–26. [55] *Id.*, at 95 ff.

> While there does not exist any institution of mankind which is as violative of the inherent right to life and its protection as a war or other armed conflict, article 6 of the Covenant applies also in time of armed conflict, and the Covenant does not permit derogations from it. Its text, corroborated by its legislative history, demonstrates that article 6 of the Covenant would not guarantee the right to life as an absolute right without exceptions. Its examination in paragraphs 26 to 52 above has led to the conclusion that to the extent that in present international law "lawful acts of war" are recognized, such lawful acts are deemed not to be prohibited by article 6 of the Covenant if they do not violate internationally recognized laws and customs of war. However, even if this far-reaching exception is read into article 6 of the Covenant and even if death resulting from "lawful acts of war" or "lawful acts of armed conflict" are not considered "arbitrary" deprivations of life, article 6, nevertheless, contains a number of very important humanitarian provisions protecting human rights against acts other than "lawful acts of war."[56]

The study does not expressly address the same problem under the very different text of Article 2 ECHR, but its discussion of derogations to my eyes at least implies that Article 15(2) ECHR would have been seen as the solution. Again, no mention was made of *lex specialis*.

What then of the scholarship that grew with and after these U.N. initiatives? First, the vast majority thereof was in general agreement with the proposition that human rights continue applying during armed conflict. In that regard, the classical distinction between the law of war and the law of peace was regarded as obsolete by all of the scholars whose work I reviewed. Second, most scholars also pointed to the derogation clauses in human rights treaties as a crucial element for their application in armed conflict. Third, there was some pushback against the project to integrate IHL and IHRL on the part of a (vocal) minority of scholars who felt that it was too political in nature. This could be damaging for IHL, because, in the wonderfully premodern words of one ICRC lawyer: "le droit humanitaire est souvent mieux accepte que les droits de l'homme car il ne souleve pas de problemes ideologiques."[57]

The liveliest example of this pushback was a veritable human rights skeptic tirade written in 1972 by Henri Meyrowitz, who argued in the strongest possible terms for the need to maintain the disciplinary purity of the law of armed conflict. He regarded IHL and IHRL as two radically different regimes, with different histories, resting on different philosophical foundations, protecting different interests, and positively railed

[56] *Id.*, at 104, para. 46. [57] Junod, *supra* note 39, at 262.

against what he termed "confusionism." But his reason for doing so was not simply doctrinal and ideological puritanism, but was firmly grounded in his belief that the law of armed conflict was *stronger* than IHRL and could only be weakened in the admixture.[58]

But, and this brings me to my main point, not even Meyrowitz the ur-skeptic relied on any variant of the *lex specialis* principle.[59] This is not to say that the scholars of the day thought IHRL to be universally applicable to every situation in armed conflict. For example, some reservations were expressed about the territorial and personal scope of human rights treaties, particularly with regard to Article 2(1) ICCPR. In addition to the derogation clauses in the treaties, human rights provisions were seen to be broad and vague while IHL treaties contained much more detailed regulation. Similarly, the potential for any norm conflict was less obvious simply because of the then-paucity of human rights case law.[60] The European Court's leading right to life case, *McCann*, did not come until 1995,[61] while at the time of the UNSG's two reports the only human rights treaty actually in force was the ECHR.

[58] See Meyrowitz, *supra* note 39, at 1105 (noting [rather poetically] the fact that, despite its weaknesses, "le droit de la guerre est plus vigoureux que les droits de l'homme. Il est pourvu d'un armament qui fait défaut aux conventions relatives à ces derniers: les sanctions, consistant dans la responsabilité international des États belligérants et dans la responsabilité pénale individuelle; le régime des puissances protectrices; enfin, et surtout, cette institution incomparable, inimitable et non transposable que constitue le Comité international de la Croix-Rouge, avec les prerogatives qui lui sont reconnues").

[59] See Meyrowitz, *supra* note 39, at 1185 ff. Meyrowitz's argument rather was that the ICCPR excluded the very idea of war and that it could never apply to relations between enemies. He acknowledged that this argument was contradicted by ICCPR's derogation clause and its drafting history, i.e., that the concept of public emergency threatening the life of the nation in Article 4 ICCPR could encompass war, and that during the drafting a number of states expressly said so. He thus immediately qualified the argument by stating that the ICCPR would, without any doubt, apply to *internal* armed conflicts (at 1086). His problem was with IACs, as he considered that the application of the ICCPR's derogation clause to belligerents would be an "intellectually impossible operation" (at 1087). He further argued that both the population of an occupied territory and prisoners of war, even if imprisoned on the territory of the adversary, would fall outside the scope of the jurisdiction clause of Article 2(1) ICCPR (at 1087–1088). When it came to the ECHR, he relied on its derogation clause in Article 15, arguing that because of that clause the ECHR would itself not add anything to the applicable rules of IHL in IACs (at 1091).

[60] A notable, but relatively late exception is Hampson, *Using International Human Rights Machinery. . .*, *supra* note 38 (focusing on derogation and the arbitrariness standard in the ICCPR).

[61] McCann and Others v. United Kingdom, App. No. 18984/91, September 27, 1995.

Even so, it is striking that no scholar whose pre-1996 work I have reviewed endorsed the rigid classical division between the law of war and the law of peace, nor some kind of overarching principle whereby special law overrode the general one. Indeed, of the thirty-five works reviewed whose predominant subject was the relationship between IHL and IHRL, there were only two – *two* – uses of the term *lex specialis*, and even these were descriptive, isolated references rather than statements of some general principle on norm conflict resolution of avoidance. The first was in a monograph by Aristidis Calogeropoulos-Stratis, where he argued that:

> En revanche, l'application des droits de l'homme ne présente aucune difficulté apparente. Leurs conditions d'application sont en principe les mêmes pour la période de paix et pour celle de conflit armé, les clauses de derogation permettant cependant de tenir compte de l'existence d'un conflit et de "moduler" les obligations de l'Etat selon lex exigences de la situation. . . . Toutefois, l'acte de qualification dans le droit humanitaire se rapproche de l'acte d'invocation de la clause de dérogation dans les droits de l'homme dans la mesure où l'un et l'autre revêtent dans une certaine mesure un caractère constitutif. Or, on peut se demander s'il n'y a pas entre les deux une relation automatique. Nous pourrions admettre que, du moment qu'un gouvernement suspend les droits de l'homme prévus dans une convention en invoquant la clause de derogation pour faire face à une situation exceptionelle, en l'occurrence un conflict armé, il reconnaît de ce fait la situation juridique du conflict et par là l'applicabilité du droit humanitaire, droit tout spécialement applicable dans cette situation et en quelque sorte "*lex specialis.*" Il serait toutefois difficile d'aller plus loin et il n'existe pas à vrai dire de subsidiarité automatique entre droit humanitaire et droits de l'homme: leurs conditions d'applicabilité restent autonomes et indépendantes l'une de l'autre.[62]

Note again how *lex specialis* is used purely descriptively; indeed the author relies on *derogations* to effect any modification to IHRL in times of armed conflict, not some principle external to human rights treaties.[63]

The second reference was in a 1983 *AJIL* article by Theodor Meron, who was broadly sympathetic to the idea of integration between IHL and IHRL.[64] While noting that there might be difficulties with applying

[62] Calogeropoulos-Stratis (1980), *supra* note 39, at 95–96.

[63] See also *ibid.*, at 128–137 (discussing derogations generally), 144 (derogation under Article 15(2) from the right to life in armed conflict, coupled with a *renvoi* to IHL).

[64] Meron, *supra* note 38, at 594: "The fact that these two systems of law have different historical and doctrinal origins must not deter us from realizing that a tremendous

the ICCPR extraterritorially and to foreign nationals, Meron stated that "[t]here may also be limitations of applicability of human rights instruments based on preemption by a different and, on the whole, less generous *lex specialis*, as in the case of prisoners of war."[65] But Meron again did not use this as some overarching principle of normative hierarchy. He later extensively discussed derogations and the potential for their abuse by states,[66] and then touched upon the issue of the right to life in armed conflict, endorsing the U.N. Secretary-General's analysis that an IHL-compliant killing in armed conflict would not be considered to be "arbitrary" in the sense of Article 6 ICCPR, without mentioning *lex specialis*.[67]

I was also able to find three further passing references to *lex specialis* with regard to the relationship between IHL and IHRL in works that did *not* predominantly deal with the IHL/IHRL issue. First, in an article on conflicts between law-making treaties by Wilfred Jenks, who, referring to Grotius, generally discusses the *lex specialis* principle on a page-and-a-half, commenting that the principle is more difficult to apply to treaties than it is to domestic statutes[68] and notes that:

> A clear illustration of its applicability is afforded by instruments relating to the laws of war which, in the absence of evidence of a contrary intention or other special circumstances, must clearly be regarded as a *leges speciales* in relation to instruments laying down peace-time norms concerning the same subjects. Apart from relatively simple cases of this kind, the limits of the principle must be regarded as doubtful.[69]

Jenks' position seems to echo the classical divide between the law of war and the law of peace, which is only natural in a piece published in 1953. But even so Jenks confines the *lex specialis* principle only to "relatively simple cases," while otherwise its limits are doubtful. He does not specifically discuss human rights in wartime.

Second, in a book by Glen Plant on environmental protection in armed conflict:

rapprochement has already taken place between them and that the trends point to an ever greater reliance on the shared idea of humanity."

65 *Id.* 66 *Id.*, at 600–602. 67 *Id.*, at 604, n. 78.

68 See Wilfred Jenks, *The Conflict of Law-Making Treaties*, 30 Brit. Y.B. Int'l L. 401, 446–447 (1953).

69 *Id.*, at 446.

> As between belligerents it is generally agreed that the law of war applies as *lex specialis* and that their normal peacetime relationship is suspended, with the exception of only a few norms which continue to operate exceptionally, such as certain human rights norms.[70]

Note how at the time there most certainly was no general agreement about the continued validity of the classical position on the suspension of normal peacetime relations in wartime, but also how Plant does not use *lex specialis* to override human rights, which continue to apply. The third reference was in Leslie Green's book on the contemporary law of armed conflict. When discussing the history of IHL, he noted the General Assembly's affirmation that fundamental human rights continued to apply fully in armed conflict, and remarked that:

> This is something of a departure from previous understanding for it would normally be thought that the Hague and Geneva Law constitute *lex specialis* which overrides the *lex generalis* to be found in human rights instruments and which might be considered as applicable in time of peace, though these instruments do recognise that most of their provisions, but not all, are derogable in time of emergency, which would include an armed conflict.[71]

Green provided no references for the stated "previous understanding" or the use of *lex specialis*, nor any clear description of what that principle does and where it comes from, although my impression was that he was mainly responding to the proposition that fundamental human rights would *fully* apply during armed conflict. He was in any event something of a *lex specialis* aficionado – in the same book he uses the term in describing the relationship between IHL and the UN Convention on the Law of the Sea,[72] having done the same in an earlier article.[73]

[70] Glen Plant, Environmental Protection and the Law of War: A Fifth Geneva Convention on the Protection of the Environment in the Time of Armed Conflict? 14 (1992).

[71] Leslie Green, The Contemporary Law of Armed Conflict 47 (1994).

[72] *Id.*, at 156–157: "If it is suggested that UNCLOS constitutes *lex generalis* it must be pointed out that it cannot invalidate any rights arising under *lex specialis* such as the law of armed conflict, unless there is incontrovertible evidence in the text that it was intended to override such *lex specialis.* To the extent that UNCLOS may itself be considered as *lex specialis* it clearly cannot invalidate any principle of another *lex specialis*, especially when so much of the latter arises from custom and therefore is not affected by any application of the principle that later potentially inconsistent law invalidates any earlier principles."

[73] Leslie Green, *The Environment and the Law of Conventional Warfare*, 29 Canadian Yearbook of International Law 222, 226 (1991): "Article 87 [UNCLOS] merely

All of the other references to *lex specialis* as some kind of principle of norm conflict avoidance or resolution that I was able to find were isolated or sporadic, used in several different senses, and not applied to the relationship between IHL and IHRL.[74]

D. *Conclusion*

I hope to have demonstrated that the *lex specialis* principle was not part of mainstream thinking on the relationship between IHL and IHRL before 1996. Again, I fully acknowledge the limitations of my literature review, since I did not look at works written in say German, Italian, or Spanish, and obviously there may well have been some references to *lex specialis* that I have missed. Nonetheless, if the *lex specialis* principle enjoyed general acceptance it would have been simply impossible for it to

confirms the established rule of international law that the high seas are open to all states, while Article 88 specifically provides that 'the high seas shall be reserved for peaceful purposes'. This implies that not even the normal activities of maritime warfare would be compatible with the obligations imposed by the 1982 Convention if conducted outside the territorial sea of the belligerents. However, the Convention has not yet entered into force and – of major significance – while the Convention is *lex generalis,* the law of war is *lex specialis* and, to the extent that its provisions are contrary to those of the *lex generalis,* they prevail."

74 See, in chronological order, J.A. Roach, *Certain Conventional Weapons Convention: Arms Control or Humanitarian Law?*, 105 MIL. L. REV. 3, 31–35 (1984) (weapons protocols are *lex specialis* to Additional Protocol I); THEODOR MERON, HUMAN RIGHTS AND HUMANITARIAN NORMS AS CUSTOMARY LAW (1989), at 161 (speaking of *lex specialis* rules of attribution as a matter of state responsibility); William Hayes Parks, *Air War and the Law of War*, 32 AIR FORCE L. REV. 1, 13, at n. 52 (1990) (nuclear weapons are *lex specialis* to the rules on conventional bombing); Francoise Hampson, *The Geneva Conventions and the Detention of Civilians and Alleged Prisoners of War*, (1991) PUBLIC LAW 507, 519 (UK Geneva Conventions Act as *lex specialis* to the Immigration Act); Stephanie Simonds, *Conventional Warfare and Environmental Protection: A Proposal for International Legal Reform*, 29 STAN. J. INT'L L. 165, 188 (1992) (environmental law is specialized enough that it can apply in wartime and not be trumped as *lex generalis* by IHL, responding to Green, *supra* note 73); Dalibor Jilek, *Human Rights Treaties and the New Constitution*, 8 CONN. J. INT'L L. 407, 418 (1993) (referring to *lex specialis* in the context of the relationship between human rights protections under the dedicated treaties and under the U.N. Charter); Amit Mukherjee, *International Protection of Journalists: Problem, Practice, and Prospects*, 11 ARIZ. J. INT'L & COMP. L. 339, 354 (1994) (wartime rules on the protection of journalists override peacetime rules as *lex specialis*); Richard D. Glick, *Lip Service to the Laws of War: Humanitarian Law and United Nations Armed Forces*, 17 MICH. J. INT'L L. 53, 92 (1995) (referring to the U.N. Security Council's decisions as *lex specialis*).

make but a single appearance in the *Nuclear Weapons* case and the few isolated appearances in pre-1996 scholarship that I have identified.

As I have explained earlier, that scholarship examined the relationship between IHL and IHRL from a high altitude, often in very general philosophical terms. Examinations of potential conflicts between the specific norms of these two regimes, as in the Secretary-General second report regarding the right to life in armed conflict, were rare indeed.[75] While the rejection of the rigid classical divide between the law of war and the law of peace and the complementarity between IHL and IHRL emerged as the mainstream position, if with some pushback, little thinking was devoted to the problem of norm conflict. The vast majority of scholars were oblivious to the issue's importance or even its existence, other than through extensive analyses of the derogation mechanisms under IHRL treaties.

I do not doubt that *lex specialis* was mainstreamed after the ICJ's *Nuclear Weapons* opinion, but this was largely because of the opinion itself. The timing of that mainstreaming should not be forgotten. It is simply factually incorrect to say that *lex specialis* was always "there" somewhere in the ether, that it represents the "traditional" position that its alternatives have the burden of disproving, or that is entrenched in long-standing custom. Such ahistorical narratives should be rejected for, as Robert Kolb well put it:

> The precise relation of IHL and [IHRL] and the reasons for their coming closer one to the other can be grasped only in the light of an historical analysis. This is particularly true since the closer ties witnessed today between the two branches of the law are not in any sense natural or necessary. They are the result of forces and interests, as well as profound ideological shifts, whose careful evaluation only allows giving the relationship found to exist today its full sense and its most articulate understanding.[76]

One could object to my analysis by saying that even if officials and scholars did not use the *words lex specialis* before 1996, they *did* somehow express and endorse the *ideas* behind these words. There is some small truth in that observation. For instance, I do not think anyone seriously disputed that IHRL was generally made for peacetime conditions of normalcy, while IHL was designed to regulate armed conduct – that is after all simply a fact. The whole point of the integrationist project was that the newly rebranded IHL was somehow an extension of human

[75] See *supra* note 56 and accompanying text.

[76] Robert Kolb, *Human Rights and Humanitarian Law*, in MAX PLANCK ENCYCLOPEDIA OF PUBLIC INTERNATIONAL LAW, available with subscription at http://opil.ouplaw.com/home/EPIL, para. 3.

rights to armed conflict, or an exceptional, specialized part of IHRL. But the real problem is that the *lex specialis* terminology, *as it is used today*, can denote at least *three different ideas*, i.e., those same Latin words can mean different things to different people. This at the very least creates potential for miscommunication. Drawing on my earlier work,[77] I will now try to unpack these different conceptions in the following section. And because the mainstreaming of *lex specialis* happened only after the *Nuclear Weapons* opinion, it will also be important to establish precisely which of these conceptions was argued for by the UK in the advisory proceedings and adopted by the Court, as well as whether we can observe the influence of these three different ideas in pre-1996 scholarship.

3. The Different Conceptions of *Lex Specialis*

For our purposes there are three relevant conceptions of *lex specialis*: as a rule of *total displacement*; as a rule of *partial displacement* or norm conflict resolution; and as a mere *interpretative tool* or rule of norm conflict avoidance.[78] Let me address each in turn.

First, *lex specialis as total displacement* is a purported rule under which IHL applies to the complete exclusion of IHRL. This variant is essentially a restatement, if in different terminology, of the classical divide between the law of war and the law of peace. But that classical divide applied to *all* of international law, which was rigidly separated into two halves, and turned on the existence of "war" as a formal, technical legal condition.[79] And it is precisely as a *general* matter that this position has been abandoned, at least after the Second World War. Most recently, in its 2011 Draft Articles on the Effects of Armed Conflict on Treaties the International Law Commission affirmed the general principle that the "existence of an armed conflict does not *ipso facto* terminate or suspend the operation of treaties: (a) as between States parties to the conflict; (b)

[77] See Milanovic, *supra* note 3, at 229 ff.

[78] See generally Anja Lindroos, *Addressing Norm Conflicts in a Fragmented Legal System: The Doctrine of Lex Specialis*, 74 Nord. J. Int'l L. 27 (2005), esp. at 46; Nancie Prud'homme, *Lex Specialis: Oversimplifying a More Complex and Multifaceted Relationship?*, 40 Israel L. Rev. 355, 366ff (2007); Milanovic, *supra* note 3, at 249 ff. See also Serdar Mohammed v. Ministry of Defence [2014] EWHC 1369 (QB), para. 273 ff.

[79] See more Stephen Neff, War and the Law of Nations: A General History 178 ff (2005).

as between a State party to the conflict and a State that is not."[80] In doing so the ILC followed a long line of authorities, including the 1980s work of the *Institut de Droit international*.[81]

Similarly, the total displacement variant of *lex specialis* is directly contradicted by the text of the derogation clauses of human rights treaties, some of which expressly mention "war" as a public emergency justifying derogation measures.[82] These provisions would make absolutely no sense if human rights treaties automatically ceased to apply in wartime.[83] And indeed in its 2011 Draft Articles the ILC included human rights treaties in an indicative list of treaties "the subject-matter of which involves an implication that they continue in operation, in whole or in part, during armed conflict."[84] The ICJ's *Nuclear Weapons* opinion and its progeny likewise stand for the proposition that IHRL treaties continue to apply during armed conflict.[85]

In the IHL/IHRL context the total displacement variant of *lex specialis* today has few advocates. It was first articulated in its modern form by the George W. Bush administration during its "war on terror," in what was an attempt to rearticulate the classical divide while using the ICJ's *lex specialis* terminology, coupled with the rejection of the extraterritorial application of the relevant IHRL treaties.[86] In effect the argument was

[80] Art. 3, ILC Draft Articles on the Effects of Armed Conflict on Treaties, U.N. Doc. A/66/10, para. 100.

[81] See ILC commentary to Art. 3, *ibid.*, para. 101.

[82] See, e.g., Art. 15 ECHR and Art. 27 ACHR. See also Art. 2(2) CAT, under which "[n]o exceptional circumstances whatsoever, whether a state of war or a threat of war, internal political instability or any other public emergency, may be invoked as a justification of torture."

[83] See Serdar Mohammed v. Ministry of Defence, para. 281: "it is impossible to maintain that in a situation of armed conflict IHL, by reason of the principle of *lex specialis*, displaces Convention rights altogether."

[84] Art. 7 and Annex, item (f), U.N. Doc. A/66/10, para. 100.

[85] See *Nuclear Weapons*, para. 25; *Legal Consequences of the Construction of a Wall in the Occupied Palestinian Territory*, Advisory Opinion, 2004 ICJ Rep. 136, para. 106; *Case Concerning Armed Activities on the Territory of the Congo* (DRC v. Uganda), 2005 ICJ Rep. 168, para. 216.

[86] See, e.g., Response of the U.S. to the request for Precautionary Measures on behalf of the detainees in Guantanamo Bay, Cuba, April 15, 2002, reprinted in 41 ILM 1015 (2002), available at www.derechos.org/nizkor/excep/usresp1.html: "international human rights law is not applicable to the conduct of hostilities or the capture and detention of enemy combatants, which are governed by the more specific laws of armed conflict . . . It is humanitarian law, and not human rights law, that governs the capture and detention of enemy combatants in armed conflict. To the extent the ICJ's decision in the *Nuclear Weapons Case* implies otherwise, the United States reserves its judgment"; Comments by

that IHL operated to the exclusion of IHRL. The only other states espousing a similar position have been Israel[87] and Russia,[88] and even then inconsistently and sporadically. The U.S. position softened in the latter years of the Bush administration and in the Obama administration, so that *lex specialis* is now conceived of as partial, rather than total displacement,[89] and it is this variant that I turn to next.

the Government of the United States of America on the concluding observations of the Human Rights Committee, U.N. Doc. CCPR/C/USA/CO/3/Rev.1/Add.112, October 10, 2007: "The United States is engaged in an armed conflict with al Qaida, the Taliban, and their supporters. As part of this conflict, the United States captures and detains enemy combatants, and is entitled under the law of war to hold them until the end of hostilities. The law of war, and not the Covenant, is the applicable legal framework governing these detentions." See also the Opening Remarks by John Bellinger, Legal Adviser, U.S. Department of State, before the U.N. Committee Against Torture, May 5, 2006, available at www.state.gov/g/drl/rls/68557.htm; Opening Statement of Matthew Waxman, Head of U.S. Delegation before the U.N. Human Rights Committee, July 17, 2006, available at http://2001-2009.state.gov/g/drl/rls/70392.htm.

87 See, e.g., Second Period Report of Israel, UN Doc. CCPR/C/ISR/2001/2, December 4, 2001, para. 8: "Israel has consistently maintained that the Covenant does not apply to areas that are not subject to its sovereign territory and jurisdiction. This position is based on the well-established distinction between human rights and humanitarian law under international law. Accordingly, in Israel's view, the Committee's mandate cannot relate to events in the West Bank and the Gaza Strip, inasmuch as they are part and parcel of the context of armed conflict as distinct from a relationship of human rights." See also Comments by the Government of Israel on the concluding observations of the Human Rights Committee, U.N. Doc. CCPR/CO/78/ISR/Add.1, January 24, 2007, para. 15; Fourth Periodic Report of Israel, U.N. Doc. CCPR/C/ISR/4, December 12, 2013, para. 47: "The relationship between different legal spheres, primarily the Law of Armed Conflict and Human Rights Law remains a subject of serious academic and practical debate. For its part, Israel recognizes that there is a profound connection between human rights and the Law of Armed Conflict, and that there may well be a convergence between these two bodies-of-law in some respects. However, in the current state of international law and state-practice worldwide, it is Israel's view that these two systems-of-law, which are codified in separate instruments, remain distinct and apply in different circumstances."

88 See, e.g., the European Court's summary of Russia's arguments in Georgia v. Russia (II) (dec.), App. No. 38263/08, December 13, 2011, para. 69: "the Convention did not apply to a situation of international armed conflict where a State Party's forces were engaged in national defence, including in respect of any required operations abroad. In such circumstances the conduct of the State Party's forces was governed exclusively by international humanitarian law."

89 See, e.g., Fourth Periodic Report of the United States, U.N. Doc. CCPR/C/USA/4, May 22, 2012, paras. 506 & 507:

With respect to the application of the Covenant and the international law of armed conflict (also referred to as international humanitarian law or "IHL"), the United States has not taken the position that the Covenant does not apply "in time of war." Indeed, a time of war does not suspend the operation of the Covenant to matters within its scope of application. To cite but two obvious examples from among many, a State Party's

The partial displacement variant of *lex specialis* concedes that IHRL and IHL both apply in armed conflict and even accepts the basic position of human rights bodies that "both spheres of law are complementary, not mutually exclusive."[90] It is certainly true that in the vast majority of situations IHRL and IHL will complement each other well, either by both having norms going in the same direction (e.g., their parallel prohibitions of torture and ill-treatment) or by performing a gap-filling function (e.g., IHL says nothing about the freedom of expression or of the press in occupied territory). So far so good. But the real bite of the partial displacement variant of *lex specialis* comes in those few situations in which the specific norms of IHRL and IHL *can* conflict, i.e., would govern the same situation *differently*, and such norm conflict was genuine and could not be avoided through interpretation. The two cases in which such norm conflicts would arise most frequently would be killing and detention. If such conflict was unavoidable *lex specialis* would operate as a rule of norm conflict resolution, so that IHL would displace or qualify the conflicting rule of IHRL *to the extent strictly required* to resolve the conflict. Thus, a killing that would in principle violate IHRL (e.g., because nonlethal means to neutralize the target were not exhausted), but was compliant with the rules of IHL (on targeting,

participation in a war would in no way excuse it from respecting and ensuring rights to have or adopt a religion or belief of one's choice or the right and opportunity of every citizen to vote and to be elected at genuine periodic elections.

More complex issues arise with respect to the relevant body of law that determines whether a State's actions in the actual conduct of an armed conflict comport with international law. Under the doctrine of *lex specialis*, the applicable rules for the protection of individuals and conduct of hostilities in armed conflict are typically found in international humanitarian law, including the Geneva Conventions of 1949, the Hague Regulations of 1907, and other international humanitarian law instruments, as well as in the customary international law of armed conflict. In this context, it is important to bear in mind that international human rights law and the law of armed conflict are in many respects complementary and mutually reinforcing. These two bodies of law contain many similar protections. For example, prohibitions on torture and cruel treatment exist in both, and the drafters in each area have drawn from the other in developing aspects of new instruments; the Commentaries to Additional Protocol II to the Geneva Conventions make clear that a number of provisions in the Protocol were modeled on comparable provisions in the ICCPR. Determining the international law rule that applies to a particular action taken by a government in the context of an armed conflict is a fact-specific determination, which cannot be easily generalized, and raises especially complex issues in the context of noninternational armed conflicts occurring within a State's own territory.

[90] Human Rights Committee, General Comment 31 (2004), para. 11.

weapons, etc.), would now also become compliant with IHRL by virtue of *lex specialis.*[91]

This brings me to the third variant of *lex specialis* as a tool of norm conflict avoidance. In this conception the scope of the principle is limited to *interpretation only.* In essence, *lex specialis* would simply be an articulation of the more general principle stated in Article 31(3)(c) VCLT that in interpreting treaties we should take into account other relevant rules of international law applicable between the parties. For example, IHL could help us interpret the arbitrariness standard in Articles 6 and 9 ICCPR during armed conflict. But this relationship would not be a one-way street, since in *some* cases it is IHRL that might be more specific and thus useful for the interpretation of more general IHL.[92] For instance, the fair trial provisions of IHRL treaties and the jurisprudence of human rights bodies would inform our interpretation of the Common Article 3 requirement that sentences should not be passed "without previous judgment pronounced by a regularly constituted court affording *all the judicial guarantees which are recognized as indispensable by civilized peoples.*"

Note that under this conception IHL would need to be *taken into account*, but that it would not necessarily be *dispositive* for the interpretation of IHRL. Thus, while it makes perfect sense to generally interpret the arbitrariness standard in Article 6 ICCPR in line with IHL during armed conflict, in some circumstances that standard might require *more* than just compliance with IHL.[93] Consider, in that regard, the *Targeted Killings* judgment of the Israeli Supreme Court, in which the Court applied human rights jurisprudence to require the exhaustion of

[91] See, e.g., Heike Krieger, *A Conflict of Norms: The Relationship between Humanitarian Law and Human Rights Law in the ICRC Customary Law Study*, 11 JCSL 265 (2006), at 272; Cordula Droege, *Elective Affinities? Human Rights and Humanitarian Law*, 90 IRRC 501, 524 (2008).

[92] See Kolb, *supra* note 76, paras. 35–37 (discussing *lex specialis* as a *renvoi* from IHRL to IHL, and vice versa).

[93] *See*, in that regard, Louise Doswald-Beck, *International Humanitarian Law and the Advisory Opinion of the International Court of Justice on the Legality of the Threat or Use of Nuclear Weapons*, 37 IRRC 35, 50–51 (1997) (examining the ICJ's reference to *lex specialis*, and concluding that "it means that humanitarian law is to be used to actually interpret a human rights rule. Conversely, it also means that, at least in the context of the conduct of hostilities, human rights law cannot be interpreted differently from humanitarian law.") The distinction between the strong and weak variants of *lex specialis* is actually in Doswald-Beck's second sentence: taking IHL into account is not in question, but under the weak variant of *lex specialis* IHRL *can* be interpreted differently from IHL if the circumstances so warrant.

nonlethal means, i.e., a capture before kill approach, in targeting suspected terrorists in the occupied Palestinian territories, even though it considered these terrorists to be lawful targets under IHL, with the Court justifying this approach by referring to the comprehensiveness of the control that Israel exercises over these territories.[94]

The third variant of *lex specialis* does not give IHL the power to *ipso facto* override, displace, or qualify conflicting norms of IHRL (or of any other part of international law). While IHL would be a crucially important interpretative factor, it would still remain only one factor among many, and would not invariably determine the outcome of the interpretative process. This variant also presupposes the existence of (an admittedly elusive) boundary between interpretation and amendment, i.e., that interpretation can only go so far without committing violence against a treaty's text, object, and purpose. Thus, for instance, IHL as *lex specialis* could influence the interpretation of the arbitrariness standards in the ICCPR far more than that of the categorical rules and closed lists in Articles 2 and 5 ECHR, at least absent a derogation from these provisions.[95]

These then are the three variants of *lex specialis* relevant to describing the relationship between the norms of IHL and IHRL.[96] But as we have seen *lex specialis* as total displacement simply has no place in modern international law. The choice is therefore down to the second and the third variants, i.e., strong *lex specialis* as partial displacement and weak *lex specialis* as a purely interpretative tool. The third variant is

[94] The Public Committee against Torture in Israel et al. v. The Government of Israel et al., HCJ 769/02, Judgment, December 11, 2006, para. 40 (relying on the European Court's *McCann* judgment). See further Marko Milanovic, *Lessons for Human Rights and Humanitarian Law in the War on Terror: Comparing Hamdan and the Israeli Targeted Killings Case*, 89 IRRC 373 (2007).

[95] *See* Milanovic, *supra* note 3, at 249 ff.

[96] Note that there are many other ways of using the term, which only adds to the possibility for confusion. For instance, it can be used purely descriptively, as a label for specialized subregimes within a legal system (labor law, environmental law, trade law as *leges specialis*), or as a reference to specific provisions within the same instrument, or in relation to the *ejusdem generis* technique of interpretation, or to describe the relationship between custom and treaties, so that custom is *lex generalis* and treaties are *leges specialis*, which is really describing the idea of contracting out of custom or *jus dispositivum*, etc. See also Fragmentation of International Law: Difficulties Arising from the Diversification and Expansion of International Law, Report of the Study Group of the International Law Commission, finalized by Martti Koskenniemi, U.N. Doc. A/CN.4/L.682, April 13, 2006 (hereinafter "ILC Fragmentation Study"), para. 61 ff. The three variants analyzed in the text are the only ones relevant for discussing the *relationship between IHL and IHRL*.

unobjectionable in and of itself,[97] with the main issue again being what the proper limits of interpretation are. It is essentially our default option if the second, strong variant of the principle is shown to be unconvincing – so let us now examine its foundations in more detail.

The strong conception of *lex specialis* as a rule of norm conflict resolution rests on a simple premise: the legislator could not possibly have intended to legislate two hierarchically equal norms that are ultimately contradictory.[98] In particular, the primary legislators of international law – states – could not possibly have intended to agree to more general norms of IHRL that would both apply in armed conflict *and* be more restrictive than the rules of IHL that were designed precisely to regulate armed conflict. This premise is then buttressed by two arguments grounded in fact. First, states have historically not behaved in a way that would demonstrate that they have agreed to more restrictions in armed conflict than IHL provides. Second, imposing such restrictions would undermine the balance struck by IHL between humanitarianism and military necessity, it would introduce real uncertainties, and could never truly work in the "real world."

I have argued elsewhere that the premise, at least, is flawed.[99] The idea that the legislator could not possibly have intended for his norms to produce two contradictory outcomes is a fiction even in centralized domestic legal systems, and it is entirely misplaced in the heterogeneous and decentralized international one.[100] When state representatives (often different individuals, depending on the subject area) sit down to draft treaties, they do not have in their minds a comprehensive list of all possible applications of that treaty to concrete problems, and even less so how the treaty would interact with other norms of international law in every conceivable permutation. Their agreement is reflected in the text of the treaty and its object and purpose, not in the thousands of possible applications of that treaty that they supposedly envisaged and mentally

97 *See also* Serdar Mohammed v. Ministry of Defence, para. 289: "I can see no difficulty with this, most modest version of the argument that IHL operates as *lex specialis*."

98 *See* Joost Pauwelyn, Conflict of Norms in Public International Law: How WTO Law Relates to other Rules of International Law 388 (2003).

99 See Marko Milanovic, *Norm Conflict in International Law: Whither Human Rights?*, 20 Duke J. Comp. & Int'l L. 69 (2009); Milanovic, *supra* note 3, at 229 ff.

100 "There is no single legislative will behind international law. Treaties and custom come about as a result of conflicting motives and objectives—they are 'bargains' and 'package-deals' and often result from spontaneous reactions to events in the environment." ILC Fragmentation Study, para. 34.

ticked off. And just like any ordinary individual can of their own free will assume two contradictory commitments (e.g., paint two different houses on the same day, or contract the same book with two different publishers), so can states conclude (multilateral) treaties that, once interpreted and applied to specific problems, can ultimately conflict. This is not an outcome that is normatively desirable, and it preferably should be avoided, but it can and does happen.

Prioritizing between contradictory but hierarchically equal norms on the grounds that one is special and the other general is exceptionally rare even in domestic systems. Consider for a moment the normal course of dealing with normative conflicts in municipal law. Courts will first attempt to *avoid* such conflicts through interpretation, but they will not always be successful in doing so – again because there are some limits on what interpretation alone can achieve. When a conflict is genuine and unavoidable, courts will look at the hierarchical status of the source of the norms in question: the constitution will trump statute, statute will trump executive decrees, which will trump local ordinances, and so forth. The exact hierarchical pyramid will of course depend on the constitutional system of each given state.

Things get trickier when the two conflicting instruments are hierarchically equal, say two statutes passed by the U.S. Congress or by the British Parliament, and when the instruments themselves do not contain clauses that regulate their mutual interaction, e.g., provisions on express repeal. Courts will then prioritize the instrument which is later in time, the *lex posterior*, which will be regarded as having implicitly repealed the prior instrument. This general approach is justified not simply in terms of legal reasoning or logic, or the (supposed) intentions of the legislator, but in political and democratic theory: a constitution prevails over statute because it is the expression of a democratic super-majority which had the right to entrench its norms, while the later in time statute is the current expression of the will of an ordinary democratic majority, which is not shackled by the simple majorities of the past.[101]

What then of *lex specialis*? It would be used in domestic systems as a true rule of *norm conflict resolution* if and *only* if all of the following

[101] For an overview of issues of legislative entrenchment and implied repeal as an aspect of the overarching principle of Parliamentary sovereignty in the UK, where the only power Parliament lacks is the one to bind its successors, see the contributions by Bradley, Lester, and Craig in THE CHANGING CONSTITUTION (Jeffrey Jowell and Dawn Oliver eds., 2011), as well as the classical articles by William Wade, *Sovereignty – Revolution or Evolution*, 112 LQR 568 (1996) and T.R.S. Allan, *Parliamentary Sovereignty: Law, Politics and Revolution*, 113 LQR 443 (1997).

conditions are met: (1) there is an apparent conflict between norms stemming from two different instruments; (2) the norm conflict cannot be avoided through interpretation, and thus becomes genuine; (3) the two instruments are hierarchically of the same level or standing; (4) there is no clear provision in either instrument as to how any normative conflicts between them are to be reconciled; (5) one instrument is "general" and the other is "special" (however exactly we define these concepts); (6) the general instrument was enacted *after* the special one; but even so (7) the prior special law prevails over the later general law by virtue of the *lex specialis* principle. In this chain of reasoning *lex specialis* is really an exception to *lex posterior* – if the "special" law is later in time than the general one, then it will prevail over the general one *because* it was later in time, rather than on grounds of specialty. In a centralized legal order, therefore, *lex specialis* makes sense as a rule of norm conflict resolution only if the special law is prior in time than the general law, but will still not be considered as having been implicitly repealed.[102]

Now, how many examples of this chain of reasoning can you think of in whatever domestic system? How many cases are there where a domestic court applied an earlier statute in lieu of a later-in-time statute on the grounds that the earlier statute was more specific or special and that the legislature could not possibly have intended to impliedly repeal it? I am sure there must be *some* such examples, but I at least cannot think of any in the municipal systems that I am familiar with (nor could easily find one).[103] Whatever its general validity, the strong variant of *lex specialis* is a rarity even in centralized domestic legal systems.

And what then are we to make of the fragmented and decentralized international system, in which many steps of this reasoning chain simply break down? Unlike domestic law, the vast majority of international law is not hierarchical in nature, with its principal sources – treaties and custom – being of equal standing. What few elements of hierarchy we have, such as *jus cogens* and Article 103 of the U.N. Charter (which is

[102] It is, of course, perfectly possible for the *lex posterior* and *lex specialis* maxims to point in the same direction, but *lex specialis* is then not operating as an independent rule of norm conflict resolution.

[103] In English law, at least, some prior statutes have been regarded as immune from implied repeal because of the constitutional importance of their subject matter (e.g., the European Communities Act 1972 or the Human Rights Act 1998), not because of some relationship of the special to the general – *see* R (Factortame Ltd) v Secretary of State for Transport (No 2) [1992] 1 AC 603; Thoburn v Sunderland City Council [2002] EWHC 195 (Admin).

not truly hierarchical in nature anyway, since unlike *jus cogens* it does not invalidate the conflicting norm), are not useful for analyzing the relationship between the norms of IHL and IHRL. That treaties generally prevail over custom is not due to their higher hierarchical status, but because most customary rules are *jus dispositivum*, i.e., they apply unless states agree to do something different and contract out of them.[104] Similarly, *lex posterior* is much harder to apply in the international system, in which its basic premise (the supposed "intent" of the unified legislator) is lacking, especially with multilateral treaties adopted by different groups of states, drafted by different individuals, and for different purposes. Even a quick glance at Article 30 VCLT demonstrates just how difficult it is to apply *lex posterior* in the international order, despite how naturally the later in time rule comes to lawyers in municipal systems.[105] And there is no way to meaningfully apply that principle to IHL and IHRL treaties, which were concluded in several overlapping waves. It simply makes no sense to say that the 1950 ECHR should prevail over the 1949 Geneva Conventions, or that the 1977 Additional Protocols should prevail over the ECHR just because of the timing of their conclusion.

What we are left with, therefore, is *lex specialis* detached both from *lex superior* and *lex posterior*. And how many examples in international practice do we actually have of *lex specialis* being used as a rule of norm conflict resolution? Few if any. In its extensive study on the fragmentation of international law the ILC mentions precisely zero.[106] It does so even though it acknowledges that *lex specialis* can be conceptualized either as an elaboration of a more general norm (i.e., weak *lex specialis* as interpretative norm conflict avoidance) or as its displacement (i.e., strong *lex specialis* as norm conflict resolution), but rather tries to downplay the importance of that distinction.[107] But as we have seen that distinction is of paramount importance, at least in dealing with the differences in the text and structure between the relevant provisions of the ICCPR and the ECHR.

Lex specialis of whatever type is of course not mentioned in the VCLT (unlike *lex posterior*). Nor is it mentioned in any other relevant treaty. And if we go back to the principle's genesis in the *Nuclear Weapons* case, we can only observe that the Court employed the weak version of the

[104] *See more* ILC Fragmentation Study, para. 79 ff. [105] *See more Id.*, para. 223 ff.
[106] *See* ILC Fragmentation Study, paras. 46–122, esp. paras. 103–107.
[107] *See Id.*, paras. 56–57, 88, 96–97.

principle, relying on IHL to interpret the arbitrariness standard in Article 6 ICCPR.[108] But the Court said *nothing* about the principle's application to categorical texts such as Article 2 ECHR, which do not have the same open window through which IHL could enter. When we look at how *states* argued the issue before the Court, we can see that they relied precisely on the fact that ICCPR's arbitrariness standard could be interpreted in line with IHL.[109] This was especially the case with the UK, who as we have seen was the only state to use the *lex specialis* language.[110] And when these states touched on the ECHR, they did not argue that the categorical provision in Article 2 ECHR was *ipso facto* displaced by IHL in armed conflict, but referred to the Article 15(2) derogation clause.[111] We can make the same observations with regard to pre-1996 scholarship, which also focused on derogation and the open language of the ICCPR.[112] Indeed, a strong version of *lex specialis* would render the derogation clauses entirely superfluous, especially Article 15(2) ECHR.[113]

It is in my view hard to dispute that the strong version *lex specialis* as some kind of overarching principle of international law rests on very shaky formal foundations. But if we are left only with the third, weak interpretative version of *lex specialis* (for which we do not need the Latin anyway), how then do we square the normative applicability of IHRL with the reality of the need to resort say to status-based targeting and preventive security detention in armed conflict? Here I think there is less daylight between the proponents of the weak and strong versions of *lex*

[108] *Nuclear Weapons*, para. 25. See *supra* note 8 and accompanying text. This is also how the ILC read the opinion – see ILC Fragmentation Study, para. 104: "The Court was careful to point out that human rights law *continued to apply* within armed conflict. The exception – humanitarian law – only affected one (albeit important) aspect of it, namely the relative assessment of 'arbitrariness'. Humanitarian law as *lex specialis* did not suggest that human rights were abolished in war. It did not function in a formal or absolute way but as an aspect of the pragmatics of the Court's reasoning. However desirable it might be to discard the difference between peace and armed conflict, the exception that war continues to be to the normality of peace could not be simply overlooked when determining what standards should be used to judge behaviour in those (exceptional) circumstances." Like the Court, the ILC did not examine the same issue from the standpoint of Article 2 ECHR.

[109] *See supra*, Section 2.B. [110] *See supra* notes 25–36 and accompanying text.

[111] *Id.* [112] *See supra*, Section 2.C.

[113] *See also* Serdar Mohammed v. Ministry of Defence, para. 284: "in circumstances where the Convention itself defines the conditions in which and the extent to which derogation from its obligations is permitted, and makes specific provision for derogation in time of war, it is difficult to see that there is any room for the *lex specialis* principle to operate as a basis for disapplying the Convention when it conflicts with IHL."

specialis then might first appear. First, even under more modest interpretative approaches the arbitrariness language of the ICCPR allows for harmonious interpretation with IHL, at least in the vast majority of cases. Second, the limitations clauses that characterize a number of other substantive rights similarly allow for the adaptation of these rights to the specific requirements of armed conflict. Third, states can and should resort to derogations more frequently in order to introduce flexibility into IHRL that can take account of IHL, and this is particularly the case for the ECHR.

However, crucially, neither interpretation nor derogations would necessarily always allow for complete harmony between IHL and IHRL. When it comes to the conduct of hostilities, there may be some, truly exceptional cases where IHRL will impose additional restrictions which go beyond the targeting rules of IHL, e.g., the requirement to take all reasonable steps to capture an adversary before resorting to lethal force. The likelihood of that will increase the less the case at issue resembles a traditional battlefield situation, and the greater the capacity of the relevant state is to comply with additional restrictions (think, for instance, of the U.S. operation to kill Osama bin Laden in Pakistan). When it comes to detention, IHRL could accommodate some forms of internment, but it would not normally allow for the removal of any judicial review of detention, no matter what IHL might say.[114]

4. Moving Forward

The appeal of *lex specialis* lies in the veneer of antiquity of its Latin formula,[115] in its apparent formality, simplicity, and objectivity. But all it really does is disguise a series of policy judgments about what outcomes are the most sensible, realistic, and practicable in any given situation. The strong variant of *lex specialis* is neither old, nor established, nor formally sound. The Latin formula is no more than a crutch used to make oneself

114 *See more* Milanovic, *supra* note 3, at 249–261.

115 Much as with the (admittedly non-obfuscating) terms *jus ad bellum* and *jus in bello* – see Robert Kolb, *Origin of the Twin Terms* Jus ad Bellum/Jus in Bello, 37 IRRC 553 (1997) (arguing that the "august solemnity of Latin confers on the terms *jus ad helium* and *jus in bello* the misleading appearance of being centuries old. In fact, these expressions were only coined at the time of the League of Nations and were rarely used in doctrine or practice until after the Second World War.")

feel better, as not overstepping one's bounds as an objective, supposedly apolitical lawyer while actually making that series of policy judgments.[116]

I would thus favor dropping the *lex specialis* language even in its third, conceptually unproblematic variant – it is in my view sufficient to say that IHL and IHRL should be taken into account when interpreting one another, in accordance with Article 31(3)(c) VCLT, without having to inquire into which one is special and which general. Similarly, I am prepared to accept the possibility that the European Court might eventually find in some future case that at least in international armed conflicts the categorical norms of Articles 2 and 5 ECHR should give way to IHL and enable status-based targeting and security detention, even without a formal derogation under Article 15. But if the Court did so (and in my view it should *not* do so in the absence of derogation), it would do so not because of some *lex specialis* principle extraneous to the Convention (even if it invoked it), but because it made a policy judgment and decided to "read down" the categorical text into a more flexible standard such as arbitrariness.[117] Whether the Court would have the *authority* to make such an interpretative decision, or it would stray into impermissible amendment, is an arguable point – and the debate worth having.[118]

[116] *See also* Lindroos, *supra* note 78, at 66 (arguing that *lex specialis* "is a descriptive principle that has little independent normative force," which can only be applied once highly political and value-related issues are resolved).

[117] I would argue that this is precisely what the most sophisticated advocates of *lex specialis* are actually doing – *see especially* Marco Sassòli and Laura Olson, *The Relationship between International Humanitarian and Human Rights Law where it Matters: Admissible Killing and Internment of Fighters in Non-International Armed Conflicts*, 90 IRRC 599 (2008).

[118] On this I will only say that the boundary between permissible interpretation and impermissible amendment is more set by the set of social practices that underpin a given legal system than by legal rules themselves. Compare, in that regard, s. 3(1) of the UK Human Rights Act, under which "*[s]o far as it is possible to do so*, primary legislation and subordinate legislation must be read and given effect in a way which is compatible with the [ECHR]" (emphasis mine). What the limits of the *possible* are has been the object of much case law and academic writing – *see esp.* Ghaidan v Godin-Mendoza [2004] 2 AC 557, where the House of Lords read the word "spouse" in a statute to include a cohabitating same-sex partner, in order to avoid discrimination and the incompatibility of the statute with the ECHR. British judges generally justify this very aggressive interpretative approach by referring to the grant of authority to them by Parliament and the expectation that incompatibility will be avoided in the vast majority of cases, although there are still *some* limits on what is "possible," in which case they will make a declaration of incompatibility which does not invalidate the incompatible statute. See also Aileen Kavanagh, *The Elusive Divide between Interpretation and Legislation under the Human Rights Act 1998*, 24 OJLS 259 (2004).

Obviously I am aware that not everyone will agree with my critique of *lex specialis*. How then to move forward the debate between the human rights skeptics and the human rights enthusiasts while avoiding its derailment? To do that we would need to agree on *something*. I would say that we can genuinely do so on three basic principles:

First, that fundamentalism of either the enthusiast or the skeptic kind is unhelpful and counterproductive. In other words, both camps must acknowledge that the adherents of the other camp make some valid arguments, and that a crude, simplistic dismissal of all of these arguments is persuasive only in one's own echo chamber. Similarly, we must acknowledge the extent to which all of us driven by our own policy preferences and essentially moral judgments as to what particular rules provide a better fit for a given situation.

Second, that applying human rights in armed conflict involves striking a balance between the universality of human rights on the one hand and considerations of effectiveness on the other, just like IHL itself embodies a balance between humanitarianism and military necessity. In particular, the corpus of human rights law, developed over decades by courts and treaty bodies primarily in times of normalcy, must be adjusted and applied more flexibly in extraordinary situations in order to avoid imposing excessive, unrealistic burdens on states. As argued earlier, the really difficult question is how far do normal tools of interpretation allow us to go in order to achieve this flexibility. The watering down of human rights during armed conflict certainly must not go too far, so as to render them completely ineffectual or to compromise the integrity of the regime as a whole. We must also arrive at specific rules applying to specific problems that are clear and predictable, rather than endlessly ruminate on the relationship between IHL and IHRL as a whole. Derogations have the potential of being a powerful (if under-utilized) tool for achieving these goals of flexibility, regime integrity, and clarity.

Third, and finally, we must try to isolate as much as possible the issue of the interaction between IHRL and IHL from other issues that can arise simultaneously, primarily but not exclusively the *jus ad bellum*. For example, one could legitimately argue that a killing would be "arbitrary" within the meaning of Article 6 ICCPR if in the process of invading state A without a valid *ad bellum* justification state B deprives individuals of their lives *even if the killing was otherwise IHL compliant* (e.g., B killed A's combatants). In other words, while *jus ad bellum* legality does not influence *jus in bello* legality, it *might* influence IHRL legality. Indeed, states considering the issue in the *Nuclear Weapons* case generally agreed that nonarbitrariness under the ICCPR would require both *ad bellum* and *in bello* compliance. In the words of the U.S. representatives in the WHO case: "it is inconceivable that the various human rights instruments cited could have been intended to abridge that right [of self-defence] so long as the rules of armed conflict *and the limitations of the U.N. Charter are observed.*"[119] But whether this is a good idea, or whether IHRL in wartime should be separated from the *jus ad bellum* just like IHL, is not something I wish to discuss in this piece, and it is certainly an issue to be addressed only *after* the relationship between IHRL and the *jus in bello*. Conceptual clarity is crucial if we are to avoid misunderstandings and derailment, and to be able to assess the consequences of one particular course of action over another. In particular, those relying on the *lex specialis* principle must appreciate that there are several different ways of conceptualizing that principle, and must clearly articulate which version of that principle they are invoking and on what precise basis.

[119] *See* Written Comments of the United States, June 20, 1995, at 20 (emphasis added). *See also supra* Section 2.B. For arguments along these lines *see, e.g.*, William Schabas, Lex Specialis? *Belt and Suspenders? The Parallel Operation of Human Rights Law and the Law of Armed Conflict, and the Conundrum of* Jus ad Bellum, 40 Israel L. Rev. 592 (2007); Karima Bennoune, *Toward a Human Rights Approach to Armed Conflict: Iraq 2003*, 11 U.C. Davis J. Int'l L. & Policy 171, 213–216 (2004); Ralph Wilde, *The Extraterritorial Application of International Human Rights Law on Civil and Political Rights*, *in* Routledge Handbook of International Human Rights Law 635, 652–656 (Scott Sheeran and Nigel Rodley eds., 2014); Erik Roxstrom, Mark Gibney, and Terje Einarsen, *The NATO Bombing Case* (Bankovic et al. v. Belgium et al.) *and the Limits of Western Human Rights Protection*, 23 B.U. Int'l L. J. 55, 118–119 (2005). For the opposite view *see* Ronald St. J. Macdonald, *Derogations under Article 15 of the European Convention on Human Rights*, 36 Colum. J. Transnat'l L. 225, 247 (1997); David Harris et al., Law of the European Convention on Human Rights 638 (2009); Rusen Ergec, Les droits de l'homme à l'épreuve des circonstances exceptionnelles: Étude sur l'article 15 de la Convention européenne des droits de l'homme 129–134 (1987).

4

Acting as a Sovereign versus Acting as a Belligerent

JENS DAVID OHLIN*

Introduction

In assessing the legality of targeted killings, or almost any other lethal action, the outcome of the legal analysis will frequently turn on which body of law applies to the action. Under the frame of reference provided by International Humanitarian Law (IHL), lethal attacks are judged by a permissive standard: attacks against legitimate military targets are presumptively lawful, as long as the weapon in question does not violate a particular rule of *jus in bello* (such as chemical weapons). While attacks directed against civilians are unlawful, civilian deaths that are the incidental result of attacks against military targets are still lawful as long as the damage is not disproportionate to the value of the military target.[1] These rules are highly permissive: they sanction killing writ large, subject only to the principles of distinction, necessity, and proportionality. While it is true that there exists some intramural squabbling over exactly how permissive the principle of necessity should be understood (more on that later), the simple fact is that critics of targeted killings have lost conceptual ground once they concede (if they concede) that the legality of a particular drone strike is governed by IHL.[2]

On the other hand, some critics insist that International Human Rights Law (IHRL) governs drone strikes (depending on their location).[3]

* The author acknowledges helpful suggestions from Marty Lederman, Marko Milanovic, John Dehn, Janina Dill, Naz K. Modirzadeh, Brian Orend, Jonathan Horowitz, and Adil Haque.

1 *See, e.g.*, Customary International Humanitarian Law, Volume 1, Rules 46–50 (Jean-Marie Henckaerts & Louise Doswald-Beck eds., 2005).

2 The exception here is the argument made by Ryan Goodman, who argues that IHL does not license lethal force when non-lethal alternatives are available. *See, e.g.*, Ryan Goodman, *The Power to Kill or Capture Enemy Combatants*, 24 Euro. J. Int'l L. (manuscript at 33–34) (2013).

3 *See, e.g.*, Mary Ellen O'Connell, *Unlawful Killing with Combat Drones: A Case Study of Pakistan, 2004–2009*, *in* Shooting to Kill: Socio-Legal Perspectives on the Use of Lethal Force (Simon Bronitt et al. eds., 2012).

Under this framework, the basic standard is flipped: killing is presumptively illegal. All human beings have the right to life, and generally speaking, there is no principle of necessity that allows the government to kill large numbers of people. The default rule is that the government should arrest, prosecute, and imprison individuals who threaten the state. Killing is subject to the demands of exigency – an imminent threat against the police, the public, and the state. Moreover, killing the threatening individual, say in the course of a police chase, must meet the demands of the least-harmful-means test. State agents must be faced with an extreme situation where no other action less than lethal force can alleviate the threat to innocent bystanders. Police officers who kill instead of arresting subjects are therefore subject to the highest scrutiny that human rights law has to offer.[4] When judged against these standards, it is more likely that any particular drone strike will be judged illegal. Of course, these are comparative statements. I do not mean to suggest that IHL will always justify a drone strike; nor will IHRL always condemn it. Rather, the point is simply that IHL is far more likely to justify a strike than IHRL. Consequently, the choice of framework represents half (or even most) of the battle. The choice of framework is usually, though not always, outcome determinative.

It is no surprise, then, that the choice of framework question is contentious and bitter. What is surprising, however, is how intractable the debate has become and how little law there is to resolve the question of which legal framework applies.[5] In a sense, the problem stems from the lack of a metalegal framework – a legal framework that determines which legal framework applies. There is nothing of the sort, though perhaps one can be inferred from the content of the two legal regimes, working outward from their object and purpose to determine when and how they apply and whether they can be applied together.[6] The following chapter is an example of this methodology.

[4] *See, e.g.*, McCann v. United Kingdom, 21 Eur. Ct. H.R. (ser. A) at 91 (1995).

[5] Some scholars have also suggested that the application of human rights norms in armed conflict may not necessarily generate the improved conditions for civilians (when compared to IHL) that human rights activists assume will flow from the co-application of the two legal regimes. *See* Naz K. Modirzadeh, *The Dark Sides of Convergence: A Pro-civilian Critique of the Extraterritorial Application of Human Rights Law in Armed Conflict*, 86 INT'L L. STUD. 349, 350 (2010).

[6] For a discussion of this important issue, see MARKO MILANOVIC, *Norm Conflicts, International Humanitarian Law, and Human Rights Law*, *in* INTERNATIONAL HUMANITARIAN LAW AND INTERNATIONAL HUMAN RIGHTS LAW (Orna Ben-Naftali ed., 2011).

I. The Lex Specialis Principle

Recently, the U.S. softened its previously categorical claim that IHRL never applies in armed conflict, and concluded that:

> With respect to the application of the Covenant and the international law of armed conflict (also referred to as international humanitarian law or "IHL"), the United States has not taken the position that the Covenant does not apply "in time of war." Indeed, a time of war does not suspend the operation of the Covenant to matters within its scope of application. To cite but two obvious examples from among many, a State Party's participation in a war would in no way excuse it from respecting and ensuring rights to have or adopt a religion or belief of one's choice or the right and opportunity of every citizen to vote and to be elected at genuine periodic elections.[7]

Although this sounds like a substantial retreat from prior positions of the U.S. government, the details reveal more similarity than departure.[8] The fact that armed conflict does not abrogate the human right to freedom of religion or equal opportunity in voting in no way tells you whether there is room for human rights to regulate who and in what way the United States may target with a drone in Yemen, Afghanistan, Pakistan, or Somalia.

As for more pertinent restrictions stemming from IHRL, the U.S. conceded that some IHRL protections are co-extensive with protections from IHL, so there will be no conflict. An example is the prohibition against torture and cruel or degrading treatment, which is illegal under any framework, human rights or armed conflict.[9] Outside of this relatively clear example, however, the U.S. could only muster the following vague statement: "Determining the international law rule that applies to a particular action taken by a government in the context of an armed conflict is a fact-specific determination, which cannot be easily

See also Marko Milanovic, Extraterritorial Application of Human Rights Treaties (2011).

[7] Fourth Periodic Report at para. 506.

[8] The exact nature of the U.S. legal position appears to be in flux. Legal Advisor Harold Koh authored a memorandum just before he left the State Department arguing that the ICCPR applies extraterritorially. *See* Harold H. Koh, Legal Advisor, U.S. Department of State, *Memorandum Opinion on the Geographic Scope of the International Covenant on Civil and Political Rights* (October 19, 2010). For a discussion, see Beth Van Schaack, *The United States' Position on the Extraterritorial Application of Human Rights Obligations: Now is the Time for Change*, 90 Int'l L. Stud. 20 (2014).

[9] Convention Against Torture and Other Cruel, Inhuman or Degrading Treatment or Punishment, December 10, 1984, 1465 U.N.T.S. 85 (entered into force June 26, 1987). *See also* Jens David Ohlin, *The Torture Lawyers*, 51 Harv. Int'l L.J. 193 (2010).

generalized, and raises especially complex issues in the context of non-international armed conflicts occurring within a State's own territory."[10] What this means is anyone's guess. The U.S. could only reassure the Human Rights Committee that the U.S. pledges to comply with the demands of IHL with regard to its armed conflict against al-Qaeda, and that in many respects the relevant IHL provisions run "parallel" to the provisions of the ICCPR.[11] This deliberately leaves vague the question of *opinio juris*: Is the U.S. complying with the underlying norm because it emanates from IHRL or because it simultaneously emanates from IHL?

In its report, the United States gestured toward a nuanced view of IHL as *lex specialis* toward IHRL. This is not to suggest that IHRL has no role to play in the application of legal norms in armed conflict, as an extreme reading of the principle of *lex specialis* might imply. Rather, it suggests that IHL provides the content of what IHRL requires during times of armed conflict. This way of talking subsumes IHL under the larger rubric of IHRL as a specialized field of law with particular subdisciplines that apply in different contexts. Given the unique nature of armed conflict, and every state's interest in seeing it effectively regulated, armed conflict has responded to significant pressure toward codification, perhaps more so than other areas of the law.

There are, however, limitations of this nuanced *lex specialis* talk. First, it is somewhat ahistorical since it views IHL as a sub-branch of IHRL even though IHL is historically prior. By this I mean that the great push toward IHL codification happened at the very beginning of the twentieth century. While it is true that the Four Geneva Conventions were negotiated and signed in 1949 and entered into force in 1950,[12] the Hague Conventions were drafted in 1899 and 1907.[13] When compared with the modern rise of human rights codification in the aftermath of World War II (with the Universal Declaration of Human Rights coming in 1948),

[10] Fourth Periodic Report at para. 507. [11] *Id.* at para. 509.

[12] *See* Convention for the Amelioration of the Condition of the Wounded and Sick in Armed Forces in the Field, August 12, 1949, art. 2, 6 U.S.T. 3114, 75 U.N.T.S. 31, 32 [hereinafter First Geneva Convention]; Convention for the Amelioration of the Condition of the Wounded, Sick, and Shipwrecked Members of Armed Forces at Sea, August 12, 1949, art. 2, 6 U.S.T. 3217, 75 U.N.T.S. 85, 86 [hereinafter Second Geneva Convention]; Convention Relative to the Treatment of Prisoners of War, August 12, 1949, art. 2, 6 U.S.T. 3316, 75 U.N.T.S. 135, 136 [Third Geneva Convention]; Convention Relative to the Protection of Civilian Persons in Time of War, August 12, 1949, art. 2, 6 U.S.T. 3516, 75 U.N.T.S. 287, 288 [Fourth Geneva Convention].

[13] *See, e.g.*, Hague Convention Respecting The Laws and Customs of War on Land, with Annexed Regulations, October 18, 1907, 36 Stat. 2277.

IHL is ancient. That being said, concepts are not always historical and there might be good reasons to think that IHL is conceptually subordinated to IHRL *today* even if its historical development stands in some tension with that conceptual reality.

The bigger problem with the *lex specialis* story is that it fails to provide an answer to the gap-filling quandary. Specifically, the laws of war, like any legal norms, are not self-applying and capable of covering all situations. Furthermore, the gap is even larger in non-international armed conflicts (NIACs), whose legal restrictions are only codified in Common Article 3 and Additional Protocol II. The abstract notion of *lex specialis* does not – indeed cannot – provide an answer on how to fill these gaps. Should one look to IHRL to fill the gap or provide scope and context to the legal norms, under the rationale that IHL is subsumed under IHRL? Or is the special nature of IHL such that IHL is a part of – but in some sense normatively separate from – IHRL at the same time? Shouting *lex specialis* offers no answers to these crucial questions.

Indeed, the question is in part determined by one's view regarding the legal significance of *absence*. Is the absence of a codified rule *ipso facto* evidence that all is permitted?[14] This was the view taken by the Permanent Court of Justice in *S.S. Lotus*, which generally assumed that in the absence of a specific international prohibition to the contrary, states may act as they wish.[15] In other words, the default is permission; and prohibitions must be established by reference to a clearly established rule. On the other hand, one might take the opposite view: states acting extraterritorially must appeal to a particular norm or principle of international law to justify their behavior, and in the absence of a legal foundation they are not permitted to act. In the end, the only way to solve this problem is to appeal to a conceptual framework that will demarcate IHRL and IHL. This is the task of the next two sections.

II. Sovereignty Versus Belligerency

First, a point about the work that this conceptual framework will provide: it is not meant to provide a foundational account of human rights. For

[14] *Cf.* Arnulf Becker Lorca, *Rules for the "Global War on Terror": Implying Consent and Presuming Conditions for Intervention*, 45 N.Y.U. J. Int'l L. & Pol. 1, 76 (2012) (arguing that the *Lotus* principle is no longer fully applicable).

[15] *But see* Separate Opinion of Judge Alvarez, (U.K. v. Norway), 1951 I.C.J. 145, ¶ 10 (December 18, 1951), cited with approval in Lorca, *supra* note 14, at 76 n.179.

that one must appeal to the dignity of human persons that marks them out as centers of moral concern. Many human rights theorists unpack this aspect of humanity in explicitly Kantian or contractarian terms. The framework proposed in this chapter is not meant to displace or crowd-out these deontological accounts that are relevant at a deeper level of abstraction. Rather, the sovereignty versus belligerency framework proposed in this chapter is designed to explain when each body of positive law applies, since IHL and IHRL are potentially in conflict when the state deploys military or quasi-military force. But none of this is meant to displace a philosophical account of human rights that relies on the dignity of the human person.

Recently, it has become fashionable for philosophers writing about war and armed conflict to deny that armed conflict presents any special moral problem that requires the creation of a distinct body of rules that apply only during armed conflict (*jus in bello*). This revisionist view contrasts sharply with the traditional Just War Tradition view, ably articulated in its modern variation by Michael Walzer in *Just and Unjust Wars*. The revisionists, most famously Jeff McMahan, argue that morality is more or less individualistic, and that each soldier must make an individual claim of self-defense against an unjust attack if he is to be justified for killing enemy soldiers during an armed attack.[16] This view conflicts sharply with the more collectivist impulse of IHL, which allows all soldiers with the combatants' privilege to kill enemy soldiers and remain immune from criminal prosecution for it.[17] In this sense, the IHL framework assumes that an individual's membership in a collective group engaged in a bona fide armed conflict is sufficient to allow that individual to engage in lawful acts of combatancy.

The present essay takes the collective approach as given in the sense that the collective approach embodies the governing legal framework underlying IHL. For the moment, I do not take a position on the deeper question of whether the moral foundation of the law of war should be individual or collective. Rather, it is sufficient to note that in positive law the rules of *jus in bello* are applied to an individual soldier just as long as the soldier belongs to a party to an armed conflict, irrespective of whether that conflictive party is the aggressor or the victim of the conflict. This

[16] JEFF MCMAHAN, KILLING IN WAR (2011).

[17] See RICHARD BAXTER, *So-Called 'Unprivileged Belligerency': Spies, Guerrillas, and Saboteurs*, in HUMANIZING THE LAWS OF WAR: SELECTED WRITINGS OF RICHARD BAXTER 37–38 (2013).

background throws into sharp relief the tension between the laws of war and human rights law, since the former is based on the existence of an armed conflict between collectives, while the latter is based on the inalienable rights of individuals. During times of armed conflict when *jus in bello* is triggered, what happens to human rights law? Where does it go?

On deeper inspection, the respective legal spheres include principles that demarcate their conceptual boundaries. Human rights law is designed to limit the behavior of sovereigns as they regulate the actions of their subjects. In contrast, IHL is designed to constrain the military activities of co-equal belligerents engaged in an armed conflict against each other.[18] Here is historian Stephen Neff's explanation of the distinction, which he terms a Janus-faced affair:

> In very brief terms, sovereign rights are peacetime rights, arising from the Constitutions and the ordinary laws of the land. Belligerent rights are peculiar to a state of war. Their source is international law, and they spring automatically into action when a state of war takes effect. Sovereign rights and powers are applied to citizens of the law-making power in question, whereas belligerent rights and powers are invoked against enemy nationals. In the concrete terms, this meant that the Union authorities sometimes treated the Confederates as enemies in an "ordinary" armed conflict—that is, virtually as foreign nationals—while at other times treating them as rebellious citizens of the Union itself. In other words, the Confederates were treated sometimes as enemies and sometimes as criminals, with the Union government correspondingly functioning sometimes as a belligerent and sometimes as a sovereign. When acting in a belligerent capacity, the Union was guided by the international rules on the conduct of war. When operating in its sovereign capacity, it was constrained by the statutory law of the land and, ultimately, by the strictures of the Constitution.[19]

Neff takes this distinction as the central answer that will solve the riddle of the American Civil War: Lincoln treated the Confederacy as an illegal rebellion *and* a recognized belligerency triggering the laws of war.

I adopt this distinction as a framework for understanding the distinction between human rights and IHL. However, there are two key differences with my application of the distinction that depart from its application to the

[18] The distinction between acting as a sovereign versus acting as a belligerent is introduced in Stephen C. Neff, Justice in Blue and Gray: A Legal History of the Civil War (2010).

[19] Neff at 4–5.

U.S. Civil War. First, Neff's account does not involve the application of international human rights law as a constraint on sovereign action. Rather, the relevant body of law is domestic law and the Constitution. With "In Lincoln's time, basic principles of human rights had not yet solidified into the robust and complete body of law that it is today. But the distinction still holds even though the relevant body of law for regulating sovereign action was once purely domestic. Regardless of its source as domestic or international, the peacetime law represents a *constraint* on governmental action against its own subjects – a relationship that contains the same inner logic regardless of which source of law (IHRL or domestic constitutional law) regulates sovereign behavior.

Second, the U.S. Civil War triggered a particularly penetrating collision of sovereign and belligerent rights because it was a *civil war* that involved an internal belligerency. This produced the uncertainty regarding whether the Union's treatment of confederate individuals constituted sovereign or belligerent action. In contrast, much of the current debate surrounding the interaction of IHRL and IHL applies in situations that extend beyond the context of civil wars to transnational conflicts. Is the sovereign-belligerency framework limited to civil wars and NIACs or can it be applied to international armed conflicts (IACs) as well?

In principle the distinction applies in all armed conflicts, regardless of their classification. Although the collision between the belligerent and sovereign modes of action will be most keenly felt in civil wars, when the government engages in belligerent actions on its own territory, the conceptual distinction is not tethered in any way to the NIAC context. Indeed, IACs or extraterritorial NIACs will trigger comparatively modest collisions of the sovereign and belligerent modes of action, though they still exist. The following sections of this chapter will now unpack and apply this legal distinction.

A. *Acting as a Sovereign*

First, let us explain the concept of *acting as a sovereign*. Governments act in this mode whenever they are engaged in the regular activity of governmental regulation and constraining the conduct of their subjects. The term *subject* here is not used to denote the member of a monarchical kingdom, as the phrase was once used during the American Revolution. At that time, the term "subject" referred to government by monarchy, as opposed to "citizens" participating in a Republic. This is a technical distinction not relevant to our discussion here.[20] Rather, the term "subject" also has a more general meaning: an individual ruled by a sovereign government regardless of its type or form.[21]

The government is acting as a sovereign when it controls its subjects. That control can take many forms, including the implementation of general laws and regulations and the enforcement of the same against the individual. This inherently unequal relationship between sovereign and subject is capable of immense corruption and abuse. Ideally, citizens themselves form the core of their own government through representative democracy, which in so doing provides a check on government abuse. However, this still leaves open the possibility of a tyranny of the majority. And it also leaves open the possibility of abuse from non-democratic or illiberal nations that do not engage in robust citizen decision-making. In these countries, government power is truly unchecked. Since there is nothing in international law that preserves an explicit right to democracy, international law is faced with a diverse plurality of different types of governance structures.[22] Human rights law provides a valuable constraint on government behavior especially in non-democratic regimes where citizens and subjects have little contribution to governmental decisions.

In this context, human rights law emerged as the central body of law designed to curb governmental abuses against its own subjects. The content of the individual rights reflect this object and purpose. The ICCPR protects the right to be free from discrimination, equal protection for men and women, freedom from slavery, free exercise of religion, access to education, and a lengthy list of other protections.[23] Individuals can assert these protections as a trump against government conduct as a way of mitigating the harshness of the unequal relationship between ruler

[20] BLACK'S LAW DICTIONARY 1561 (9th ed. 2009); JOHN SALMOND, JURISPRUDENCE 133 n.e (Glanville L. Williams ed., 10th ed. 1947).

[21] *See* Jens David Ohlin, *The Duty to Capture*, 97 MINN. L. REV. 1268 (2013).

[22] Although a right to democracy is well theorized in the philosophical literature, it is absent from codified international law. *But see* JOSHUA COHEN, *Is There a Human Right to Democracy?*, *in* THE EGALITARIAN CONSCIENCE (2006) ("A world with more democracy would be a more just world, because it gives people the treatment as equals to which all are entitled. But democracy, with its equal right to participate, is not part of the common standard of achievement, defensible on the terrain of global public reason, to which global public responsibility extends."); SEYLA BENHABIB, IS THERE A HUMAN RIGHT TO DEMOCRACY?: BEYOND INTERVENTIONISM AND INDIFFERENCE (2008).

[23] *See generally* LOUIS HENKIN, THE AGE OF RIGHTS (1990).

and ruled.[24] In exchange for reciprocal promises from other sovereigns regarding their own behavior, sovereigns have voluntarily consented to constraints on their behavior. In some cases the rights in question may even transcend voluntarism insofar as they are *jus cogens* obligations that apply in the absence of consent. In that situation, the rights must emanate not from the consent of the sovereign but rather from the dignity of the individual, or some other conceptual account that explains the moral and legal value of the individual human being.[25] In either case, however, the rights mitigate the fundamentally unequal relationship between the sovereign and her subjects.

B. Acting as a Belligerent

We might compare this with belligerency – a status that obtains between collectives engaged in armed conflict. Like human rights law, IHL also constrains the behavior of governments. However, it does so in different ways: it regulates how they engage in belligerency. And the key element of belligerency is embodied in the relationship of formal equality between parties to an armed conflict. Instead of the unequal relationship of sovereign to subject, belligerents stand against each other as co-equal participants following the same constraints regarding their behavior in armed conflict. Whichever side is victorious in battle becomes the winner of the contest, as Jim Whitman has explored in his recent book.[26] The content of IHL provides the legal restrictions regarding this military contest.

In reality, of course, belligerency rarely tracks *factual* equality. One side of the conflict usually has greater strength in terms of military assets, technology, techniques or strategies, and territory. However, one needs to distinguish between factual equality and formal equality. The formal equality of belligerents during armed conflict stems not from factual predicates but rather from the law's decision to treat both sides of the conflict as subject to the same rules, a situation that does not obtain in the field of human rights. The government needs to protect an individual's right of religion, but the individual is not under a reciprocal duty to protect the government's right of religion. That does not even make sense. It is a category mistake; individuals are the bearers of human rights and sovereign states bear the corresponding obligations. (If there

[24] *See* Ronald Dworkin, Taking Rights Seriously (1978).
[25] *See* Henkin, *supra* note 23, at 186–87.
[26] *See generally* James Whitman, The Verdict of Battle (2012).

are reciprocal duties owed in IHRL, it is between sovereign states for mutual compliance with IHRL norms). In contrast, both parties to an armed conflict enjoy the same responsibilities toward each other with regard to their compliance with the demands of *jus in bello*.

The formal equality of belligerents is reinforced by the separation of *jus in bello* and *jus ad bellum* under the law of war.[27] The application of *jus in bello* is insensitive to determinations regarding justification under *jus ad bellum*. As such, it does not matter whether a state is the aggressor or the victim under *jus ad bellum*; both are required to comply with the demands of *jus in bello*. Questions of aggression, prohibitions on the use of force under Article 2(4) of the U.N. Charter, and self-defense under Article 51 of the Charter have nothing to do with the regulations regarding permissible conduct during warfare.[28] The formal *de jure* equality of belligerents (with regard to *jus in bello*) is so deep that it transcends all questions regarding the resort to force under international law.

Some examples might be helpful. Consider the government's power to tax citizens and residents. This clearly represents a sovereign action since it is a regulatory power that runs from the sovereign to all subjects. But not all seizures represent sovereign action. A government's seizure of an individual's property for non-payment of taxes constitutes sovereign action. However, the government's seizure of a shipping vessel pursuant to the rules of capture is belligerent in nature because the action is taken by one belligerent party against a formally co-equal belligerent during armed conflict. In contrast, a seizure for non-payment of taxes is a purely sovereign action.

Consider a second example: the announcement and enforcement of a naval blockade. In 1861, Lincoln declared a blockade of Southern ports.[29] This decision implicated not only domestic law but also international law, since it interfered not only with the South's ability to engage in commerce but also restricted the ability of foreign states to engage in trading with Southern ports.[30] Lincoln's authority to blockade Southern ports stemmed not from sovereign authority – which would have required congressional legislation – but rather from the Confederacy's

[27] Some Just War Theorists have recently questioned this separation, though it is undeniably a fixture of the existing law. The strong push in Just War Theory is then best viewed as a revolutionary proposal. *See, e.g.*, Jeff McMahan, Killing in War (2011).

[28] *See* Jens David Ohlin & George P. Fletcher, Defending Humanity: When Force is Justified and Why (2008).

[29] Neff at 20. [30] Neff at 21.

status as a belligerent power. Consequently, under international law, the Union was justified in blockading the ports of an enemy belligerent power.[31] The Supreme Court upheld the resulting captures in the *Prize Cases* because the Court concluded that an armed conflict existed with the Confederacy and that the existence of the armed conflict was a matter of law for the Supreme Court to decide rather than a political question for Congress to decide under the Article 1 Declaration Clause.[32] As Neff puts the point, Lincoln had a "dualistic approach" to the legal nature of the conflict because it occasionally regulated the South with sovereign powers and at other times with belligerent powers. This, for example, allowed the Union to label Confederate soldiers as treasonous (under sovereign regulation) but also allowed them to voluntarily treat Confederate soldiers as lawful combatants entitled to POW status.[33] Lincoln was therefore switching between sovereign and belligerent methods "as a matter of free choice and not of legal obligation."[34]

I employ the distinction between sovereign and belligerent powers to slightly different effect. Unlike Lincoln, I do not believe that the two modes are a matter of free choice to be selected by the executive. As the analysis in the rest of this chapter will demonstrate, belligerent powers flow from actions that regulate the armed conflict between two co-equal belligerents, while sovereign powers regulate the subjects under the government's control. The distinction between the modes of action might overlap in discrete situations – requiring a legal principle (such as *lex specialis*) to resolve the potential conflict. For example, it is conceptually possible that a government might exercise sovereign control under circumstances that are also regulated by the law of armed conflict and stem from belligerent powers. The interplay between the two spheres requires a legal framework for resolving tensions between the two spheres. What should be sufficiently clear, at this point, is that the two frameworks stem from different powers and trigger different legal frameworks, a human-rights-oriented framework that constrains sovereign actions versus a belligerency framework that constrains the behavior of both belligerent parties during an armed conflict. The latter regulations are reciprocal in the sense that they apply to both parties to the armed conflict (even non-state actors), whereas the former are asymmetrical because they only apply to governmental entities capable of exercising sovereign power.[35]

[31] Neff at 22–23. [32] The Prize Cases, 67 U.S. 635 (1863). [33] Neff at 157.
[34] Neff at 21. [35] *See* Neff at 28.

C. *Individuals versus Collectives*

Implicitly, IHRL constrains a government's relationship with individuals, while IHL constraints government conduct against a warring collective. That collective is usually a foreign power, though in the case of a NIAC the warring collective might be an armed rebel group. The enemy need not be a formal recognized government under international law, though they must be capable of fulfilling the basic criteria for belligerency under international law: capacity to launch military attacks, exhibiting command and control hierarchy, and capacity to follow the rules of *jus in bello* (if they wish).[36]

Individuals are incapable of fulfilling these criteria. In theory, an individual *might* satisfy the first criteria: the capacity to launch a military attack that threatens the rival belligerent power.[37] Although this is unlikely, recent advances in military technology (and terrorism) make it increasingly likely that an individual might procure a Weapon of Mass Destruction capable of producing devastating casualties against a belligerent power. If the individual purchases several weapons, the attacks might be ongoing and constitute a sustained threat. This need not be a nuclear attack; biological and chemical weapons might be built and deployed by a single individual with a particular antagonism toward a particular state. This factual scenario is unlikely but conceptually possible.[38]

However, individuals are incapable of maintaining a hierarchical command structure or following the rules of warfare. Simply put, both criteria assume the existence of a collective and the requirements make no sense when applied to individuals. An individual is incapable of following a command structure, which requires commanders and underlings. Theorists often exaggerate the requirements of a system of hierarchy, which does not require a linear, vertical, or conventional arrangement; terrorist cells might be hierarchical as long as there is a leader that controls each cell.[39] What is required, however, is a *collective*

36 *See* Protocol Additional to the Geneva Conventions of August 12, 1949, and Relating to the Protection of Victims of Non-International Armed Conflicts (Protocol II) Art. 1, June 8, 1977, 1125 U.N.T.S. 609 [hereinafter Additional Protocol II].

37 *See* William A. Schabas, *Prosecuting Dr Strangelove, Goldfinger, and the Joker at the International Criminal Court: Closing the Loopholes*, 23 Leiden J. Int'l L. 847–49 (2010).

38 *See, e.g.*, Bond v. United States, 564 U.S. (2011), involving a chemical attack by a single individual against another individual as part of a romantic dispute. This is for more likely than an individual attack against a state.

39 *See* Kai Ambos & Josef Alkatout, *Has "Justice Been Done?" The Legality of Bin Laden's Killing Under International Law*, 45 Isr. L. Rev. 341, 347–50 (2012).

in which the individuals are embedded. The law then looks to the internal structure of that collective and determines whether it represents a hierarchical relationship allowing commanders to exercise sufficient control over underlings.

Consider also the third prong: the capacity to comply with the laws of war. These do not make sense outside of the collective context. Can an individual comply with the laws of war, fighting as a single individual against a state belligerent? The laws of war require that a lawful belligerent identify himself as a belligerent by wearing a uniform or displaying a fixed emblem recognizable at a distance. These uniforms and symbols identify the belligerent as belonging to a particular belligerent fighting force on whose behalf the individual is acting. This triggers collective responsibility for the belligerent's actions, or in Lieber's famous phrase, the two "bear, enjoy, suffer, advance and retrograde together, in peace and in war."[40] There is no such thing as a belligerent who identifies himself as a belligerent *simpliciter*, fully divorced from a belligerent force. How would this be accomplished? There is no uniform for a lone fighter *in abstracto*, no hypothetical military force of *one* with which the individual could associate himself. Perhaps he belongs to the imaginary college of independent belligerents? No, belligerency is a collective enterprise.

III. The Concept of Control

How do we distinguish between the state acting in the two modes of belligerency and sovereignty? The ICCPR is illustrative in how it explains the relationship between ruler and ruled. Article 2 of the Covenant states that the state parties are obligated to secure the individual human rights of all individuals "within its territory and subject to its jurisdiction." Jurisdiction is, fundamentally, a concept of *control*. So IHRL applies when the state is acting as a sovereign and governing its subjects who are under its control, as opposed to situations where the sovereign is acting as a co-equal belligerent against an enemy belligerent force. But *control* is not a self-applying concept. It differs in degrees and flavor and requires further conceptual analysis. This section unpacks the concept.

[40] *See* Francis Lieber, Instructions for the Government of Armies of the United States in the Field, General Order No. 100 [Lieber Code], Art. 20 (April 24, 1863).

A. *The Problem of Segmentation*

One can understand control with regard to the territory in question. Establishing jurisdiction is obtained once the state controls the territory on which the individual rests and imposes its will on its residents by exclusively regulating their behavior. The first question is the required breadth of control: does the state need to exercise control over the entire territory of the state, and how comprehensive should the control be? Total control is an illusion and there will always be non-compliant subjects. In fact, control is demonstrated in the breach as the state imposes its coercive power on citizens and subjects who refuse to comply with state directives. The non-compliant individuals are subject to a governmental or legal process that enforces collective interests. This shows evidence of precisely the type of control that triggers the machinery of human rights.

In some situations the state may only enjoy limited control over a small stamp of territory and outside that territory another sovereign reigns, or there may be no sovereign ruler at all. Furthermore, in some situations the state may only exercise limited *temporal* control. On Monday the state is in control but on Tuesday the control evaporates. Then on Wednesday the state reestablishes control, which is extinguished again on Thursday. Is the state in a position to exercise sufficient jurisdiction to trigger IHRL?

The ICCPR does not offer an answer to these questions, though at first glance these hypothetical scenarios sound like impermissible segmentation. One ought to be skeptical of this segmentation because it proves too much. If one allows segmented control to meet the standard for IHRL, then any situation will meet the requirement. One can always, in a single moment or slice of territory the size of a postage stamp, declare that the state is exercising control over the individual because they are capable of imposing their will on the individual (say by military force). But this is "control" only in the most trivial sense, an impoverished notion segmented down to single individuals without regard for the fact that states engage in jurisdiction and control over their subjects *as an entire class*, not jurisdiction over isolated individuals at isolated moments in time standing on isolated chunks of territory. Whatever control is, it represents a wider and deeper phenomenon.

A good example is the type of *de jure* control that the Supreme Court recognized in *Rasul* and *Boumediene*.[41] In these cases the Supreme Court concluded that the U.S. exercised de facto jurisdiction over Guantanamo

[41] Boumediene v. Bush, 553 U.S. 723 (2008).

Bay, a legal finding that triggered the writ of habeas corpus to the military base.[42] If the U.S. enjoys *de facto* sovereignty, then the Great Writ runs to the base. Nonetheless, it is important to remember that the control is merely *de facto*, not *de jure;* Cuba retains formal sovereignty over the base and the U.S. continues to make payments to Cuba under the original lease agreement signed between the two nations.[43] That being said, the level of U.S. control over the territory is total and complete. In the famous phrase from the Supreme Court oral arguments, a Cuban postage stamp will not get a letter off the base.[44] Although the military base is not large, it is sufficiently widespread to generate the conclusion that the U.S. enjoys control and jurisdiction over the physical territory. And control can be established even in the absence of *de jure* sovereignty.

Based on this theory there is a colorable argument that the Bush Administration was wrong when it claimed that IHL and law of war principles exclusively governed detention at Guantanamo Bay.[45] The United States had sufficient control and jurisdiction over the detainees at Guantanamo that the basic relationship of ruler–ruled was satisfied. This suggests that human rights law has a role to play with regard to interpreting the requirements of detainee treatment. Whether the ICCPR applies as a matter of treaty interpretation depends on the correct interpretation of the word "territory" in Article 2 of the Covenant. So the bare text of Article 2 might diverge from the basic principles underlying human rights theory. However, even if Article 2 of the Covenant does not apply based on the possibility that Guantanamo Bay is not the *de jure* territory of the United States, there is a possible argument that Guantanamo Bay represents *de facto* territory of the United States on the basis of the jurisdiction and control that the U.S. enjoyed over the military base.

The analysis might be extended to other detention facilities overseas, though the outcome of the analysis is less certain. Bagram Air Force Base was located in Afghanistan; enemy combatants captured in the

[42] *See* Anthony Colangelo, "*De Facto Sovereignty*": *Boumediene and Beyond*, 77 Geo. Wash. L. Rev. 623 (2009).

[43] Boumediene, 553 U.S. 723, at 753.

[44] *See* Oral Argument Transcript (April 20, 2004), Rasul v. Bush, Case No. 03–334 & 03–343, at 23 (comment by John Gibbons that a "stamp with Fidel Castro's picture on it wouldn't get a letter off the base")

[45] Third Periodic Report at para. 130; Response of the United States for Request for Provisional Measures – Detainees in Guantanamo Bay, Cuba, Inter-American Commission of Human Rights. *See also* Van Schaack, *supra* note 8, at 55.

Afghanistan theater of operations were housed at this location. At one point in time, the U.S. government exercised exclusive control over Bagram Air Force Base after the invasion of Afghanistan. On the basis of U.S. control over the military base, does human rights law apply to the treatment of the detainees there? Although there was a substantial level of control, it never rose to the level of Guantanamo Bay, Cuba. First, Bagram is located within the Afghanistan theater of operations; although it was relatively secure it remained under threat of attack from enemy belligerents. It was within the territory of Afghanistan and remained a military base from which ongoing military operations were planned and conducted. Although the U.S. remained in control of the base, it was only in control insofar as *any* military base during an armed conflict is under the "control" of the party who constructed and used it. Furthermore, Afghanistan retained de facto sovereignty over the base and was engaged in some non-military regulation of the space, in the sense that Afghanistan officials were permitted on the base (unlike Guantanamo Bay where Cuban officials are not permitted). This suggests that the level of control was operational at Bagram but did not go deeper. Whether this level of control was *enough* to trigger application of human rights law is unclear.

In contrast, Guantanamo Bay is not within an active theater of war, and U.S. jurisdiction over the base is more significant than the pedestrian level of control that any military force exerts over their military bases. Indeed, this was precisely the inspiration for the U.S. decision to locate the detention facility there. By housing the detainees extraterritorially (as opposed to military brigs in the U.S.), the Executive Branch hoped to avoid judicial scrutiny under the writ of habeas corpus. In *Rasul*, Justice Scalia noted this reliance and argued that if the Executive Branch had known that the judicial branch would interfere in detainee affairs at Guantanamo Bay, President Bush would never have sent the detainees there.[46] That being said, it is unclear why a reliance theory should make any difference to the outcome of the constitutional or international law analysis. The U.S. retains exclusive control over the territory and as such

[46] Rasul v. Bush, 542 U.S. 466 (2004) (Scalia, J., dissenting) ("The fact that extraterritorially located detainees lack the district of detention that the statute requires has been converted from a factor that precludes their ability to bring a petition at all into a factor that frees them to petition wherever they wish – and, as a result, to forum shop. For this Court to create such a monstrous scheme in time of war, and in frustration of our military commanders' reliance upon clearly stated prior law, is judicial adventurism of the worst sort.").

there is a credible argument that its operations are subject to the joint application of human rights law and IHL.

B. *Spatial Control versus Personal Control*

Although the preceding analysis makes clear that control is the central concept in this inquiry, the more controversial question is how to understand and define control. The recent jurisprudence from the ECHR is illustrative.[47] In deciding whether the European Convention applies extraterritorially, the ECHR has analyzed what counts as sufficient control for the purposes of evaluating whether an individual falls under the jurisdiction of the state in question.

For example, in *al-Saadoon*, the ECHR applied the European Convention against the United Kingdom with regard to its detention of Iraqi individuals detained in Basra.[48] The United Kingdom transferred the individuals to Iraqi authorities where they faced the death penalty, a prospect that potentially violated the *non-refoulement* provisions of the European Convention.[49] In its 2010 opinion, the ECHR considered that al-Saadoon fell under the protections of the ECHR because the United Kingdom exercised jurisdiction over the prison in which al-Saadoon was detained. The United Kingdom's spatial control over the prison complex provided a geographical definition of jurisdiction that triggered the Convention's application.[50] Although it was unclear how far spatial control could be segmented, it was clear in *al-Saadoon* that spatial control could be defined down to the level of a single physical complex – at least in the prison context.

But what is the logical limit of this argument? In *Banković*, the ECHR concluded that the rights of the Convention were not divisible.[51] By this it meant that there was no mini-Convention that applied in situations

[47] The best legal analysis of these decisions is found in Marko Milanovic, *Al-Skeini and Al-Jedda in Strasbourg*, 23 Euro. J. Int'l L. 121 (2012).

[48] *See* Al-Saadoon and Mufdhi v. United Kingdom (App. No. 61498/08), ECHR (July 3, 2009).

[49] Al-Saadoon, para. 88. [50] *Id.*

[51] Banković and Others v. Belgium and Others (App. No. 52207/99), ECHR Grand Chamber (December 12, 2001), para. 75 ("However, the Court is of the view that the wording of Article 1 does not provide any support for the applicants' suggestion that the positive obligation in Article 1 to secure 'the rights and freedoms defined in Section I of this Convention' can be divided and tailored in accordance with the particular circumstances of the extra-territorial act in question and, it considers its view in this respect supported by the text of Article 19 of the Convention.").

where there was only partial jurisdiction or control by the state. So there was no sliding scale of jurisdiction that triggered a greater or lesser percentage of human rights. It was all or nothing; either the Convention applied or it did not.[52] The *Banković* action was filed by Serbian nationals who claimed that Belgium violated their human rights by participating in NATO airstrikes designed to pressure Milosevic into compliance with international demands regarding resolution of the Kosovo crisis. This was a parallel action to the ICJ case filed by Serbia against NATO countries, a case that was dismissed on jurisdictional grounds by the ICJ.

The ECHR action in *Banković* was similarly dismissed on the grounds that Belgium had no jurisdiction over the individuals.[53] Applying the rules of the Vienna Convention on the Law of Treaties, the court concluded that jurisdiction is "primarily territorial" and that examples of extra-territorial jurisdiction under public international law (whether passive or active nationality, or universal jurisdiction) were "exceptional" and required "special justification."[54] The Court also took notice of the fact that state parties to the ECHR did not generally file derogations with regard to their extra-territorial war-time conduct, a fact that supported the general view that state parties did not view themselves as extra-territorially bound by the ECHR.[55]

That being said, the Court was willing to countenance the possibility of extra-territorial jurisdiction in discrete situations, though the conditions for this jurisdiction were substantial: The state party would need to exercise "effective control" over the territory in question.[56] This followed logically from the *Cyprus v. Turkey* decision, which held that Turkey had sufficient jurisdiction over the territory of Northern Cyprus by virtue of the number of troops it had deployed and its close relationship with the Turkish Republic of Northern Cyprus government. Consequently, Turkey was responsible for ensuring the full panoply of ECHR rights.[57] This was the basis for future interpretations of *Banković* as suggesting an all-or-nothing scheme.[58] According to the ECHR itself in *Banković*, the

[52] *Id.* For a discussion, see Sarah Joseph & Adam Fletcher, *Scope of Application*, *in* International Human Rights Law 119, 137 (D. Moeckli, S. Shah, S. Sivakumaran, & D. Harris eds., 2014).

[53] Banković, para. 82. [54] Banković, para. 61. [55] Banković, para. 62.

[56] Banković, para. 71.

[57] Cyprus v. Turkey (App. no. 25781/94), ECHR Grand Chamber (May 10, 2001), para. 80.

[58] Banković appears to preclude the possibility of a sliding scale of jurisdiction. For an example of this approach, see John Cerone, *Human Dignity in the Line of Fire: The Application of International Human Rights Law During Armed Conflict, Occupation, and*

extra-territorial application of the ECHR is only triggered when the state party "exercises all or some of the public powers normally to be exercised by that Government."[59] Under this standard, there was no possible way that the individuals fell under the jurisdiction of the NATO forces, and the only possible way to find jurisdiction was under an implausible and incoherent "cause-and-effect" notion of jurisdiction whereby jurisdiction was established whenever the individual was adversely affected by the actions of the government agents.[60] This would destroy "jurisdiction" as a limiting principle and would make all actions of the government subject to ECHR regulation. If this were the correct interpretation of the concept of jurisdiction in the treaty, it would perform no work whatsoever and then trigger the question of why the drafters would have placed it in the treaty in the first place.

The issue re-arose with a different resolution in *al-Skeini*, which involved Iraqi citizens shot and killed by British forces in occupied Iraq. In the British courts, the Court of Appeals concluded that the state enjoyed no jurisdiction over the individuals because none of the recognized exceptions to territorial jurisdiction was present, such as diplomatic affairs or naval vessels flying under the state's flag.[61] In addition, the British courts considered the notion of "state agent authority" as the basis for jurisdiction, whereby the agent's authority triggers the exercise of jurisdiction. The court concluded, however, that the petitioners were not subject to the jurisdiction of Britain under either the effective control theory *or* the state agent authority theory.[62] Specifically, the situation in Britain did not rise to the level of Turkey's control in Cyprus, a recognized precedent regarding extra-territorial jurisdiction.[63] Furthermore, the British courts noted the implications of extending the application of the ECHR to individuals in Iraq during the occupation. Under the *Banković* line of analysis, this conclusion would trigger the application

Peace Operations, 39 Vanderbilt Journal of Transnational Law 1447 (2006); John Cerone, *Jurisdiction and Power: The Intersection of Human Rights Law & the Law of Non-International Armed Conflict in an Extraterritorial Context*, 40 Israel Law Review (2007).

[59] Banković, para. 72. [60] Banković, para. 75.

[61] R. (on the application of Al-Skeini and others) v. Secretary of State for Defence, EWCA Civ. 1609 (2005), All ER (D) 337 (2005) (hereinafter cited as Al-Skeini, Court of Appeals), para. 48.

[62] Al-Skeini, Court of Appeals, para. 49.

[63] Al-Skeini, Court of Appeals, para. 123–127., citing Loizidou v. Turkey, 23 EHRR 513 (DC 175) (1997).

of the entire convention, and British forces would be required to secure to all individuals in that territory the full panoply of ECHR rights.[64]

On appeal to Strasbourg, the ECHR refused to follow the conclusions of the British Courts, and the court applied the Convention to the killings of the Iraqi civilians. Specifically, the court rejected that spatial control was the sine qua non of jurisdiction: "The Court does not consider that jurisdiction in the above cases arose solely from the control exercised by the Contracting State over the buildings, aircraft or ship in which the individuals were held. What is decisive in such cases is the exercise of physical power and control over the person in question."[65] This style of analysis was also followed in the more recent decision of *Al-Saadoon and Others* by the High Court of Justice of England and Wales.[66] In *Al-Saadoon*, the British court found that any amount of physical force against an individual human being triggers the human rights obligations of the European Convention on Human Rights. The court noted:

> Whether the exercise of physical control over an individual outside a state's own territory should be sufficient to bring that individual within the scope of the Convention is far from obvious. However, once that principle is established, as it now is, I find it impossible to say that shooting someone dead does not involve the exercise of physical power and control over that person. Using force to kill is indeed the ultimate exercise of physical control over another human being. Nor as it seems to me can a principled system of human rights law draw a distinction between killing an individual after arresting him and simply shooting him without arresting him first, such that in the first case there is an obligation to respect the person's right to life yet in the second case there is not.[67]

In other words, the reasoning in *Al-Saadoon* stands for the proposition that the negative obligation under the ECHR to refrain from depriving someone of life applies even in the *absence* of detention or other

[64] Al-Skeini, Court of Appeals, para. 124 ("In my judgment it is quite impossible to hold that the U.K., although an occupying power for the purposes of the Hague Regulations and Geneva IV, was in effective control of Basrah City for the purposes of ECHR jurisprudence at the material time. If it had been, it would have been obliged, pursuant to the Banković judgment, to secure to everyone in Basrah City the rights and freedoms guaranteed by the ECHR.").

[65] Al-Skeini and Others v. United Kingdom (App. No. 55721/07), ECHR Grand Chamber (July 7, 2011), para. 136.

[66] Al-Saadoon and Others v. Secretary of State for Defence, 2015 EWHC 715 (High Court of Justice of England and Wales, March 17, 2015).

[67] *Id.* at para. 95.

meaningful control of the person's movements or behavior. However, it is unclear if this maximalist interpretation of the jurisdiction of the European Convention will be upheld on appeal to higher British courts or even the European Court of Human Rights, which might balk at the extreme consequences of taking the principles of *Al-Skeini* this far.[68]

At first glance, the ECHR's endorsement of personal control (rather than spatial control) looks like an improvement. As a theory of jurisdiction, personal control had a longer history and there is much to recommend it. It avoids the most pernicious aspect of the problem of segmentation: deciding how small a slice of territory one might consider in finding jurisdiction. Is a small building or a bedroom sufficiently large that controlling it constitutes the type of jurisdiction that triggers the application of a human rights regime? The switch to personal jurisdiction would sidestep that question and replace it with a more probative inquiry regarding control over individuals: whether the state exercised effective control over the petitioner in the case. This *sounds* like a conceptual improvement.

This conclusion should be resisted. On deeper reflection, the improvements are mostly illusory. Think again of the concept of territorial jurisdiction and what it means. The most obvious definition is that it constitutes effective control over a piece of territory. But what does *that* mean? Control over territory can only mean the capacity to control the individuals who reside on that slice of territory. Consider uninhabited territory, i.e., when a state exercises control over an empty island. What does this statement mean? To say that the state exercises control over the empty island means that it could exclude incoming individuals from the installations it builds on the island. Spatial control *is* personal control once you drill down one level and ask for more details about the nature of the control.

Of course, the difference between spatial control and personal control must have some significance otherwise litigants would not fight so fiercely over it. And there is a difference, although it often remains unacknowledged. Spatial control invites a particular style of analysis that implies that jurisdiction requires control over an aggregation of individuals living on a piece of territory. So it covertly provides a backstop against excessive segmentation in the sense that spatial control usually involves control over multiple individuals, rather than single individuals.

[68] For a discussion, see David Goddard, *Britain's Al-Saadoon Case: A Matter of Human Rights Law and the use of Military Force Overseas*, Just Security (July 16, 2015).

But there really isn't much that is irreducibly *spatial* about it. The idea that spatial control and personal control are fundamentally different is a conceptual fiction.

What the distinction between spatial control and personal control obscures is the question of how much and what type of control the state must have in order to trigger the application of human rights. Of course the legal standard is "effective control," but one needs a further theory to cash out what constitutes "effective control." With a single individual, the state's control might range over a very limited set of functions, such as whether the individual will be detained or killed in the case of an armed occupation. On the other hand, if the state has control over a large number of individuals, then it is more likely, though by no means certain, that the state's control might range over a large set of functions, including decisions to regulate health care, education, religion, and privacy of the effected individuals. So spatial control, by implying a large number of persons, is effectively a proxy for a more complete type of control ranging over a far more diverse set of daily activities and regulations pertinent to them. But the underlying significance stems from the nature of the underlying control, and how much and what type of control the state has over the individual, not how many individuals are involved in the jurisdiction and the territory on which they are located. These latter factors all function to obscure the more relevant phenomenon: What matters is how widely the state can regulate the lives of particular individuals.

So we are left then with a concept of jurisdiction that entails the ability of the state to regulate the life of the individual in the usual way that a government will exercise governing control.[69] There is a risk of circularity in this definition: a state has control when it exercises the typical controls of government. The concept of control appears on both sides of the equation. However, the circularity is certainly not vicious; the explanatory cycle looks to the *typical* cases of control exercised by sovereign governments and then asks whether the extra-territorial control exercised by the sovereign government involves the same types of power and regulation that exist in the former case. If they both involve

[69] For a similar view, see Orna Ben-Naftali, *The Extraterritorial Application of Human Rights to Occupied Territories*, 100 Am. Soc. Int'l L. Proc. 90, 92 (2006) (concluding that "jurisdiction" for purposes of human rights law "signifies the ability to rule, to exercise the powers of government vis-à-vis individuals who are affected by these powers.") Ben-Naftali rejects spatial control in favor of personal control.

effective control then the basic human rights regime constrains the government regardless of whether the control is exercised on its home territory or not.[70]

In *al-Skeini*, the ECHR concluded that the individuals fell under the jurisdiction of the British government, despite the fact that the soldiers' control over the victims did not involve a wide array of activities. How could this be? The answer stems from the ECHR's analysis regarding the relationship between the British Government and the Coalition Provisional Authority led by L. Paul Bremer.[71] The court viewed the CPA as the functional equivalent of a U.S.-U.K. occupational regime, and by virtue of this fact, the British government exercised effective control, via the CPA, over the territory of Iraq.[72] In this sense the holding in *al-Skeini* may be consistent with the all-or-nothing approach in *Banković* simply because the CPA had effective control over Iraq and therefore the full panoply of ECHR rights applied. But without the British link to the CPA, it is hard to see how this conclusion could be sustained.

One might object that even a limited type of control is nonetheless significant and ought to be constrained by human rights law. Is not the power of the state at its apex when it is capable of killing the individual, even if this is the only action the state can take against the individual? In

[70] *See* Naz, *supra* note 5, at 375–76 (suggesting that "there are no coherent legal grounds" for the limitation implied by the extraterritorial application of IHRL in armed conflict "that human rights really apply only when the invading/attacking/belligerent State is in a quasi-governing stance vis-à-vis my population."). One might view the current chapter and its standard for "acting as a sovereign" as providing one such coherent ground at the level of abstract legal theory.

[71] Al-Skeini, ECHR Grand Chamber, para. 149 ("It can be seen, therefore, that following the removal from power of the Ba'ath regime and until the accession of the Interim Government, the United Kingdom (together with the United States) assumed in Iraq the exercise of some of the public powers normally to be exercised by a sovereign government. In particular, the United Kingdom assumed authority and responsibility for the maintenance of security in South East Iraq. In these exceptional circumstances, the Court considers that the United Kingdom, through its soldiers engaged in security operations in Basrah during the period in question, exercised authority and control over individuals killed in the course of such security operations, so as to establish a jurisdictional link between the deceased and the United Kingdom for the purposes of Article 1 of the Convention.").

[72] *Id.* Incidentally, the Court never addressed the significance of the *joint* exercise of control between the U.S. and the UK, and whether the presence of the U.S. in some way negated the UK control via the CPA. In international criminal law there are numerous doctrines to express this relationship (joint perpetration, co-perpetration, etc.) though the Court did not appear to have any legal concepts at its disposal to consider the normative consequences of joint control with a non-ECHR party.

other words, control over life and death is not just a *type* of control but is, in fact, the most *elementary* form of existential control. Although this view has some rhetorical appeal, it is based more on a folk conception of control over an individual's fate, rather than the type of control exercised by a sovereign government.[73] Control in the jurisdictional sense requires that the state be capable of subjecting an individual to the full scope of governmental regulation, rather than simply capable of submitting an individual to its will (via killing). The latter type of control is one-dimensional and has little to do with the powers of governmental action. As evidence, consider the lawful use of force by a justified defender in the regular criminal context. It would be fallacious to assert that the victim has jurisdiction over the aggressor simply because the victim's bullet is capable of controlling the fate of the aggressor and whether he lives or dies. Control for purposes of jurisdiction is at once richer and more complex.

IV. Applying Principles of Control to Armed Conflict

The prior section developed an account of control that was necessarily abstract. It is in its application that the concept of control gains its full content. Consequently, this section applies the concept of control to the two most serious issues addressed by the law of armed conflict: detention and targeting. Detention and targeting necessarily involve different levels of control. As a final matter, this section also addresses the application of principles of control to the law of occupation, a military and legal environment that creates a liminal space in between armed conflict and a permanent regime of peacetime human rights.

A. Control and Targeting

Consider lethal attacks conducted during targeted killing operations. Do human rights have a role to play with regard to the lawfulness of targeted killings? The situation here is markedly different than the detention context. In most situations the killings take place in areas where the U.S. exercises little control or jurisdiction over the targeted individuals. In Yemen, for example, al-Qaeda-inspired forces engaged in a protracted

[73] For example, the U.S. jurisprudence on the Fourth Amendment is based on the assumption that police killings may constitute a "seizure" for purposes of Fourth Amendment scrutiny.

armed conflict with the government of Yemen. The U.S. enjoyed no control or jurisdiction over the territory; it does not impose its sovereign will over any subjects in that time or place. Similarly, the U.S. did not enjoy control over the tribal regions in Afghanistan or Pakistan where drone operations were regularly conducted.[74] A similar situation obtained in Somalia where al-Shabaab militants controlled most of the relevant territory for a significant period of time. Consequently, the control that triggers human rights obligations in the detention context is usually absent from the targeting context.

This raises a natural question regarding the legal geography of armed conflict. Scholars who favor the application of human rights law argue that it applies wherever and whenever the state is projecting its military power. Under this view, IHL only applies when the state acts on so-called hot battlefield zones, i.e., discrete zones of active hostilities. Outside of these zones, the obligations of human rights law apply in full force. Support for the legal geography of armed conflict is allegedly drawn from the ICTY *Tadic* judgment, which defines armed conflict (thus triggering IHL) when there is sufficient scope and intensity of armed attacks.[75] As I have argued elsewhere, the *Tadic* judgment is persistently misread since the chamber concluded that IHL applied to the entire area of the party's territory and also held that it was wrong to limit the definition of armed conflict to the discrete area where the hostilities were taking place.[76] The Trial Chamber explicitly rejected the narrow view favored by the defense.

However, it is also important to approach the question from the opposite direction: in situations where IHL does not apply, does human rights law automatically apply? This conclusion is hasty and represents a conceptual mistake. Human rights law is not a default international legal regime that applies wherever the state is acting. Constitutional law occasionally follows the flag but not so human rights law.[77] Rather, human rights law applies when the state is engaged in control over its

[74] Indeed, it is not even clear whether *Pakistan* enjoyed full control and sovereignty over the so-called Af-Pak tribal regions, given the limited practical reach of the central government in those areas.

[75] *See* Prosecutor v. Tadić, Case No. IT-94-1-T, Judgment, para. 557–60 (Int'l Crim. Trib. for the Former Yugoslavia May 7, 1997).

[76] *Id.*

[77] For the application of constitutional provisions to extra-territorial conduct, see KAL RAUSTIALA, DOES THE CONSTITUTION FOLLOW THE FLAG?: THE EVOLUTION OF TERRITORIALITY IN AMERICAN LAW 241–47 (2009)

subjects, and in most targeted killing operations the state has no control in the time and place where the strike occurs. Even with an impermissible segmentation argument that we dismissed earlier, it seems unlikely that the state would have sufficient sovereign control over the subject to trigger the application of human rights law. In hypothetical situations discussed by the Israeli Supreme Court in *Targeted Killings*, the argument might be different.[78] If a terrorist is sitting in a café in an area without open hostilities, then it seems clear that the government has enough control to trigger the machinery of human rights law. The same might be said of a potential terrorist located in the United States. In these situations, killing would only be appropriate as a last resort under a least-harmful-means interpretation of the principle of necessity, if capture and trial under the criminal law proved impossible or infeasible.[79] The requirements of imminence and danger to the public would also have to be met under basic principles of domestic law enforcement or human rights law before lethal force would be justified.[80]

The two points are conceptually related. Drone critics sometimes take an overly narrow view of IHL's application; this leads them to take a correspondingly expansive view of human rights law. One way of expressing the problem is that they should reign in human rights law; the corollary is that they should expand their understanding of IHL. In the main, IHL applies during situations of armed conflict when the state is acting as a belligerent against enemy forces. However, it is false to assume that the application of IHL, or the rules regarding NIAC, is limited to so-called hot battlefield zones. Only a misreading of the *Tadic* standard supports this view. Rather, the laws of war constrain any military action taken by the state in furtherance of its belligerency in an armed conflict. The correct frame of reference is not the legal geography but rather the *event* of armed conflict because the obligations stem from the state's status as a belligerent in the conflict.

It may also be the case that IHL applies to military actions taken before the situation rises to a full-blown armed conflict. Although this sounds paradoxical, it becomes necessary when one understands the basic principles of belligerency. If the first military strike during a military

[78] HCJ 769/02 Pub. Comm. Against Torture in Isr. v. Gov't of Isr. 53(4) PD 459 [2006] (Israel).

[79] *See* Goodman, *supra* note 2, at 3–5.

[80] *See, e.g.*, Scott v. Harris, 550 U.S. 372, 376 (2007); Tennessee v. Garner, 471 U.S. 1, 11–12 (1985).

campaign is isolated, and the opposing state has not yet engaged in a counter-response, then the original military strike does not meet the standards for armed conflict. As such, IHL would not apply. But this is always the case when belligerents trigger armed conflicts. Someone always shoots first, *by definition*. Until there is sufficient intensity to meet the putative armed conflict standard, the original attacks would be classified as violations of human rights law, which seems implausible. These proto-armed-conflict attacks are paradigmatic examples of military activity that ought to be governed by IHL. To suggest that all armed conflicts governed by IHL begin with attacks that *cannot* be governed by IHL in the first instance sounds like a paradox. The better view is that the beginning stages of military attacks *triggering* the armed conflict are also covered by IHL, on pain of contradiction (or at least absurdity).

There is an important objection here. One might argue that the first side to fire its weapons, thus triggering an armed conflict, *has* violated international law. The attacking soldiers are the aggressors and ought to be condemned for their resort to force. But this is precisely the point. They are not guilty of violating IHL or human rights law. A state in this situation is guilty of violating *jus ad bellum* if the underlying justification for infringing another state's sovereignty does not accord with the U.N. Charter's prohibition on the use of force and Article 51's allowance for self-defense.[81] The correct legal response is to hold the state liable for the crime of aggression. This is just one reason why it is so important that the ICC Assembly of State Parties amended the Rome Statute to adopt a definition of aggression and confer jurisdiction on the ICC (even if the jurisdiction is severely constrained by the mechanisms expressed in article 8 *bis*) to prosecute these cases. Aggression is crucial because IHL and human rights law often leave a gap here. There is so much talk of using human rights law to "fill the gap" in many cases, though the correct legal conclusion is that there is already a powerful body of law to generate legal scrutiny, i.e., *jus ad bellum*.

B. *The Outsourcing Problem*

Another objection becomes apparent at this point. In some situations an intervening state may deflect the negative consequences of *jus ad bellum* by operating with the consent of the host nation. Although this consent

[81] Or Security Council authorization under Article 39 of the U.N. Charter.

negates any intrusion of sovereignty and the *jus ad bellum* issues that come with it, this leaves a vacuum of legal regulation over the behavior in question. The intervening state is not subject to human rights law because they are not in control over the territory. And the host state is not subject to human rights law because, although it is in control over its own territory, it is not the agent of the particular actions. In a sense, the host state appears to be extracting itself from the bounds of human rights law by outsourcing the actions in question to a foreign state. This outsourcing arguably represents an end-run around the demands of human rights law. Unable to act in a lawful way itself, the host state authorizes an intervening state to do their bidding. If this is the case, the legal analysis has taken a wrong turn.

There are strong prudential reasons for international law to prohibit host states from outsourcing their human rights violations. One solution is to craft a specific rule to prohibit the pre-textual use of third-party interventionist states as a means of reaching around human rights constraints. But this solution is not necessary. The problem originally flows from a narrow reading of IHL. The intervening state should be subject to IHL if they exercise military force when they act as a belligerent against an enemy party to an armed conflict. Although the application of IHL will not necessarily impose the restrictive demands of IHRL, including its least-harmful-means interpretation of necessity, it will nonetheless impose serious constraints on belligerent behavior that violates *jus in bello*.

From the perspective of the subjects of the host nation, this may be of little consolation. Legitimate belligerent targets will be subject to lethal force under the basic rules of *jus in bello* – force that would be subject to greater constraints under human rights law. However, if the belligerents are also engaged in an armed conflict with their own government, the government would be entitled to invoke the legal framework of IHL in its dealings with the belligerent force anyway. If the subjects of the host nation are not engaged in an armed conflict, then they are not subject to lethal targeting under either IHL or IHRL.

Ashley Deeks has recently suggested that international law should develop strict standards for evaluating state claims of consent for the use of force.[82] When the host state is silent, how should the world community interpret this silence? New standards might resolve anxieties stemming from private consent that is never publicly articulated by the

[82] *See* Ashley Deeks, *Consent to the Use of Force and International Law Supremacy*, Harv. Int'l L. J. 1(2013).

target state, leaving uncertainty over how the world community should judge claims by the intervening state that they were acting with host state authority. Deeks also suggested that the *jus ad bellum* constraints of necessity and proportionality could be applied to all extra-territorial uses of force, regardless of whether Article 51 is triggered or not.[83] Under this proposal, consent would be irrelevant for purposes of whether necessity and proportionality (in the jus ad bellum sense of these terms) apply to the intervening state as legal constraints on their behavior.

These are coherent alternatives *de lege ferenda* that would mitigate the harshness of the doctrinal and conceptual consequence that the intervening state would be immune from the human rights constraints imposed on the host state if they were to engage in the very same military actions against their own citizens. Resorting to a broader reading of IHRL is not necessary to solve this problem.

C. *The Law of Occupation and Jus Post Bellum*

Two final points remain. Does the distinction between acting as a sovereign and acting as a belligerent provide an answer to when the IHL framework *ceases* to apply at the end of an armed conflict? As the tide of war changes, a belligerent force may become so successful in its military effort that it begins to consolidate control over the territory on which the armed conflict occurs. During the course of ongoing fighting the state is still acting as a belligerent. At some point, however, the level and intensity of fighting diminishes and the state consolidates its control over the territory as it successfully degrades the fighting capacity of the enemy belligerent party. At that moment in time, the state may yet again act as a sovereign over new subjects; a new ruler-ruled relationship applies between the state and individuals on that territory.

International law is well aware of this framework and has developed a specialized body to codify these obligations. This is the law of occupation.[84] Although the law of occupation is formally distinct from human rights law as a matter of codified law, it rests upon the same conceptual foundation as human rights law. Just as human rights law is based on the state's operation as a sovereign in control of its subjects, so too the law of occupation is based on the state's operation as *de facto* sovereign over the subjects under its dominion. The law of occupation

[83] *Id.* [84] *See generally* Eyal Benvenisti, The Law of Occupation (2012).

imposes a series of affirmative obligations that constrain conduct; the law also imposes positive obligations to protect the civilian infrastructure of the nation, preserve law and order, and even protect important cultural artifacts. The crucial difference is that the law of occupation imposes these obligations as temporary constraints designed to facilitate the return to normal governance on the occupied territory.[85] While human rights law applies in a permanent way to a sovereign's exercise of authority over its subjects, the law of occupation applies to the temporary occupation of foreign territory when the occupying power acts as a *de facto* sovereign over the foreign subjects. If, at some point, a state of occupation is transformed into the denial of the former state's sovereignty, and the imposition of a new state governed by the invading forces, then human rights law would again apply to the behavior of the governing state. But in that instant the conceptual foundation would not have substantially changed. The state would have transitioned from *de facto* sovereign to *de jure* sovereign, though in both cases the state would be acting as a sovereign over subjects under its control. In that sense, the law of occupation is conceptually closer to human rights law than it is to the law of armed conflict.

D. *The Irrelevance of Citizenship*

A final point remains regarding the definition of "subject." Occasionally the state may find it necessary to engage in lethal force against one of its own citizens. It would be hasty to conclude on this basis alone that IHRL applies simply because the state is acting as a sovereign over one of its subjects. The classic example here is the U.S. military strike against Anwar al-Awlaki in Yemen.[86] At the time of the strike, the U.S. was engaged in an armed conflict against AQAP, of which Awlaki was a top commander. According to the U.S. government, he was more than just a propagandist at the time; he had turned "operational" because he approved specific terrorist plots against U.S. citizens.[87] He also happened to be a U.S. citizen and spent much of his youth in New Mexico. For

[85] *Id.* at 42 (occupation as a "temporary and limited regime" emerged in the early twentieth century).

[86] *See* Peter Finn, *In Secret Memo, Justice Department Sanctioned Strike*, WASHINGTON POST, October 1, 2011, at A9; Charlie Savage, *Secret U.S. Memo Made Legal Case to Kill a Citizen*, N.Y. TIMES, October 9, 2011, at A1.

[87] *See* U.S. Department of Justice, *Lawfulness of a Lethal Operation Directed Against a U.S. Citizen Who is a Senior Operational Leaders of Al-Qa'ida or an Associated Force* (2011), *available at* www.fas.org/irp/eprint/doj-lethal.pdf.

some critics of the strike, his status as a U.S. citizen provided an extra level of constraint against U.S. military action in Yemen. The U.S. Constitution might provide one such framework by imposing a due-process overlay for targeting citizens. But this argument is belied by the fact that in *Hamdi* the content of the constitutional protections was provided mostly by the international obligations imposed on the U.S. during armed conflict.[88]

This pushes the argument back down to international law to determine which body of law applies. Under the proposed framework presented in this chapter – acting as a sovereign or belligerent – it might appear that the U.S. was acting as a sovereign against one of its citizens. But this conclusion would be too hasty. The sovereign-subject relationship is determined not by citizenship but by the degree of control that the sovereign exercises over the individual in question. In the case of Awlaki, or another citizen that has voluntarily joined an enemy belligerent force, the state enjoys no control over the individual. That is why states have generally not provided an extra level of due process protection to enemy citizens that they encounter on the battlefield.[89]

This analysis is confirmed by the nature of civil wars. In the case of a putative secession or rebel attempt to take over the government, the rebel force organizes itself as a collective belligerency. To the extent that the belligerent force succeeds in marshaling enough support to mount a sophisticated military operation, and also destroy the control that the government enjoys over the territory in question, then the state is no longer in a sovereign-subject relation with the individuals that constitute the rebel force. By creating a collective fighting force and disrupting the control that the state exercises over the territory in question, the enemy fighters have destroyed the factual predicate that triggers the application of human rights law to their relationship with the government. Their belligerency has transformed the relationship from one of sovereign obedience to one of co-equal belligerency as a matter of international law. Citizenship is simply irrelevant to these status-based relationships, which rely far more on *functional* criteria.

E. The Irrelevance of Due Process in Targeting

The sovereign versus belligerency framework can also resolve a much broader question regarding the applicability of due process norms

[88] Hamdi v. Rumsfeld, 542 U.S. 507, 539–40 (2004).
[89] *See* Ohlin, *Duty to Capture*, *supra* note 21, at 1335.

generally in military operations, regardless of the citizenship of the target. When the U.S. military killed Awlaki, critics complained that the killing violated his due process rights because he had no opportunity to contest, via judicial review, the executive branch determinations regarding him. Although some critics pegged this right to Awlaki's status as an American citizen, others maintained that the due process right applied regardless of citizenship, especially if the military operation ought to be regulated by IHRL.

Historically, targets of military operations have never been offered an *ex ante* opportunity to contest the executive branch's determination that they constitute a legitimate target. Traditionally, the law has been limited to *ex post* determinations regarding the appropriateness of targeting decisions; unlawful targeting can trigger a prosecution for the war crime of intentionally targeting civilians (if there is a forum with jurisdiction over the conflict). However, the mere fact that militaries are not accustomed to offering robust due process protections is not dispositive of the legal issue. Nor can one simply *assume* that IHL applies and that IHRL is irrelevant – that is precisely the issue to be decided. Rather, the legal issue is determined by asking whether the state is acting as a sovereign or a belligerent. In targeting a single individual who belongs to a formally co-equal belligerent who is party to an armed conflict, the state is in no way acting as a sovereign over its subjects, and as such no right of due process constrains the government conduct. The right of due process is simply irrelevant to the analysis because IHRL does not govern the situation.

However, the opposite may be true in the detention context. When the state exercises total control over the individual by virtue of its jurisdiction over an entire prison complex, then the state is acting as a sovereign over its subjects. It has the ability to regulate, with the full array of governmental regulations, the affairs of the individual. This triggers the application of IHRL, and with it, some right of due process. In these situations, IHRL may have a role to play in governing the conduct of the state, in addition to the other detention regulations that stem from IHL. This leaves unresolved, however, the question of how to interpret the IHRL norm of due process during armed conflict. Specifically, must the state provide the detained combatant with the same procedural opportunities available in the normal civilian context? Or do the procedural regulations already embodied in IHL provide enough of the substance of a due process right? Under IHL, detainees have a right to contest the legality of their detention through a neutral decision-maker, though these tribunals need not contain the more robust procedures of a domestic trial.[90] But the question is whether the IHL rule exhausts the content of the IHRL due process right in situations of armed conflict, or whether the IHL rule is insufficient to meet the criteria demanded by IHRL.[91] This issue need not be resolved here.

Conclusion

The distinction between acting as a sovereign and acting as a belligerent provides a useful analytical framework for determining when IHRL and IHL apply. The distinction is not only normatively convincing but also descriptively pertinent. The relevant prohibitions in IHRL and IHL track this basic distinction. In applying this framework, this chapter defended the following conclusions. First, during armed conflict, the legal regulation of targeting is governed exclusively by IHL, because the state is acting as belligerent. Second, detention may involve (in some circumstances) a sufficient level of control to trigger the application of basic principles of human rights. Third, situations of belligerent occupation involve the greatest level of functional control short of full government, and therefore trigger the widest application of human rights principles in situations of armed conflict.

However, it would be wrong to assume that all legal rules from IHRL should apply in the detention and occupation contexts. In both of these situations, there are other bodies of law – IHL and the law of belligerent occupation – that regulate state behavior. At issue in these situations is how to resolve any potential conflict between IHRL and the rules from the more specific body of law. This is a complex question not addressed by this chapter. Nonetheless, a few basic observations are in order as a way of framing this debate.

In the current literature, there is pressure to "fill the gap" in situations under-regulated by IHL. The greatest temptation to fill the gap with human rights norms applies in situations where codified IHL is notoriously thin: non-international armed conflicts. The extent of codification is limited to Common Article 3 and Additional Protocol II. But the lack of codification does not necessarily entail a lack of *law* entirely, given that

90 *See, e.g.*, Hamdi v. Rumsfeld, 542 U.S. 507, 520–21 (2004).

91 *See* Larry May, Global Justice and Due Process (2011) (arguing that the right to due process is protected not just by domestic legal systems but also by international law).

an entire array of customary rules, based on state practice, may apply to non-international armed conflicts (NIACs).[92] Generally speaking the literature has brushed past this point, giving insufficient recognition to the role that customary law may play in NIACs. So the lack of codified law does not by itself provide a strong reason to appeal to what remains a conceptually distinct body of law – human rights law.

Even in the absence of customary law on point, the appeal to human rights law to fill the gap is conceptually problematic, given the distinct nature of the two fields of law. If the state is genuinely acting as a sovereign over its subjects then the importation is hardly controversial as a means of filling the gap when no operative rule of IHL governs the conduct in question. But the application of human rights norms when the state is acting as a belligerent risks conceptual confusion; such importations run counter to the animating spirit of each body of law which are designed to regulate different activities and different modes of action. Human rights law deals with the unequal imposition of state power of ruled subjects, while the law of armed conflict regulates formally co-equal belligerents engaged in armed conflict. The two bodies of law could not be more different.

In contrast, some scholars and governments argue that the rules from IACs should apply *by analogy* to NIACs.[93] While I would prefer to rely on customary rules applicable to NIACs as a first resort, the preceding argument demonstrates that the application of IAC rules by analogy to NIACs is normatively superior to the importation of human rights as gap-fillers. Better to import by analogy a body of rules (from IACs) that share the same conceptual foundation, rather than import a body of rules (from IHRL) that rest on a completely different conceptual framework, i.e., the relationship of a sovereign over its subjects.

[92] *See, e.g.*, Jens Iverson, *The Drone Reports: Can Members of Armed Groups Be Targeted?*, Opinio Juris (November 6, 2013), *available at* http://opiniojuris.org/2013/11/06/drone-reports-can-members-armed-groups-targeted/ (discussing the need for customary law analysis based on state practice).

[93] *See* Kenneth Watkin & Andrew J. Norris, *Preface*, *in* Non-International Armed Conflict in the Twenty-First Century xxii (2012). *Compare* Ryan Goodman, *Al-Qaeda, the Law on Associated Forces and "Belonging to" a Party (did the new U.N. drones reports get it right?)*, Just Security (October 18, 2013), *available at* http://justsecurity.org/2013/10/18/al-qaeda-law-forces-belonging-to-party-drones-reports/, *with* Kevin Jon Heller, *The Problematic "Belonging To" Analogy: A Response to Goodman*, Just Security (October 23, 2013), *available at* http://justsecurity.org/2013/10/23/guest-post-problematic-belonging-to-analogy-response-goodman/.

The only situation where reference to human rights law is appropriate is when the government is acting as a sovereign over its subject – a situation that may well occur in some detention scenarios where the state exercises regulatory control over the individuals in question. The result of this analysis is an asymmetry between detention and targeting. Since detention potentially involves the state acting as a sovereign, human rights law has a role to play in filling the gaps where IHL or the law of occupation under-regulates the situation, especially in NIACs, which are governed by relatively few rules regarding detention. In contrast, targeting during an armed conflict is a situation of pure belligerency; since the state is acting as a belligerent, none of the legal machinery associated with the sovereign mode is triggered. However, this conclusion assumes that there are no *pre-existing bodies of law* that already regulate the conduct, working out the demands of human rights law that are applicable during times of armed conflict. Where there is a specific rule on point in IHL or the law of occupation, these fields of law provide the content for human rights law in these situations.[94] These bodies of law become *lex specialis* insofar as they provide the normative content of human rights law in specialized circumstances.[95] Consequently, the approach in this chapter supports a *minimalist* co-application view,

[94] The ICJ envisioned this approach in its *Nuclear Weapons* and *Wall* opinions.

[95] *See also* Oona Hathaway et al., *Which Law Governs During Armed Conflict? The Relationship Between International Humanitarian Law and Human Rights Law*, 96 Minn. L. Rev. 1883, 1886 (2012), who argue that a Conflict Resolution Model allows IHL and IHRL to co-apply during armed conflict if the rules converge, but if they conflict a decision-rule must determine which rule should govern. They consider three decision rules for resolving the conflict: event-specific displacement, reverse event-specific displacement, and specificity. In the first, IHL trumps IHRL in armed conflict when their rules conflict; in the second, IHRL trumps IHL when their norms conflict. Neither of these options is particularly nuanced; they involve competing claims of primacy that are difficult if not impossible to resolve. The third rule – specificity – dictates "the law more specifically tailored to the situation prevails." *Id.* at 1910. In practice, the rule privileges IHL by virtue of its *lex specialis* nature in most situations, though leaves open the possibility that more specific rules of IHRL (if they were developed) might conceivably trump IHL rules. One benefit of the specificity rule is that it privileges the most detailed legal rule applicable, thus prioritizing greater regulation regardless of its source. One deficit of the rule is the fluctuating and mercurial nature of its application: at one moment IHL might apply, seconds later IHRL could apply. *Id.* at 1911. Soldiers and civilians alike may face difficulty predicting which regime applies if the frameworks constantly shift based on their comparative degree of specificity. For a slightly different rendering of the decision rules covertly residing under the umbrella of *lex specialis*, see Milanovic, Extraterritorial Application of Human Rights Treaties, *supra* note 6, at 229.

where IHRL can provide supplement only in those situations where the state is acting as a sovereign and no definitive rule from either IHL or the law of occupation applies. This may be a small universe, perhaps even a null set. In all other situations when the state is acting as a belligerent, IHL applies exclusively.[96]

[96] This produces a more conceptually satisfying answer than relying exclusively on the level of specificity of the competing rules, which has little or nothing to do with the nature of the government's action. *Cf.* Hathaway, *supra* note 95, at 1911.

PART II

Conceptual Limits of the Law of War Framework

5

Ending the Global War

The Power of Human Rights in a Time of Unrestrained Armed Conflict

JONATHAN HOROWITZ*

ABSTRACT

A notion that there exists under international law the possibility of a "global" or "transnational" non-international armed conflict (or "global NIAC") rests on the assertion that a state that is party to a NIAC may use the law of armed conflict (LOAC) to target an enemy fighter anywhere he or she goes in the world. If true, a global NIAC may permit a state to lawfully drop a bomb on an enemy fighter who sits for a coffee in the middle of a peaceful city, say London, Rabat, or Hong Kong. Amongst a series of concerns this chapter highlights, a global NIAC would also permit, under the LOAC principle of proportionality, incidental civilian harm and destruction of civilian property. A global NIAC makes war omnipresent and forever looming. These consequences are unsettling and require a serious evaluation to determine if international law does in fact permit such an expansive understanding of war. Utilizing the public international law of interstate use of force, human rights, and LOAC, this chapter concludes that the concept of a global NIAC cannot exist without there being a violation of international law, although notably the violation that this chapter focuses on is that of the territorial state rather than the attacking state. This does not mean that a state cannot respond to attacks and threats from non-state groups abroad. It means that concepts other than a global NIAC must be relied upon to justify extraterritorial use of force.

* Legal Officer, Open Society Justice Initiative, jonathan.horowitz@opensocietyfoundations.org. This chapter was written in the author's personal capacity. The author thanks Ralph Mamiya, Naz Modirzadeh, Jens David Ohlin, Andrea Prasow, Christopher Rogers, and Gabor Rona for their comments and Harshani Dharmadasa and Alex Porter for their research assistance. All errors remain his own.

Introduction

This chapter assesses the impact that international human rights law has on the legality of what has been called a global non-international armed conflict ("global NIAC"). A global NIAC is based on the premise that a state that is party to a NIAC may use the law of armed conflict (LOAC, also known as international humanitarian law) to target an enemy fighter with lethal force anywhere he or she goes in the world. John O. Brennan, when serving as assistant to the U.S. president for homeland security and counterterrorism, articulated the notion of a global NIAC when he stated that the United States was in an armed conflict with al-Qa'ida, the Taliban, and associated forces and "[t]here is nothing in international law that ... prohibits us from using lethal force against our enemies outside of an active battlefield, at least when the country involved consents or is unable or unwilling to take action against the threat."[1]

Here, to better demonstrate what a global NIAC permits, is a hypothetical:

> *The state of Arcadia is engaged in a NIAC with a rebel group on the territory of Desmonda. A rebel sub-commander boards a plane in Desmonda and travels to Franconia, which is a country that is not engaged in any armed conflict and is located thousands of miles from Arcadia and Desmonda.*
>
> *In Franconia, the sub-commander plans to meet with various arms dealers and will determine from which of them he will purchase dozens of rocket propelled grenades, hundreds of AK-47s, and components for improvised explosive devices. The sub-commander plans to use those weapons in his armed conflict with Arcadia. Franconia's intelligence service learns that the sub-commander is within its territory and informs Arcadia. Arcadia, in turn, asks for Franconia's consent to target the sub-commander using lethal*

[1] John O. Brennan, The Ethics and Efficacy of the President's Counterterrorism Strategy, Speech at Woodrow Wilson International Center, Washington, D.C. (Apr. 30, 2012), *available at* www.wilsoncenter.org/event/the-efficacy-and-ethics-us-counterterrorism-strategy. *See also* Applicability of Federal Criminal Laws and the Constitution to Contemplated Lethal Operations Against Shaykh Anwar al-Aulaqi, Op. Off. Legal Counsel, at 24 (Jul. 16, 2010), *available at* http://fas.org/irp/agency/doj/olc/aulaqi.pdf ("[T]he contemplated DoD operation would occur in Yemen, a location that is far from the most active theater of combat between the United States and al-Qaida. That does not affect our conclusion, however, that the combination of facts present here would make the DoD operation in Yemen part of the non-international armed conflict with al-Qaida."). For another articulation of a global NIAC *see generally* KENNETH ANDERSON, *Targeted Killing and Drone Warfare: How We Came to Debate Whether There Is a 'Legal Geography of War,' in* FUTURE CHALLENGES IN NATIONAL SECURITY AND LAW (Peter Berkowitz ed., 2011).

force due to Arcadia's determination that he is a legally targetable individual under LOAC.

Franconia agrees to Arcadia's request. Five days later Arcadia kills the sub-commander with a missile fired from one of its armed unmanned aerial vehicles. This takes place a few days before the sub-commander's meeting with the first arms dealer he was scheduled to meet.

Due to falling debris from a nearby building caused by the attack, a family of three Franconians was killed. Arcadia knew of their presence and the risk posed by falling debris, but determined, in accordance with the principle of proportionality, that the three lost lives would be outweighed by the military advantage gained by killing the sub-commander.

The far reaching consequences of a global NIAC are obvious from this scenario. As the ICRC put it, such a paradigm "would mean that the whole world is potentially a battlefield and that people moving around the world could be legitimate targets under international humanitarian law wherever they might be."[2] A global NIAC permits a state to claim it is lawful to drop a bomb on an enemy fighter who sits for a coffee in the middle of a peaceful city, say London, Rabat, or Hong Kong. The global NIAC paradigm also permits the LOAC rules of proportionality to apply. This would make permissible incidental civilian harm and destruction of civilian property if it did not outweigh the military advantage anticipated. A global NIAC would even permit the attacking state to invite other states into its NIAC to carry out attacks on its behalf through the doctrine of collective self-defense.

From a historical and political perspective, the notion of a global NIAC brings to an end the view that war, as Yoram Dinstein put it, "would appear every once in a while, leave death and devastation in its wake, and temporarily pass away to return at a later date."[3] Instead, a global NIAC makes war omnipresent and forever looming – both geographically and temporally. The notion of a global NIAC has other consequences. It creates a "backdoor" that allows Franconia to escape its

[2] Peter Maurer, President of International Committee of the Red Cross, Interview, The use of armed drones must comply with laws (May 10, 2013), *available at* www.icrc.org/eng/resources/documents/interview/2013/05-10-drone-weapons-ihl.htm.

[3] Yoram Dinstein, War, Aggression and Self-Defense 76 (5th ed. 2012); Christof Heyns, Report of the Special Rapporteur on extrajudicial, summary or arbitrary executions, U.N. Doc. A/68/382, at 16 (Sept. 13, 2013) ("Peace should be the norm, yet such scenarios risk making its derogation the rule by privileging force over long-term peaceful alternatives. The expansive use of armed drones by the first States to acquire them, if not challenged, can do structural damage to the cornerstones of international security and set precedents that undermine the protection of life across the globe in the longer term.").

human rights obligations. Take for example a situation where Franconia, which is not a party to a NIAC, wishes to kill someone on its territory who is participating in a NIAC with Arcadia. Under the rules of a global NIAC, Franconia could subvert its human rights obligations by requesting Arcadia to carry out the killing. A global NIAC can also put an attacking state in direct competition with the territorial state's domestic laws.[4] If Franconia permitted an Arcadia agent to kill someone in a manner that is unlawful under Franconia's domestic law, that Arcadia agent could be held criminally liable.[5] Franconia agents involved in the operation could also be exposed to criminal liability for allowing Arcadia to break its domestic laws.[6] Additionally,

[4] Ashley Deeks, *Drone Strikes in Pakistan: Consent and Obfuscation?*, Lawfareblog.com, Mar. 7, 2013, *available at* www.lawfareblog.com/2013/03/drone-strikes-in-pakistan-consent-and-obfuscation/ ("My argument, in short, is that we are seeing an increasing number of incidents in which a state seeks another state's consent to use force in the latter's territory. And we also are seeing territorial states provide that consent, even in the face of limitations that may exist in their own laws – such as restrictions on the presence of foreign troops in its territory, or prohibitions on the use of particular weapons, or due process requirements. That move by territorial states stands in tension with the usual understanding of consent in law generally, which is that an actor only may consent to that which the actor could do herself."). *See also* Ashley Deeks, *Consent to the Use of Force and International Law Supremacy*, 45:1 Harv. Int'l L.J. 2, 33 (2013) ("international law should recognize consent as a legal basis for using force only where a state's consent authorizes actions the state itself could lawfully undertake").

[5] This is far from a hypothetical scenario. In 1980, when the U.S. Department of Justice Office of Legal Counsel (OLC) considered the legal implications of conducting extraterritorial law enforcement apprehensions without the consent of the foreign state, the OLC noted the possibility that federal officials may be extraditable to the foreign state for kidnapping. Extraterritorial Apprehension by the Federal Bureau of Investigation, 4B Op. Off. Legal Counsel 543, 556 (1980), *available at* www.justice.gov/olc/docs/op-olc-04b.pdf. In June 2005, an Italian judge issued arrest warrants for Americans, mostly CIA agents, suspected of involvement in the unlawful kidnapping of Egyptian Abu Omar in Italy in 2003. As of 2013, Italian courts had convicted twenty-six Americans *in abstensia* and sentenced them to prison. Alessio Vinci, *Italy seeks Americans over abduction*, CNN.COM, Jun. 24, 2005, *available at* www.cnn.com/2005/WORLD/europe/06/24/italy.arrests/; Max Fisher, *The story of how a Milan CIA station chief became a fugitive, now caught in Panama*, Washington Post, Jul. 18, 2013, *available at* www.washingtonpost.com/blogs/worldviews/wp/2013/07/18/the-story-of-how-a-milan-cia-station-chief-became-a-fugitive-now-caught-in-panama/; Jeffrey Castelli, *Ex-CIA Rome Chief, Sentenced To Jail In Abu Omar Kidnapping Case*, Reuters, Feb. 13, 2013, *available at* www.huffingtonpost.com/2013/02/01/jeffrey-castelli_n_2599831.html.

[6] In addition to Italian courts trying and convicting Americans for the 2003 kidnapping of Egyptian Abu Omar in Italy, the courts tried and convicted Italy's former intelligence chief Nicolo Pollari and sentenced him to ten years imprisonment for his role in the kidnapping. The court also sentenced his former deputy to nine years. However, in February 2014, those convictions and the convictions of other Italian nationals were overturned by

Franconia would be liable for allowing Arcadia to breach its international human rights obligations.

How the U.S. government and many U.S. international and national security lawyers and scholars arrived at the conclusion that there existed a thing called a "global NIAC" is discussed in this volume by Kevin Jon Heller and Naz K. Modirzadeh – who point out that vying for policy making influence; overreliance on LOAC as the dominating legal framework to combat terrorism; and blindly transposing international armed conflict (IAC) rules onto NIACs have all been significant contributing factors.[7] The result has been, as demonstrated, a series of consequences that are unsettling and require a serious evaluation to determine if international law does in fact provide for a regime that permits for such an expansive understanding of war. This is not to say that practitioners and scholars have failed to put forward strong arguments that undercut claims that global NIACs exist.[8] But this chapter makes a contribution to

the Court of Cassation due to the secret nature of the information surrounding the case. *Italy's ex-spy chief convicted over 2003 CIA rendition*, BBC News - Europe, Feb. 12, 2013, *available at* www.bbc.co.uk/news/world-europe-21435632; *Convictions of 5 Italians thrown out in CIA case*, Associated Press, Feb. 24, 2014, *available at* http://news.yahoo.com/convictions-5-italians-thrown-cia-case-190156876.html.

7 Kevin Jon Heller, *The Use and Abuse of Analogy in IHL and IHRL*, *in* Theoretical Boundaries of Armed Conflict and Human Rights (Jens David Ohlin ed., 2016); Naz K. Modirzadeh, *Folk International Law, in* Theoretical Boundaries of Armed Conflict and Human Rights (Jens David Ohlin ed., 2016).

8 *See, for example*, Rogier Bartels, *Guest Post: Bartels–Temporal Scope of Application of IHL: When do Non-International Armed Conflicts End? Part 1,* OpinioJuris.org, Feb. 17, 2014, *available at* http://opiniojuris.org/2014/02/18/guest-post-bartels-temporal-scope-application-ihl-non-international-armed-conflicts-end-part-1/ ("If a NIAC only starts when organised groups are engaged in fighting of certain intensity, then logically, the armed conflict ends when these two criteria are no longer both present. This would also make clear that the United States' so-called NIAC against Al-Qaeda cannot be a 'perpetual war'."); Noam Lubell and Nathan Derejko, *A Global Battlefield? Drones and the Geographical Scope of Armed Conflict*, 11 J. Int'l Crim. Just. 65, 87 (2013) ("in many cases the existence of armed conflict between the striking state and the targeted group can be cast in doubt; nowhere is this clearer than in the so-called global war on terror or war on Al-Qaida [as opposed to the distinct conflict in Afghanistan]. The nexus to an existing and identifiable conflict meeting the threshold requirements for classification as such, to which the state and group are Party, must exist; if there is no armed conflict to which the drone strikes are attached, then in most cases the legitimacy for direct lethal strikes will disappear."); Gabor Rona, *Debate (Round 1): The 'Lutte' Against Terrorism,* JustSecurity.org, Sept. 30, 2013, *available at* http://justsecurity.org/1378/lutte-terrorism/ (arguing that Al Qaeda does not meet the legal threshold of a "party to the armed conflict" and also arguing that the term "associated forces" is not an appropriate label for who other than members of Al Qaeda can be targeted under the rules of LOAC); Yoram Dinstein, *Concluding Remarks on Non-International Armed Conflicts*, 88 Int'l L. Stud. 399, 400 (2012)

this literature by utilizing the public international law of interstate use of force, human rights, and LOAC to uniquely demonstrate that the concept of a global NIAC cannot be carried out in compliance with international law. This chapter reaches this conclusion by focusing primarily on the international legal obligations of the state in which the attack is occurring (e.g., the territorial state) rather than the obligations of the attacking state.

In doing so, this chapter addresses a lacuna in the scholarship highlighted by John Dehn, who has noted that "little to no attention has been paid to the international obligations of the state in which a violent non-state actor is located and targeted."[9] When evaluating the concept of a global NIAC from this angle, this chapter shows that the territorial state's human rights obligations prohibit it from giving its consent to an attacking state that wishes to apply LOAC on an enemy who is not in an armed conflict with the territorial state. As a result, human rights law creates a legal barrier that prevents LOAC from jumping from one state to another, which is the defining characteristic of a global NIAC. To be sure, this chapter acknowledges circumstances when a state is permitted to chase its enemy across international borders, but this is permissible

("Virtually all commonly used definitions of a NIAC are restrictive in that the armed conflict is circumscribed to a single State [the common locution in the past was 'civil war']. Admittedly, a majority of the Supreme Court of the United States, in the *Hamdan* case of 2006, seems to have arrived at the conclusion that the post-9/11 transnational 'war on terrorism' should be deemed a NIAC. However, the idea that a NIAC can be global in nature is oxymoronic: an armed conflict can be a NIAC and it can be global, but it cannot be both."); Maurer, *supra* note 2 (responding to the question of "Who may be targeted under international humanitarian law?" as follows: "In armed conflict lethal force may, under international humanitarian law, be used against combatants or fighters, and against civilians taking a direct part in hostilities. What is much more complex is the situation that arises when a person participates directly in hostilities from the territory of a non-belligerent State, or moves to the territory of a non-belligerent State after having taken part in an armed conflict. The question is whether lethal force may lawfully be used against such a person and under what legal framework. Opinions diverge. The ICRC holds the view that international humanitarian law would not be applicable in such a situation, meaning that this person should not be considered a legitimate target under the laws of war. Advising otherwise would mean that the whole world is potentially a battlefield and that people moving around the world could be legitimate targets under international humanitarian law wherever they might be. Of course, the person described can be held accountable for his or her actions, and, in our view, human rights law would apply to any use of force that may be necessary."). *See also* Jelena Pejic, *Extraterritorial targeting by means of armed drones: Some legal implications*, 96:893 INT'L REV. RED CROSS 67 (2015).

9 John C. Dehn, *Targeted Killing, Human Rights and Ungoverned Spaces: Considering Territorial State Human Rights Obligations*, 54 HARV. INT'L L.J. 84 (2012).

through accepted legal frameworks of international law, and not through the notion of a "global NIAC."

In support of its argument against a global NIAC, this chapter outlines the applicable human rights obligations that the territorial state has to respect and protect the prohibition on arbitrary deprivation of life. It also draws attention to the legal principle that one may not transfer more legal rights than one has (*nemo plus iuris ad alium transferre potest quam ipse habet*).[10] Under this principle the territorial state cannot permit the attacking state to target an individual who the territorial state is not in an armed conflict with. This is because, whereas the attacking state may wish to make the claim that it can rely on LOAC rules because it is in an armed conflict with its target, the territorial state cannot make a similar claim because it is in no such armed conflict with the target and, therefore, the territorial state does not have the legal authority that is required to permit, through its consent or otherwise, the targeting state to use LOAC on its territory. In drawing this conclusion, this chapter does not address – due to a lack of space – whether the territorial state's human rights violations (i.e., by means of providing its consent to the attacking state) impacts the lawfulness of the attacking state's subsequent strike.

If the territorial state refuses to provide its consent (as it should), but the attacking state nonetheless wishes to carry out the strike, new issues of international law arise, in particular with respect to the *jus ad bellum*. While one might expect the attacking state to assert that its involvement in a NIAC trumps all else, this is not a convincing argument under international law. When a state uses extraterritorial force anew, it must do so through the authority of the U.N. Security Council, doctrine of self-defense, or the territorial state's consent to the use of force. Whether

[10] *See, for example,* Legal Consequences for States of the Continued Presence of South Africa in Namibia (South West Africa) notwithstanding Security Council Resolution 276 (1970), 1971 I.C.J. 16 (Jun. 21) at 264 (dissenting opinion of Judge Fitzmaurice) (referring to "*nemo dare potest quod ipse non habet,* or (the corollary) *nemo accipere potest id quod ipse donator nunquam habuit*" as an "elementary yet fundamental principle of law" and an "incontestable legal principle"). *See also* Lighthouses Case (Fr. v. Greece), 1934 P.C.I.J. (ser. A/B) No. 62 (Mar. 17) (separate opinion of Judge Seferiades) at 49–50 (referring to "*nemo dat quod non habet*" as a general principle of law); Situation in the Democratic Republic of Congo, I.C.C., ICC-01/04–455, at 24 (fn. 28) (Feb. 18, 2008) ("The OPCD refers to the principle of *nemo plus iuris ad alium transferre potest quam ipse habet* [one may not transfer more legal rights than one has], which is considered to be a general principle of international law."). *See also* Maarten Bos, A Methodology of International Law 5, 73, 277 (1984).

a state is in an armed conflict is therefore not in and of itself sufficient to determine if a state can use lethal force against an enemy. Thus, if the territorial state's human rights obligations prevent it from granting consent to the attacking state, the attacking state must look to U.N. Security Council authorization or the doctrine of self-defense to use extraterritorial force.[11]

Sections I, II, and III of this chapter set out in greater detail the public international law of interstate use of force, human rights law, and LOAC. This review is necessary for assessing, as is done in Section IV, their relationship to one another. What can be concluded from this assessment is that a global NIAC is not able to exist without there being a breach of international law. In recognition of the needs of states to protect themselves and their populations from attack, Section IV also describes ways that states can respond to attacks and threats from non-state groups while complying with international law.

I Sovereignty and Consent-based Use of Force

In our assessment of the legality of a global NIAC under international law, it is important to first consider under what circumstances a state is legally permitted to use force in another state. The general rule is found in Article 2(4) of the Charter of the United Nations, which requires states to refrain from "the threat or use of force against the territorial integrity or political independence of any state, or in any other manner inconsistent with the Purposes of the United Nations."[12] It follows that a lethal attack on one state's territory by another state engages Article 2(4). The content of Article 2(4) – the prohibition on the use of force – has, by some, been regarded as a peremptory norm (a rule *jus cogens*) and others as reflecting customary international law.[13]

[11] It is important to note at this point, and throughout, that while this chapter explores the intersection of three areas of public international law, any legal assessment of issues pertaining to the *jus ad bellum* are distinct from legal assessments pertaining to the law of armed conflict or human rights law.

[12] U.N. Charter, art. 2, para. 4.

[13] *See* Military and Paramilitary Activities (Nicar. v. U.S.), 1984 I.C.J. 392 (Nov. 26) (dissenting opinion of Judge Schwebel) at 615 ("While there is little agreement on the scope of *jus cogens*, it is important to recall that in the International Law Commission and at the Vienna Conference on the Law of Treaties there was general agreement that, if *jus cogens* has any agreed core, it is Article 2, paragraph 4."); Oliver Dörr & Albrecht Randelzhofer, *Article 2(4)*, *in* The Charter of the United Nations:

There are, however, three clear exceptions to Article 2(4). The first exception is Article 39 of the U.N. Charter, which is of limited concern to this chapter. It permits the Security Council to sanction the use of force or other measures when it makes a determination of the existence of a "threat to the peace, breach of the peace, or act of aggression."[14] The second exception to Article 2(4) is found in Article 51, which recognizes the inherent right that states have to use force against another state in self-defense. The full text of Article 51 reads,

> Nothing in the present Charter shall impair the inherent right of individual or collective self-defence if an armed attack occurs against a Member of the United Nations, until the Security Council has taken measures necessary to maintain international peace and security. Measures taken by Members in the exercise of this right of self-defence shall be immediately reported to the Security Council and shall not in any way affect the authority and responsibility of the Security Council under the present Charter to take at any time such action as it deems necessary in order to maintain or restore international peace and security.[15]

Article 51 is important to the discussion of a global NIAC because it requires any state that uses force in the name of the *jus in bello* to also consider whether that use of force is in compliance with the separate rules of state sovereignty.[16] The third exception to Article 2(4), which is

A COMMENTARY, VOLUME I 231 (Bruno Simma, Daniel-Erasmus Khan, Georg Nolte, and Andreas Paulus eds., 3rd ed., 2012) ("the prohibition on the use of force laid down in Art. 2 (4) is usually acknowledged in State practice and legal doctrine to have a peremptory character, and thus to be part of the international *ius cogens*."); RESTATEMENT (THIRD) OF FOREIGN RELATIONS LAW OF THE UNITED STATE § 102 (1987). *See generally* for additional discussion for and against regarding Article 2(4) as reflecting a rule *jus cogens*, James A. Green, *Questioning the Peremptory Status of the Prohibition of the Use of Force*, 32:2 MICH. J. INT'L L. 215 (2011).

14 U.N. CHARTER, arts. 39, 41 & 42.

15 U.N. CHARTER, art. 51.

16 *See* Lubell & Derejko, *supra* note 8, at 80 (noting that an attacking state has two separate legal decisions to make: one relating to the *jus ad bellum* and another relating to the *jus in bello*: "while the transgression of borders is key for determinations in the *ius ad bellum*, it is not the key determining factor for the finding of an armed conflict and the applicability of the *ius in bello*."); Michael N. Schmitt, *Charting the Legal Geography of Non-International Armed Conflict*, 90 INT'L L. STUD. 1, 17 (2014) ("even when an individual may lawfully be targeted under IHL, a separate legal basis to cross the border of the State into which the operation is to be mounted must exist [the two most likely being consent and self-defense].") *See also* General Counsel of the Department of Defense Jeh Charles Johnson, National security law, lawyers and lawyering in the Obama Administration, Speech at Yale Law School (Feb. 22, 2012), *available at* www.cfr.org/defense-and-security/jeh-johnsons-speech-national-security-law-lawyers-lawyering-obama-administration/p27448 ("International legal principles, including respect for a state's sovereignty and the

most important to this chapter, is that international law permits an attacking state to use force on the territory of another state when the territorial state provides its consent.[17] Consent, when considered in this context has been said to effectively wash away the sovereignty issues described earlier.[18]

Less discussed in the literature on consent, but relevant to examining the legality of a global NIAC under international law, is the situation where the attacking state wishes to conduct LOAC targeting operations

laws of war, impose important limits on our ability to act unilaterally, and on the way in which we can use force in foreign territories.").

This chapter does not address the myriad of issues associated with Article 51, many of which have been covered in detail elsewhere. *See, for example,* Dapo Akande and Thomas Liefländer, *Clarifying Necessity, Imminence, and Proportionality in the Law of Self-Defense*, 107:3 AM. J. INT'L L. 563 (2013); Deeks, *Consent to the Use of Force and International Law Supremacy, supra* note 4; DINSTEIN, *supra* note 3; Dire Tladi, *The Nonconsenting Innocent State: The Problem with Bethlehem's Principle* 12, 107:3 AM. J. INT'L L. 570 (2013).

[17] For discussions on the role of consent-based military assistance in the context of armed conflict interventions *see, for example,* JOHN LAWRENCE HARGROVE, *Intervention by Invitation and the Politics of the New World Order*, *in* LAW AND FORCE IN THE NEW INTERNATIONAL ORDER (Lori F. Damrosch & David J. Scheffer eds., 1991); REIN MULLERSON, *Intervention by Invitation*, *in* LAW AND FORCE IN THE NEW INTERNATIONAL ORDER (Lori F. Damrosch & David J. Scheffer eds., 1991); David Wippman, *Military Intervention, Regional Organizations, and Host-State Consent*, 7 DUKE J. COMP. & INT'L L. 209 (1996); Eliav Lieblich, *Intervention and Consent: Consensual Forcible Interventions in Internal Armed Conflicts as International Agreements*, 29 B.U. INT'L L.J. 337 (2011). *See also,* IAN BROWNLIE, PRINCIPLES OF PUBLIC INTERNATIONAL LAW 309 (7th ed., 2008) (arguing that there exists under international law a "governing principle . . . that a state cannot take measures on the territory of another state by way of enforcement of national laws without the consent of the latter. Persons may not be arrested, a summons may not be served, police or tax investigations may not be mounted, orders for production of documents may not be executed, on the territory of another state, except under the terms of a treaty or other consent given.").

[18] See, *Draft articles on Responsibility of States for Internationally Wrongful Acts*, International Law Commission, art. 20 ("Valid consent by a State to the commission of a given act by another State precludes the wrongfulness of that act in relation to the former State to the extent that the act remains within the limits of that consent."). This is not to say intervention through consent is without its problems. There have been numerous examples where a foreign state asserted that it gained consent on either false or very shaky grounds. *See, for example,* Wippman, *supra* note 17, at 211 ("when the Soviet Union invoked the principle of state consent to justify invasions of Hungary in 1956, Czechoslovakia in 1968, and Afghanistan in 1979, it met with widespread criticism on the ground that the invitations at issue were either manufactured or coerced."). For a discussion on specific rules that could be applied to giving and obtaining consent, *see* Deeks, *Consent to the Use of Force and International Law Supremacy, supra* note 4; HARGROVE, *supra* note 17, at 116–8.

in the territorial state when the territorial state is not in an armed conflict with the attacking state's targets. This reflects the scenario provided at the beginning of this chapter. To conduct such targeting operations without the territorial state's consent would be, as explained earlier, an unlawful breach of its sovereignty, unless of course permission is given by the Security Council or the attacking state makes a lawful claim to act in self-defense. But, assuming that the territorial state is willing to grant its consent, the question remains: what obligations and rights shape what this consent should look like when another state wishes to use lethal force on its territory?

As Ashley Deeks and others have pointed out, rules for operationalizing consent under international law are largely unclear and what exists often lacks precision.[19] There appear to be, however, general principles that can help to interpret what a territorial state can and cannot do when it comes to granting its consent to another state's use of force on its territory.[20]

One general principle is that the state is entitled to place limits on the consent it grants. This reflects the core nature of sovereignty. Status of Forces Agreements (SOFAs) provide classic examples where territorial states limit the use of force and non-use of force activities of foreign states,[21] something that Iraq did extensively in its 2008 SOFA with the United States. Article 3, for example, regulated:

1. While conducting military operations pursuant to this Agreement, it is the duty of members of the United States Forces and of the civilian component to respect Iraqi laws . . .

[19] Deeks, *Consent to the Use of Force and International Law Supremacy*, *supra* note 4, at 16 ("If consent to the use of force remains a complicated proposition for scholars, it also remains one for states, which have been imprecise or silent about their views."). *See also generally* Hargrove, *supra* note 17, at 114–8; *see generally* Mullerson, *supra* note 17.

[20] These principles are based on the author's assumption that a territorial state's consent to the use of force should be regarded as an international agreement and interpreted, in part, through the rules set out in the 1969 Vienna Convention on the Laws of Treaties. *See* Lieblich, *supra* note 17, at 357–63 *and* Deeks, *Consent to the Use of Force and International Law Supremacy*, *supra* note 4, at 18–9.

[21] R. Chuck Mason, Status of Forces Agreement (SOFA): What Is It, and How Has It Been Utilized?, 3 (Congressional Research Service, Jun. 16, 2008), *available at* www.fas.org/sgp/crs/natsec/RL34531.pdf ("A SOFA may include many provisions, but the most common issue addressed is which country may exercise criminal jurisdiction over U.S. personnel. Other provisions that may be found in a SOFA include, but are not limited to, the wearing of uniforms, taxes and fees, carrying of weapons, use of radio frequencies, licenses, and customs regulations.").

2. With the exception of members of the United States Forces and of the civilian component, the United States Forces may not transfer any person into or out of Iraq on vehicles, vessels, or aircraft covered by this Agreement, unless in accordance with applicable Iraqi laws and regulations, including implementing arrangements as may be agreed to by the Government of Iraq.[22]

A second principle of consent is that the consenting state holds the right to withdraw its consent.[23] So it went when President Kabila of the Democratic Republic of Congo withdrew his consent that had allowed the presence of foreign forces in the DRC.[24] Withdrawal of consent may also arise when the terms of the agreement are breached.[25]

A third general principle that applies to consent is that states cannot enter into agreements that conflict with a peremptory norm of international law (*jus cogens*).[26] For example, two states may never agree to form a "torture pact" or a "slavery pact" in which the territorial state

[22] Agreement Between the United States of America and the Republic of Iraq On the Withdrawal of United States Forces from Iraq and the Organization of Their Activities during Their Temporary Presence in Iraq, Nov. 17, 2008, art. 3, *available at* http://graphics8.nytimes.com/packages/pdf/world/20081119_SOFA_FINAL_AGREED_TEXT.pdf.

[23] Lieblich, *supra* note 17, at 374 ("Withdrawal of consent to a forcible intervention by a state is all but an absolute right.").

[24] *Id.* at 364–5.

[25] This is in keeping with the general principle of treaty law *pacta sunt servanda. See* Vienna Convention on the Law of Treaties of 1969, art. 60, 1155 UNTS 331; 8 ILM 679 (1969) (entered into force Jan. 27, 1980) ("1. A material breach of a bilateral treaty by one of the parties entitles the other to invoke the breach as a ground for terminating the treaty or suspending its operation in whole or in part."); *Draft articles on Responsibility of States for Internationally Wrongful Acts, supra* note 18, at art. 20 ("Valid consent by a State to the commission of a given act by another State precludes the wrongfulness of that act in relation to the former State to the extent that the act remains within the limits of that consent."); *Id.* at 363–4 ("When the presence of the intervener becomes unwanted,. . .or when the nature of the intervention deviates from what was agreed upon, the intervention might become wrongful and the intervener, accordingly, incurs state responsibility.").

[26] *See, for example,* Vienna Convention on the Law of Treaties of 1969, *supra* note 25, at art. 53 ("A treaty is void if, at the time of its conclusion, it conflicts with a peremptory norm of general international law. For the purposes of the present Convention, a peremptory norm of general international law is a norm accepted and recognized by the international community of States as a whole as a norm from which no derogation is permitted and which can be modified only by a subsequent norm of general international law having the same character."); *Fragmentation of International Law: Difficulties Arising from the Diversification and Expansion of International Law: Report of the Study Group of the International Law Commission*, International Law Commission, 58th Sess., at 14(10) & 14(32), U.N. Doc A/CN.4/L.702 (Jul. 18, 2006), *available at* www.un.org/ga/search/view_doc.asp?symbol=A/CN.4/L.702; Lieblich, *supra* note 17, at 364.

allows another state to commit acts of torture or slavery on its territory due to the *jus cogens* status of the prohibitions against torture and slavery.[27]

A fourth general principle that appears to apply to consent is that a state may not allow another state to do what the consenting state is not permitted to do. This reflects the legal principle that one may not transfer more legal rights than one has.[28] Hargrove raised this issue in his discussions of intervention by invitation; Deeks has too, pointing out that there is a "usual understanding of consent in law generally, which is that an actor only may consent to that which the actor could do herself."[29] This issue goes to the question that the rest of the chapter will address: Can the territorial state permit the attacking state to kill someone if the territorial state is not allowed to kill that same person?

II Human Rights Obligations of the Territorial State

While it may be a foregone conclusion that a state may permit, through its consent, another state to conduct activities on its territory, there remains the question of what other sources of international law must the territorial state - which in our scenario is not in an armed conflict with the targeted individual - take under consideration when determining whether it should permit another state to carry out lethal targeting operations on its soil. This is a discussion that has received little attention in the academic writings on global NIAC and it is a discussion where international human rights law plays an important role. Whereas much of the discussion about global NIAC has focused on the attacking state (e.g., the United States), this section of the chapter will demonstrate that the territorial state's human rights obligations play a decisive role in understanding the legal impermissibility of a global NIAC under international law.

27 *See Fragmentation of International Law*, *supra* note 26, at 21 ("The most frequently cited examples of *jus cogens* norms are the prohibition of aggression, slavery and the slave trade, genocide, racial discrimination apartheid and torture, as well as basic rules of international humanitarian law applicable in armed conflict, and the right to self-determination.").

28 *Supra* note 10.

29 Hargrove, *supra* note 17, at 121; Deeks, *Drone Strikes in Pakistan*, *supra* note 4. *See also* Deeks, *Consent to the Use of Force and International Law Supremacy*, *supra* note 4, at 33 ("international law should recognize consent as a legal basis for using force only where a state's consent authorizes actions the state itself could lawfully undertake.").

One of the most frequent human rights that a global NIAC engages is the right to life. The International Covenant on Civil and Political Rights (ICCPR) and the three major regional human rights treaties – the African Charter on Human and Peoples' Rights (ACHPR), European Convention for the Protection of Human Rights and Fundamental Freedoms (ECHR), and American Convention on Human Rights (ACHR) – all prohibit the unlawful and arbitrary deprivation of life.[30] Article 6 of the ICCPR reads, for example, "Every human being has the inherent right to life. This right shall be protected by law. No one shall be arbitrarily deprived of his life."[31]

All four treaties assign this right non-derogable status, which means there are no circumstances in which the state may limit the right beyond the limits that the treaty expressly states.[32] These treaties and their case law also make it clear that a territorial state has the responsibility to respect and protect the right to life of an individual when that individual is located on its territory. There is, therefore, little doubt that a state's

[30] While the European Convention for the Protection of Human Rights and Fundamental Freedoms does not use the term "arbitrary," the Court has routinely referred to a prohibition on arbitrary deprivation of life.

[31] International Covenant on Civil and Political Rights, art. 6, Dec. 16, 1966, 999 U.N.T.S. 171; S. Exec. Doc. E, 95-2 (1978); S. Treaty Doc. 95-20, 6 I.L.M. 368 (1967) (entered into force Mar. 23, 1976) [hereinafter ICCPR]. The language on the right to life in regional treaties is as follows: American Convention on Human Rights, art. 4, para. 1, Nov. 21, 1969, O.A.S. T.S. No. 36; 1144 U.N.T.S. 143; S. Treaty Doc. No. 95-21, 9 I.L.M. 99 (entered into force Jul. 18, 1978) [hereinafter ACHR] ("Every person has the right to have his life respected. This right shall be protected by law and, in general, from the moment of conception. No one shall be arbitrarily deprived of his life."); African Charter on Human and Peoples' Rights, art. 4, Jun. 27, 1981, 1520 U.N.T.S. 217, 245; 21 I.L.M. 58, 59 (1982) (entered into force Oct. 21, 1986) [hereinafter ACHPR] ("Human beings are inviolable. Every human being shall be entitled to respect for his life and the integrity of his person. No one may be arbitrarily deprived of this right."); European Convention for the Protection of Human Rights and Fundamental Freedoms, art. 2, Nov. 4, 1950, Europ.T.S. No. 5, 213 U.N.T.S. 221 (entered into force Sept. 3, 1953) [hereinafter ECHR] ("1. Everyone's right to life shall be protected by law. No one shall be deprived of his life intentionally save in the execution of a sentence of a court following his conviction of a crime for which this penalty is provided by law. 2. Deprivation of life shall not be regarded as inflicted in contravention of this Article when it results from the use of force which is no more than absolutely necessary: (a) in defence of any person from unlawful violence; (b) in order to effect a lawful arrest or to prevent the escape of a person lawfully detained; (c) in action lawfully taken for the purpose of quelling a riot or insurrection.").

[32] See, ICCPR, art. 4, para. 2, and ACHR, art. 27. ECHR, art. 15, para. 2 permits "No derogation from Article 2, except in respect of deaths resulting from lawful acts of war." The ACHPR has no derogation clause, thus article 4 cannot be derogated from.

human rights obligations are engaged when another state carries out a lethal targeting operation on its territory. What exactly those obligations are is, however, a separate issue, which we will now discuss.

1 "Unlawful" and "Arbitrary" under Human Rights Law

One important component of the prohibition on the deprivation of life for the purposes of our discussion of a global NIAC is how international human rights law defines the terms "unlawful" and "arbitrary." Human rights law is adamant that the state must not be permitted to kill as a general rule, but states were also adamant that human rights law needed to account for special exceptions. Two clear examples were the death penalty[33] and – more relevant to this chapter – a state agent's ability to use lethal force in the name of self-defense or to protect others.[34] As a result, human rights treaty law does not prohibit *all* deprivation of life; it prohibits *unlawful* and *arbitrary* deprivation of life. These terms make clear that a state must have in place adequate regulations for when deprivation of life is permissible and that any deprivation of life that takes place outside the law is prohibited.[35]

International human rights law also dictates that when force is used to take a life, it must have been necessary and proportionate. The European Court of Human Rights (ECtHR) in fact uses the terms "absolutely necessary" and "strictly proportionate," and takes an interdependent interpretation of these two rules. In *Nachova and Others v. Bulgaria*,

[33] *See, for example*, ACHR, art. 4, paras. 2–6; and ICCPR, art. 6, paras., 2, 4 & 5 (acknowledging the rights of states to impose the death penalty, but regulating its application).

[34] *See, for example*, ECHR, art. 2, para. 2.

[35] For the European Court of Human Rights' (ECtHR's) interpretation of "arbitrary" see Simsek and Others v. Turkey, Eur. Ct. H.R. 104 (2005) ("As the text of Article 2 itself shows, the use of lethal force by police officers may be justified in certain circumstances. Nonetheless, Article 2 does not grant a *carte blanche*. It goes without saying that a balance must be struck between the aim pursued and the means employed to achieve it. Unregulated and arbitrary action by State officials is incompatible with effective respect for human rights. This means that, as well as being authorised under national law, police operations must be sufficiently regulated by it, within the framework of a system of adequate and effective safeguards against arbitrariness and abuse of force."). *See also* Bozano v. France, Eur. Ct. H.R. 54 (1986) (In the context of arbitrary detention: "The main issue to be determined is whether the disputed detention was 'lawful', including whether it was in accordance with 'a procedure prescribed by law'. The Convention here refers essentially to national law and establishes the need to apply its rules, but it also requires that any measure depriving the individual of his liberty must be compatible with the purpose of Article 5 [art. 5], namely to protect the individual from arbitrariness.").

the Court stated, "any use of force must be 'no more than absolutely necessary', that is to say it must be strictly proportionate in the circumstances."[36] In simplest terms, lethal targeting – that is to say, the suppression of an enemy using lethal force as a means of first resort – is strictly prohibited under international human rights law due, in large part, to the rules of necessity and proportionality. Some of the clearest elaborations on these human rights rules are found in the United Nations Code of Conduct for Law Enforcement Officials (hereinafter, Code of Conduct) and the United Nations Basic Principles on the Use of Force and Firearms by Law Enforcement Officials (hereinafter, Basic Principles). Both have the status of soft law but have been regarded by human rights tribunals as providing instructive interpretation.[37] The Basic Principles explain the notion of necessity this way:

> Law enforcement officials shall not use firearms against persons except in self-defence or defence of others against the imminent threat of death or serious injury, to prevent the perpetration of a particularly serious crime involving grave threat to life, to arrest a person presenting such a danger and resisting their authority, or to prevent his or her escape, and only when less extreme means are insufficient to achieve these objectives. In any event, intentional lethal use of firearms may only be made when strictly unavoidable in order to protect life.[38]

The Basic Principles explain the proportionality requirement in this manner:

> Whenever the lawful use of force and firearms is unavoidable, law enforcement officials shall: (a) Exercise restraint in such use and act in proportion to the seriousness of the offence and the legitimate objective to be achieved; (b) Minimize damage and injury, and respect and preserve human life.[39]

[36] Nachova and Others v. Bulgaria, Eur. Ct. H.R. 94 (2005). For summaries of ECtHR case law on excessive use of force, see European Court of Human Rights, *Factsheet – Right to life* (Jun. 2013), *available at* www.echr.coe.int/Documents/FS_Life_ENG.pdf.

[37] Gabriel Shumba v. Republic of Zimbabwe, Af. Comm. H.R., Comm. 288/2004 136 (2012) (the African Commission on Human and Peoples' Rights cited the Code of Conduct for Law Enforcement Officials and the United Nations Basic Principles on the Use of Force and Firearms by Law Enforcement Officials as "international jurisprudence" that has "shed some light in the interpretation of the right to life"). *See also* Giuliani and Gaggio v. Italy, Eur. Ct. H.R. 209 (2011); Simsek and Others v. Turkey, *supra* note 25, at 91–2.

[38] Basic Principles on the Use of Force and Firearms by Law Enforcement Officials, art. 9, adopted by the Eighth United Nations Congress on the Prevention of Crime and the Treatment of Offenders, Havana, Cuba, Aug. 27 to Sept. 7, 1990.

[39] *Id.* at art. 5, paras. a & b.

The Code of Conduct articulates in Article 3 the principle of necessity and proportionality as follows: "Law enforcement officials may use force only when strictly necessary and to the extent required for the performance of their duty."[40] The accompanying commentary to Article 3 states, in part:

> The use of firearms is considered an extreme measure.... In general, firearms should not be used except when a suspected offender offers armed resistance or otherwise jeopardizes the lives of others and less extreme measures are not sufficient to restrain or apprehend the suspected offender.[41]

Notwithstanding the strict prohibitions on the deprivation of life, there are exceptional moments when the prohibition must be reinterpreted through the rules of a more specialized legal regime, namely in times of armed conflict through LOAC. These rules are discussed next, but suffice it to say here that a state in an armed conflict is not bound by the "ordinary" human rights principles of necessity and proportionality.[42] Instead, while human rights law continues to apply in armed conflict, some tribunals have held that LOAC rules define what constitutes an arbitrary deprivation of life of your enemy. This relationship between LOAC and human rights law is most famously articulated in the International Court of Justice's 1996 Advisory Opinion on the *Legality of the Threat or Use of Nuclear Weapons*. In the Opinion, the Court declared that human rights law is applicable during times of armed conflict, but that,

> whether a particular loss of life, through the use of a certain weapon in warfare, is to be considered an arbitrary deprivation of life contrary to Article 6 of the Covenant [on Civil and Political Rights], can only be decided by reference to the law applicable in armed conflict and not deduced from the terms of the Covenant itself.[43]

40 Code of conduct for law enforcement officials, art. 3, U.N. Doc A/RES/34/169 (Feb. 5, 1980).

41 *Id.*

42 The term "ordinary" is used to denote the application of human rights law outside of armed conflict.

43 Legality of the Threat or Use of Nuclear Weapons, 1996 I.C.J. 226 (Jul. 8), at 25. For further discussion on the relationship between international human rights law and the law of armed conflict, see, Santo Domingo Massacre v. Colombia, Preliminary Objections, Merits and Reparations, Judgment, Inter-Am. Ct. H.R. (ser C.) No. 259, para. 24 (Nov. 30, 2012); Sir Daniel Bethlehem QC, *The Relationship between International Humanitarian Law and International Human Rights Law in Situations of Armed Conflict,*

While this and other understandings of the relationship between human rights law and LOAC are important for determining the international legal obligations of a state that is party to an armed conflict, they are of limited relevance to this chapter since the "clash" of human rights law and LOAC we are dealing with does not pertain to the actions of a single state, but pertains to a clash of legal norms between two states: one being the attacking state that asserts LOAC authorities and the other being the territorial state that does not have LOAC authorities, but human rights obligations to the individual who the attacking state wishes to target with lethal force.

2 *Scope of the Prohibition on the Unlawful and Arbitrary Deprivation of Life*

The negative and positive obligations that human rights law place on states is a second component of the prohibition on the unlawful and arbitrary deprivation of life that is important to consider in our discussion of a global NIAC. Negative obligations require the state to refrain from the commission of human rights abuses against people on its territory. In simplest terms, the state is prohibited from carrying out such acts as unlawful and arbitrary killings, torture, rape, slavery, denial of due process, and other abuses. Positive obligations require the state to ensure, through legislative, judicial, administrative, educative, and other appropriate measures, the protection of individuals from human rights abuses, be it by the state, another state, or private individuals or entities.[44] As a result, under human rights law a state is prohibited from permitting another state to carry out a human rights abuse on its territory and also has obligations to prevent another state from carrying out a human rights abuse on its territory.

The obligation that the state has to protect individuals on its territory from human rights abuses committed by third parties emerged most prominently in the Inter-American human rights system. The system was confronted with a situation in which unidentified men abducted

2:2 CAMBRIDGE J. INT'L & COMP. L. 180 (2013); Jonathan Horowitz, *Human Rights, Positive Obligations, and Armed Conflict: Implementing the Right to Education in Occupied Territories*, 1:2 INT'L HUMANITARIAN LEGAL STUD. 304 (2010); Nancie Prud'homme, *Lex Specialis: Oversimplifying a More Complex and Multifaceted Relationship?*, 40:2 ISR. L. REV. 355 (2007).

[44] *See* General Comment 31: The Nature of the General Legal Obligation Imposed on States Parties to the Covenant, at 6 & 8, U.N. Doc CCPR/C/21/Rev.1/Add. 13 (2004).

people who were never to be seen again.[45] The families of the victims believed that it was most likely state agents carrying out these acts of "disappearances," many of which ended in the death of the victim. From a state liability perspective it was difficult however for the families of the disappeared to prove state involvement due to the clandestine nature of the disappearances. The Inter-American Court of Human Rights addressed this protection gap by holding the state responsible not for the disappearance *per se*, but for its failure to ensure the victim's protection from the multitude of rights that disappearances breached.[46] In the landmark case *Velasquez Rodriguez v. Honduras* the Court came to find a violation of the American Convention on Human Rights after noting that the

> obligation of the States Parties is to "ensure" the free and full exercise of the rights recognized by the Convention to every person subject to its jurisdiction. This obligation implies the duty of the States Parties to organize the governmental apparatus and, in general, all the structures through which public power is exercised, so that they are capable of juridically ensuring the free and full enjoyment of human rights. As a consequence of this obligation, the States must prevent, investigate and punish any violation of the rights recognized by the Convention and, moreover, if possible attempt to restore the right violated and provide compensation as warranted for damages resulting from the violation.[47]

The obligation on the state to ensure the enjoyment of human rights is now firmly entrenched as a mode of state liability under international and regional human rights law. For example, in *Zimbabwe Human Rights NGO Forum v. Zimbabwe*, the African Commission on Human and Peoples' Rights held that "human rights law imposes obligations on States to protect citizens or individuals under their jurisdiction from the harmful acts of others."[48] The ECtHR has taken a similar

[45] Velasquez Rodriguez v. Honduras, Judgment, Inter-Am.Ct.H.R. (ser. C) No. 4, para. 149 (Jul. 29, 1988) ("Disappearances are not new in the history of human rights violations. However, their systematic and repeated nature and their use not only for causing certain individuals to disappear, either briefly or permanently, but also as a means of creating a general state of anguish, insecurity and fear, is a recent phenomenon. Although this practice exists virtually worldwide, it has occurred with exceptional intensity in Latin America in the last few years.").

[46] *Id.* [47] *Id.* at para. 166.

[48] Zimbabwe Human Rights NGO Forum v. Zimbabwe, Af. Comm. H.R., Comm. 245/02 143 (2006). *See also* Commission nationale des droits de l'Homme et des libertés v. Chad, Af. Comm. H.R., Comm. 74/92 20 (1995) ("if a State neglects to ensure the rights in the

approach.[49] These examples speak strongly to a territorial state's obligation to prevent abuses by third parties that are regarded as being outside the sphere of state control. The obligation has been articulated in a practical fashion, recognizing that the state is not capable of preventing all crime all the time. For a finding of a violation, the ECtHR said that the state must have known or ought to have known "of the existence of a real and immediate risk to the life of an identified individual or individuals from the criminal acts of a third party and that they failed to take measures within the scope of their powers which, judged reasonably, might have been expected to avoid that risk."[50]

Relatedly, international human rights law prohibits a state to consent to – effectively enabling – another state's human rights abuses on its territory. This was demonstrated in *El-Masri v. the former Yugoslav Republic of Macedonia*, where the ECtHR found Macedonia in violation of the ECHR for permitting the United States to carry out torture and an illegal detention and transfer on its territory.[51] In that case the Court noted, a state "must be regarded as responsible under the Convention for acts performed by foreign officials on its territory with the acquiescence or connivance of its authorities."[52] It is quite likely then that the Court would not only find a territorial state at fault for permitting an unlawful and arbitrary killing by a foreign state to take place on its territory, but it might also determine that the actual consent agreement was itself a violation of the Convention. This is indicated by various decisions that have found violations based on faulty regulatory systems and operational planning that permitted, or at least failed to prevent, human rights abuses. In *McCann v. U.K.*, for example, a case relating to the United Kingdom's use of lethal force against an alleged terrorist threat, the Court outlined that a state's obligations on the use of force applied not only to when force is used, but also to pre-operation stages, noting that, "in determining whether the force used was compatible with Article 2 (art. 2), the Court must carefully scrutinize. . .whether the anti-terrorist operation was planned and controlled by the authorities so as to minimise, to the greatest extent possible, recourse to lethal force."[53] Similarly, in

African Charter, this can constitute a violation, even if the State or its agents are not the immediate cause of the violation.").

[49] *See, for example,* Osman v. United Kingdom, Eur. Ct. H.R. (1998) and Ilaşcu and Others v. Moldova and Russia, Eur. Ct. H.R. 318 (2004).

[50] Osman v. United Kingdom, *supra* note 49, at 116.

[51] El-Masri v. former Yugoslav Republic of Macedonia, Eur. Ct. H.R. (2012).

[52] *Id.* at 116. [53] McCann and Others v. United Kingdom, Eur. Ct. H.R. 193 (1995).

Giuliani and Gaggio v. Italy, the ECtHR looked at Italy's use of force regulatory system to determine if there was an Article 2 violation: "The primary duty on the State to secure the right to life entails, in particular, putting in place an appropriate legal and administrative framework defining the limited circumstances in which law enforcement officials may use force and firearms, in the light of the relevant international standards."[54] Indeed, when viewed as part of a pre-operation stage or as the regulatory system under which an attack was subject, a granting of consent that allows a foreign state to kill as a means of first resort on a host state's territory would seem to run contrary to the Court's jurisprudence on how a state must secure the right to life.

In summation, human rights law prohibits the unlawful and arbitrary deprivation of life and requires that any use of force be necessary and proportionate. These requirements necessarily prohibit lethal targeting as a means of first resort for suppressing an enemy. Human rights law also places both negative and positive obligations on the state with respect to the right to life. This includes the obligation on the state not to carry out unlawful and arbitrary killings and to take measures to protect an individual's right to life both from the state and third parties. When we apply these rules to the context of a global NIAC, we see that a state with ordinary human rights obligations to individuals within its territory is not permitted to kill unlawfully or arbitrarily, not permitted to allow a third party to kill unlawfully or arbitrarily, and must take reasonable measures to prevent unlawful and arbitrary killings generally. For these reasons, a state cannot consent to another state carrying out a killing that would amount to an unlawful or arbitrary deprivation of life on its territory.

Finally, our brief assessment of the right to life demonstrates that when a state is in an armed conflict, the prohibition on the arbitrary deprivation of life under human rights law is to be interpreted in light of relevant LOAC rules. This is of limited value to our discussion of a global NIAC however, since we are dealing with two states with competing legal regimes rather than one state trying to resolve its own competing rules. We will now turn to discuss LOAC targeting rules and privileges to gain a stronger understanding of their incompatibilities with human rights law in a global NIAC and what the corresponding consequences are of those incompatibilities.

[54] Giuliani and Gaggio v. Italy, *supra* note 37, at 209.

III Relationship Between the Territorial State's Human Rights Obligations and LOAC

Whereas human rights law applies to states in times of peace and armed conflict (and the times in between), LOAC targeting rules and privileges apply only to a state that is engaged in an armed conflict.[55] There are, generally speaking, two legal classifications of armed conflict.[56] One is IAC, which exists when two or more states are engaged in an armed conflict with one another.[57] There is also NIAC, which takes place between a state actor (or actors) and a non-state armed group (or groups), or between two or more non-state armed groups. It is worth noting that a state may be involved in both an IAC and a NIAC in the same time and place.[58]

LOAC targeting rules and privileges immediately flow once an armed conflict exists. A considerable amount of scholarly attention has been given to the issue of what constitutes a NIAC and the nature of a NIAC's geographic scope. But what is important to our discussion now is the fact that a state may only consider using its LOAC targeting privileges against those fighters who are engaged in that state's armed conflict. This is true even when there are other states involved in other armed

[55] Arts. 2 & 3 common to the Geneva Convention for the Amelioration of the Condition of the Wounded and Sick in Armed Forces in the Field, Aug. 12, 1949, 6 U.S.T. 3114, 75 U.N.T.S. 31; Geneva Convention for the Amelioration of the Condition of Wounded, Sick, and Shipwrecked Members of Armed Forces at Sea, Aug. 12, 1949, 6 U.T.S. 3217, 75 U.N.T.S. 85; Geneva Convention Relative to the Treatment of Prisoners of War, Aug. 12, 1949, 6 U.S.T. 3316, 75 U.N.T.S. 135; Geneva Convention Relative to the Protection of Civilian Persons in Time of War, Aug. 12, 1949, 6 U.S.T. 3516, 75 U.N.T.S. 287 [hereinafter Common art. 2 and Common art. 3]

[56] Despite there being two legal classifications of armed conflicts, all IACs and all NIACs are not the same. For a discussion on armed conflict typologies *see, for example*, Sylvain Vité, *Typology of armed conflicts in international humanitarian law: legal concepts and actual situations*, 91:873 INT'L REV. RED CROSS 69 (2009).

[57] With respect to the applicability of LOAC in international armed conflict, Common art. 2 also states that, "The Convention shall also apply to all cases of partial or total occupation of the territory of a High Contracting Party, even if the said occupation meets with no armed resistance."

Protocol Additional to the Geneva Conventions of 12 August 1949, and Relating to the Protection of Victims of International Armed Conflicts, art. 1(4), Jun. 8, 1977, 1125 U.N.T.S. 3 also notes that its rules apply in "armed conflicts in which peoples are fighting against colonial domination and alien occupation and against racist régimes in the exercise of their right to self-determination."

[58] Tadić v. Prosecutor, Case No. IT-94-1-AR72; 35 ILM (1996) 32, I.C.T.Y. (Oct. 2, 1995), at 73 (Noting that the parties to the conflict in the former Yugoslavia considered the situations, "at different times and places as either internal or international armed conflicts, or as a mixed internal-international conflict.") *See also* Vité, *supra* note 56, at 85–7.

conflicts all on the same territory. Franconia, which in our hypothetical is not engaged in an armed conflict with Arcadia's enemy, therefore does not have a LOAC relationship with respect to Arcadia's enemy.

A second aspect of LOAC that is important to our discussion is that LOAC, as noted briefly above, provides more permissible rules for how and when a state may kill compared to "ordinary" human rights law. This is relevant to our discussion because it reveals a significant tension between the territorial state's human rights obligations and the attacking state's targeting privileges under LOAC. This tension can be described as follows: A territorial state that is not a party to the attacking state's so-called global NIAC has obligations to prevent the arbitrary deprivation of life as a matter strictly of human rights law, whereas the attacking state is seeking the consent of the territorial state to take life under the more permissible rules of LOAC.

The tension between the attacking state's claim to LOAC targeting privileges and the territorial state's human rights obligations is largely a result of LOAC having no principles of necessity and proportionality analogous to those found in ordinary human rights law. As Geoffrey S. Corn explained, "peacetime self-defense. . .justifies a State's use of deadly military force only as a measure of last resort. In contrast, *jus in bello* necessity authorizes the use of deadly combat power against an enemy as a measure of first resort."[59] LOAC, thus, does contain a rule of necessity (commonly referred to as "military necessity"), but it relates to the fighting force's necessity to destroy its adversary. For example, under LOAC, a military force may attack, with lethal force, a non-state fighter who is planning to destroy the military's communications towers while putting no person's safety directly or immediately at risk. Similarly, LOAC may permit the killing of an enemy as they sleep in their barracks, something that ordinary human rights law would never permit a state to do. This concept of "military necessity," when applied to armed conflict targeting rules, is radically dissimilar to the concept of "necessity" under ordinary human rights law, which is tested against an imminent risk to life or serious injury. As Corn concluded, "armed conflict triggers authority to employ force in a manner that would rarely (if ever) be tolerated in peacetime."[60]

59 Geoffrey F. Corn, *Self-defense Targeting: Blurring the Line between the Jus ad Bellum and the Jus in Bello*, 88 Int'l L. Stud. 57, 68 (2012) (the full quote is, "Like peacetime self-defense, jus ad bellum self-defense justifies a State's use of deadly military force only as a measure of last resort.").

60 *Id.* at 68.

LOAC also has no analogous definition of proportionality as it exists under ordinary human rights law. The rule of proportionality in LOAC – one of LOAC's core principles – is of an entirely different nature, one that regulates the relationship between military advantage and incidental civilian harm.[61] LOAC permits a degree of incidental harm to civilian and civilian property as a consequence of an attack against a military objective. Thus, warring parties are prohibited only from carrying out "an attack which may be expected to cause incidental loss of civilian life, injury to civilians, damage to civilian objects, or a combination thereof, which would be excessive in relation to the concrete and direct military advantage anticipated."[62] Ordinary human rights law, in contrast, uses the term "proportionality" most often to regulate the amount of force that can be used against the threat itself as well as to assess whether it was justifiable for bystanders to be harmed. In other words, human rights law requires the state to ask itself: Must I use rubber bullets instead of live ammunition against a group of approaching violent protesters?[63] Must I first shoot warning shots before I shoot at them directly? LOAC requires the state to ask: When I kill my enemy (by almost whatever means I chose), what will be the civilian harm?

IV The Legal Impermissibility of a "Global NIAC" and Legally Permissible Alternatives

1 The Impermissible Global NIAC

Now that we have reviewed the various rules of public international law that are at play in a so-called global NIAC, we will now turn to an evaluation of whether a global NIAC can be legally permissible. An

[61] *See, for example, Id.* at 70–2.

[62] Protocol Additional to the Geneva Conventions of 12 August 1949, *supra* note 57, at art. 51(5)(b). This is an accepted rule of customary international law in both NIACs and IACs. For supporting materials see JEAN-MARIE HENCKAERTS & LOUISE DOSWALD-BECK, CUSTOMARY INTERNATIONAL HUMANITARIAN LAW, VOLUME I: RULES 46–7 (2005).

[63] *See, for example,* Simsek and Others v. Turkey, *supra* note 25, at 108 ("The Court repeats that the use of force may be justified under Article 2 § 2 (c), in cases where the action is taken for the purpose of quelling a riot or insurrection. However in the instant case, the submissions of the applicants and the decision of the Trabzon Assize Court show that, in order to disperse the crowd, officers shot directly at the demonstrators without first having recourse to less life-threatening methods, such as tear gas, water cannons or rubber bullets. In this connection, the Court observes that Turkish legislation allows police officers to use firearms only in limited and special circumstances. However, it appears that this principle was not applied during the Gazi and Ümraniye incidents.").

evaluation of the legal permissibility of a global NIAC is especially important because the claim that "[t]here is nothing in international law that . . .prohibits us from using lethal force against our enemies outside of an active battlefield, at least when the country involved consents or is unable or unwilling to take action against the threat,"[64] has far reaching concerns and consequences, as set out in the introduction. Given these implications, is such extensive legal disarray really what international law permits? Or, is the notion of a global NIAC flawed? And, if so, why is a global NIAC legally flawed?

For the proponents of a global NIAC who believe that an attacking state does not require the consent of the territorial state to target its enemy, this chapter has shown that such a claim incorrectly places LOAC (and the attacking state's national interests) above one of the most basic principles of international law, namely the prohibition on the use of force against another state. A "no-consent global NIAC" is, therefore, directly at odds with the requirement under international law that each time a state in a NIAC wishes to cross an international border to use force anew it must press the proverbial "start over" button and reassess the rules of applicable international law. This requires the state to question: Does the U.N. Security Council, doctrine of self-defense, or the territorial state's consent permit me to use force? The wrong question to ask first is: Am I in an armed conflict?

Several scholars and experts have recognized the need for taking a holistic approach to evaluating extraterritorial use of force and have noted that "other bodies of international law may well limit where operations attendant to such conflict may be conducted."[65] Sean Murphy also took into consideration all relevant parts of international law when he assessed the legality of U.S. premeditated cross-border operations from Afghanistan into another country; its "hot pursuit" cross-border operations from Afghanistan into Pakistan; and its unmanned aerial vehicle attacks in Pakistan. For each one of these categories of operations, Murphy took into account the prohibition on the use of force; the right to self-defense; whether Pakistan provided its

[64] Brennan, *supra* note 1. *See also* Applicability of Federal Criminal Laws and the Constitution to Contemplated Lethal Operations Against Shaykh Anwar al-Aulaqi, *supra* note 1.

[65] Schmitt, *supra* note 16, at 19; and Michael N. Schmitt, *Guest Post: A Step in the Wrong Direction: The EU Parliament's Drone Resolution*, JustSecurity.org, Mar. 7, 2014, *available at* http://justsecurity.org/7926/step-wrong-direction-eu-parliaments-drone-resolution-schmitt/.

consent; whether the U.N. Security Council sanctioned the cross-border operations; the target's status (i.e., a member of the Taliban or Al Qaeda); and the threat that the target posed.[66] Christof Heyns, the United Nations Special Rapporteur on extrajudicial, summary, or arbitrary executions, similarly agrees that a proper assessment of the lawfulness of extraterritorial use of force can only be accomplished in such a holistic and comprehensive manner.[67] In the context of "drone" strikes, he wrote:

> A central point made by the Special Rapporteur is that a holistic approach is needed in order to protect the right to life. For a particular drone strike to be lawful under international law it must satisfy the legal requirements under all applicable international legal regimes. Although a particular drone strike may satisfy the requirements for the use of inter-State force, it may nevertheless be inconsistent with applicable rules of international humanitarian law and international human rights law, or vice versa, and thus unlawful under international law. The right to life can be adequately secured only if all the distinct requirements posed by the various constitutive parts of international law are met.[68]

For those who believe that consent is required in a global NIAC, the question then turns to whether international law permits the territorial state to allow the attacking state to target an enemy who is 1) within the territorial state's borders and 2) is not in an armed conflict with the territorial state. Dehn answered this question in the following manner: "The international human rights obligations of a territorial state should be understood to place constraints [on] the use of force by an attacking state, particularly when the territorial state consents to the attacks but is not party to an armed conflict with the relevant non-state actor."[69] Heyns has also added his voice to those who recognize that human rights law

[66] *See generally* Sean D. Murphy, *The International Legality of US Military Cross-Border Operations from Afghanistan into Pakistan*, 85 Int'l L. Stud. 109 (2009).

[67] Heyns, *supra* note 3, at 24.

[68] *Id. See also* European Parliament, resolution on the use of armed drones, 2014/2567(RSP) (Feb. 27, 2014), at E & F ("E. whereas drone strikes outside a declared war by a state on the territory of another state without the consent of the latter or of the UN Security Council constitute a violation of international law and of the territorial integrity and sovereignty of that country; F. whereas international human rights law prohibits arbitrary killings in any situation; whereas international humanitarian law does not permit the targeted killing of persons who are located in non-belligerent states.").

[69] Dehn, *supra* note 9, at 90. For a similar discussion on the relationship between human rights obligations and consent, *see generally* Rijie Ernie Gao, *Between a Rock and a Hard Place: Tensions Between the U.S.-ROK Status of Forces Agreement and the Duty to Ensure Individual Rights Under the ICCPR*, 33:2 Fordham Int'l L.J. 585 (2009) (arguing that the Republic of Korea's human rights obligations are at odds with the contents of the SOFA it

may have limiting factors on a geographically unconstrained application of LOAC. With a focus on the relationship between targeted killings, human rights, and consent, he explained:

> States cannot consent to the violation of their obligations under international humanitarian law or international human rights law. A State that consents to the activities of another State on its territory remains bound by its own human rights obligations, including to ensure respect for human rights and thus to prevent violations of the right to life, to the extent that it is able to do so.[70]

These conclusions, in the author's view, give proper deference to the territorial state's human rights obligations when it is not a party to the same armed conflict as the attacking state. The conclusions are also in keeping with the legal principle that one may not transfer more legal rights than one has, which Hargrove and Deeks have cited in their articles on consent-based use of force abroad.[71] Under this principle a territorial state (Franconia) cannot permit the attacking state (Arcadia) to target an individual who the territorial state is not in an armed conflict with. Whereas Arcadia may claim that it can rely on LOAC rules because it is in an armed conflict with its target, Franconia cannot make a similar claim because it is in no such armed conflict with that same target. Franconia does not have the legal authority to permit Arcadia to conduct LOAC targeting operations on its territory because Franconia has no LOAC rights to "give away."

In assessing the relationship between the attacking state's claim to LOAC targeting privileges and the territorial state's obligations under human rights law, it is also important to recall that we are being presented with a competition between those things that a state claims it has the *authority* to do, and those things that a state is *required* to do. LOAC grants a state the permission to target its enemies, but it leaves it up to the state to choose whether it wants to do so or not. To put it bluntly, LOAC does not require a state at war to kill. It merely allows it to do so. Laurie Blank points out, "Military necessity is . . . a principle of authority: the authority to use force to accomplish strategic and national security goals."[72] This is in contrast to human rights law, which requires

signed with the United States pertaining to criminal jurisdiction over U.S. military personnel).

[70] Heyns, *supra* note 3, at 38. [71] *Supra* note 29.

[72] *See* Laurie R. Blank, *Chapter 11: Debates and Dichotomies: Exploring the Presumptions Underlying Contentions About the Geography of Armed Conflict*, 16 Y.B. INT'L HUMANITARIAN L. 297, 305 (2013).

the state to respect the prohibition on the arbitrary deprivation of life. This includes the negative obligation not to carry out an arbitrary deprivation of life and the positive obligation to prevent an arbitrary deprivation of life. In determining the relationship between *privileges* and *obligations*, it would seem logical that it is the obligations that take priority, however unfortunate that may be for the attacking state.[73]

2 *Issues of Normative Conflict*

All this being said, is not uncommon for a single state to enter into competing legal agreements. In the case before us, these competing legal agreements (the territorial state's human rights treaty and its subsequent bilateral agreement with the attacking state) bring rise to an apparent norm conflict. Therefore, it is necessary to consider what international law says about such situations.[74]

The International Law Commission's "Study Group on the Fragmentation of International Law: difficulties arising from the diversification and expansion of international law," noted, "It is by now well settled that in cases of conflict, the issue is not with invalidity but relative priority between treaties." It goes on to recognize, however, that it is clearly unsatisfactory that Article 30 of the Vienna Convention on the Law of Treaties (VCLT) "leaves open some of the most difficult questions" and that a "party that has concluded incompatible agreements will have a

[73] For a discussion on how this issue is resolved in a single-state scenario, *see* Marko Milanović, *Norm Conflict in International Law: Whither Human Rights?*, 20 Duke J. Comp. & Int'l L. 69, 72 (2009) (noting that some have argued that when competition arises for a State between an obligation and a right, a norm conflict does not need to result in a breach because "the state can choose not to exercise its right pursuant to one norm, and thus comply with its obligation from the other"). *See also* Wilfred Jenks, *The Conflict of Law-Making Treaties*, 30 Brit. Y.B. Int'l L. 401, 451 (1953) ("There is no conflict if the obligation of one instrument are stricter than, but not incompatible with, those of another, or if it is possible to comply with the obligations of one instrument by refraining from exercising a privilege or discretion accorded by another . . .").

[74] This topic has received significant scholarly and judicial attention. *See, for example*, The Vienna Conventions on the Law of Treaties: A Commentary, Volume 1 (Olivier Corten & Pierre Klein eds., 2011); Isabel Feichtner, *The Waiver Power of the WTO: Opening the WTO for Political Debate on the Reconciliation of Competing Interests*, 20:3 Eur. J. Int'l L. 615 (2009); Jenks, *supra* note 73, at 452; Ralf Michaels & Joost Pauwelyn, *Conflict of Norms or Conflict of Laws?: Different Techniques in the Fragmentation of Public International Law*, 22 Duke J. Comp. & Int'l L. 349 (2012); Milanović, *supra* note 73.

right of election as to which agreement it will fulfil and which of its parties will have to satisfy itself with State responsibility."[75]

While the VCLT may produce an unsatisfactory result with regard to harmonizing norm conflicts generally, the VCLT and human rights jurisprudence seems to be not so ambiguous when it comes to human rights law. As noted earlier, states cannot enter into agreements that violate peremptory norms, which would include such human rights violations as torture and slavery. Also, Article 41 of the VCLT, which addresses agreements that states can make to modify multilateral treaties between certain but not all parties, does not pertain to the modification of "a provision, derogation from which is incompatible with the effective execution of the object and purpose of the treaty as a whole."[76] Certainly, the protections afforded to the non-derogable right to life in international and regional human rights treaties would appear to be a major component of the object and purpose of regional and international human rights treaties.[77] Therefore a state party to the ICCPR could not opt out of its Article 6 obligations in order to enter into an agreement that allows a foreign state to kill someone on its territory.

Human rights obligations are afforded special protection in other ways. Alexander Orakhelashvili has noted that agreements with a humanitarian character receive special protections under Article 60 of the VCLT that guard them from being terminated by a bilateral agreement that is not of a humanitarian character.[78] He has concluded, "Practice has formulated an approach implicitly based on hierarchical priority of human rights and humanitarian treaties over other conflicting

[75] *Fragmentation of International Law: Difficulties Arising from the Diversification and Expansion of International Law: Report of the Study Group of the International Law Commission*, International Law Commission, 58th Sess., at 320, A/CN.4/L.682 (Apr. 13, 2006).

[76] Vienna Convention on the Law of Treaties of 1969, *supra* note 25, art. 41.

[77] *See, for example*, General Comment 24: Issues Relating to Reservations Made upon Ratification or Accession to the Covenant or the Optional Protocols thereto, or in Relation to Declarations under Article 41 of the Covenant, U.N. Doc. CCPR/C/21/Rev.1/Add.6, at 10 (1994) (explaining that a reservation to the prohibition on the right to life would offend against the object and purpose of the Covenant both because of its non-derogable status and its status as a peremptory norm).

[78] Alexander Orakhelashvili, *Article 30 (1969)*, *in* The Vienna Conventions on the Law of Treaties: A Commentary, Volume 1 793 (Olivier Corten & Pierre Klein eds., 2011). *See also* Thomas Giegerich, *Article 60. Termination or suspension of the operation of a treaty as a consequence of its breach*, *in* The Vienna Conventions on the Law of Treaties: A Commentary, Volume 1 1045–7 (Oliver Dörr & Kirsten Schmalenbach eds., 2012).

treaties."[79] The Human Rights Committee, for example, has recognized that states may find themselves in situations of conflicting norms, but that the ICCPR prevails. In *Kindler v. Canada*, the Committee held,

> States parties to the Covenant will often also be party to various bilateral obligations, including those under extradition treaties. A State party to the Covenant is required to ensure that it carries out all its other legal commitments in a manner consistent with the Covenant. The starting point for an examination of this issue must be the obligation of the State party under article 2, paragraph 1, of the Covenant, namely, to ensure to all individuals within its territory and subject to its jurisdiction the rights recognized in the Covenant. The right to life is the most essential of these rights.
>
> If a State party extradites a person within its jurisdiction in circumstances such that as a result there is a real risk that his or her rights under the Covenant will be violated in another jurisdiction, the State party itself may be in violation of the Covenant.[80]

The ECtHR has taken a similar approach when the issue has arisen with respect to extradition agreements between states[81] and state agreements with international organizations.[82] The current case law seems to rest on the Court's interpretation that "[t]he State is considered to retain Convention liability in respect of treaty commitments subsequent to the entry into force of the Convention."[83] A consequence – indeed the purpose – of the Court's rulings on this issue was to ensure that states did not evade their ECHR responsibilities by allowing another entity to do what the consenting state itself was prohibited from doing. Thus, a state's consent to another state's action does not relieve the consenting state from liability for the actions that the other state may undertake. As the Court held in *Bosphorus Hava Yollari Turizm Ve Ticaret Anonim Şirketi v. Ireland*, "the Court has recognised that absolving Contracting States completely from their Convention responsibility in the areas covered by such

[79] Orakhelashvili, *supra* note 78, at 793.

[80] Kindler v. Canada, H.R.C, at 13.1–2, U.N. Doc. CCPR/C/48/D/470/1991 (1993).

[81] *See generally* Soering v. United Kingdom, Eur. Ct. H.R. (1989).

[82] *See generally* Matthews v. United Kingdom, Eur. Ct. H.R. (1999).

[83] Al-Saadoon and Mufdhi v. United Kingdom, Eur. Ct. H.R. 128 (2010) (The Court also stated, "the obligation under Article 3 of the Convention not to surrender a fugitive to another State where there were substantial grounds for believing that he would be in danger of being subjected to torture or inhuman or degrading treatment or punishment was held to override the United Kingdom's obligations under the Extradition Treaty it had concluded with the United States in 1972").

a transfer [of sovereign powers] would be incompatible with the purpose and object of the Convention; the guarantees of the Convention could be limited or excluded at will, thereby depriving it of its peremptory character and undermining the practical and effective nature of its safeguards."[84] Antonios Tzanakopoulos noted that this type of argumentation "could be seen as an implementation of the maxim *nemo plus juris transferre potest quam ipse habet*. One may not circumvent limitations on the exercise of power by conferring the power to someone else."[85]

What can be concluded from this is that public international law may not resolve in its entirety the problem of conflicting international norms, but there appears to be a strong resistance, reflected through the content of the VCLT and judicial practice, that states that enter into agreements that conflict with their human rights treaty obligations, be it through their own actions or through the powers they bestow upon others, can be found to be in breach of those human rights obligations. If this is the case, then a bilateral agreement that allows the attacking state to carry out LOAC targeting would not invalidate the territorial state's human rights obligations, nor would priority be given to the bilateral agreement. Instead, the territorial state's consent to the LOAC operation would be a violation of its human rights obligations if the territorial state were not in an armed conflict with the targeted individual. It is therefore hard to imagine how a global NIAC can be made permissible under international law if the territorial state's consent is necessarily a breach of its obligations under international human rights law.

3 *Legally Permissible Alternatives*

This chapter, while concluding that a consent-based global NIAC is made impermissible under international law by the territorial state's human rights obligations, does not seek to challenge other rules under international law that permit a state to defend itself from a non-state group acting abroad. It is quite possible in fact that many of the actions that a state may wish to undertake under the banner of a global NIAC could be

[84] Bosphorus Hava Yollari Turizm Ve Ticaret Anonim Şirketi v. Ireland, Eur. Ct. H.R. 154 (2005).

[85] Antonios Tzanakopoulos, *Kadi and the Solange Argument in International Law*, EJIL-Talk.org, Jan. 15, 2013, *available at* www.ejiltalk.org/kadi-and-the-solange-argument-in-international-law-2/.

taken through other legally permissible use-of-force frameworks. For example, if Franconia was in an armed conflict with the sub-commander with whom Arcadia wished to target, Arcadia could carry out a LOAC attack if it became a party to Franconia's armed conflict. Or, if Franconia were not in an armed conflict with the sub-commander with whom Arcadia wished to target, Arcadia could, without Franconia's consent, target the sub-commander – though not necessarily lethally – if his actions met the self-defense test under the laws of sovereignty.

The distinction between using a legally permissible framework or a legally impermissible framework is critically important even if the material difference is negligible. This is because the concept of a global NIAC stands for something far greater than the consequences of any single lethal attack or group of lethal attacks that a state may wish to carry out. A global NIAC, if it were to be legally permissible, would permit a state to engage in a never-ending war in which human rights law would be sidelined and the more permissible LOAC targeting rules would be routinely applied without geographic constraint. What comes with this is a legal framework that dramatically expands state use of force beyond what international law had envisaged to date. This is most acutely seen by the global NIAC's assertion that LOAC rules can apply nearly everywhere, despite their generally intended use for scenarios where a state is under such threat that the normal machinery of law enforcement and due process guarantees is not enough to defeat a well-organized enemy that has the resources and capabilities to jeopardize the security of the state.

To better illustrate alternatives to a global NIAC, here are several legal avenues permissible under international law that states may use to defend themselves from violent non-state groups:

- *Territorial State Action*: The attacking state, instead of carrying out an operation, may ask the territorial state to take action. This has to be done within the confines of the law, and might result in, *inter alia*, the territorial state detaining, arresting, prosecuting, or extraditing the targeted individual. In exceptional circumstances, the use of force, including lethal force, may result lawfully when done proportionately and out of necessity, as those terms are defined under human rights law. It is not beyond the realm of possibility that situations could arise where the territorial state could derogate from its human rights treaty obligations, thereby allowing it to carry out a more "robust" law enforcement operation. But such derogation can be made only in so far as the derogation is within the bounds of what is permissible under relevant international law.[86]

- *Consent-Based Armed Conflict*: In instances where the territorial state is engaged in a NIAC with the same individual(s) who the foreign state wishes to target, the territorial state may request the foreign state to join its armed conflict. The territorial state may also accept offers of a foreign state's armed support to the armed conflict. Under these conditions, the foreign state may find itself becoming a party to the territorial state's armed conflict and, implicitly, be permitted to rely on LOAC targeting rules.
- *Inherent Right to Self-Defense*: Some have argued that a state that is the object of an armed attack by a non-state group may claim an inherent right to self-defense. This right would exist regardless of the territorial state's consent. Important to the invocation of self-defense, but not discussed in this chapter, is both a consideration of what constitutes an "armed attack" and what amount and type of force is permitted when a claim of self-defense is made.[87]
- *United Nations Security Council Authorization*: An attacking state may seek and obtain Security Council authorization to respond with force to an armed attack by a non-state group.[88]
- *"Law Enforcement" Consent*: A territorial state may allow another state to use force on its territory provided that the consent only permits the attacking state to operate within the confines of the law, in particular international human rights law. To do this, the consent agreement must, amongst a myriad of issues, recognize that there is a prioritization of capture over kill and, therefore, the consent agreement would necessarily have to include a detailed detention scheme. It is not beyond the realm of possibility that situations could arise where the territorial state could derogate from its human rights treaty obligations,

[86] *See generally* General Comment 29: States of Emergency (Article 4), U.N. Doc CCPR/C/21/Rev.1/Add.11 (2001); A. and Others v. the United Kingdom, Eur. Ct. H.R. 173–90 (2009).

[87] The author recognizes that there is debate over whether a state can invoke a right to self-defense under Article 51 in response to an attack by a non-state group. The U.N. Security Council seems to have determined that it can, having passed resolutions that recognize the right to self-defense in the context of non-state terrorist attacks. *See* S.C. Res. 1368, U.N. Doc. S/RES/1368 (2001) ("Recognizing the inherent right of individual or collective self-defence in accordance with the Charter"). *See also* S.C. Res. 1373, U.N. Doc. S/RES/1373 (2001). For further discussion, *see* John Cerone, *Misplaced Reliance on the "Law of War,"* 14:1 New Eng. J. Int'l & Comp. L. 57, 59–60 (2007).

[88] Dinstein, *supra* note 3, at 308–9.

thereby allowing the territorial state to permit the attacking state to conduct a more "robust" law enforcement operation. But such derogations can be made only in so far as the derogation is within the bounds of what is permissible under relevant international law.[89]

- *Emergence of Armed Conflict*: It is conceivable that any of the aforementioned scenarios could develop into a NIAC where the full breadth of applicable LOAC comes into force (alongside international human rights law). For this to occur the threshold for a NIAC would have to be reached and LOAC's permissive targeting rules would then apply between the relevant parties and individuals.

V Conclusion

This chapter analyzes the public international law of interstate use of force, human rights law, and LOAC to demonstrate that the concept of a global NIAC cannot exist without there being a violation of international law, although notably the violation that this chapter focuses on is that of the territorial state rather than the attacking state. This conclusion is based on the following argumentation, as applied to the hypothetical scenario from the introduction:

Franconia has human rights obligations to the people in its territory. These include negative obligations that prohibit Franconia from committing unlawful and arbitrary killings and positive obligations that require Franconia to prevent Arcadia from committing unlawful and arbitrary killings. Because Franconia is not in an armed conflict, Franconia must carry out these obligations under the ordinary interpretations of human rights law and not through LOAC interpretations. Based on these obligations, Franconia must therefore refuse to grant its consent to Arcadia's requests to use LOAC targeting rules to kill the rebel sub-commander who is on Franconia's territory. This is because LOAC targeting rules, which do not apply to Franconia, are inherently incompatible with the ordinary human rights obligations that apply to Franconia. It is equally clear that if Arcadia carries out the attack without Franconia's consent, it would be doing so in breach of international law, unless Arcadia can make a claim that the attack was carried out lawfully under the rules of self-defense or with United Nations Security Council authorization.

[89] *Supra* note 86.

As this demonstrates, human rights law creates a legal barrier that prevents LOAC from jumping from one state to another, which is the defining characteristic of a global NIAC. This does not mean, as this chapter explains, that states cannot respond to attacks and threats from non-state groups while complying with international law. It means that advocates of a global NIAC must use other sources of international law to justify the extraterritorial use of force that they think a global NIAC makes legally possible. Whether states will take such action to render the concept of a global NIAC extinct is a different matter. It would require nothing less than the territorial state respecting its human rights obligations and asserting its sovereignty within the extremely politicized and highly insecure sphere of terrorism, counterterrorism, and armed conflict. This is a particularly tall order for a territorial state when the request comes from an attacking state that has considerable military, political, and economic resources to provide or withhold. To ensure the territorial state complies with international law will require sustained focus and intensified discussions on the legal obligations of the territorial state and will have to include holding the territorial states accountable for its breach of international law. It is equally important that territorial states and attacking states utilize and strengthen the various lawful means outlined in this chapter to address non-state actors. Not to do so threatens to make the global NIAC the default framework that states use to address the real (and sometimes not so real) threats that non-state actors pose.

6

Folk International Law

9/11 Lawyering and the Transformation of the Law of Armed Conflict to Human Rights Policy and Human Rights Law to War Governance

NAZ K. MODIRZADEH*

"We're in a new kind of war, and we've made very clear that it is important that this new kind of war be fought on different battlefields."

– Condoleezza Rice, November 2002[1]

"The United States agrees that it must conform its actions to all applicable law. As I have explained, as a matter of international law, the United States is in an armed conflict with al-Qaeda, as well as the Taliban and associated forces, in response to the horrific 9/11 attacks, and may use force consistent with its inherent right to self-defense under international law."

– Harold Hongju Koh, March 2010[2]

Introduction

On March 25, 2010, State Department Legal Adviser Harold Koh, a prominent and well-respected international lawyer, human rights scholar, and former Dean of the Yale Law School, gave an address at the American Society of International Law Annual Meeting, laying out, for the first time, the Obama Administration's perspective on the legality of the so-called

* This chapter is an abridged version of Naz K. Modirzadeh, *Folk International Law: 9/11 Lawyering and the Transformation of the Law of Armed Conflict to Human Rights Policy and Human Rights Law to War Governance*, 5 Harv. Nat. Sec. J. 225–304 (2014), and is republished with the permission of the journal. For reasons of space, many non-essential citations, references, and qualifying comments were removed.

1 Condoleezza Rice on Fox News Sunday, Fox News (November 11, 2002), www.foxnews.com/story/0,2933,69783,00.html [http://perma.law.harvard.edu/04pjFndWstN].

2 Harold Koh, Legal Advisor to the U.S. Dep't of State, Speech at the American Society of International Law: The Obama Administration and International Law (March 25, 2010), available at www.state.gov/s/l/releases/remarks/139119.htm [hereafter: ASIL Speech].

"war on terror." It was a heavy moment. By that time, news had come out that President Obama and his team had approved a massive increase in the use of CIA-led weaponized unmanned aerial vehicles (drones) outside the conflict in Afghanistan, with numerous strikes in Pakistan and elsewhere. Many in the fields of international humanitarian law ("IHL") and international human rights law ("IHRL") had high expectations for both the Obama Administration and Harold Koh. Indeed, many hoped that Dean Koh would restate the commitment of the U.S. to international law, distance the Obama Administration from these secretive attacks, and mark the firm and final end to the Bush-era "global war on terrorism."

That did not happen. Instead, Koh articulated the "Law of 9/11,"[3] largely reiterated the previous Administration's understanding of an ongoing armed conflict between the United States and al Qaeda and justified the use of lethal force across multiple "battlefields" spanning the globe. Many in IHL and IHRL, by that point, had struggled for years with the U.S. government against the claim that international law was "quaint," with the Bush Administration seeming to reject the idea that international law – as law – had any place in this new war. International law certainly played a role in Koh's speech that March day, but in ways that those who had long awaited that moment could not have expected. It was, for many, a depressing day in what had been a depressing decade. Three years later, as the end of the Obama Administration's first term neared, the executive's publicly asserted legal basis for key facets of the prosecution of the "war on terrorism" – not least, the targeted killing of Americans and foreigners "associated" with al-Qaeda anywhere at any time – remained strikingly opaque and strikingly innovative in comparison to well-established international humanitarian law, *jus ad bellum*, and international human rights law.

But that is the end of the story. This chapter starts with the beginning.

This chapter seeks to track the debates within the two disciplines central to the international legal regulation of the U.S. use of force that led to this moment. Debates within and across the fields of IHL and IHRL, and the disintegration of the boundaries between these two fields of law, seemed to have played, if unwittingly, into arguments that Koh made that day and that the Obama Administration continues to promote as of this writing.

[3] Koh appears to have coined this term, referring to "what I call the Law of 9/11: detentions, use of force, and prosecution." ASIL Speech.

The arc of this story demonstrates a real-world convergence between international human rights law, as interpreted and applied largely through U.S. constitutional law, and international humanitarian law. This convergence conflates and confounds long-standing principles and rules of both branches of public international law. Convergence of IHL and IHRL is often presented as a victory for humanitarianism - a move toward a single body of international law that protects individuals in all circumstances, in all places, in an almost borderless conception of the world. In a previous article,[4] I raised a number of criticisms of the extraterritorial application of human rights law in armed conflict, and I questioned the theoretical and practical grounds for full extraterritorial application of human rights on top of and within IHL. One of the main doctrinal and operational criticisms of convergence is that it dilutes the clarity of the law of armed conflict. A far less common critique is that it also dilutes the clarity and moral resonance of human rights law and human rights advocacy by introducing IHL's often brutal balance between military necessity and humanity into situations that would otherwise be governed by more restrictive approaches, especially regarding the right not to be arbitrarily deprived of life.

This chapter develops that criticism by pointing to a practical cost of convergence: the dilution and weakening of international law-based arguments against the U.S. government's legal construction of the "war on terror." The thickly legal construction of the Obama Administration's global war on al-Qaeda, the Taliban, and associated forces was enabled in part by U.S.-based human rights and IHL lawyers who, over the past decade and in the face of a perceived existential threat to their relevance, traded in certain principles for (potential) influence on executive decision-making. These lawyers and advocates helped to fuel the Obama Administration's articulation of its legal basis for the use of force against al-Qaeda and others by making use of "folk international law," a law-like discourse that relies on a confusing and soft admixture of IHL, *jus ad bellum*, and IHRL to frame operations that do not, ultimately, seem to be bound by international law - or at least by any conception of international law recognizable to international lawyers, especially non-Americans.

[4] Naz K. Modirzadeh, *The Dark Sides of Convergence: A Pro-Civilian Critique of the Extraterritorial Application of Human Rights Law in Armed Conflict*, 86 Int'l L. Stud. Ser. U.S. Naval War Col. 349 (2010).

The practical impact of convergence and the extent to which convergence has confused and diluted the sharpness of law, as well as the division of labor between two fields of legal professionals, must be seen against the backdrop of the incredibly intense debate over central concepts of international law and the "war on terror" since September 2001. As will be demonstrated, while this debate and this major shift occurred within the field of elite international lawyers working in the United States, the Bush and Obama Administrations developed a number of legal strategies that depended on diluting the boundaries between various fields of international law and diminishing the clarity of binding rules and fields of legal application.

Two narratives fuel this story. The first is the uneasy relationship between U.S.-focused IHL and IHRL legal professionals and scholars and the rather thinly articulated doctrine of convergence, being worked out while each field was also marshaling its resources to fight the battle of its life against the Bush Administration's attack on international law in the early 2000s. The second is the government's position that international law and the boundaries it prescribed needed to be made more flexible in order to facilitate the fight against a transnational terrorist organization that had made clear its intent to murder many thousands of individuals across the world. As these two narratives collided, human rights law and humanitarian law themselves changed, as did their practices.

This chapter presents a chronological journey through these shifts and proceeds in four parts. It examines three discourses: the position of the Bush and Obama Administrations; the simultaneous and often overlapping debates within and between international humanitarian law and human rights law; and the key themes that were the focus of pitched battles. The debate among lawyers in this intense period is significant for its impact on international legal discourse, and as a demonstration of how international legal projects forged in crisis can influence and reshape not only the state, but also the disciplines themselves.

Part I of the chapter focuses on the immediate aftermath of 9/11 (2001–2003), and presents the key international legal theme of that era as focused on the debate over whether the "war on terror" should be properly thought of as a "war" or as a global law enforcement operation. Part II explores the next phase (2003–2006), beginning with the war in Iraq and ending with the U.S. Supreme Court decision in *Hamdan v. Rumsfeld*. It explores the debate over what law applied to detainees captured during the "war on terror," and how that war, if it was one, ought to be classified within IHL. Part III covers the period directly after *Hamdan* through the early months of the Obama Administration (2006–2009), and presents the stakes of the highly technical debate over the notion of the direct participation of civilians in hostilities. Part IV moves to the period of 2009 to the present, focusing on the changes in rhetoric and legal discourse of the Obama Administration and the two disciplines' responses. This last part submits that the field of argumentation over the use of CIA-led lethal operations – also known as "targeted killings" – away from the recognized battlefield is profoundly diminished as a result of the compromises made within and between the disciplines along the way. It concludes that four outcomes emerge from a decade of debate within and between IHL and IHRL: convergence as purported law, convergence as lawyering, the flattening of the distinction between international and non-international armed conflict, and the blurring of civilian immunity and combatant targetability.

I. 2001–2003: The War Versus Law Enforcement Model

A. U.S. Government

As the government's arguments from this period are well-known, for present purposes I merely note the central claims and legal rhetorical positions, which were often perceived by those receiving them less as legal arguments and more as the international law equivalent of being told to take a hike:

- The United States is at war. In this war, the President is authorized to "use all necessary and appropriate force against those nations, organizations, or persons he determines planned, authorized, committed, or aided" the attacks of September 11th carried out by al-Qaeda.[5]
- Everything is up for grabs. The Administration may or may not utilize existing international and domestic law in order to pursue its aims, but all of this is being reevaluated and reconsidered in light of the current threat.[6] The executive branch is the only decision-maker in determining the legal framework applicable to the war on terror, and it alone

[5] Authorization for Use of Military Force, S.J. Res. 23, 107th Cong. § 2(a) (2001) [hereafter: AUMF].

[6] Memorandum from George W. Bush, President, to Richard B. Cheney, Vice President, et al., Humane Treatment of al Qaeda and Taliban Detainees, para. 1 (February 7, 2002) [hereafter: Bush Memo on Detainees].

will determine how international law regulates (if at all) the behavior of the United States.[7]

- International law does not apply as law, but it may *or may not* apply as a matter of policy.[8]
- The United States is faced with a new war. This new war is materially different from any war that has come before it, and therefore a new war needs either new law or no law or some mysterious set of laws that are found in the perceived gaps between existing laws.[9]

As this general approach to international law and IHL was tested out and articulated, two more specific legal arguments were put forward. First, the U.S. argued that while international armed conflict ("IAC") rules applied to the overall execution of hostilities in Afghanistan, the individuals captured and the party against which the United States was fighting there (meaning members of both the Taliban and al-Qaeda) did not enjoy any privileges under the laws of war. This argument was then expanded to cover the entire "war on terror." It was at this point that the Bush Administration put forward the argument that the global war on terror was classified as an international armed conflict *globally*, but that the principal enemy in this war, al-Qaeda, did not enjoy any privileges under the law applicable to international armed conflict, including the right to conduct hostilities, immunity from prosecution for acts conducted in compliance with IHL, and treatment as Prisoners of War upon

[7] See Memorandum from John C. Yoo, Deputy Assistant Att'y Gen., Office of Legal Counsel, U.S. Dep't of Justice, to William J. Haynes II, Gen. Counsel of the U.S. Dep't of Def., Military Interrogation of Alien Unlawful Combatants Held Outside the United States 47 (March 14, 2003) [hereafter: Yoo Memo on Military Interrogation].

[8] This is best captured in President Bush's executive order stating that, "[a]s a matter of policy, the United States Armed Forces shall continue to treat detainees humanely and, to the extent appropriate and consistent with military necessity, in a manner consistent with the principles of Geneva." Bush Memo on Detainees, para. 3. See also Memorandum from Alberto R. Gonzales to the President, Decision Re Application of the Geneva Convention on Prisoners of War to the Conflict With al Qaeda and the Taliban (January 25, 2002) (advising the President that, "[o]f course, you could nevertheless, as a matter of policy, decide to apply the principles of [Geneva Convention III] to the conflict with al Qaeda and the Taliban" (emphasis added)) [hereafter: Gonzales Memo on Application of Geneva Conventions].

[9] See, e.g., Memorandum from the President to the Vice President et al., on the Humane Treatment of al Qaeda and Taliban Detainees (February 7, 2002) (Appx. C to Independent Panel to Review DoD Detention Operations, Chairman the Honorable James R. Schlesinger to U.S. Secretary of Defense Donald Rumsfeld (August 24, 2004)); Gonzales Memo on Application of Geneva Conventions, p. 2; Brief for Respondents, Hamdan v. Rumsfeld, 548 U.S. 557 (2006) (No. 05-184), 2006 WL 460875, pp. *38-40, *48.

capture. At the time, many characterized this argument as a perversion of IHL to provide all available privileges of killing and indefinite detention to the government with none of the obligations in terms of treatment of the enemy.

B. International Humanitarian Law and Lawyers

On September 10th, 2001, the IHL discipline was focused on a number of issues, largely unnoticed by other international lawyers (and not crucial for present purposes). The post-9/11 arguments of the Bush Administration, summarized earlier, came crashing into the discipline of IHL like a wrecking ball. As statements from President Bush and his top officials came out on an almost weekly basis questioning the very applicability of IHL to the United States, there was a very real sense, one that must be deeply appreciated in order to understand the choices made by leading IHL lawyers and institutions in the years to come, that the United States might simply walk away from the law and burn down the house on its way out the door. For individuals who had negotiated with Chechen fighters to bring lifesaving humanitarian goods to individuals in Grozny, or who had spoken with Congolese militias about the basic distinction between civilians and combatants, the possibility that IHL as they knew it could be destroyed seemed very real and very terrifying.

IHL lawyers felt there needed to be a swift response, one that would reassert the power, reassurance, and calm majesty of IHL. Led by the ICRC, the reactions and responses that made up the legal discourse from IHL lawyers at the time can be characterized as follows:

- "Humanitarian law is basically fine."[10]
- Interstate conflict (with states as belligerents against other states) is a precondition for the existence of international armed conflict ("IAC"); therefore, the global war on terror cannot be classified as an armed conflict to which IHL applicable to IAC applies.
- There are very clear lines between IHL and other fields of law, and it is critical that these lines be maintained. IHL allows for lawful killing, collateral damage, the indefinite detention of individuals (until the end of hostilities), and the massive lawful destruction of property. Therefore, any reference to IHL rules must be made in the context that the

[10] Gabor Rona, *Interesting Times for International Humanitarian Law: Challenges from the "War on Terror,"* 27 FLETCHER F. WORLD AFF. 55, 69 (2003).

entire corpus and field of application of IHL are relevant: The U.S. cannot simply utilize IHL in a context where the threshold of armed conflict has not been reached, and it cannot apply the rules of IHL to an abstract conflict with a common noun. If it were allowed to do so, a host of activities which would otherwise be illegal under IHRL would be legally sanctioned as part of armed conflict.

- There is no new war. The threat of terrorism can be analogized to many historic conflicts and threats, and international humanitarian law and international law more generally were crafted to deal with precisely such threats. Because there is no new war, there is no need for new law.
- It is critical that lawyers and legal scholars committed to IHL and its survival create a unified front, one that does not allow for any incursion by Bush Administration arguments. This mode of argumentation is captured by the statement (almost rising to the level of a creedal claim): "International humanitarian law, in its current form, is, on the whole, adequate as a legal basis for responding to the challenges of contemporary international armed conflicts."[11] Anyone who suggests that IHL ought to be reformed, revised, updated, or reexamined in the current political crisis is effectively siding with the Bush Administration.
- The conflict in Afghanistan (but *not* the global war on terror or the war against al-Qaeda more generally) is properly classified as an international armed conflict, to which the full Geneva Conventions and those provisions of the First Additional Protocol recognized as customary international law apply to the United States. This means that members of the Taliban who are captured should be treated as Prisoners of War ("PoW").

The main technical debates of this time focused on *jus ad bellum* arguments about whether 9/11 could be considered an armed attack under the U.N. Charter (not an arena in which IHL lawyers as such would intervene, recognizing this as the domain of public international lawyers more generally), and the classification of detainees taken during the war in Afghanistan (the debate over PoW status). For the small discipline of IHL, shot into the headlines by 9/11 and its immediate aftermath, the major concern was to defend the law – gapless and suited to any conflict that might be envisioned as parts of the global war on terror – and to ensure that the United States did not do significant and lasting damage to the entire corpus of rules.

[11] See, e.g., Jakob Kellenberger, President, Int'l Comm. of the Red Cross, Address at the 28th International Conference of the Red Cross and Red Crescent (December 3, 2003), available at www.icrc.org/eng/resources/z3temp/traning%20tests/5tvhu9.htm.

C. *Human Rights Law and Lawyers*

The story was very different for human rights lawyers, who could immediately engage on a range of detailed substantive law questions raised by the Bush Administration's approach to the global war on terror. In some sense, the moment of impact hit human rights lawyers very differently than their IHL counterparts. For U.S.-based human rights lawyers,[12] the immediate aftermath of 9/11 was not yet experienced as an existential threat to their discipline.

At this stage, human rights advocates argued:

- The global war on terror is not a war, and it should not be framed as a war. It is a law enforcement operation that will manifest in a variety of domestic and international forms and should be primarily focused on prosecution or extradition of alleged terrorists and their supporters, while complying with all applicable human rights protections.
- Criminal law and domestic courts are fully equipped to handle the problem of al-Qaeda and transnational terrorism, and should be the central approach to dealing with the fight against what is essentially an international criminal network.[13]
- The global war on terror implies significant violations of central human rights, such as the right to be free from torture, the right to a fair trial, the right to privacy, and the rights of immigrants and refugees.
- Provisions such as the U.S.A. PATRIOT Act and other law enforcement approaches adopted in a dangerous war mentality may lead to discrimination against minority groups and denial of key rights of the accused.

While human rights advocates thought it was important to reiterate the ICRC's main position that IHL is completely coherent and gapless and that the law does not need to be revised or reconsidered in light of the threat of terrorism, this issue was not a significant substantive project for human rights lawyers. Human rights law was generally seen as being far

[12] This chapter focuses solely on human rights lawyers either based in the United States or focused on U.S. advocacy and analyzes the American debates within and between the IHL and IHRL disciplines over the period discussed.

[13] See Rona, *Interesting Times for International Humanitarian Law*, p. 69 ("There is little evidence that domestic and international laws and institutions of crime and punishment are not up to the task when terrorism and the War on Terror do not rise to the level of armed conflict.").

more powerful in arguing against war as such and against the types of detention and treatment that were occurring in the broader context of the global war on terror.

D. *Summary*

This phase of the international law response to the global war on terror is captured most clearly in the debate over whether a law enforcement or war model was more appropriate for understanding the "war on terror." For IHL lawyers, at this point in the story the debate was as much about where IHL *should not apply* as about where it should. For human rights lawyers, the debate was relevant principally as a matter of rhetoric. Unfamiliar with the details of IHL, many human rights law advocates simply saw the use of the term "war" as a way to justify human rights abuses and as a framework that would allow the U.S. to become a bad actor on the world stage. There was little sense then that the two fields would approach the crisis together.

II. 2003–2006: Detention and Classification

This phase in the story involves perhaps the darkest days for international lawyers working on the war on terror. With the start of the Iraq war on March 19, 2003, the release of graphic photographs of abuse of detainees in Abu Ghraib prison on April 28, 2004, and the release of what are now known as the "Torture Memos,"[14] the scope of the early Bush Administration's assertion of executive power and manipulation of existing legal regimes began to emerge.[15] Against a nightmarish background in which international law was perceived to be entering a black void, a number of significant concessions were made to some of the most radical early Bush Administration policies and abstract proposals.

[14] See generally The Torture Papers: The Road to Abu Ghraib (Karen J. Greenberg & Joshua L. Dratel eds., 2005).

[15] A sentiment typical of the time is captured in an amicus brief filed by three human rights experts (two academics, one practitioner), two of whom would within five years find themselves acting as government lawyers: "In amici's experience, the Executive's rhetoric and practice evoke not so much our own Government's historical practices as those of dictatorial foreign governments that the U.S. State Department has traditionally condemned." Brief for Louis Henken, Harold Hongju Koh, & Michael H. Posner as Amici Curiae Supporting Respondents, Rumsfeld v. Padilla, 542 U.S. 426 (2004) (No. 03-1027), p. 17.

Whether this was for pragmatic reasons[16] (a last-ditch effort to save the broader corpus of international law by granting what were then seen as narrow concessions) or an effort to regulate the exception by bringing it into the realm of law, what emerged from this period is a very different approach to IHL and IHRL than seen in the last phase. Out of all of the issues that occupied lawyers during this time, one key theme shoots through these debates: the response to a massive worldwide detention operation, justified through a vague and innovative quasi-legal qualification of international armed conflict.

A. U.S. Government

As the Bush Administration sought to articulate how broad, vague, and rhetorical positions on the global war on terror would be turned into domestic and foreign policy, and as they provided more detailed justification for their legal positions, lawyers saw for the first time the scope of the Bush Administration's vision of itself and its approach to law. In government filings responding to litigation, previously secret memoranda, President Bush's acknowledgment of the extensive role of the intelligence service in detention, and investigations of abuse, we see a number of key arguments and positions emerge on the relationship between IHL and the global war on terror. The executive saw the global war on terror as an international armed conflict, subject to the "common laws of war." According to the Bush Administration:

- This international armed conflict was, however, not regulated by IHL and the Geneva Conventions nor by the domestic War Crimes Act, because neither Common Article 2 nor Common Article 3 of the Geneva Conventions applied to the war with al-Qaeda and its associates.
- As such, individuals captured and detained during the global war were neither subject to domestic criminal and constitutional law (because they were enemy combatants), nor protected by the Third or Fourth Geneva Conventions, either as Prisoners of War or as civilian internees.

[16] That is, international law is meaningless if a state simply refuses to understand it as international law; therefore we have to interpret rules in a plausible manner that will at least create the grounds for conversation and compliance.

- The President, at a time of war, has vast unitary power. It is necessary for him to be able to carry out these powers with swiftness and dispatch. In carrying out these powers, all decisions regarding the interpretation of law, conduct during war, capture, incommunicado detention, transfer of detainees, and judicial process of detainees is entirely within the discretion of the President.
- By dint of this power, the President has the authority to authorize interrogations of detainees (held in secret CIA locations as well as in Guantánamo) and – aside from not being bound by the Geneva Conventions and customary IHL – would be able to authorize "harsh" procedures that would assist in obtaining information.
- The Geneva Conventions applied to the armed conflict in Iraq, at least vis-à-vis the United States and Iraq, as well as to the occupation of Iraq and any protected persons in Iraq. But they did not apply to non-Iraqi al-Qaeda operatives who were found in Iraq during the course of the international armed conflict and occupation.
- Individuals have been, are being, and will be held in secret CIA detention sites (in undisclosed locations outside the United States). Rules developed to apply to military interrogations in the wake of the Abu Ghraib scandal did not apply to the CIA interrogations, but the CIA was not authorized to "torture" detainees.

B. International Humanitarian Law and Lawyering

In responding to the aforementioned policies and legal claims, an important shift occurred on the part of IHL lawyers (from the ICRC to U.S. military lawyers). Many began to consider whether the initial position that IHL does not need to be modified would need to give way to a compromise that would in some way accommodate the Administration's view. As we will see, the push for compromise may have been hastened by what was happening in the arena of human rights law, as coalitions of lawyers in the United States began to bring cases against the government on behalf of individual detainees, significantly heightening the intensity and the demand for some kind of workable legal framework.

In the course of the debates over detention and qualification of conflict, three key arguments, positions, and professional moves may be observed: first, the concept of civilian "direct participation in hostilities" and its implications for detention; second, the release of the ICRC's Customary International Humanitarian Law Study; third, the emergence of the concept of a "transnational non-international armed conflict" to regulate military operations in Iraq and Afghanistan.

Direct Participation in Hostilities: In its September 2003 report for States and Delegates for the twenty-eighth International Conference of the Red Cross and Red Crescent, the ICRC the paper addressed the topic of "direct participation in hostilities" (based on a provision in Article 51 (3) of Additional Protocol I) and noted that "under humanitarian law applicable in international armed conflicts, civilians enjoy immunity from attack 'unless and for such time as they take a direct part in hostilities.' ... [Civilians] do not enjoy the combatant's or belligerent's 'privilege' of not being liable for prosecution for taking up arms and are thus sometimes referred to as 'unlawful' or 'unprivileged' combatants or belligerents."[17] I argue that this can be read as a direct response to the Bush Administration's introduction of the term "unprivileged combatants" or "unlawful combatants" into almost all discussion of the global war on terror, and perhaps also a reaction to the fact that, two years into the crisis, the term did not seem to be going away. Thus, the ICRC opened the door to a discussion and indeed an evaluation of the critical concept of direct participation right at the height of its disputes with the Bush Administration, despite its significant concerns that *any* opening of debate on *any* core issue of IHL at that time would create an opportunity for the Administration to denigrate and diminish the protective shield of IHL.

ICRC's Customary International Humanitarian Law Study: This study[18] is a high point of the positivist search for law through state practice and *opinio juris*, involved detailed review of many state military manuals, court decisions, official government statements, and other relevant materials. Importantly for developments in this period, the study submitted that "many rules applicable in international armed conflicts have also become applicable in internal armed conflicts as customary international law."[19] The Customary International Humanitarian Law Study and its approach to the customary rules applicable to NIAC may

[17] The International Committee of the Red Cross, International Humanitarian Law and the Challenges of Contemporary Armed Conflicts 9 (2003), available at www.icrc.org/eng/assets/files/other/ihlcontemp_armedconflicts_final_ang.pdf, [hereafter ICRC Report].

[18] Jean-Marie Henckaerts & Louise Doswald-Beck, Customary International Humanitarian Law (2005), available at www.icrc.org/eng/assets/files/other/customary-international-humanitarian-law-i-icrc-eng.pdf, [hereinafter CIHL Study].

[19] ICRC Report, p. 15; see also CIHL Study, p. xxxv.

have prepared the ground for IHL lawyers to be open, later in the story, to accept the notion that situations that they previously would have seen as IACs could be classified as NIACs without diminishing legal protections. The Customary International Humanitarian Law Study served to create the feeling (although not espoused by the authors of the Study) that IAC and NIAC rules were, for the most part, "essentially the same." This motto seemed to become a refrain used more and more once the study was released.

***Transnational Non-International Armed Conflict*:** In response to the claim of Bush Administration lawyers that the Geneva Conventions did not regulate the war with al-Qaeda because al-Qaeda was not a state, a number of scholarly articles suggested that a mutated form of non-international armed conflict, generally referred to as "transnational non-international armed conflict," might apply to some formulation of the "war on terror."[20] At that point, IHL scholars and practitioners saw the idea as relatively narrow in its practical application *as far as IHL was concerned*. The idea began to gain more support once it appeared that there was general agreement that the 2006 Israeli war in Lebanon against Hezbollah fell into this category.[21] Given the urgent need to create a regulatory framework that could plausibly deal with the now thousands of detainees in U.S. custody, the ability to apply some form of NIAC rules became more appealing. The sense of crisis for IHL lawyering, and the overall mood at the time that an agreed-upon framework was desperately needed, may have prematurely shoved this theory into the heart of the practice.

What pushed this new, under-explained concept of transnational armed conflict from academic theory to practice? What was the main demand for such a framework? For this part of the debate, we cross disciplines.

[20] There was vast disagreement about what this might mean. A very early articulation of the notion suggests that there might be some sort of global non-international armed conflict with al-Qaeda, see Derek Jinks, *September 11 and the Laws of War*, 28 YALE J. INT'L L. 1 (2003), but that had little traction at the time. A highly respected ICRC lawyer then suggested that there might be some ways in which the core rules of NIAC might apply to conflicts with terrorist groups. See Jelena Pejic, *Terrorist Acts and Groups: A Role for International Law?*, 75 BRIT. Y.B. INT'L L. 71 (2004).

[21] See, e.g., Human Rights Watch, Questions and Answers on Hostilities between Israel and Hezbollah (August 2, 2006), www.hrw.org/news/2006/08/01/questions-and-answers-hostilities-between-israel-and-hezbollah.

C. *International Human Rights Law and Lawyering*

It is at this phase that IHL went to trial in the U.S., mediated through constitutional law and human rights lawyering. The main concern of U.S. human rights lawyers was the Administration's introduction of military commissions through executive order, and the claim that the Authorization for Use of Military Force extended to any individuals that the U.S. chose to detain anywhere in the world.[22] In addition, there were significant concerns regarding U.S. citizens taken into custody as "enemy combatants" and slated to appear before military commissions.

The concerns of U.S. human rights lawyers bringing cases on behalf of detainees were very different from those of IHL lawyers. Lawyers who likely had had little or no contact with the laws of war prior to their engagement on the war on terror may well have not been very impressed with that body of law's due process safeguards. IHL was at best a set of tools that could be operationalized alongside constitutional law, human rights law, and criminal law and procedure in order to advocate on behalf of their clients. Whatever one thinks of the outcome of the cases or their jurisprudence, it is clear that neither a majority of lawyers litigating the cases nor the judges deciding them had a great deal of familiarity with IHL and its inner workings. IHL rules and concepts were often watered down in order to fit within the methodology, form, and language of U.S. courts. But, more importantly, lawyers and judges were often unaware of what impact beyond the cases at hand the transformation of IHL concepts was to have. One case tells this story better than any other: *Hamdan v. Rumsfeld.*

On June 29, 2006, the U.S. Supreme Court decided, in a landmark moment in our story and one of the first real meaningful victories for those challenging the Bush Administration's framing and execution of the war on terror, that there were some constraints on the power of the President.[23]

[22] See, e.g., Harold Koh, *Setting the World Right*, 115 Yale L.J. 2350, 2355 (2005–2006) (explaining that the Bush Administration "rejects human rights universalism in favor of executive efforts to create law-free zones: extralegal spaces (Guantánamo), extralegal courts (military commissions), extralegal persons (enemy combatants) and extralegal practices (extraordinary rendition) . . .").

[23] The case centered on a habeas corpus petition filed by Salim Hamdan, a Yemeni national captured in Afghanistan in 2001 while acting as Osama bin Laden's driver. He was brought to the detention facility at Guantánamo Bay, Cuba, in 2002 as an "enemy combatant," and President Bush ordered he be brought before a military commission in 2003 on charges that were later specified as "conspiracy to commit offenses triable by

The Court received numerous amici briefs from IHL and IHRL experts, and the Court's decision can be read as being highly influenced by these submissions.

The Supreme Court ultimately adopted the most innovative argument of the amici. Building on a number of other detainee cases, the experts drafting the Law of War amici brief in *Hamdan* adopted a theory that had been percolating for at least five years by this point: none other than the notion of *global transnational non-international armed conflict.*[24] As one of the most important instances of human rights lawyering through IHL during that time (and perhaps to this day), the Brief's legal arguments and approaches merit close attention both as signposting a shift in discourse and as impacting the framing of how law applied in the conflict.

In order to reach the desired legal conclusion that Hamdan's military commission trial violated Common Article 3, the Law of War amicus brief made three main arguments. First, Hamdan was captured during an international armed conflict, to which the Third Geneva Convention was applicable. For that reason, he should benefit from Prisoner of War status, even if his status is in doubt. So far, classic IHL. Second, Hamdan's military commission was unlawful under IHL (and here the amici depart from traditional understandings of classification) *because* "Common Article 3 applies to trans-territorial non-international armed conflict."[25] Third, even if the government was correct and the war against al-Qaeda was an "international armed conflict," Common Article 3 also applied to such a conflict. In putting forward the argument that non-international

military commission." Hamdan argued that that the military commission was unlawful under the Uniform Code of Military Justice and the Geneva Conventions, and that the commission was not authorized by Congress. The government argued that Hamdan could not access the federal courts because he was not a Prisoner of War (but rather an enemy combatant), and that the Geneva Conventions did not apply to his detention or trial (because the conflict with al Qaeda is not with a signatory to the Conventions, yet is also not a Common Article 3 conflict because it is international in character). See generally Hamdan v. Rumsfeld, 548 U.S. 557 (2006).

[24] One of the authors of the amicus brief was a very early promoter of the notion that Common Article 3 should apply to the entire global war against terror/war against al-Qaeda. See Jinks, *September 11 and the Laws of War.* (Although it does not appear that Jinks had in mind a global regulatory framework that would a priori recognize any exertion of lethal force by the United States as falling within an already existing Common Article 3 NIAC.)

[25] Brief of Professors Ryan Goodman, Derek Jinks & Anne-Marie Slaughter as amicus Curiae Supporting Reversal (Geneva - Applicability), Hamdan v. Rumsfeld, 548 U.S. 557 (2006) (No. 05–184), p. 18.

armed conflicts have always been thought of as including trans-territorial conflicts, the amici help lay the foundation of a claim that will become important under very different circumstances a mere five years later.[26]

In attempting to counter the government's argument that international law effectively applied *nowhere* in its conflict with al-Qaeda, the amici took on the position that the law applied *everywhere* in the U.S. conflict with al-Qaeda. It is important to note that the brief did not actually say (and arguably, though it is a source of debate, neither did the Court[27]) that the United States is in a global conflict with al-Qaeda, and that global conflict is transnational non-international as a matter of IHL classification. However, the amici did say: "The Government maintains *correctly* that at least since September 11th, an armed conflict exists between the United States and al Qaeda,"[28] and "Common Article 3 applies to armed conflicts that extend across state borders."[29] With these two sentences we see a nascent scholarly concept in IHL shift to human rights advocacy and then to *the* landmark decision of the U.S. Supreme Court on these issues.

The decision came to stand for the idea that the U.S. was bound to apply international law, and thus, in a sense, that the Court had somehow redeemed lawyering itself. Yet it did so at a great potential cost, for the decision seemed to accept that the U.S. was in a potentially global war against al-Qaeda. In IHL terms, *Hamdan* provides the imprimatur of the highest court in the land to extending Common Article 3 beyond Afghanistan to the world – and with Common Article 3, as with all applications of IHL, comes not only a set of restraints on how states must treat people in their power but also a set of rights for states to kill lawfully. Thus, by the end of this phase the firmament of IHL had been loosened in a way that might not have seemed particularly significant at that time but was to prove crucial for the development of the discourse of "folk international law."

[26] "International bodies have consistently and unequivocally maintained that Common Article 3 applies to trans-territorial conflicts." *Id.* at 23.

[27] My sense is that the Court's opinion on the IHL element to the case is far narrower than it has been read. Essentially, the Court is saying that there is a war and that the individuals in Guantánamo have Common Article 3 protection. One of the downsides of moving from IHL to IHRL lawyering, however, is that it may well be that the Court failed to understand properly that this is now how IHL works.

[28] Brief of Goodman, Jinks & Slaughter, p. 18 (emphasis added).

[29] *Id.* at 18.

III. 2006–2009: Distinction and Direct Participation in Hostilities

After *Hamdan*, the ground beneath both disciplines shifted. Most IHL lawyers harbored deep concerns about the classification of the war against al-Qaeda as a global non-international armed conflict to which Common Article 3 applied, but at least there was no longer a need to convince the Administration that IHL mattered *at all*. For human rights lawyers, *Hamdan* and related cases (notably *Rasul*[30] and *Hamdi*[31]) opened the door to litigating the contours of the Administration's approach to detention, treatment, access to justice, and applicable law, in an attempt to secure sufficient safeguards and due process for all detainees.

Dilemmas relating to the conduct of hostilities rose to the top of the IHL agenda, largely due to trends in Afghanistan and Iraq. As U.S. and allied forces faced the task of conducting a massive conventional ground war within the rubric of a "multinational" NIAC, significant questions arose as to how the framework of NIAC would provide a regulatory regime for detention operations, both in terms of grounds for detention and in terms of the process and protections that must legally be afforded to detainees. At this stage, the POW debate on newly captured detainees was all but concluded, given that by this point everyone seemed to accept that there was no POW status available in either Afghanistan or Iraq for insurgents and other security detainees.

A. U.S. Government

Facing multiple military fronts, legal challenges domestically, as well as a change in administrations, the government's position was more varied and slightly more tentative across this phase. In general, however, the trend of asserting executive power and discretion over the war on terror continued, as did the overall global armed conflict approach. As the Obama Administration came to power, it attempted

[30] Rasul v. Bush, 542 U.S. 466 (2004) (holding that the federal habeas corpus statute provides federal courts with jurisdiction to hear habeas corpus petitions brought by or on behalf of individuals detained at Guantánamo).

[31] Hamdi v. Rumsfeld, 542 U.S. 507 (2004) (holding that while the AUMF permits the President to detain U.S. citizens as enemy combatants, due process considerations permit Hamdi to challenge his classification as an enemy combatant in federal court).

to signal a commitment to international law and to indicate clear distinctions from the Bush Administration while also maintaining as much flexibility and permissiveness within the rules as possible.

The government's key positions and arguments during this time may be summarized as follows:

- The new version of the Military Commissions Act and the Detainee Treatment Act attempt to resolve some of the constitutional flaws of the laws at issue in the detainee cases, providing some basic protections for detainees, yet still far away from both Uniform Code of Military Justice and criminal due process baselines.[32]
- The term "enemy combatant" is used less frequently, and abandoned by mid to late 2009.[33]
- The Authorization for the Use of Military Force ("AUMF") – expanded, restricted, enhanced, or unaffected by (depending on who is speaking and at what point) IHL – is the sole and sufficient basis for legal authority to detain in the war against al-Qaeda.[34]
- Detainees in the Guantánamo Bay detention center should not, despite the Supreme Court decision in *Hamdan*, have access to habeas corpus review, nor should they be able to access domestic courts or criminal law in order to challenge their detention.
- The basis for the detention of civilians in the wars in Iraq and Afghanistan is legally framed by *analogy* to international armed conflict,[35] in which

[32] See generally Hamdan, 548 U.S. 557 (holding that the military commissions established by President Bush did not comply with the Uniform Code of Military Justice or IHL).

[33] The term was never meaningful as a matter of IHL (it simply means a combatant who fights for enemy forces) but was for some time utilized as a designation for people, including U.S. citizens, who were placed under the authority of the Department of Defense for detention purposes (either within the United States or in Guantánamo). See ASIL Speech (explaining that the United States has "based our authority to detain not on conclusory labels, like 'enemy combatant', but on whether the factual record in the particular case meets the legal standard").

[34] *Id.* (explaining that, "as a matter of domestic law, the Obama Administration has not based its claim of authority to detain those at GITMO and Bagram on the President's Article II authority as Commander-in-Chief," as was claimed by the previous Administration, but rather "on legislative authority expressly granted to the President by Congress in the 2001 AUMF") (emphasis in original). Furthermore, Koh explains that the Administration interprets the scope of its detention authority "on authority authorized by Congress in the AUMF as informed by the laws of war." *Id.* (emphasis in original).

[35] Brief of Respondents at 1, In Re Guantánamo Bay Detainee Litigation, No. 08–442 (D.D.C. March 13, 2009) (emphasizing that "[p]rinciples derived from law-of-war rules governing international armed conflicts ... must inform the interpretation of the detention authority Congress has authorized for the current armed conflict").

protected persons can be interned "if the security of the Detaining Power makes it absolutely necessary."[36]

- In 2009, it is announced that the term "global war on terror" will no longer be utilized by the Administration. It is unclear at the time of this announcement whether this has any legal implications or whether this will alter the approach of the government vis-à-vis the key legal and practical debates of the time.[37]
- An overly narrow approach to the notion of civilian direct participation in hostilities, in either IAC or NIAC, is not acceptable to the United States and is not practical for states fighting complex wars around the world.[38]

B. *International Humanitarian Law and Lawyering*

During this period, perhaps unlike the preceding two, IHL lawyers were required to address how their body of law regulated its area of core concern and highest relevance: the conduct of hostilities and treatment of civilians in armed conflict, as traditionally understood. Two developments bear emphasis. First, the consensus that emerged around classification of Afghanistan and Iraq as NIACs, despite tremendous international involvement and control, profoundly narrowed the range of binding IHL applicable to the U.S. in each of those conflicts. Second, the notoriously complex question of whether there was any kind of combatancy recognized in NIAC needed to be quickly addressed. Scholars and military practitioners had long discussed that the notion

[36] Geneva Convention Relative to the Protection of Civilian Persons in Time of War, Art. 42, August 12, 1949, 6 U.S.T. 3516, 75 U.N.T.S. 287 [hereinafter Geneva Convention IV].

[37] For instance, see Ryan Goodman, *Flip Flops: The Conflict with Al Qaeda is (Not) a War*, Just Security (September 23, 2013), available at http://justsecurity.org/2013/09/23/flip-flops-conflict-al-qaeda-not-war/ (explaining that, over time, the answer to the question of whether the United States is at war with al-Qaeda has depended upon the various interests at stake).

[38] See Military Commissions Act of 2006, Pub. L. No. 109–366, § 3(a), 120 Stat. 2600, 2601 (codified at 10 U.S.C. 948(a)(1)(A) (2006)) (defining one who directly participates in hostilities, or an "unlawful enemy combatant," as "a person who has engaged in hostilities or who has purposefully and materially supported hostilities against the United States or its co-belligerents who is not a lawful enemy combatant (including a person who is part of the Taliban, al Qaeda, or associated forces)"). But see Ryan Goodman & Derek Jinks, *International Law, U.S. War Powers, and the Global War on Terrorism*, 118 Harv. L. Rev. 2653, 2657–58 (2005) (finding that "the President's notion of 'enemy combatants' in [the global war on terror] exceeds the scope of LOAC [the law of armed conflict]").

of "direct participation in hostilities" by civilians[39] required further elaboration and understanding. The lack of uniformed, state-led armed forces fighting on behalf of either Iraq or Afghanistan brought the question to the fore. For IHL to remain relevant to U.S. decision makers in this mode, lawyers and proponents of the law had to be able to present a plausible account of how NIAC rules could be utilized to target, detain, and protect civilians.

In May 2009, the ICRC published the Interpretive Guidance on the Notion of Direct Participation in Hostilities Under International Humanitarian Law ("Interpretive Guidance").[40] By this time, the central focus of the study had changed significantly: It had narrowed from detention *and* targeting to focusing solely on lawful targets, and it had expanded from exclusively addressing IAC to both IAC and NIAC.[41]

The Interpretive Guidance formulated a fairly classical standard for the principle of distinction for IAC and a more innovative one for NIAC. In IAC, anyone who was not a member of the armed forces of a party to the conflict (or a member of a levée en masse), and in NIAC, anyone who was not a "member of State armed forces or organized armed groups of a party to the conflict," was a civilian entitled to protection against direct attack unless and for such time as he took a direct part in hostilities. The Interpretive Guidance defined organized armed groups as consisting "only of individuals whose continuous function it is to take a direct part in hostilities (continuous combat function or 'CCF')."[42] The ICRC enumerated three "constitutive elements of direct participation in hostilities," which essentially required that the specific act must have a certain threshold of harm, a direct causation to that harm, and a belligerent nexus.

[39] See Protocol Additional to the Geneva Conventions of 12 August, 1949 and Relating to the Protection of Victims of International Armed Conflicts (Protocol I), June 8, 1977, 1125 U.N.T.S. 3 [hereinafter Protocol I]; Protocol II Additional to the Geneva Conventions of 12 August, 1949 and Relating to the Protection of Victims of Non-International Armed Conflicts, opened for signature December 12, 1977, reprinted in 16 I.L.M. 1442 [hereinafter Protocol II].

[40] See ICRC, *Interpretive Guidance on the Notion of Direct Participation in Hostilities Under International Humanitarian Law*, 90 Int'l Rev. Red Cross 991 (2008), available at www.icrc.org/eng/assets/files/other/irrc-872-reports-documents.pdf [hereinafter ICRC Interpretive Guidance].

[41] *See* Kenneth Watkin, *Opportunity Lost: Organized Armed Groups and the ICRC "Direct Participation in Hostilities" Interpretive Guidance*, 42 N.Y.U. J. Int'l L. & Pol. 641, 643 (2010).

[42] ICRC Interpretive Guidance, p. 995.

Despite the political environment surrounding the Interpretive Guidance drafting process, and the ongoing public debate over terms like "unlawful enemy combatant," a general consensus emerged around the concept of "functional membership" in an organized armed group. Some experts voiced strong concerns that this concept would create a third category of status outside of civilians and combatants. The most contentious issues of the Interpretive Guidance, and those that finally broke the group, included the requirement of a belligerent nexus with a party to the conflict and the restraints on the kind and degree of force that could be used against someone not entitled to protection against direct attack.

It is clear that the process had the impact of drawing and focusing tremendous scholarly and practitioner interest on the question of the definition of a civilian, and the determination of what constitutes membership and function in an organized armed group, such that a member could be targeted in the same way as a combatant under IHL applicable to IAC. In putting before the expert group the contested question of whether IHL maintained a bifurcated approach to status,[43] IHL lawyers were in a position to air a range of views on this question. While ultimately articulating what many on the "military" side of the profession saw as far too narrow and restrictive a model of DPH, the Interpretive Guidance *process* provided a high-level forum for, and possibly legitimized, a series of alternative conceptions of direct participation. The process opened up questions of who is a "real" civilian, and of the continued relevance of blanket status determinations for targeting (as opposed to a functional analysis of every individual's contribution to the enemy's war effort).

C. *International Human Rights Law and Lawyering*

The U.S. Supreme Court, in the cases following *Hamdan*, indicated that it expected the lower courts to determine the substantive boundaries imposed on the government in habeas trials and to provide a more detailed analysis of the legality of various Administration approaches to detention. After *Boumediene*,[44] as a glut of cases reached the courts,

43 Meaning that all individuals on the battlefield are either combatants or civilians.

44 Boumediene v. Bush, 553 U.S. 723 (2008) (holding that foreign nationals detained at Guantánamo had a constitutional right to habeas review of their continued detention, and that provisions denying habeas review to these individuals, as contained in the 2006 Military Commissions Act, were unconstitutional).

contested IHL concepts began to appear in human rights lawyering and argumentation. This was an important moment with significant potential consequences. The notion of direct participation in hostilities took on a different life when channeled into human rights litigation by way of constitutional law arguments for individual clients. What did the concept of DPH do for human rights argumentation and how was it used by amici and by justices in some of the decisions?

While the ICRC and most IHL lawyers would deny that there is any such thing as a standard of DPH for detention, that is precisely the issue that lawyers, amici experts, and courts faced during this period. As "law of war concepts" were brought to bear in detainees' cases, the concept of DPH moved from a purely IHL *conduct of hostilities* notion to a measure of whether the government had the authority to *detain* (or continue to detain). This is true despite the fact that IHL was not a body of law crafted for individual standing and provided no means for individuals to bring claims against state parties to armed conflict.

The NIAC detention regime did not provide a regulatory model for major detention operations or the management of individual detainee cases. As such, all those engaged in these cases (the Administration, the military, lawyers for the detainees, and judges) relied on some combination of IAC, NIAC, and IHRL, including domestic criminal law, to come up with an evolving kaleidoscopic system. DPH for *targeting* implicates the juridical space of Iraq or Afghanistan, providing a general set of legal interpretations that will inform how commanders and their legal advisers determine targeting decisions, attack strategies, and air campaigns. DPH for *detention* imagines Guantánamo as its key space of argumentation. The archetypal detainee in most of the cases in this period was captured well before the litigation (many in Afghanistan or the U.S. in 2001–2002) and had been held in Guantánamo for a significant period of time. Therefore, when talking about direct participation in this mode, there was little concern that these individuals were going to be *targeted* in Chicago or Peoria or Cuba.

By this phase, whether or not the *Hamdan* Court wished to indicate that the United States was in fact engaged in global armed conflict, courts seemed to have applied that decision as such.[45] So, given that the government relied on the AUMF as the authority to detain individuals

[45] According to the Hamlily Court, "To begin with, the U.S. conflict with al Qaeda is a non-international armed conflict; hence, Article 4 and Additional Protocol I do not apply." Hamlily v. Obama, 616 F. Supp. 2d 63, 73 (D.D.C. 2009).

captured during the war on terror, the question became how and to what extent IHL could be read into or could be read to supplement the AUMF in order to determine both the standard for authority to detain and the basis for continued detention. This is where the very fresh debate over DPH came to be utilized. A review of legal proceedings from this period reveals four arguments relating to DPH. First, there was no basis in NIAC to detain other than domestic criminal law. Second, there *was* authority to detain under NIAC, but this authority stemmed only from DPH (the contours of which seem to diverge by various degrees from that presented by the Interpretive Guidance). This meant that simple membership in an armed group was not enough. Rather, the government must actually demonstrate that the detainee was participating in hostilities. Third, there *was* authority to detain under NIAC, based on the very formal Interpretive Guidance direct targeting standard of performing a "continuous combat function" in an organized armed group. Fourth, in order to continue detaining a person captured in a NIAC, the government must demonstrate that he was likely to rejoin the fight, again using standards derived from DPH.

The arguments used by human rights lawyers produced strange outcomes and an overall confusing jurisprudence of the significance of the IAC/NIAC distinction in terms of authority to detain and protections owed to detainees. As IHL went to court in human rights mode, it was clear that complex debates over DPH influenced the detainee cases and the arguments being put before courts by international law experts. However, because these cases all focused on authority to detain in the past and grounds for continued detention in the present, they took DPH concepts and translated them from questions of status and targetability to questions of conduct, membership, and "guilt" for purposes of detention. Given that the question of DPH for purposes of detention was abandoned at the very early stages of the ICRC process, this type of argumentation and brief drafting lead not only to some bizarre interpretations of settled IHL (like the notion that there are no grounds in IHL to detain combatants in an IAC), but also to confusing conclusions regarding whether a very restrictive or a very permissive DPH would be a basis for detention. While this may be fascinating as a matter of federal courts jurisprudence, given that these decisions and arguments were occurring during several ongoing armed conflicts, one might have wondered at this point how all this uncertainty would impact commanders and JAGs on the battlefield.

IV. 2009 to Early 2013: Targeted Killing

> *"Over time, a consensus will likely evolve that targeted killing of suspected terrorists under some circumstances is legal under IHL. If this is the likely evolution of the law, it is all the more important to determine how IHL, assuming it applies, should regulate targeted killing."*[46]

This brings us to the end of our story. At this point, a major break occurred. After eight difficult, traumatic years, it appeared that light shone once again on international law in the U.S. government. The Administration of Barack Obama began to articulate its positions on the war on terror. From the outset, expectations among international lawyers were high and everything seemed very, very different. It was perhaps for this reason that many in the IHL and IHRL disciplines, particularly in the U.S., were taken by surprise when the Obama Administration decided during this period to take the fight to al-Qaeda: a fight not carried out through detention, rendering, and interrogation, but through Predator drones and Hellfire missiles. This iteration of the war on terror was, in short, about killing.

A. U.S. Government

There has been, and will continue to be, a tremendous amount of debate regarding to what extent, if at all, the Obama Administration actually rejected or moved away from Bush-era policies regarding the war on terror. In focusing on the legal arguments and rhetorical moves articulated around the issues of concern to our inquiry, the change in tone and approach is certainly striking. There are a number of positions, decisions, and arguments that typify the early Obama Administration approach to the war on terror:

- The Administration explicitly recognized the armed conflict with al-Qaeda as a NIAC[47] and has said "we are indeed at war with al Qaeda

[46] Radsan & Murphy, Measure Twice, Shoot Once, p. 1203.

[47] See Harold Koh, *Powerpoint for Keynote Address at the U.S. Naval War College International Law Department: International Law and Armed Conflict in the Obama Administration* (June 22, 2011), available at www.usnwc.edu/getattachment/f53eec9c-1e22-48bb-8fb2-85f6f70b9c9b/ [http://perma.law.harvard.edu/0JyvnFk45HL/] [hereafter NWC PPT], (stating that "[u]nder domestic law, we rest our detention authority in the NIAC with Al Qaeda on a statute – the 2001 AUMF – as informed by the principles of the laws of war") (emphasis added). Other executive branch officials, including David Kris, John O. Brennan, Jeh C. Johnson, Eric Holder, and Stephen W. Preston, made similar statements.

and its affiliates."[48] It articulated for the first time the concept of the "Law of 9/11."[49]

- The Administration based its authority to detain under international law on self-defense and, at least in Afghanistan, on the consent of the territorial state, as well as on a United Nations Security Council resolution authorizing the use of "all necessary measures."[50] Furthermore, the Obama Administration explicitly tied its approach to detention, which seemed unchanged in terms of operations on the ground in Iraq and Afghanistan, to the ICRC DPH Interpretive Guidance[51] and has said it is "not asserting an unlimited detention authority."[52] However, the Administration also stated that the authority to detain is rooted in IAC rules "by analogy."[53]
- The President explicitly prohibited torture as a tool of interrogation, explicitly rejected the legal reasoning of the "torture memos," and instructed the CIA to discontinue its use of "black sites."[54]
- The Obama Administration stated it would no longer utilize the term "enemy combatant," but would rather take a "facts-based" approach to determining whether individuals have a DPH-style functional membership in al-Qaeda and associated forces.[55]

48 President Barack Obama, *Remarks by the President on National Security, National Archives* (May 21, 2009) available at www.whitehouse.gov/the_press_office/Remarks-by-the-President-On-National-Security-5-21-09/.

49 ASIL Speech; see also Harold Koh, *Powerpoint for Keynote Address at the U.S. Naval War College International Law Department: International Law and Armed Conflict in the Obama Administration* (June 22, 2011), available at www.usnwc.edu/getattachment/f53eec9c-1e22-48bb-8fb2-85f6f70b9c9b/.

50 ASIL Speech. 51 *Id.* See also NWC PPT. 52 ASIL Speech.

53 See Respondent's Memorandum at 2, In Re Guantánamo Bay Detainee Litigation, D.D.C. March 13, 2009, (No. 08–442), stating: "Principles derived from law-of-war rules governing international armed conflicts, therefore, must inform the interpretation of the detention authority Congress has authorized for the current armed conflict. . . . The President also has the authority under the AUMF to detain in this armed conflict those persons whose relationship to al-Qaida or the Taliban would, in appropriately analogous circumstances in a traditional international armed conflict, render them detainable." In addition, the Obama Administration believes that there is a separate set of NIAC black-letter rules that support authority to detain. See NWC PPT ("Common Article 3 and APII recognize – and U.S. Supreme Court recognized in Hamdi – detention of enemy belligerents to prevent them from returning to hostilities is a well-recognized feature of armed conflict.").

54 See Exec. Order No. 13491, 74 Fed. Reg. 4893 (January 22, 2009).

55 In re-articulating detention authority as resting on the AUMF, the Department of Justice stated that "individuals who supported al Qaeda or the Taliban are detainable only if the support was substantial. And it does not employ the phrase 'enemy combatant.'" Press

- The Administration significantly increased, but did not openly acknowledge, CIA-controlled or CIA-led drone strikes on targets in Afghanistan, Pakistan, Yemen, Somalia, and possibly a number of other countries. The relationship and chain-of-command structure between the military and the CIA was kept vague, but many observers suggested that CIA control of the program was critical in order to avoid legal exposure and maintain legal flexibility.
- As to the *jus ad bellum*, the government based its authority to attack targets outside of the armed conflicts in Iraq and Afghanistan on three incredibly complex and difficult-to-follow arguments. The government has not articulated which of these principles it relied upon or how the three concepts legally interacted. First, the U.S. is engaged in an ongoing non-international armed conflict with al-Qaeda, the Taliban, and associated forces around the world, authorized by the AUMF. Second, the U.S. may be operating within a given territorial state, such as Yemen or Pakistan, with that state's (explicit, tacit, or even private) consent. Third, the U.S. maintains a seemingly separate legal justification for attacks against al-Qaeda, the Taliban, and/or associated forces targets in *any country* based on self-defense. Such self-defense would allow the United States to attack if the territorial state is "unable or unwilling" to obviate the threat from terrorists on its territory. Furthermore, a self-defense claim may be legally sound if a state cannot control its own territory, or is a "failed state." Meanwhile, some American academics began to argue for a theory – reportedly developed by Koh – of "elongated imminence" based on "battered spouse syndrome."[56]
- As to *jus in bello* rules applicable to the geographically unbounded NIAC against al Qaeda, the Taliban, and/or associated forces, and associated targeting operations, including against U.S. citizens, the government "takes great care to adhere to the principles" of distinction and proportionality, as defined in IHL. While the CIA and any military agencies acting under its orders or authority are to act in accordance

Release, Department of Justice, Department of Justice Withdraws "Enemy Combatant" Definition for Guantánamo Detainees (March 13, 2009), available at www.justice.gov/opa/pr/2009/March/09-ag-232.html.

56 Daniel Klaidman argues that Koh's theory was that "[i]f a husband demonstrated a consistent pattern of activity before beating his wife, it wasn't necessary to wait until the husband's hand was raised before the wife could act in self-defense." DANIEL KLAIDMAN, KILL OR CAPTURE: THE WAR ON TERROR AND THE SOUL OF THE OBAMA ADMINISTRATION 219–223 (2012).

with IHL "principles" in their targeting, it is not clear whether the CIA can or will be held accountable for any violations of IHL, or whether, particularly when acting in "covert operations," they would be subject to criminal liability under the Uniform Code of Military Justice or the War Crimes Act.[57]

- In February 2013, an unsigned and undated Department of Justice White Paper on "The Lawfulness of a Lethal Operation Directed Against a U.S. Citizen Who Is a Senior Operational Leader of Al-Qaida or an Associated Force" publicly surfaced.[58] While the White Paper does not provide the DOJ's comprehensive legal analysis, it does serve as a sort of "folk international law" primer, conflating concepts, rules, and principles from IHL, IHRL, and *jus ad bellum.*[59] For instance, the White Paper invokes a concept of imminence that appears to be unrecognizable under long-standing IHRL and *jus ad*

57 One prolific former assistant general counsel to the CIA has suggested in numerous publications and testimony before the House of Representatives that the CIA should utilize the office of the Investigator General to provide "internal due process" according to principles of IHL. See Afsheen John Radsan, *Loftier Standards for the CIA's Remote-Control Killing: Hearing Before the Subcomm. on National Security and Foreign Affairs of the H. Comm. on the Judiciary*, William Mitchell College of Law Legal Studies Research Paper 2010–11 (April 28, 2010), available at http://papers.ssrn.com/sol3/papers.cfm?abstract_id=1604745.

58 Department of Justice, Lawfulness of a Lethal Operation Directed Against a U.S. Citizen Who is a Senior Operational Leader of Al-Qaida or an Associated Force, White Paper (November 8, 2011), available at www.fas.org/irp/eprint/doj-lethal.pdf.

59 In addition, much of the detailed support for the legality of U.S. targeted killing/global NIAC has come from a small group of scholars writing during this phase. I would classify these scholars as a third category, neither IHL lawyers nor human rights lawyers, but national security lawyers in a particular post-9/11 mold. This field does not see itself as defined by either discipline and displays little dogmatic attention to its texts. National security law may turn to IHL because it is part of the international legal infrastructure around the United States' response to the terrorist attacks, and its primary intellectual and disciplinary commitment is to a broader field that has emerged since 9/11, which encompasses some mélange of constitutional law, criminal law, IHL, IHRL-lite, and jus ad bellum/Security Council law. For now, while the national security law lawyers may share a great deal with their IHL counterparts, and may even hold similar political commitments, they are kept at arms' length from the heart of the discipline. However, this small sub-discipline is critical to this last chapter insofar as its members may be more comfortable moving between legal fields, questioning traditionalist approaches to the field of application of the law of armed conflict, and do so with great attention to legal complexity, the rigors of legal scholarship, and reference to multiple fields of international legal literature. See, e.g., Robert Chesney, *Who May Be Killed? Anwar al-Awlaki as a Case Study in the International Legal Regulation of Lethal Force*, 13 Y.B. of Int'l Humanitarian L. 3 (2011) (providing a detailed analysis of the legality of targeted killing in Yemen according to all of the categories listed in this Section).

bellum.[60] It also seems to take an extraordinarily narrow view under international law of the Administration's obligation to seek the capture of terrorists away from "hot" battlefields before using lethal force. Finally, it argues for territorially unbounded NIAC by way of analogy.

These legal arguments and positions indicate that while the Bush Administration coined and regularly used the term "war on terror," the Obama Administration much more actively pursues an armed conflict with al-Qaeda, the Taliban, and associated forces in a *global context.*[61] In doing so, the Obama Administration purportedly expands the scope of the applicability of IHL to any place that the United States targets these individuals, typically with only a passing reference to the "sovereignty" of the state on which the terrorist is being targeted. It then states that certain IHL principles are being applied – or at least considered – by a clandestine branch of the government whose accountability to the rules of IHL is unclear.[62]

Yet these developments have occurred after the Obama Administration appointed some of the country's finest international lawyers, many of them well known to the IHL and human rights lawyers who have been fighting against the war on terror throughout this story. Indeed, many of the international lawyers who joined the Obama Administration have been involved in legal or scholarly efforts to curtail the Bush Administration's pursuit of the global war on terror. In this sense, as we head into the reactions by IHL and IHRL to these positions, there seems to be far more benefit of the doubt granted to this Administration's approach to the conflict.[63]

60 White Paper, pp. 7–8 (explaining that the threat posed by al-Qaeda "demands a broader concept of imminence," one that "must incorporate considerations of the relevant window of opportunity, the possibility of reducing collateral damage to civilians, and the likelihood of heading off disastrous attacks on Americans").

61 See, e.g., ASIL Speech.

62 But see John T. Bennett, *White House Quietly Shifts Armed Drone Program from CIA to DoD*, Defense News (May 24, 2013), www.defensenews.com/article/20130524/DEFREG02/305240010/ (citing senior Administration officials and new presidential policy guidance indicating "a preference for the Department of Defense" to conduct drone strikes (emphasis added)).

63 See, e.g., Human Rights Institute, Colum. Univ., *Background Note for American Society of International Law Annual Meeting, Targeting Operations with Drone Technology: Humanitarian Law Implications* (March 25, 2011), p. 8, available at www.law.columbia.edu/ipimages/Human_Rights_Institute/BackgroundNoteASILColumbia.pdf ("[I]t is not clear whether the Administration would characterize all hostilities beyond Afghanistan as part of a singular war. Even if it did, it is unclear whether the Administrations [sic] uses 'war'

B. *International Humanitarian Law and Lawyering*

As IHL scholars and practitioners take in these unexpected developments under the Obama Administration, they expand and dilute IHL in a number of ways. First, many take the position that ascertaining whether each instance of targeted killing is illegal is a matter solely of *jus ad bellum*. This position essentially holds that the legality of the use of force in the attacks is not at issue for IHL, and instead focuses on whether the attacks may violate the sovereignty of the territorial state or on whether the consent of the territorial state or whether that state is "unable and unwilling" to obviate threats emanating from its territory may be problematic.[64] Others in the field appear to focus not on the lawfulness of the resort to force but on compliance *during* the attacks and with reference to IHL principles, as opposed to binding conduct-of-hostilities rules. In this way, many IHL lawyers can engage the government and each other on technical legal issues of proportionality, distinction, and DPH as to specific operations despite the enormous implications in expanding the battlefield to include any corner of the globe where a senior member of al-Qaeda or an associated force may be. Still others focus on the conduct-of-hostilities issues, largely avoiding the question of whether they are raised as "a matter of policy" or as "fundamental principles," as opposed to law, holding that IHL can be discussed and applied in each attack as a discrete NIAC.

C. *International Human Rights Law and Lawyering*

Human rights lawyers, when faced with leading members of their profession within the Obama Administration supporting a much more muscular version of the war against al-Qaeda, respond in a number of surprising ways given their positions at the outset of the global war on terror. Chiefly, having gained a degree of fluency in IHL concepts over the course of the war on terror debates, many respond to the challenge of CIA-led targeted killing occurring outside Iraq and Afghanistan by pointing to the role that human rights can play in regulating the killing

synonymously with the term 'armed conflict'; thus, the United States may refer to a single 'war,' as a rhetorical matter, but regard itself as engaging in multiple armed conflicts.").

64 See, e.g., International Committee of the Red Cross, *The Use of Armed Drones Must Comply with Laws* (May 10, 2013), www.icrc.org/eng/resources/documents/interview/2013/05-10-drone-weapons-ihl.htm.

of terrorists.[65] This may be explained by an effort to maintain a dialogue with the government, and a desire to take advantage of the friendlier posture toward international law discourse and concepts by proffering practical ways that law can regulate killing. While some do articulate a clear position that human rights law makes targeted killing illegal, this argument – made almost exclusively by non-Americans – is rarely presented on its own.[66] Indeed, few U.S.-based human rights lawyers suggest that the entire targeted killing program outside Iraq and Afghanistan is illegal and that thus there is no legitimate role that human rights law or human rights discourse can play in regulating the attacks themselves. Instead, often arguing conditionally or in the alternative, human rights advocates present IHL-like arguments about targetability, which focus on whether specific individuals satisfy the criteria for DPH by analogy to a situation of armed conflict, or focus on the need for obtaining additional information from the government before making a final judgment regarding the legality of strikes.[67] In short, for many

[65] Notable statements arguing that IHRL might permit the use of lethal force outside of zones of armed conflict include *Letter from Kenneth Roth to President Barack Obama* (December 7, 2010), available at www.hrw.org/en/news/2010/12/07/letter-obama-targeted-killings, and Tom Malinowski, *Human Rights Watch Responds*, Lawfare Blog (October 26, 2010), www.lawfareblog.com/2010/10/human-rights-watch-responds/. In the new spirit of agreement between those who might in earlier years have viciously disputed one another's views, national security law experts have endorsed the Human Rights Watch position [Robert Chesney, *Malinowski on IHL Away from the Battlefield and on the Meaning of Imminence*, Lawfare Blog (December 14, 2010), www.lawfareblog.com/2010/12/malinowski-on-ihl-away-from-the-battlefield-and-on-the-meaning-of-imminence/ and carried out their own IHRL analyses on targeted killing.

[66] Philip Alston, Report of the Special Rapporteur on Extrajudicial, Summary or Arbitrary Executions, A/HRC/14/24/Add.6 (May 28, 2010), available at http://www2.ohchr.org/english/bodies/hrcouncil/docs/14session/A.HRC.14.24.Add6.pdf.

[67] A joint letter from leading human rights organizations calls upon the Administration publicly to disclose key targeted killing standards and criteria; ensure that U.S. lethal force operations abroad comply with international law; enable meaningful congressional oversight and judicial review; and ensure effective investigations, tracking, and response to civilian harm. In asking the Administration to make public information about the targeted killing program, the letter states, "In fact, improved transparency may serve national security by demonstrating the legal bases for targeted killing policies and practices." American Civil Liberties Union et al, *Statement Of Shared Concerns Regarding U.S. Drone Strikes and Targeted Killings* 2 (April 11, 2013), available at www.hrw.org/sites/default/files/related_material/4-11-13_US_LetterToPresidentObamaOnTargetedKillings.pdf. Finally, on the issue of international law, the document – rather uncharacteristically for human rights and advocacy organizations – does not appear to make any actual statements about the legality of the Administration's actions. This approach would likely have surprised and disappointed many of the same organizations in 2002.

U.S.-based human rights advocates, a pragmatic assessment of access to power begins to make human rights as war policy look more and more appealing; a blend of vague IHL concepts and human rights standards seems as though it is the only way that these advocates will maintain a meaningful role in the policy discussion.

This approach to law and style of argumentation seem to take the form of seeking out grounds for agreement with the government, jumping over the question of whether the overall framing of the war against al-Qaeda is anathema to human rights law and entering into the regulation of the killing itself. The discourse seems both to accept that the Administration's commitment to international law is genuine and to seek to accommodate this commitment by focusing on restraining the *types* and *frequency* of strikes and expanding available public information regarding the hostilities associated with the war against al-Qaeda.

V. Conclusion: Stitching the Threads Together

It now appears that the conflict formerly known as the "Global War on Terror" will continue for some time, and that the use of special forces, drones, and small elite commando units will take the place of massive ground troop commitments in a variety of countries where al-Qaeda and its affiliates are active. If international human rights or humanitarian lawyers were therefore to respond to the government today by simply saying, "We refuse to acknowledge that this is armed conflict; we refuse to acknowledge that this is NIAC; and we will not participate in arguing in the alternative," there is a chance that the state would simply forge ahead in conducting lethal strikes in a variety of sovereign states around the world, covertly and overtly. It may be that to the extent humanitarian lawyers and, increasingly, human rights lawyers are involved in this discussion, they are able to at the very least ensure that minimum standards are applied to operations involving targeting and detention.

However, it does seem clear that whatever international law is doing in this new formulation of global armed conflict, it is certainly outside the boundaries of long-established IHL and IHRL as understood at the outset of our story. The Obama Administration appears to be engaging in conduct that in 2001 would have been seen as a manipulation and instrumentalization of IHL and a co-optation and violation of IHRL. Further, these operations are presented as framed through a confusing admixture of IHL-like language, human rights rhetoric, and conduct-of-hostilities principles. In this mode, IHL functions not as binding international law regulating the behavior of the armed forces and armed groups in a territorially bounded and externally recognizable armed conflict, but rather as a free-floating and shifting set of principles that provide guidance for how to kill ethically. Unbound from its very narrow field of application, and delinked from the predicate political and factual tests that allow for its operation, this distinct body of international law thereby becomes what could be called "folk international humanitarian law," a set of concepts spoken and interpreted by a broad range of actors to provide a loose moral restraint on the organized use of lethal force.

I argue in this Section that the compromises, as well as the strategic and tactical professional choices, made over the course of the key debates presented herein played a role in constructing "folk international law."

1. *Convergence as Law*

The central purpose of the convergence of IHL and IHRL is to increase the protection of individuals in armed conflict. The notion behind the insistence that IHL and IHRL are part of the same discipline suggests that IHL is *part of* the far larger and more broadly applicable legal realm of IHRL. Indeed, the very idea of the "humanization of humanitarian law"[68] is that the cold, brutal balancing of IHL, its perceived deference to the military and the needs of the state is opened up and mitigated by a body of law that protects the individual's human rights against the state. Yet here the story flips: It is IHRL that seems to become part of IHL. It is IHRL that, by the end of our narrative, seems to be brought into the service of conflict, to act *not* as a powerful check on the brute force of the sovereign, *not* as the voice of the international community against those who wish to prioritize national security over individual liberties, but rather as a *means to regulate the use of lethal violence*. Having argued vociferously that IHRL applies in all situations of armed conflict at all times in order to protect individuals, the argument suddenly turns in the other direction. It becomes possible to say that IHRL can be utilized to allow for one state to invade another state's territory in order to murder individuals without an attempt to arrest, detain, charge, and try these individuals. What is so striking in this view is how well – if that is the

[68] Theodor Meron, *Editorial Comment, Revival of Customary International Humanitarian Law*, 99 AM. J. INT'L L. 817 (2005).

right word – the convergence argument worked, or at least how much work convergence ended up doing. Remarkably, many who wish to justify a far broader and even more aggressive CIA drone program cite convergence as a basis for doing so.[69]

For the application of IHL, on the other hand, the dominant assumption of convergence – that human rights law and IHL are part of the same general field, that they apply simultaneously, and that they are part of the same conversation – may have had the effect of loosening the boundaries around the field of application of IHL. As the two bodies of law began to be used interchangeably – as an attack utilizing a five-hundred-pound bomb is analogized to a police officer using a weapon when faced with the imminent danger of a hostage situation – one effect on the perception of IHL may be that it is no longer seen as a tightly controlled body of law. As many leading IHL lawyers warned in 2001 and 2002, once IHL is applied, many ugly things that we generally see as illegal, as outside the realm of rule of law, suddenly become lawful.

Those IHRL lawyers who argued that IHRL applies simultaneously to IHL during armed conflict may have contributed to the blurring of the line between war and not-war.

2. *Convergence as Lawyering*

We began this story with two distinct professions on September 10, 2001, and a description of what made them distinct. By 2013, this is certainly no longer the case. That IHL and IHRL are no longer discrete areas of practice has an impact on the kinds of arguments we see presented by the final stage, and creates a smaller universe of possible arguments that we will see in the future.

By 2013, once there is systematic killing going on outside of Iraq or Afghanistan, and as the government frames that killing in a law-sounding manner, it is highly appealing to turn to IHL. That is, after all, what IHL regulates: armed conflict. But this is where IHL as a discipline and a profession is so critical, and that may have been lost in the turn of human rights discourse toward IHL. Human rights lawyers, by invoking IHL standards of proportionality and distinction into situations that do not

[69] See, e.g., Radsan & Murphy, Measure Twice, Shoot Once, p. 1208 ("Analyzing the legality of targeted killing can be difficult because the practice falls between the two dominant legal models that generally are understood to control the state's use of force: human rights law and IHL.").

satisfy the material field of application of IHL, move into a mode of engaging with the state that is foreign to traditional approaches.

IHL assumes that everyone is on a very particular, very peculiar field: armed conflict. It is already a place where everyday life has been, to some extent, suspended. It is a place where most of our assumptions about the way in which human beings interact have been upended. Humanitarian lawyers understand that theirs is not a law that they will practice every day – indeed, they hope they do not – and it is not a law whose criteria for application they seek to expand.[70] They are not engaged in a broad institution-building project, and they are deliberate about constructing new law – due in part to concern that newer norms may diminish legal restraints applicable in armed conflict. IHRL takes a different approach to norm development and diffusion.

Human rights lawyers take an expansive approach to their discipline, to its institutions, and to its growth: More law is good, as are more institutions, more debate, and more people engaging in disparate projects that nominally fly the flag of the discipline. Practitioners are much less concerned with the idea that IHRL begins to apply at a particular moment. Human rights lawyers are accustomed to overlapping norms and to dealing with multiple municipal laws and regional systems.

By 2013, the human rights profession was attempting to utilize a new set of norms and principles derived from IHL, but not always with the level of nuance humanitarian lawyers would apply. This style, when applied to the finely calibrated concepts and balances of violence and humanity held within IHL, inadvertently expand the battlefield and may ultimately allow concepts of distinction, proportionality, and precautionary measures to supplant more protective human rights provisions. The collapse of multiple disciplines and fields of application into the "Law of 9/11" is not simply the product of a manipulative move by the government to justify its actions (although it is that). It is also the result of a particular approach to legal argumentation, mapped through various tactical moves made through the course of the legal battle over the war on terror.

[70] "The broadest, most significant criticism of humanitarian law seems to be that it should adopt provisions to cover so-called 'new forms of conflict.' Those who take this view are either wittingly or unwittingly calling for expansion of the concept of armed conflict, or the expansion of the scope of application of humanitarian law beyond armed conflict." Rona, *Interesting Times for International Humanitarian Law*, p. 63.

3. *The Flattening of the IAC/NIAC Distinction*

Another theme that emerges from this decade of 9/11 lawyering is the move away from two clear sub-species of armed conflict: that applicable to wars between states (international armed conflict) and that applicable in internal conflicts (non-international armed conflict) between states and rebels or between armed groups within the territory of a state.

For IHL lawyers, facing the danger of an angry superpower ready to walk away from the rules altogether, the functional merging of the body of rules applicable to each type of armed conflict served to ensure two things. First, it averted the risk that the United States would push for a new body of law at a time when it seemed nearly certain that any such law-making enterprise would result in a far less civilian-protective regime. Second, it ensured that at least some set of norms, even if not recognized as binding law, would apply to Afghanistan, and later Iraq, as those wars transitioned from classic international armed conflicts into far more complex, multinational engagements.

For its part, the ICRC clearly never accepted the notion of a global Common Article 3 NIAC, and continues to reject such a notion to this day.[71] It argues that you can have a multinational or transnational NIAC against a non-state actor, but that any determination regarding whether a NIAC exists must be subject to a case-by-case analysis of the facts.[72] It further argues, here in the mode of law as policy, that the *rules* applicable in IAC would nonetheless be applicable in almost all ways to NIAC, and that in this sense, the difference matters far less than it once did.[73]

For human rights lawyers, the flattening of the distinction between the rules of IAC and NIAC may not have been as carefully considered, but it functioned to provide discrete legal arguments in the many cases of individual detainees brought before U.S. courts. The decision to argue that Common Article 3 applied to the war against al-Qaeda was made in the context of a specific case against a government that argued it was fighting a global war with no rules derived from international law, as it

71 See, e.g., International Committee of the Red Cross, Opinion Paper, *How is the Term "Armed Conflict" Defined in International Humanitarian Law* (March 2008), pp. 3–5, available at www.icrc.org/eng/assets/files/other/opinion-paper-armed-conflict.pdf (describing the parameters of NIACs within the context of Common Article 3).

72 Interview by ICRC with Kathleen Lawand (December 10, 2012), available at www.icrc.org/eng/resources/documents/interview/2012/12-10-niac-non-international-armed-conflict.htm.

73 CIHL Study, p. 198 (noting that some customary rules of IHL "are indicated as being 'arguably' applicable [in NIACs as well as IACs] because practice generally pointed in that direction but was less extensive").

took hundreds of people into detention marked by brutal interrogations and secret transfers across borders.

Today, many non-IHL specialists see *Hamdan* as contributing to a solution to the problem of the war on terror by regulating the U.S. conflict with al-Qaeda through Common Article 3. The reasons and motivations for going beyond existing law to argue that IAC and NIAC are essentially the same *and* to argue that NIAC could apply were understandable. But with the further shift from NIAC to "*Transnational* NIAC" (that jurisprudence like *Hamdan* perhaps facilitated) we see some unintended consequences.

The law of NIAC assumes, as its paradigmatic case, that a state is fighting against rebels who seek to take power, to take over the state as the new government. Unlike IAC, a key background assumption of NIAC is that unless you have a sociopathic head of state, the state wants to get things back to peace as soon as possible. The concept of "Transnational NIAC" does not rest on this assumption. It now serves to provide the sense that some set of "minimal rules" or "foundational IHL principles" can be applied to conduct of hostilities in a range of countries, and even in a single instance of attack. In this way, it flips the purpose of opening up the boundaries of classification and softening the line between the two types of conflict: Rather than increasing restraints on the state, it serves as simultaneous *jus ad bellum* and *jus in bello* permissiveness, allowing the government to argue that any action is already in an armed conflict context, and that as such some subset of IHL rules applies.

As we look at the debate over targeted killing, it is clear that the "non-territorially strict material field of application of IHL" approach preferred by some who support expansion of the CIA drone program finds much support in arguments made in the heat of the struggle against the Bush Administration.

4. *Blurring of the Distinction between Combatants and Civilians through DPH*

The debates over the distinction between combatant and civilian – the rise of the concept of direct participation in hostilities and, particularly, the notion of a "continuous combat function" in an organized armed group – came similarly out of a discrete set of arguments with the government.

For IHL lawyers, the fact that the Bush Administration seemed to refuse to recognize *any* conventional definition of combatancy, particularly in the first two stages when it defined the war on terror as an international armed conflict unrestricted by IHL rules on detainees, meant that there was a high degree of pressure to ensure that existing law could be made plausible for the United States. IHL divides the battlefield into civilians and combatants, with a presumption in favor of civilian status. In the war on terror, this stringency seemed ever more unsustainable, even – in the eyes of some – allowing Osama bin Laden to enjoy the protections of civilian immunity. Whether this was correct as a matter of law, by 2006 many thought that revisiting the concept of direct participation in hostilities would maintain the relevance of IHL. The hoped-for consensus was never reached. Out of the debates, two points emerged. First, one of the world's leading promoters of IHL had, at the very least, identified a category of individuals who did not enjoy the privilege of combatancy but who could be targeted and killed as though they were combatants. Second, the distinction between civilians and combatants, often framed as the very bedrock, nearly absolute principle of IHL, was now seen by many as a disputed concept, one that was open to multiple reasonable interpretations.

For human rights lawyers, this topic, one of the most complex concepts of IHL and little known to those outside of the discipline, was borrowed as a tool for challenging the detention authority of the government, particularly as to whether specific detainees had in fact served as fighting members of al-Qaeda or the Taliban. As these arguments were made before the courts, human rights lawyers translated DPH and CCF from determinations of targetability in situations of armed conflict into standards for capture and detention.

Seen from the vantage point of 2013, the DPH debate, both in terms of the ultimate legal outcome and in terms of the ideas and disagreements that were fleshed out through the process of drafting the Interpretive Guidance, has come to play out in a much broader arena. When coupled with the increasingly fuzzy boundaries around the field of application of IHL (or between war and law enforcement), and the concept of transnational Common Article 3 NIAC, DPH has come to stand for the idea that individuals anywhere can be identified as targetable and therefore subject to the IHL principles for targeting.

5. *Conclusion*

Much has been written about the role of government lawyers in the war on terror, and surely the debates over the past ten years confirm that their work is critical to the ways that the state presents its choices through or against international law.[74] Our story, however, has focused on the role of IHL and IHRL as disciplines, as communities of lawyers, and as people who were involved in a decade of lawyering that many saw as a battle to save the very existence of international law in, and as a constraint on the behavior of, the U.S. Their engagements continue with the government, with each other, and with divisive and profoundly important substantive questions of law: When is a situation of violence a war, and when is it a policing exercise? When is a conflict "international" in some meaningful sense, and when is it bounded within the control of a single sovereign? Who can be killed, whose liberty can be deprived, and for what reasons? In some sense, neither discipline could nor wished to answer fully these questions, yet both desired to be deeply relevant to the regulatory framework that restrained and licensed the state's behavior and its legal justifications for that behavior. Both disciplines wished to capture the actions of the U.S. within their legal texts, their interpretive tools, and their normative commitments. To do so, each discipline had to make significant compromises, to shift its doctrinal boundaries, and to imagine how old definitions would come to accommodate new kinds of fighting, imprisonment, and force.

Ultimately, the fields of international humanitarian law and human rights impacted one another and the government, and the debates within and between the disciplines had important consequences. In the phases identified in this chapter, we see new terms and concepts used on the battlefield; we see disputed theories move from scholarly works to the highest court in the land; and we see many who began the decade disputing the arguments of government lawyers becoming government lawyers themselves.

Amid the muddle, what seems clear is that neither IHL nor IHRL are the disciplines that they were in 2001, and neither form of lawyering has remained untouched by the debates that took place. What remains most unclear is what will happen next. As these fields look forward, at least three significant questions arise. Will clarity be lost once again in order to

[74] See, e.g., Michael B. Mukasey, *The Role of Lawyers in the Global War on Terrorism*, 32 B.C. Int'l & Comp. L. Rev. 179 (2009).

make room for new authorities and new approaches? Will rigor diminish in order to gain and maintain access to government interlocutors? Will more lines be blurred in attempts to ensure that IHL and IHRL are able to maintain the hard-earned place they now have at the table of deciding how war will be fought into the second decade of the twenty-first century? The answers may be shaped by a coming legal elite forged in the battles of the last twelve years, perhaps defined more by responding to the demands of policy than by fealty to international law. The extent to which international law can meaningfully constrain authority during the tumult of armed conflict and other situations of lethal force may be at stake.

7

The Use and Abuse of Analogy in IHL

KEVIN JON HELLER[1]

Introduction

It is a truism to say that conventional international humanitarian law (IHL) regulates international armed conflict (IAC) far more extensively than non-international armed conflict (NIAC). In IAC, conventional IHL – the four Geneva Conventions and the First Additional Protocol – authorizes both targeting and detention and carefully circumscribes their use. In NIAC, by contrast, conventional IHL – Common Article 3 and the Second Additional Protocol – is silent on the authorization for targeting and detention and prescribes only rudimentary limits on when individuals may be targeted or detained.

Like nature, however, international law abhors a vacuum. Many of the gaps in the conventional IHL of NIAC have been slowly filled by custom. In its groundbreaking study, for example, the ICRC concluded that 138 of the 161 customary rules of IHL now apply in both IAC and NIAC – nearly 86%.[2] A number of those customary rules simply parallel provisions in the Second Additional Protocol[3] (AP II), such as the prohibition on attacking civilians[4] and the obligation to protect the wounded and sick.[5] But others go well beyond AP II, particularly concerning "the basic principles on the conduct of hostilities and… rules on specifically protected persons and objects and specific methods of

[1] My thanks to Nastasia Bach for her exceptional research assistance.

[2] *See* Emily Crawford, *Unequal before the Law: The Case for the Elimination of the Distinction between International and Non-international Armed Conflicts*, 20 Leiden Journal of International Law 441, 457 (2007).

[3] Protocol Additional to the Geneva Conventions of 12 August 1949, and relating to the Protection of Victims of Non-International Armed Conflicts, Art. 1, 16 I.L.M. 1442, 1125 U.N.T.S. 609 (1977).

[4] Jean-Marie Henckaerts & Louise Doswald-Beck, Customary International Humanitarian Law: Volume 1: Rules, Rule 1 (2005).

[5] *Id.*, Rules 109–11.

warfare."[6] As a result, it is now common for scholars to claim that, with the notorious exceptions of the combatant's privilege and POW status, very few critical differences remain between IAC and NIAC concerning the applicable rules of IHL.[7]

From a positivist perspective, of course, the gradual harmonization of IAC and NIAC through convention and custom is unproblematic. Both are formal sources of international law.[8] Since 9/11, however, the United States has consistently taken the position that certain IAC-based rules of IHL can be applied in NIAC via a third method: analogy. The U.S. has argued, for example, that it can target members of any organized armed group that would qualify as a "co-belligerent" of al-Qaeda under IAC rules.[9] Similarly, by analogizing to the "persons accompanying" provision of the Third Geneva Convention[10] (GC III), the U.S. has argued that it can detain individuals who are not members of al-Qaeda but substantially support it.[11]

In assessing the legitimacy of such analogies, it is tempting to focus on whether it makes sense to apply a particular IAC rule in NIAC.[12] Is the Haqqani Network's relationship with al-Qaeda really equivalent to Italy's relationship with Nazi Germany? Are individuals who regularly cook for members of al-Qaeda really like supply contractors working with the U.S. Armed Forces? Emphasizing the substantive "fit" between IAC and NIAC, however, simply obscures a more fundamental question: *Where does the U.S.'s authority to analogize between IAC and NIAC come from?*

That is a critical question, for two reasons. First, targeting and detention each potentially violate the human rights of the individuals they affect. As the International Law Commission (ILC) has noted, it is not enough for targeting or detention to qualify as a legitimate act of

[6] Jean-Marie Henckaerts, *Study on Customary International Humanitarian Law*, 87 Int'l Rev. Red Cross 175, 189 (2005).

[7] *See* Crawford, *supra* note 2, at 462–65.

[8] *See* Statute of the International Court of Justice, art. 38, 59 Stat. 1055, TS No. 993 at 25, 3 Bevans 1199.

[9] *See, e.g.*, Respondents' Memorandum Regarding the Government's Detention Authority Relative to Detainees Held at Guantanamo Bay at 7, Hamlily v. Obama, 616 F. Supp. 2d 63 (D.D.C. March 13, 2009) (No. 05-763), ECF No. 175.

[10] Geneva Convention (III) Relative to the Treatment of Prisoners of War, art. 4(A)(1) and (2), August 12, 1949, 6 U.S.T. 3316, 75 U.N.T.S. 135

[11] *See, e.g.*, Department of Defense Directive Number 2310.01E (August 19, 2014), Appendix, at 14.

[12] *See, e.g.*, Duncan B. Hollis, *Re-Thinking the Boundaries of Law in Cyberspace: A Duty to Hack?*, Temple University Research Paper No. 2014-16, at 16 (May 27, 2014) (noting that "[a]nalogical reasoning requires that the context from which the analogy originates shares sufficiently relevant similarities (and no relevant dissimilarities) with the targeted context").

self-defense under Art. 51 of the U.N. Charter; that targeting or detention must also be consistent with either IHL or international human rights law (IHRL), depending on which legal regime applies.[13] By expanding its ability to target and detain, therefore, the U.S.'s use of analogy increases the number of acts that it must justify under IHL or IHRL.

Second, because all of the targeting and detention activities that occur in the NIAC between the U.S. and al-Qaeda take place extraterritorially, each U.S. use of force and each capture operation potentially violates the sovereignty of the state on whose territory it takes place. The U.S.'s analogies between IAC and NIAC greatly expand its ability to target and detain extraterritorially; its use of analogy thus significantly increases the number of acts that it must defend as legitimate self-defense.

Put more simply, by relying on analogized rules of IHL to justify expanded targeting and detention of al-Qaeda, the U.S. potentially runs afoul of a number of prohibitive rules of international law: the principle of non-intervention; the prohibition on the use of force; and IHRL prohibitions on the arbitrary deprivation of life and liberty. What, then, is the legal basis for those analogies?

This chapter's answer is straightforward: *nothing*. There is no basis in international law for taking rules of IHL that apply as a matter of convention and custom only in IAC and applying them in NIAC by analogy. The U.S. is thus systematically violating international law by relying on those analogized rules to target and detain extraterritorially.

The chapter itself is divided into two sections. Section I traces the rise of IHRL and the evolution of what has been called "transnational armed conflict"[14] in order to explain why there must always be a conventional or customary basis for extraterritorial targeting and detention. Section II then explains why the absence of the required conventional or customary basis dooms each of the IAC-based rules of IHL that the U.S. has applied in NIAC by analogy.

I. The Necessity of Convention or Custom

Given the considerable practical impact analogized rules of IHL have had on the U.S.'s targeting and detention practices, we would expect the U.S.

[13] International Law Commission, Draft Articles on Responsibility of States for Internationally Wrongful Acts, with Commentaries, at 74, A/56/10 (2001).

[14] *See generally* Geoffrey Corn & Eric Talbot Jensen, *Transnational Armed Conflict: A "Principled" Approach to the Regulation of Counter-Terror Combat Operations*, 42 Isr. L. Rev. 46–79 (2009).

government (USG) to have provided a robust defense of the legality of analogy. After all, from a positivist standpoint, it is anything but self-evident that states are free to analogize at will between IAC and NIAC. The analogized rules are not applicable in NIAC via conventional law. They cannot be viewed as general principles of law. And although some scholars talk about analogizing IAC rules of IHL to NIAC through customary international law,[15] that is not the argument the USG is making[16] – it has never claimed that the rules it applies by analogy have achieved customary status.

In fact, the USG has never made any attempt whatsoever to explain why international law permits it to analogize between IAC and NIAC. With regard to co-belligerency, for example, Jeh Johnson has merely stated that the U.S. has "publicly defined an 'associate force' as [being]… a co-belligerent with al Qaeda in hostilities against the United States or its coalition partners."[17] Similarly, with regard to detention, the Department of Justice has simply claimed that the U.S. has the authority to detain anyone "whose relationship to al-Qaida or the Taliban would, in appropriately analogous circumstances in a traditional international armed conflict, render them detainable."[18] The USG has not even been able to articulate a rationale for analogy in response to direct questions from the judiciary; an exasperated Judge Bates noted during the *Hamlily* litigation that "[a]fter repeated attempts by the Court to elicit a more definitive justification for the 'substantial support' concept in the law of war, it became clear that the government has none."[19]

Fortunately for the USG, other judges have proven far more credulous. The DC Circuit quickly rejected Judge Bates's conclusion that

[15] *See, e.g.*, Noëlle Quénivet, *The Moscow Hostage Crisis in the Light of the Armed Conflict in Chechnya*, 4 Y.B. Int'l Humanitarian L. 348, 361–62 (2001) (noting that "a way of arguing that analogy can be made is that 'there exists, at present, a corpus of customary international law applicable to all armed conflicts irrespective of their characterisation as international or non-international armed conflicts'") (citation omitted).

[16] Silja Voneky, *Analogy in International Law, in* Max Planck Encyclopedia of International Law, ¶ 9, available at http://opil.ouplaw.com/home/EPIL ("[O]ne can and must differentiate between reasoning by analogy and the evidence of a rule of customary international law, even if there may be cases of doubt which are hard to decide.").

[17] Jeh C. Johnson, *The Conflict Against Al Qaeda and its Affiliates: How Will It End?*, Speech at the Oxford Union, Oxford University (November 30, 2012), available at www.lawfareblog.com/2012/11/jeh-johnson-speech-at-the-oxford-union/#_ftn11.

[18] Respondents' Memorandum, *supra* note 9, at 1.

[19] Memorandum Opinion, at 18, Hamlily v. Obama, Civil Action No. 05–0763 (JDB) (D.D.C. 2009).

"substantial support" did not justify detention in NIAC, and no other court – District or Court of Appeals – has ever rejected an attempt by the USG to apply an IAC rule to NIAC by analogy.[20] Like the USG itself, however, those courts have uniformly failed to explain why international law permits analogizing between IAC and NIAC in the absence of a customary basis for doing so. In *Hamlily*, for example, the same Judge Bates who showed such admirable skepticism toward the USG's "substantial support" analogy had no problem concluding that co-belligerency could be applied in NIAC. Why did he reach that conclusion, despite acknowledging that "[l]ike many other elements of the law of war, co-belligerency is a concept that has developed almost exclusively in the context of international armed conflicts"? Because – and this was the totality of his argument, itself relegated to a footnote – "there is no reason why this principle is not equally applicable to non-state actors involved in noninternational conflicts."[21]

American scholars have also generally failed to articulate a coherent rationale for analogizing between IAC and NIAC. Bradley and Goldsmith, for example, simply claim that the U.S. can target al-Qaeda's co-belligerents because "the laws of war at a minimum would deem 'neutrals' that systematically violate the laws of neutrality by supporting or assisting other terrorist organizations to be lawful military targets."[22] In a similar vein, Lederman and Vladeck have suggested that "perhaps substantial supporters of enemy forces who are apprehended while accompanying such forces can be detained on roughly the same terms as the forces themselves, just as they can be in an international conflict. Cf. Third Geneva Convention, art. 4(4)."[23] Those scholars do not explain why international law permits the analogy they endorse; they focus solely on the supposed substantive desirability of applying a particular IAC-based IHL rule to NIAC.

There is, however, one notable exception to scholarly silence on the legal basis of analogy: Ryan Goodman. Goodman defends the U.S.'s right to analogize between IAC and NIAC as follows:

[20] As discussed in more detail later, the D.C. Circuit rejected applying co-belligerency to NIAC by analogy in Al-Bihani v. Obama, 590 F.3d 866, 873 (D.C. Cir. 2010). But it did so in order to reject a habeas petition filed by a Guantánamo detainee; the USG did argue analogy in that case.

[21] Hamlily Memorandum Opinion, *supra* note 19, at 16 n 16.

[22] Curtis A. Bradley & Jack Goldsmith, *Congressional Authorization in the War on Terror*, 118 Harv. L. Rev. 2048, 2113 (2005).

[23] Marty Lederman & Steve Vladeck, *The NDAA: The Good, the Bad, and the Laws of War – Part I*, Opinio Juris (December 31, 2011), available at http://opiniojuris.org/2011/12/31/the-ndaa-the-good-the-bad-and-the-laws-of-war-part-i/ (citation in the original).

> IHL is uniformly less restrictive in internal armed conflicts than in international armed conflicts. Accordingly, if states have authority to engage in particular practices in an international armed conflict (e.g., targeting direct participants in hostilities), they a fortiori possess the authority to undertake those practices in noninternational conflict. Simply put, whatever is permitted in international armed conflict is permitted in noninternational armed conflict. Hence, if IHL permits states to detain civilians in the former domain, IHL surely permits states to pursue those actions in the latter domain.[24]

Goodman's defense of analogy appears to be based squarely on the Permanent Court of International Justice's seminal judgment in the *Lotus* case – its second principle in particular:

> It does not … follow that international law prohibits a State from exercising jurisdiction in its own territory, in respect of any case which relates to acts which have taken place abroad, and in which it cannot rely on some permissive rule of international law. Such a view would only be tenable if international law contained a general prohibition to States to extend the application of their laws and the jurisdiction of their courts to persons, property and acts outside their territory, and if, as an exception to this general prohibition, it allowed States to do so in certain specific cases. But this is certainly not the case under international law as it stands at present. Far from laying down a general prohibition to the effect that States may not extend the application of their laws and the jurisdiction of their courts to persons, property and acts outside their territory, it leaves them in this respect a wide measure of discretion, which is only limited in certain cases by prohibitive rules; as regards other cases, every State remains free to adopt the principles which it regards as best and most suitable. This discretion left to States by international law explains the great variety of rules which they have been able to adopt without objections or complaints on the part of other States.
>
> In these circumstances all that can be required of a State is that it should not overstep the limits which international law places upon its jurisdiction; within these limits, its title to exercise jurisdiction rests in its sovereignty.[25]

Goodman's argument, in other words, seems to be this: (1) the ability of states to target and detain in armed conflict is limited only by prohibitive rules of IHL; (2) because there are fewer prohibitive IHL rules concerning targeting and detention in NIAC than in IAC, any targeting or detention

[24] Ryan Goodman, *The Detention of Civilians in Armed Conflict*, 48 Am. J. Int'l L. 48, 50 (2009).

[25] *Lotus*, 1927 P.C.I.J. (ser. A) No. 10, at 19.

that is not prohibited in IAC cannot be prohibited in NIAC; (3) states are thus free to apply IAC-based targeting and detention rules to NIAC, because by definition such analogized rules cannot violate a prohibitive rule of IHL.

The key here is that Goodman is arguing – if only implicitly – that states are free to analogize between IAC and NIAC as a matter of *domestic law*, not international law.[26] He is not claiming that international law itself permits states to apply IAC-based rules to NIAC by analogy; his point is that states are free to adopt whatever targeting and detention principles they want in their domestic law unless something in international law prohibits them from doing so. That is why he can also insist that the "same logic . . . does not apply to proscriptive rules. If IHL forbids states from engaging in particular actions in international armed conflicts, it does not necessarily follow that the same prohibition applies in a noninternational conflict."[27] In terms of the second *Lotus* principle, the distinction between permissive and prohibitive rules makes sense: Although there is no need to demonstrate that a particular permissive rule exists in NIAC as well as in IAC, because states are free to organize their domestic law of targeting and detention however they want as long as they do not violate a prohibitive rule, there *is* a need to show that a particular prohibitive rule of targeting or detention applies in NIAC as well as in IAC, because – to quote another part of the *Lotus* judgment – "[r]estrictions upon the independence of States cannot . . . be presumed."[28]

This is a coherent defense of analogy – but one that is ultimately unpersuasive. Although Goodman's *Lotus*-like argument would have made sense prior to World War II, the rise of universal human rights and the evolution of transnational NIAC have rendered that argument obsolete. There are now at least *four different* prohibitive rules that limit the freedom of states to apply IAC-based targeting and detention rules to NIAC solely by analogy – namely, the principle of non-intervention, the prohibition on the use of force, and IHRL's rights to life and liberty.

[26] *Cf.* Ashley Deeks, *Domestic Humanitarian Law: Developing the Law of War in Domestic Courts*, University of Virginia School of Law Public Law and Legal Theory Research Paper Series 2013–39, at 18 (October 2013) (distinguishing between international humanitarian law and domestic humanitarian law, and including in the latter category situations where "courts must first interpret traditional IHL principles and then apply those principles analogically to a new conflict").

[27] Goodman, *Detention of Civilians*, *supra* note 24, at 50.

[28] *Lotus*, *supra* note 25, at 18.

A. *The Absence of International Law*

Until the late 1940s, international law had almost nothing to say about how a state waged what we now call a non-international armed conflict. Because such conflicts were generally fought on the state's own territory, the principle of non-intervention and the prohibition on the use of force – the latter still in its infancy anyway – did not apply. International human rights law did not yet exist. And prior to the adoption of the Geneva Conventions in 1949, IHL regulated only international armed conflicts – wars between two or more states.[29] The one exception was the rare civil war in which the insurgents were so organized and hostilities so intense that third states had both "the right and the duty to grant recognition of belligerency,"[30] which required them to treat the warring parties as if they were engaged in a traditional international armed conflict.[31]

In this early phase of NIAC's evolution, the second *Lotus* principle did indeed effectively grant a state unfettered discretion to wage war against an insurgent group. There were simply no prohibitive rules of international law that limited the kind of targeting and detention rules the state could adopt as a matter of what Deeks aptly calls "domestic humanitarian law." Indeed, the right of a state to determine how it wanted to combat an insurgency was *itself* a prohibitive rule of international law, one that prevented other states from claiming the right to interfere in the internal conflict. As Kretzmer notes, "[a]ny outside interference was regarded as incompatible with the principle of sovereignty, the linchpin of international law in the post-Westphalian era."[32]

At this point in time, then, IHL was the state's enemy, not its friend. Given that the *jus ad bellum* did not apply to internal NIACs and IHRL did not yet exist, IHL provided the only conceivable limits on a state's

[29] David Kretzmer, *Rethinking the Application of IHL in Non-International Armed Conflicts*, 42 Isr. L. Rev. 8, 13 (2012); Sandesh Sivakumaran, The Law of Non-International Armed Conflict 222 (2012).

[30] 2 Lassa Oppenheim, International Law: A Treatise § 76, at 197 (Hersch Lauterpacht ed., 6th ed. 1940).

[31] Yair M. Lootsteen, *The Concept of Belligerency in International Law*, 166 Mil L. Rev. 109, 114 (2000) ("While not conferring statehood, proper recognition of belligerency grants the rebels substantive protections under the laws of war.").

[32] Kretzmer, *Rethinking*, *supra* note 29, at 13; *see also* John Cerone, *Jurisdiction and Power: The Intersection of Human Rights Law & the Law of Non-International Armed Conflict in an Extraterritorial Context*, 40 Isr. L. Rev. 396, 402 (2007) (noting that because conflicts "other than between states" were "traditionally not the concern of international law ... [t]he principle of non-intervention generally prevented international regulation of such conflicts").

freedom to do whatever it wanted to quell an insurgency. States thus went to great lengths to prevent third states from recognizing insurgent groups as belligerents,[33] because once a state was involved in a recognized belligerency, it had to extend belligerent rights to the insurgents – most notably, combatant's privilege and POW status – or it would lose its own belligerent rights in the eyes of third states.[34] And, of course, states scrupulously resisted applying any of the major IHL conventions of the time, such as the 1907 Hague Convention IV and the 1929 Geneva Convention on the Wounded and Sick in Armies in the Field, to civil wars.[35]

B. The Rise of IHRL

After World War II, the number of prohibitive rules of international law multiplied exponentially.[36] To begin with, conventional IHL began to regulate NIAC: Common Article 3 of the 1949 Geneva Conventions protects "persons taking no active part in the hostilities" from mistreatment in any "armed conflict not of an international character occurring in the territory of one of the High Contracting Parties,"[37] while the Second Additional Protocol of 1977 regulates both detention and targeting in armed conflicts that "take place in the territory of a High Contracting Party between its armed forces and dissident armed forces or other organized armed groups which, under responsible command, exercise such control over a part of its territory."[38] Those conventions, of course, do not regulate NIAC anywhere near as comprehensively as the Geneva Conventions and First Additional Protocol regulate IAC. But customary international law has closed the gaps between the two considerably: as noted earlier, the ICRC takes the position that only 23 of 161 customary rules of IHL now apply solely in IAC.[39]

33 *See* Lootsteen, *supra* note 31, at 114 (noting that Britain's recognition of the Civil War as a belligerency was "much to the chagrin" of Lincoln).

34 *See* Hersch Lauterpacht, Recognition in International Law 232 (1947) ("[I]f the lawful government were to claim belligerent rights whilst denying them to the insurgents, such illogical and one-sided conduct would invalidate its continued recognition as a belligerent.").

35 Sivakumaran, *supra* note 29, at 222.

36 *See generally* Cerone, *supra* note 32.

37 *See, e.g.*, Geneva Convention Relative to the Protection of Civilian Persons in Time of War, Art. 3, August 12, 1949, 6 U.S.T. 3516, 75 U.N.T.S. 287.

38 AP II, *supra* note 3, Art. 1(1).

39 Crawford, *supra* note 2, at 457.

The post-war expansion of conventional and customary IHL into NIAC was mirrored by the evolution of IHRL. As Rona says, "World War II gave us the Age of Rights."[40] The watershed moment was the U.N. General Assembly's adoption of the Universal Declaration of Human Rights (UDHR) in 1948, because its affirmation that "[e]veryone has the right to life, liberty and security of person,"[41] regardless of "the political, jurisdictional or international status of the country or territory to which a person belongs,"[42] meant that "the relationship between a State and its citizens and residents was no longer regarded as being a matter in the sole prerogative of each State."[43] The UDHR was merely hortatory, but its adoption led to the rapid proliferation of international and regional human-rights conventions whose prohibitive rules were binding on the states that ratified them, such as the European Convention on Human Rights (1953),[44] the International Covenant on Civil and Political Rights (1966),[45] the American Convention on Human Rights (1969),[46] and the Convention Against Torture and Other Cruel, Inhuman or Degrading Treatment or Punishment (1984).[47] Those conventions not only include provisions that govern the use of lethal force and detention, there is also – at least now, following the ICJ's decision in the *Nuclear Weapons* case[48] – no question that they continue to apply during armed conflict.[49]

[40] Gabor Rona, *A Bull in a China Shop: The "War on Terror" and International Law in the United States*, 39 Cal. West. J. Int'l L. 101 (2008).

[41] Universal Declaration of Human Rights, Art. 3, G.A. Res. 217 (III), U.N. Doc. A/RES/217 (III) (December 10, 1948).

[42] *Id.*, art. 2. [43] Kretzmer, *Rethinking*, *supra* note 29, at 8–9.

[44] Convention for the Protection of Human Rights and Fundamental Freedoms, 213 U.N.T.S. 222 (1953).

[45] ICCPR, G.A. Res. 2200A (XXI), at 52, U.N. GAOR, 21st Sess., Supp. No. 16, U.N. Doc. A/6316 (December 16, 1966).

[46] O.A.S. Treaty Series No. 36, 1144 U.N.T.S. 123.

[47] Convention Against Torture and Other Cruel, Inhuman or Degrading Treatment or Punishment, December 10, 1984, 1465 U.N.T.S. 85 (entered into force 1987).

[48] Legality of the Threat or Use of Nuclear Weapons, Advisory Opinion, 1996 I.C.J. 226 (July 8), ¶ 25.

[49] *See, e.g.*, Noam Lubell, *Challenges of Applying Human Rights Law to Armed Conflict*, 87 Int'l Rev. Red Cross 737, 738 (2005) ("The focus of the arguments is now shifting from the question of if human rights law applies during armed conflict to that of how it applies, and to the practical problems encountered in its application."); Kretzmer, *Rethinking*, *supra* note 29, at 17 (noting that it is "quite clear that during an internal armed conflict in a State's territory that State remains bound by its human rights obligations toward those in its territory, and subject to its jurisdiction"); Louise Doswald-Beck, *The Right to Life in Armed Conflict: Does International Humanitarian Law Provide All the Answers?*, 88 Int'l

The rise of the "Age of Rights" has led states to rethink their traditional aversion to regulating NIAC through IHL. Prior to World War II, states wanted to keep IHL out of NIACs fought on their territory, because the absence of IHL meant that targeting and detention were regulated solely by domestic law. Now, however, the choice is not between no international regulation and regulation by IHL, but between regulation by IHL and regulation by IHRL. And that is no contest: as discussed in more detail in Section II, the prohibitive rules of IHRL impose far greater substantive limits on targeting and detention than the prohibitive rules of IHL. As a result, states now want to ensure that IHL applies in NIAC as broadly as possible – in order to keep IHRL out.[50]

States' preference for IHL, of course, implicates the much-debated principle of *lex specialis*. As Sivakumaran notes, "in the majority of situations, a particular norm will exist both in international human rights law as well as in international humanitarian law. In such instances, the precise relationship between the two norms will have to be ascertained."[51] Three basic versions of *lex specialis* exist: (1) *total displacement*, according to which IHL completely displaces IHRL in situations of armed conflict; (2) *partial displacement*, which accepts that both IHL and IHRL apply in armed conflict but insists that specific rules of IHL displace competing rules of IHRL (understood as rules whose application would lead to a different substantive result); and (3) *principle of norm-conflict resolution*, according to which specific rules of IHL do not "ipso facto override, displace or qualify conflicting norms of IHRL," but must always be taken into account when interpreting IHRL norms.[52]

Rev. Red Cross 881, 886 (2006) (noting that "human rights law does not make a distinction between armed conflict and peace").

50 *See, e.g.*, Claus Kress, *Some Reflections on the International Legal Framework Governing Transnational Armed Conflicts*, 15 J. Conflict & Sec. L. 245, 260 (2010) (noting that, "in light of the (perceived) threat posed by violent non-State actors, States seem to be more interested in availing themselves of the wider powers they can derive from the application of the law of non-international armed conflict (compared with international human rights law) than they are concerned by the restraining effect of the ensuing obligations"); *cf.* Kretzmer, *Rethinking*, *supra* note 29, at 39 ("While the original intention behind extension of IHL to non-international armed conflicts was to enhance the protection granted to potential victims of such conflicts, given the dramatic development of IHRL, categorization of a situation as one of armed conflict, rather than internal unrest, may serve to weaken the protection offered to potential victims rather than to strengthen it.").

51 Sivakumaran, *supra* note 29, at 89.

52 Marko Milanovic, *The Lost Origins of Lex Specialis: Rethinking the Relationship Between Human Rights and International Humanitarian Law*, this volume, at 24–28.

It is no longer possible to defend the first version of *lex specialis*, for all the reasons that Milanovic has identified – state practice, the derogation provisions in human-rights conventions like the ECHR, the ICJ's *Nuclear Weapons* opinion, and so on.[53] The crux of the debate is thus between the second and third versions. Most scholars seem to adopt the partial-displacement view,[54] though Milanovic has persuasively defended the norm-conflict-resolution view.[55]

We do not have to decide which version of *lex specialis* is correct, though, because both versions share a common assumption: namely, that an applicable rule of IHRL can be displaced or modified only by a competing rule of IHL. In the absence of a competing rule of IHL – or, differently put, in the presence of a gap in IHL – both versions of *lex specialis* agree that the rule of IHRL applies.

The key here is "competing rule of IHL." Scholars uniformly assume that the kind of IHL rule capable of displacing or modifying a competing rule of IHRL is one that is based on either convention or custom.[56] They

53 *Id.* at 24–25.

54 *See, e.g.*, Doswald-Beck, *supra* note 49, at 903–04 ("Specific, clear and well-established rules of IHL can be considered to be *lex specialis*."); Deborah Casalin, *Taking Prisoners: Reviewing the International Humanitarian Law Grounds for Deprivation of Liberty by Armed Opposition Groups*, 93 INT'L REV. RED CROSS 743, 745–46 (2011) ("IHRL still applies during NIACs to the extent that . . . an IHRL rule has not been superseded by a more specific rule of IHL operating as *lex specialis*."); Marco Sassoli, *The Relationship Between International Humanitarian and Human Rights Law Where It Matters: Admissible Killing and Internment of Fighters in Non-International Armed Conflicts*, 90 INT'L REV. RED CROSS 599 (2008) (noting that *lex specialis* "seeks to establish . . . a preferential order for two rules that apply to the same problem but regulate it differently").

55 *See generally* MILANOVIC, *Lex Specialis*, *supra* note 52.

56 *See, e.g.*, John F. Murphy, *Will-o'-the-Wisp? The Search for Law in Non-International Armed Conflicts*, 88 INT'L LAW STUD. 15, 25 (2012) (noting that IHL should ideally be extended to NIAC by convention, but accepting that "if this method of extension is a mission impossible, as the evidence convincingly demonstrates, then customary international law methodology will have to be employed"); Sean Watts, *Present and Future Conceptions of the Status of Government Forces in Non-International Armed Conflict*, 88 INT'L LAW STUD. 145, 151 (2012) ("[T]he material field of application of a number of important international law-of-war instruments has recently been expanded to NIAC. By their terms, these treaties formerly regulated only IAC. Previously, their extension to NIAC could only be achieved by proof of customary status-a technique fraught with ambiguity and subject to vexing caveat."); Jens Ohlin, *Is Jus in Bello in Crisis?* 11 J. INT'L CRIM. JUST. 27, 35 (2013) ("The gap-filling version of the co-application thesis is particularly relevant with regard to the rules applicable in NIACs which are codified only in Common Article 3 and APII, arguably leaving substantial gaps in which IHRL might be applied. However, if one argues that IAC norms apply by virtue of custom in NIAC, then the available space for IHRL to 'fill the gap' is substantially reduced.");

have never suggested that an IHL rule that applies solely by analogy is the kind of *lex* capable of representing the *lex specialis*. On the contrary, Krieger has specifically stated that IHL "does not per se override human rights law in cases where humanitarian law itself is only applied by way of analogy,"[57] while Vöneky has made the more general point that because "an argument by analogy is valid only if and as far as a lacuna exists," the issue in question "must not be covered by any rule of international law or any general principle of law."[58]

The idea that only a rule of *international law* is capable of displacing a competing rule of international law via *lex specialis* explains why the second *Lotus* principle does not, in fact, permit a state to apply an IAC-based rule of IHL to NIAC by analogy. As we have seen, the argument for analogy depends upon the idea that states have the right to organize their domestic law as they see fit, subject only to prohibitive rules of international law – that is what the PCIJ meant in *Lotus* when it said that, with reference to a state's exercise of prescriptive and enforcement jurisdiction on its own territory, "[i]n these circumstances all that can be required of a State is that it should not overstep the limits which international law places upon its jurisdiction."[59] It is true that in internal NIACs there may be no prohibitive rules of *IHL* that prevent states from analogizing between IAC and NIAC. *But there are prohibitive rules of IHRL that do so.*[60] Those rules could be displaced or modified by rules of IHL that exist as a matter of convention or custom, but they cannot be displaced or modified by permissive or less prohibitive rules of IHL that exist only as *domestic law*. A state that insists it can violate prohibitive

William Abresch, *A Human Rights Law of Internal Armed Conflict: The European Court of Human Rights in Chechnya*, 16 Eur. J. Int'l L. 741, 748 (2005) ("There is a broad consensus that Common Article 3 and Protocol II fail to effectively regulate many aspects of those conflicts, but some lawyers and advocates look to customary international law – unwritten rules that states consider to be legally binding – to fill the gaps.").

[57] Heike Krieger, *A Conflict of Norms: The Relationship Between Humanitarian Law and Human Rights Law in the ICRC Customary Law Study*, 11 J. Conflict & Sec. L. 265, 273 (2006); *see also* Crawford, *supra* note 2, at 453, ("[P]olicy arguments alone are not enough to make a viable case for the elimination of the distinction between types of armed conflict. Support for the proposition needed to be found in other sources of international law, namely from state practice and from *opinio juris*.").

[58] Voneky, *supra* note 16, at ¶ 16. [59] *Lotus*, *supra* note 25, at 19.

[60] Interestingly, Goodman acknowledges in a footnote that his argument "relates only to IHL. The application of other legal regimes – e.g., human rights law – might complicate this account, especially insofar as those rules impose obligations on the exercise of state power domestically and not extraterritorially." Goodman, *Detention of Civilians*, *supra* note 24, at 50 n. 9.

rules of IHRL because it has relied on analogy to adopt contrary rules of "domestic humanitarian law" thus *precisely* "overstep[s] the limits which international law places upon its jurisdiction."[61]

C. *Transnational NIAC*

Traditional NIACs were generally fought on "the territory of one of the High Contracting Parties," even if hostilities had a propensity to spill across state borders. Such NIACs still take place, but transnational armed conflicts – NIACs in which states are engaged in hostilities with organized armed groups located primarily, if not exclusively, on the territory of other states[62] – have become increasingly common: Israel's NIAC with Hezbollah in Lebanon in 2006; Columbia's NIAC with FARC in Ecuador in 2008; Turkey's ongoing NIAC with the PKK in Iraq; and, of course, the U.S.'s seemingly endless NIAC with al-Qaeda in Afghanistan, Pakistan, Yemen, and Somalia. As we will see, the evolution of transnational NIAC both complicates and strengthens the case against analogy.

1. IHL and IHRL

The complication involves the relationship between IHL and IHRL. As long as a NIAC is being fought primarily on a state's own territory, there is no question that the hostilities are governed by both legal regimes (via *lex specialis*, however interpreted); IHRL's application is primarily territorial.[63] But what about transnational NIACs? Are they governed solely by IHL or by both IHL and IHRL?

Answering that question, of course, requires addressing the difficult and much-debated issue of whether and to what extent IHRL applies extraterritorially. If IHRL does not apply extraterritorially, states are in an odd situation: unable to rely on analogy when fighting a NIAC on their territory (because of the limits IHRL imposes on their domestic law), but able to rely on analogy when fighting a transnational NIAC (because their domestic law would not be limited by IHRL.)

[61] *Lotus*, *supra* note 25, at 19; *see also* Hugh Handeyside, *Note, The Lotus Principle in ICJ Jurisprudence: Was the Ship Ever Afloat?*, 29 MICH. J. INT'L L. 71, 90 (2007) (noting that the ICJ in the *Nuclear Weapons* case "suggested that the only instance in which the Lotus principle would come into play would be one in which no principles or rules of international law could be said to restrict the state behavior in question").

[62] *See, e.g.*, Watts, *supra* note 56, at 155.

[63] Cerone, *supra* note 32, at 416.

The better view, however, is that IHRL does apply extraterritorially, at least with regard to the rights at issue in targeting and detention – the right to life and the right to liberty. A complete examination of that issue is beyond the scope of this chapter, but three points are worth emphasizing. First, it seems clear that conventional IHRL applies to extraterritorial detention – a proposition that Van Schaack has described as "categorical."[64] The Human Rights Committee has consistently taken that position, most recently in General Comment 35, which states that because "arrest and detention bring a person within a state's effective control, States parties must not arbitrarily or unlawfully arrest or detain individuals outside their territory."[65] That conclusion is echoed by a long line of cases decided by the European Court of Human Rights (ECtHR), such as *Issa*,[66] *Öcalan*,[67] and *Al-Skeini*,[68] as well as by the jurisprudence of the Inter-American Court of Human Rights.[69] Even high-ranking USG officials – though not the USG itself – have acknowledged that the right not to be arbitrarily deprived of liberty applies extraterritorially.[70]

Second, there is also strong support for the idea that, at a minimum, prohibitive rules of conventional IHRL – particularly the right to life – apply extraterritorially. The Human Rights Committee has consistently suggested as much,[71] and according to Van Schaack "[a] longitudinal review" of the relevant jurisprudence "reveals a distinct trend toward an understanding that States' human rights obligations follow their agents and instrumentalities offshore whenever they are in a position to respect – or to violate – the rights of individuals they confront abroad."[72] Cerone has reached a similar conclusion, adding that "the structure of Article 2(1)

64 Beth Van Schaack, *The United States' Position on the Extraterritorial Application of Human Rights Obligations: Now is the Time for Change*, 90 Int'l L. Stud. 20, 52 (2014).

65 Human Rights Committee, General Comment No. 35: Article 9: Liberty and Security of the Person, CCPR/C/GC/35, ¶ 64 (October 28, 2014) (Advanced Unedited Version).

66 Issa v. Turkey, 41 Eur. Ct. H.R. 567, ¶ 70 (2004).

67 Öcalan v. Turkey, 37 Eur. Ct. H.R. 10, ¶ 93 (2003).

68 Al-Skeini v. United Kingdom, App. No. 55721/07, 53 Eur. H.R. Rep. 589, 597, ¶ 80 (2011).

69 *See, e.g.*, Coard et al. v. United States, Case 10.951, Inter-Am. Comm'n H.R., Report No. 109/99, OEA/Ser.L/V/II.106 doc. 6 rev., ¶ 37 (1999).

70 Harold H. Koh, Legal Advisor, U.S. Department of State, Memorandum Opinion on the Geographic Scope of the International Covenant on Civil and Political Rights, at 4 (October 19, 2010), available at http://justsecurity.org/wp-content/uploads/2014/03/state-department-iccpr-memo.pdf.

71 *See* David Kretzmer, *Targeted Killing of Suspected Terrorists: Extrajudicial Executions or Legitimate Means of Defence?*, 16 Eur. J. Int'l L. 171, 184 (2005).

72 Van Schaack, *supra* note 64, at 32.

of the ICCPR supports the notion that negative obligations apply vis-à-vis all individuals everywhere, whereas positive obligations may have a more limited scope."[73]

Finally, even if the right to life does not apply extraterritorially as a matter of conventional law, it almost certainly applies extraterritorially as a matter of custom. As Kretzmer notes, "[w]hile a state party's treaty obligations are a function of the scope of application defined in the particular treaty, some of the substantive norms in human rights treaties that have been ratified by the vast majority of states in the world, have now become peremptory norms of customary international law. The duty to respect the right to life is surely one of these norms."[74] Many other scholars – of very different political persuasions – agree.[75]

Because IHRL's rights to life and liberty almost certainly apply extraterritorially, states are no more free to rely on analogy in transnational NIAC than they are in purely internal NIAC. In both situations, their freedom to adopt targeting and detention rules as domestic humanitarian law is limited by the prohibitive rules of IHRL.

2. IHL, the Principle of Non-Intervention, and the *Jus ad Bellum*

As long as states fought NIACs on their own territory, IHRL represented the only possible limitation on their targeting and detention practices. But once NIACs went transnational, the legal landscape changed dramatically:

> Transnational armed conflict greatly strains traditional territorial or politically based claims of exclusive sovereign prerogative on the part of the government under attack. Classic, non-extraterritorial NIAC has relied greatly on traditional notions of territorial sovereignty to fend off

[73] Cerone, *supra* note 32, at 446.

[74] Kretzmer, *Targeted Killing*, *supra* note 71, at 184–85.

[75] *See, e.g.*, Michael N. Schmitt, *Extraterritorial Lethal Targeting: Deconstructing the Logic of International Law*, 52 Colum. J. Trans. L. 77, 110 (2013) ("[T]here is nevertheless a customary international human rights law right to life that applies extraterritorially."); Noam Lubell, Extraterritorial Use of Force Against Non-State Actors 235 (2010) ("Since forcible measures, such as killings and torture, are in fact a subject of customary international law, extraterritorial measures of this type can amount to a violation of international human rights obligations, regardless of treaty applicability and how it is interpreted."); Cerone, *supra* note 32, at 436 (noting, with respect to conventional IHRL, that "this limitation of scope may not apply with respect to those human rights norms that have evolved into customary international law. Thus, all states may be bound by these norms in their dealings with anyone anywhere").

> international regulation. With their cross-border incursions and movements, transnational armed conflicts unmoor NIAC from many of its traditional claims to general freedom from international regulation.[76]

In particular, the extraterritorial targeting and detention that are regular aspects of transnational NIAC implicate the first *Lotus* principle, which says that states cannot exercise enforcement jurisdiction on the territory of another state unless a permissive rule of international law allows them to do so:

> The first and foremost restriction imposed by international law on a State is that – failing the existence of a permissive rule to the contrary – it may not exercise its power in any form in the territory of another State. In this sense jurisdiction is certainly territorial; it cannot be exercised by a State outside its territory except by virtue of a permissive rule derived from international custom or from a convention.
>
> Far from laying down a general prohibition to the effect that States may not extend the application of their laws and the jurisdiction of their courts to persons, property and acts outside their territory, it leaves them in this respect a wide measure of discretion, which is only limited in certain cases by prohibitive rules.[77]

All transnational NIACs have to confront the first *Lotus* principle – but its implications are particularly acute for the U.S.'s transnational NIAC with al-Qaeda, in which the USG is applying a variety of permissive IAC-based rules of IHL by analogy. At the domestic level, the U.S.'s right to use force against al-Qaeda is governed by the AUMF, which provides, in relevant part, that "the President is authorized to use all necessary and appropriate force against those nations, organizations, or persons he determines planned, authorized, committed, or aided the terrorist attacks that occurred on September 11, 2001."[78] As discussed in more detail in Section II, by analogizing between IAC and NIAC, the USG has greatly expanded the number of persons against whom it is entitled to use force extraterritorially under the AUMF – it can target al-Qaeda's "associated forces" as well as Al-Qaeda itself because of the analogy to co-belligerency; it can detain individuals who "substantially support" either because of the analogy to "persons accompanying" in GC III; and so on. More importantly, the U.S. has almost certainly *actually used* more extraterritorial force in its transnational NIAC with al-Qaeda than it would have in the absence of

[76] Watts, *supra* note 56, at 156. [77] *Lotus, supra* note 25, at ¶¶ 45, 46.
[78] Authorization for Use of Military Force, Pub. L. No. 107–40, 115 Stat. 224 (2001).

analogy. It is reasonable to assume, for example, that the drone program in Somalia would look very different if the USG could not use co-belligerency to connect al-Shabaab to al-Qaeda.

Each time it relies on the AUMF to extraterritorially target or detain a member of "al-Qaeda and its associated forces," however, the U.S. must avoid violating the first *Lotus* principle. Simply put, extraterritorial targeting and detention are each potentially limited by two different prohibitive rules of international law[79]: the prohibition on the use of force in Art. 2(4) of the UN Charter; and the principle of non-intervention, "the obligation of states to refrain from performing jurisdictional acts within the territory of other states except by virtue of general or special permission."[80] Any act that violates the prohibition on the use of force will violate the principle of non-intervention,[81] but not all acts that violate the principle of non-intervention will violate the prohibition on the use of force – the principle of non-intervention applies to extraterritorial material acts of enforcement jurisdiction generally, while the prohibition on the use of force applies only to those extraterritorial material acts that involve the "threat or use of force."[82]

It is uncontroversial that extraterritorial targeting qualifies as a "use of force" for purposes of Art. 2(4); that is the position of both the U.N.[83] and most scholars.[84] The U.S. has also acknowledged that the *jus ad bellum* applies to its targeted killings – it has always defended them by

[79] The ICJ made clear in the *Nicaragua* case that although there is substantial overlap between the prohibition on the use of force and the principle of non-intervention, they are different prohibitive rules under customary international law. *See* Military and Paramilitary (Nicar. v. U.S.), 1986 I.C.J. 14 (June 27), ¶ 185.

[80] Elihu Lauterpacht, I International Law 487–88 (1970); *see also Nicaragua*, *supra* note 79, at ¶ 202 ("The principle of non-intervention involves the right of every State to conduct its affairs without outside interference.").

[81] Michael C. Bonafede, *Note, Here, There, and Everywhere: Assessing the Proportionality Doctrine and U.S. Uses of Force in Response to Terrorism After the September 11 Attacks*, 88 Cornell L. Rev. 155, 169 (2002).

[82] *Nicaragua*, *supra* note 79, at ¶ 202.

[83] Report of the Special Rapporteur on Extrajudicial, Summary or Arbitrary Executions, Philip Alston, at ¶ 34, U.N. Doc. A/HRC/14/24/Add.6, (May 28, 2010) ("Targeted killings conducted in the territory of other States raise sovereignty concerns. Under Article 2(4) of the U.N. Charter, States are forbidden from using force in the territory of another State.").

[84] *See* Nils Melzer, Targeted Killing in International Law 51 (2008) ("Authors generally agree that, in principle, the resort by a State to targeted killings within another State falls under the prohibition on interstate force expressed in Article 2(4) U.N. Charter"); *see also* Tom Ruys, *The Meaning of "Force" and the Boundaries of the* Jus ad Bellum*: Are "Minimal" Uses of Force Excluded from UN Charter Article 2(4)?*, 108 Am J. Int'l L. 159, 209 (2014) ("[A] deliberate projection of lethal force onto the territory of

invoking self-defense under Art. 51 of the U.N. Charter, and that right exists only in relation to acts that violate Art. 2(4).[85] An unjustified act of extraterritorial targeting thus violates both the *jus ad bellum* and the principle of non-intervention.

There is some controversy, by contrast, over extraterritorial detention. The general view is that a capture operation on another state's territory qualifies as a use of force under Art. 2(4),[86] and the U.S. has specifically invoked self-defense when asked to provide a legal justification for such operations – most recently with regard to the capture of Ahmed Abu Khattalah in Libya.[87] Nevertheless, some scholars continue to insist that such operations are the kind of "[m]inimal or *de minimis* uses of force [that] fall below the threshold of the Article 2(4) prohibition."[88] The Independent International Fact-Finding Mission on the Conflict in Georgia has taken the same position.[89] That dispute is inconsequential here, however, because all scholars agree that, at a minimum, extraterritorial capture and detention can violate the principle of non-intervention.[90]

another state – even if small-scale and even if not targeting the state itself – will normally trigger Article 2(4).").

85 *See, e.g.*, Department of Justice White Paper, *Lawfulness of a Lethal Operation Directed Against a U.S. Citizen Who Is a Senior Operational Leader of Al Qa'ida or an Associated Force*, at 3 (Undated), available at http://msnbcmedia.msn.com/i/msnbc/sections/news/020413_DOJ_White_Paper.pdf ("Any operation of the sort addressed here would be conducted in a foreign country against a senior operational leader of al-Qaida or its associated forces who poses an imminent threat of violent attack against the United States. A use of force in such circumstances would be justified as an act of national self-defence.").

86 *See* Dan E. Stigall, *Ungoverned Spaces, Transnational Crime, and the Prohibition on Extraterritorial Enforcement Jurisdiction in International Law*, 3 NOTRE DAME J. INT'L L 1, 18 (2013) ("With regard to an extraterritorial arrest, such action is considered to be a use of force in the territory of another sovereign and is tantamount to abduction."); *see also* Ruys, *Use of Force*, *supra* note 84, at 197.

87 Letter from Samantha Powers to Vitaly Churkin, President of the United Nations Security Council (June 17, 2014), available at http://justsecurity.org/15436/war-powers-resolution-article-51-letters-force-syria-isil-khorasan-group/ (claiming that those actions "were taken in accordance with the United States' inherent right of self-defense"); *see also* Abraham Sofaer, *Irregular Apprehension of Criminal Suspects*, 84 AM. J. INT'L L. 725, 727 (1990) ("Arrests in foreign states without their consent have no legal justification under international law aside from self-defense.").

88 MARY ELLEN O'CONNELL, The Prohibition on the Use of Force, in Research Handbook on International Conflict and Security Law 89, 102 (Nigel White & Christian Henderson eds., 2013).

89 *See* 2 REPORT OF THE INDEPENDENT INTERNATIONAL FACT-FINDING MISSION ON THE CONFLICT IN GEORGIA 242 n. 49 (2009).

90 *See, e.g.*, ELIHU LAUTERPACHT, *supra* note 80, at 488 (noting that the principle prohibits "the sending of agents for the purpose of apprehending within foreign territory persons

Extraterritorial targeting and detention thus each potentially violate at least one prohibitive rule of international law: targeting potentially violates both the prohibition on the use of force and the principle of non-intervention; detention potentially violates either the prohibition on the use of force or the principle of non-intervention. That does not mean that the extraterritorial targeting and capture conducted pursuant to analogized rules of IHL is necessarily unlawful. But it does mean that the U.S. is not free to engage in such targeting and detention as it sees fit. On the contrary, the U.S. must a find a permissive rule of international law that legitimizes its analogy-based extraterritorial targeting and detention; as the PCIJ said in *Lotus*, "the first and foremost restriction imposed by international law on a State is that – failing the existence of a permissive rule to the contrary – it may not exercise its power in any form in the territory of another State."

Two such permissive rules, of course, immediately suggest themselves. The first is consent: extraterritorial targeting and detention do not violate either the prohibition on the use of force or the principle of non-intervention when a state is acting with the consent of the territorial state.[91] Such situations are not uncommon, but they are clearly not the norm. The U.S. is thus more likely – as indicated by past practice – to invoke the second permissive rule: self-defense. Self-defense under Art. 51 of the U.N. Charter is a prototypic exception to the prohibition on the use of force, and the ICJ suggested in the *Nicaragua* case that self-defense can also justify breaches of the principle of non-intervention.[92]

A use of force must satisfy three requirements in order to qualify as self-defense. The first two are well-known, if under-studied: necessity and proportionality.[93] As Section II discusses in detail, because many acts of

accused of having committed a crime"); Simon Chesterman, *The Spy Who Came in from the Cold War: Intelligence and International Law*, 27 MICH. J. INT'L L. 1071, 1082 (2006) (noting that the principle "would clearly cover unauthorized entry into territory" and "unauthorized use of territory, such as Italian claims that CIA agents abducted an Egyptian cleric in Milan in February 2003"); INT'L BAR ASS'N, REPORT OF THE TASK FORCE ON EXTRATERRITORIAL JURISDICTION 10 (2009) ("[A] state cannot investigate a crime, arrest a suspect, or enforce its judgment or judicial processes in another state's territory without the latter state's permission.").

91 *See, e.g.*, Alston Report, *supra* note 83, at ¶ 35; MELZER, *supra* note 84, at 51.

92 *Nicaragua*, *supra* note 79, at ¶ 210; *see also* Sofaer, *supra* note 87, at 727 ("[I]nternational law ... permits extraterritorial "arrests" in situations which permit a valid claim of self-defense.").

93 *See* TOM RUYS, "ARMED ATTACK" AND ARTICLE 51 OF THE U.N. CHARTER 94 (2010) ("Notwithstanding the broad consensus as to their limiting role, the necessity and proportionality criteria have generated relatively little (in-depth) academic interest.").

analogy-justified extraterritorial targeting and detention will violate the proportionality requirement, the U.S.'s application of those rules in transnational NIAC is problematic.

The third requirement of self-defense is of particular relevance to the legitimacy of applying IAC-based rules of IHL to NIAC by analogy: *self-defensive acts must comply with IHL in order to be lawful under the jus ad bellum.* This requirement is generally ignored in contemporary debates about self-defense under Art. 51, but it was specifically affirmed by the ICJ in the *Nuclear Weapons* case:

> [A] use of force that is proportionate under the law of self-defence, must, in order to be lawful, also meet the requirements of the law applicable in armed conflict which comprise in particular the principles and rules of humanitarian law.[94]

The ICJ's conclusion does not simply re-state the uncontroversial idea that compliance with the *jus ad bellum* does not free an attacker from the need to comply with IHL. What it means is that – as Christopher Greenwood has noted – an extraterritorial use of force that does not comply with IHL violates *both* the *jus in bello* and the *jus ad bellum*:

> [T]he logical justification for holding that a state which is entitled to use force must comply with the *jus in bello* lies in considerations of the *jus ad bellum*, namely that an act which contravened the jus in bello could not be a reasonable and proportionate measure of self-defence. In that sense, the rules of the *jus in bello* give detailed expression to one of the principles of the *jus ad bellum*.[95]

[94] *Nuclear Weapons*, *supra* note 48, at ¶ 42.

[95] Christopher Greenwood, *The Relationship Between* Ius ad Bellum *and* Ius in Bello, 9 REV. INT'L STUD. 221, 231 (1983); *see also* Andreas Zimmerman, *The Second Lebanon War:* Jus ad Bellum, Jus in Bello *and the Issue of Proportionality*, 11 MAX PLANCK Y.B. U.N. L. 99, 124 (2007) ("[A] further prerequisite relates to the fact that measures taken under Article 51 of the Charter must be also legal for purposes of jus ad bellum, i.e., must abide by applicable rules of international humanitarian law. This inter-linkage between jus ad bellum and jus in bello was unequivocally confirmed by the ICJ in its Advisory Opinion concerning the Legality of the Threat or Use of Nuclear Weapons."); Eyal Benvenisti, *Rethinking the Divide Between Jus ad Bellum and Jus in Bello in Warfare Against Nonstate Actors*, 34 YALE J. INT'L L. 541, 542 n. 6 (2009) ("Although the *jus ad bellum* assessment does not depend on *jus in bello* considerations, a response to aggression that harms noncombatants excessively would be regarded itself as a *jus ad bellum* violation."); JUDITH GARDAM, NECESSITY, PROPORTIONALITY, AND THE USE OF FORCE BY STATES 168–69 (2004) ("From time to time, there have been suggestions that issues such as the means and methods of warfare adopted by a State in the exercise of its right of self-defence are purely in the province of IHL.... However, the requirements of proportionality in its *jus ad bellum* sense must also be met."). This is also clear from

This requirement creates a serious problem for the use of analogy. As we have seen, rules of IHL that are applied in NIAC by analogy to IAC do not represent international law; they have no basis in convention or custom. Those rules are simply domestic law, their application ostensibly justified by NIAC's relative lack of prohibitive conventional and customary IHL rules. But the *jus ad bellum* (and thus presumably the principle of non-intervention) requires compliance with *international* humanitarian law – the conventional or customary laws of war. Nothing in the *Nuclear Weapons* opinion or in the writings of scholars like Greenwood suggests that a use of force satisfies the *jus ad bellum* as long as it complies with the domestic humanitarian law of the attacking state. And indeed, that idea seems fundamentally at odds with the assumption underlying the IHL-compliance requirement: namely, that a state is only entitled to use force extraterritorially when its actions are consistent with all of the prohibitive rules of international law, from the *jus ad bellum* to the *jus in bello*.

To be fair, it might be argued – drawing on Goodman's work – that as long as an analogized rule does not violate a specific prohibitive conventional or customary rule of IHL that applies in NIAC, extraterritorial targeting or detention conducted pursuant to that rule cannot be considered "inconsistent" with IHL. Such an argument, however, seems to rely on a counterintuitive understanding of consistency. As long as an analogized rule allows for the targeting or detention of individuals who could not be targeted or detained under conventional and customary rules of IHL, such targeting and detention cannot be considered consistent with – cannot "meet the requirements of" – IHL. In other words, using analogy to expand the reach of IHL in NIAC beyond conventional or customary law *is* a form of inconsistency.

That said, the response does highlight an unresolved issue in the *jus ad bellum*. The *Nuclear Weapons* case focused on armed conflict; it did not address a situation in which a state uses the kind of force that triggers the *jus ad bellum* during peacetime. Presumably, in such situations, the *jus ad bellum* requires the use of force not only to be necessary and proportionate, but also to comply with the applicable rules of IHRL. Assume, for example, that an act of self-defense involving targeted killing would be

the context of paragraph 42 in the *Nicaragua* judgment. Paragraph 40 introduced the following paragraphs by stating that "[t]he entitlement to resort to self-defence under Article 51 is subject to certain constraints. Some of these constraints are inherent in the very concept of self-defence. Other requirements are specified in Article 51." *Nicaragua*, *supra* note 79, at ¶ 40.

"arbitrary" under either IHL or IHRL. If that act would violate the *jus ad bellum* in an armed conflict, it would surely also violate the *jus ad bellum* in peacetime.

II. Specific Analogies

From an international law perspective, in short, the U.S. practice of applying IAC-based rules of IHL to NIAC by analogy is very difficult to justify. Because those analogized rules represent domestic law, not international law, *Lotus* permits the U.S. to apply them only insofar as they do not run afoul of a prohibitive rule of international law. With the rise of human rights and the evolution of transnational NIAC, however, a number of prohibitive rules now potentially limit the use of analogy in the context of targeting and detention: the rules of IHRL, which apply to all NIACs, as well as the principle of non-intervention and the prohibition on the use of force, which apply in transnational armed conflict. Insofar as an analogized rule results in targeting or detention that violates one or more of those prohibitive rules, therefore, the U.S. is violating international law.

This section now turns to specific analogies between IAC and NIAC – most applied by the U.S., but one defended by scholars who believe that analogy to IAC permits organized armed groups to detain individuals in NIAC. As we will see, because none of the analogies have a basis in conventional or customary international law, they all violate the prohibitive rules of IHRL, the prohibitive rules governing extraterritorial targeting and detention, or both.

A. "Ongoing" Self-Defense

In a speech at Harvard in 2011, John Brennan, then the Assistant to the President for Homeland Security, claimed that because the U.S. was engaged in an armed conflict with al-Qaeda, the USG "takes the legal position that – in accordance with international law – we have the authority to take action against al-Qa'ida and its associated forces without doing a separate self-defense analysis each time."[96] According to Brennan, in other words, the requirements of self-defense under

[96] John O. Brennan, *Strengthening our Security by Adhering to our Values and Laws*, Speech at Harvard University (September 16, 2011), available at www.whitehouse.gov/the-press-office/2011/09/16/remarks-john-o-brennan-strengthening-our-security-adhering-our-values-an.

Art. 51 of the U.N. Charter – necessity, proportionality, and compliance with IHL – applied only to the U.S.'s initial act of self-defense against al-Qaeda; because its response (arguably) complied with those requirements, its subsequent acts of targeting and detention against "al-Qaeda and its associated forces" were and are subject solely to IHL.

Brennan cited only "international law" for this position, which we might call "ongoing" self-defense, but it appears to be based on analogy to a particular understanding of self-defense in IAC that has been articulated by Dinstein, Ago, and Kunz. Dinstein argues that "[t]here is no support in the practice of States for the notion that proportionality remains relevant – and has to be constantly assessed – throughout the hostilities in the course of war. Once war is raging, the exercise of self-defence may bring about 'the destruction of the enemy's army', regardless of the condition of proportionality."[97] Similarly, Ago wrote – in his capacity as the ILC's Special Rapporteur for State Responsibility – that "[t]he limits inherent in the requirement of proportionality are clearly meaningless where the armed attack and the likewise armed resistance to it lead to a state of war between two countries."[98] And Kunz took the position that self-defense is not limited to repelling an armed attack, but "seems to give the state or states exercising the right of individual or collective self-defense the right to resort to a justified war, to carry this war to victory, to impose a peace treaty upon the vanquished aggressor."[99]

It is easy to see why the U.S. would want to analogize this IAC-based understanding of self-defense to its NIAC with al-Qaeda: it insulates the U.S. from the claim that although it was clearly entitled to act in self-defense in response to al-Qaeda's initial armed attack – especially an attack of the magnitude of 9/11 – its subsequent actions have exceeded the limits of proportionality. Differently put, "ongoing" self-defense permits the U.S. to completely destroy al-Qaeda and its associated forces – to "carry this war to victory" – even if a less ambitious warfighting strategy would completely neutralize the threat of armed attack posed by those groups.

Ongoing self-defense might have represented positive international law prior to World War II – the type of large-scale war that Dinstein,

[97] Yoram Dinstein, War, Aggression, and Self-Defense 237 (4th ed. 2005).
[98] Robert Ago, *Addendum to Eighth Report on State Responsibility*, [1980] II ILC Y.B. 13, 70.
[99] Josef L. Kunz, *Individual and Collective Self-Defense in Article 51 of the Charter of the United Nations*, 41 Am. J. Int'l L. 872, 876–77 (1947).

Ago, and Kunz were addressing.[100] Post-Charter practice, however, indicates that the doctrine no longer applies even in *IAC*. Ruys notes, for example, that although the international community might have been prepared to accept that the U.S. acted in self-defense when it invaded the Dominican Republic in 1965 to protect its citizens, many states unequivocally condemned the U.S.'s later decision to overthrow the left-wing regime because they believed regime change was disproportionate to that goal.[101] Similarly, Gardam points out that even if states accepted the idea that the U.S. invasion of Panama in 1989 was a legitimate act of self-defense, they did not believe that protecting American nationals justified removing General Noriega from power.[102] Indeed, the idea of ongoing self-defense is generally inconsistent with state practice that insists self-defense must be temporally limited – a proportionality factor that by definition must be assessed *in media res*.[103]

It is also worth noting that Dinstein, Ago, and Kunz are very much in the minority concerning ongoing self-defense. Most scholars believe that each and every use of force during an armed conflict is subject to the same self-defense requirements as a state's initial response to an armed attack.[104] Greenwood's position is typical:

> This requirement of proportionality ... means that it is not enough for a state to show that its initial recourse to force was a justifiable act of self-defence and that its subsequent acts have complied with the *jus in bello*. It must also show that all its measures involving the use of force,

[100] Dinstein specifically cites World War II as an example, DINSTEIN, *supra* note 97, at 240, and Kunz was writing in 1947.

[101] *See* RUYS, *supra* note 93, at 117.

[102] GARDAM, *supra* note 95, at 166–67.

[103] *See* RUYS, *supra* note 93, at 119–20.

[104] *See also Id.* at 123–24 ("There exists no neat separation between the two, in the sense that necessity would determine when defensive action would be permissible, whereas proportionality would be the standard to evaluate what could be done in self-defence: to the contrary, both standards must constantly be kept under review and overlap to a certain degree."); Robert D. Sloane, *The Cost of Conflation: Preserving the Dualism of* Jus ad Bellum *and* Jus in Bello *in the Contemporary Law of War*, 34 YALE J. INT'L L. 47, 68 (2009) ("Even more generally, the *jus ad bellum* now applies not only to the initial decision to resort to force but also to all conduct 'involving the use of force which occurs during the course of hostilities'. That conduct must be necessary and proportionate to the casus belli.") (citation omitted); GARDAM, *supra* note 95, at 156 ("Proportionality, moreover, remains relevant throughout a conflict. A State cannot assess proportionality at the time of making the decision as to the appropriate response to an armed attack and then dispense with it."); David Kretzmer, *The Inherent Right to Self-Defence and Proportionality in* Jus Ad Bellum, 24 EUR. J. INT'L L. 235, 267–68 (2013) ("War aims may have to be redefined and consideration given to the necessity of using further force as well as caused by pursuing those aims. Hence, examining the proportionality of the force may become an ongoing process.").

> throughout the conflict, are reasonable, proportionate acts of self-defence. Once its response ceases to be reasonably proportionate then it is itself guilty of a violation of the *jus ad bellum*. The fact that the modern *jus ad bellum* thus applies during a conflict has important legal consequences. It means that an attack carried out in the middle of a conflict upon what is, in terms of the *jus in bello*, a legitimate military target by methods which are not forbidden by the *jus in bello* will nevertheless be a violation of international law if it cannot be justified by reference to the principle of self-defence.[105]

It is unclear whether Ago and Kunz would disagree in the context of NIAC; both wrote long before NIAC went transnational. (Kunz wrote in 1947; Ago in 1980.) Dinstein, however, would almost certainly be skeptical of analogizing between IAC and NIAC in the context of ongoing self-defense: he specifically distinguishes between a "war of self-defense" and self-defense that responds to an "isolated armed attack" of the kind that normally triggers a transnational NIAC, suggesting that proportionality remains relevant during self-defense of the latter type.[106]

More importantly, though, state practice simply does not support the U.S. claim that ongoing self-defense applies in NIAC, as the international response to the 2006 NIAC in Lebanon fought by Israel and Hezbollah demonstrates. Initially, many states – ranging from Denmark to Japan to Tanzania – supported Israel's right to use force against Hezbollah in self-defense.[107] As the NIAC dragged on and Lebanese civilian casualties continued to mount, though, more and more states claimed that Israel's actions had become disproportionate – including states such as France and Argentina, which had supported Israel at the outbreak of the conflict.[108]

In short, and *pace* Brennan's Harvard speech, state practice in both IAC and NIAC indicate that, as most scholars believe, ongoing self-defense has no relevance in any kind of armed conflict.

[105] Greenwood, *Relationship*, *supra* note 95, at 223. It is worth noting Greenwood acknowledges that, in practice, the continuing applicability of the *jus ad bellum* would not mean much in the context of an existential conflict such as World War II. *Id.*; *see also* Ruys, *supra* note 93, at 117 ("In extreme cases (for instance, if one State were to commence an all-out war against another), this would even warrant the defending State pursuing a total military defeat of the attacking State or the removal of its regime.").

[106] Dinstein, *supra* note 97, at 238.

[107] Christine Gray, *The Bush Doctrine Revisited: The 2006 National Security Strategy of the USA*, 5 Chinese J. Int'l L. 555, 573 (2006).

[108] *Id.* at 575.

B. *Declarations of War*

This U.S. analogy is its most ambitious: relying on "declarations of war" by organized armed groups to establish the existence of a NIAC. Specifically, the U.S. has consistently argued in the *al-Nashiri* and *al-Qosi* cases that its NIAC with al-Qaeda began when Osama bin Laden declared war on the U.S. in 1996. Here, for example, is how the USG replied to the al-Qosi's argument that no NIAC existed because the U.S. did not consider itself at war with al-Qaeda prior to 9/11:

> While the events of September 11, 2001, no doubt constitute an act of war, that day was not the start of the armed conflict with al Qaeda. Rather, the United States has been engaged in a [non]international armed conflict with al Qaeda since at least the mid-1990s. Indeed, al Qaeda declared war on the United States in 1996. Importantly, a state of armed conflict exists even if one party does not recognize a state of war. Geneva Convention I, Article II (1949). Here, al Qaeda has organized, planned, and carried out attacks against United States as well as its citizens, diplomats, and military personnel around the world, consistent with its 1996 declaration of war.[109]

The USG's reliance on bin Laden's declaration of war in *al-Qosi* is clearly based on analogy to IAC, as the citation to the First Geneva Convention (GC I) indicates. Similarly, the USG has defended its position by noting that "[t]he Law of War applies to all cases of declared war or any other armed conflicts that arise between the U.S. and other nations, even if the state of war is not recognized by one of them"[110] – an explicit reference to IAC.[111]

It is not surprising that the U.S. wants to analogize between IAC and NIAC with regard to the beginning of armed conflict. Relying on bin Laden's declaration of war has three distinct advantages. First, by temporally expanding the NIAC between the U.S. and al-Qaeda, it ensures that more targeting and detention are governed by the rules of IHL instead of by IHRL's much more restrictive rules. The U.S. may not

[109] U.S. v. Al-Qosi, Government Response to Defense Motion to Dismiss the Charges for Lack of Subject Matter Jurisdiction to the Extent They Related to the Period Prior to 11 September 2001, D-013, at 1 (November 7, 2008). At least one American scholar has taken the same position. *See* Karl S. Chang, *Enemy Status and Military Detention in the War Against Al-Qaeda*, 47 Tex. Int'l L. J. 1, 57 (2011).

[110] International and Operational Law Department The Judge Advocate General's Legal Center and School, The Operational Law Handbook 15 (2007).

[111] Al-Qosi, Government Response, *supra* note 109, at 1.

accept that IHRL applies extraterritorially, but it is keenly aware that its allies, particularly in Europe, do not share its position.[112] It thus has a political interest, if not a legal one (according to its understanding of IHRL), in bringing as many acts of targeting and detention as possible within the rubric of IHL. Second, and relatedly, because IHL's rules concerning targeting and detention are far less restrictive than IHRL's rules, expanding the temporal limits of the U.S./al-Qaeda NIAC makes it easier for the U.S. to satisfy the final requirement of the *jus ad bellum* discussed earlier: demonstrating that its extraterritorial uses of force comply with the applicable rules of IHL or IHRL. Third, the U.S. must expand the temporal limits of its NIAC with al-Qaeda in order to prosecute al-Qosi and al-Nashiri in military commissions, because those commissions only have jurisdiction over acts committed during armed conflict.[113]

There is, however, no conventional or customary basis for determining the existence of NIAC by reference to "declarations of war" by an organized armed group.[114] Neither CA3 nor AP II defines NIAC, and there is widespread agreement - among scholars[115] and by the International Law Association[116]- that the ICTY's definition of NIAC in *Tadić*[117] reflects customary international law. Under *Tadić*, declarations of war are irrelevant; whether a NIAC exists is determined solely by reference to the organization of the parties and the intensity of the hostilities.[118] That is a purely objective test - a party's intent, whether

112 Koh, Memorandum Opinion, *supra* note 70, at 2–3.

113 Hamdan v. Rumsfeld, 548 U.S. 557, 639 (2006).

114 For that matter, there is no longer a basis in convention or custom for determining the existence of *IAC* by reference to declarations of war. *See* International Law Association, *Final Report on the Meaning of Armed Conflict in International Law*, at 33 (2010), available at www.ila-hq.org/download.cfm/docid/2176DC63-D268-4133–8989A664754F9F87 ("The earlier practice of states creating a *de jure* state of war by a declaration is no longer recognized in international law.").

115 Sivakumaran, *supra* note 29, at 155 (noting that the *Tadić* definition "has since been adopted by a variety of influential actors and is widely recognized as authoritative. It defines the notion of an armed conflict for the purposes of Article 3 common to the four Geneva Conventions of 1949 as well as the notion of a non-international armed conflict in customary international law").

116 *Final Report on the Meaning of Armed Conflict*, *supra* note 114, at 3. The ILA reached that conclusion based on an exhaustive multi-year study of the armed conflicts that took place between 1945 and 2010. *Id.* at 2.

117 Prosecutor v. Tadić, Case No. IT-94-1-I, Decision on Defence Motion for Interlocutory Appeal on Jurisdiction, ¶ 70 (October 2, 1995).

118 *Final Report on the Meaning of Armed Conflict*, *supra* note 114, at 28–29.

to affirm or deny the existence of NIAC, has no bearing on whether the requisite organization and intensity of hostilities exist.[119]

C. *Targeting*

The "cardinal rule" of targeting in IHL is the principle of distinction.[120] That principle, which applies in both IAC and NIAC,[121] is articulated most clearly in Art. 51(2) of AP I: "[t]he civilian population as such, as well as individual civilians, shall not be the object of attack."[122] In IAC, anyone who is neither a member of a party's armed forces nor a participant in a levée en masse is a civilian.[123] In NIAC, a civilian is anyone who is neither a member of the State's armed forces nor a member of an organized armed group.[124] As long as they are not *hors de combat*, members of the armed forces and members of organized armed groups can be targeted at any time[125] – even when they are not fighting.[126] Civilians, by contrast, are targetable only if they directly participate in hostilities (DPH), and they can only be targeted "for such time as" they are participating.[127] It is always permissible to use lethal

[119] *Id.* at 33. It is worth noting that scholars recognized that declarations of war by organized armed groups were irrelevant to the existence of armed conflict long before the ICTY decided *Tadić*. In 1932, Quincy Wright noted that insurgents, "not being recognized states, have no power to convert a state of peace into a state of war, so their declaration or recognition of war would have no legal effect." Quincy Wright, *When Does War Exist?*, 26 Am. J. Int'l L. 362, 366 (1932). Similarly, Lothar Kotzsch noted in 1956 that "any declaration of war on the part of the seditious party is bare of any relevance in international law," because "[m]aterial war" is determined "by facts alone." Lothar Kotzsch, The Concept of War in Contemporary History and International Law 231 (1956). In other words, even when declarations of war had legal effect, they mattered only insofar as they were made by states.

[120] Geoffrey Corn, *Targeting, Command Judgment, and a Proposed Quantum of Information Component*, 77 Brooklyn L. Rev. 437, 441 (2011–2012).

[121] Customary IHL Study, *supra* note 4, at 3.

[122] Protocol Additional to the Geneva Conventions of 12 August 1949, and Relating to the Protection of Victims of International Armed Conflicts, Art. 51(2), June 8, 1977, 1125 UNTS 3.

[123] ICRC, Interpretive Guidance on the Notion of Direct Participation in Hostilities Under International Humanitarian Law 20 (2009).

[124] *Id.* at 27.

[125] Yves Sandoz et al. (eds.), Commentary on the Additional Protocols of 8 June 1977 to the Geneva Conventions of 12 August 1949 § 2195 (1987).

[126] *See, e.g.*, Chris Jenks et al., The Law of Armed Conflict: An Operational Approach 165 (2012).

[127] AP II, *supra* note 3, Art. 13(3).

force against a lawful target; there is no obligation to capture or minimize the use of force in IHL.[128]

Under IHRL, by contrast, the cardinal rule of targeting is that an individual must not be arbitrarily deprived of his right to life.[129] Killing is not arbitrary as long as the use of lethal force is proportionate and necessary.[130] The proportionality requirement limits the degree of force that a state may use in a particular situation. As summarized by Philip Alston, "the criterion of proportionality between the force used and the legitimate objective for which it is used requires that the escalation of force be broken off when the consequences for the suspect of applying a higher level of force would 'outweigh' the value of the objective."[131] A state may use lethal force against a suspect, therefore, only when he poses a threat to the lives of others.[132] The necessity requirement, in turn, "imposes an obligation to minimize the level of force applied regardless of the level of force that would be proportionate."[133] If a suspect who poses a threat to life can be apprehended or deterred through non-lethal means, using lethal force against him cannot be considered necessary.[134] In practice, the necessity requirement means that the extraterritorial use of lethal force is justified only to prevent an imminent attack. Requiring imminence not only ensures that lethal force will be used only against suspects who genuinely intend to launch an attack, it also limits the use of lethal force to situations in which it is genuinely impossible to apprehend or deter the suspect.[135]

It is clearly more difficult to justify targeting under IHRL than under IHL[136]: IHRL rejects targeting based on status, strictly limits how much

[128] Ian Henderson, The Contemporary Law of Targeting 79 (2009).

[129] *See, e.g.*, ICCPR, *supra* note 45, Art. 6. [130] Alston Report, *supra* note 83, ¶ 32.

[131] Extrajudicial, Summary or Arbitrary Executions, Note by the Secretary-General, U.N. Doc. A/61/311 (September 5, 2006), ¶ 42.

[132] *Id.*; *see also* Basic Principles on the Use of Force and Firearms by Law Enforcement Officials, Adopted by the Eighth United Nations Congress on the Prevention of Crime and the Treatment of Offenders, Principle 9 (1990), available at www.unrol.org/doc.aspx?d=2246.

[133] Secretary-General's Note, *supra* note 131, ¶ 41.

[134] *See, e.g.*, Kretzmer, *Targeted Killing, supra* note 71, at 179; Michael Ramsden, *Targeted Killings and International Human Rights Law: The Case of Anwar Al-Awlaki*, 16 J. Conflict & Sec. L. 385, 400 (2011).

[135] Kretzmer, *Targeted Killing, supra* note 71, at 182.

[136] *See, e.g.*, Christian Tomuschat, *Human Rights and International Humanitarian Law*, 21 Eur. J. Int'l L. 15, 32 (2010); Marko Milanovic, *A Norm Conflict Perspective on the Relationship between International Humanitarian Law and Human Rights Law*, J. Confl. & Sec. L. 459, 478 (2009); Expert Meeting on the Right to Life in Armed

force can be used against a suspect, imposes a narrow time-frame on targeting, and requires capture when possible. Moreover, IHRL requires states to conduct "an independent and objective inquiry" whenever an individual is killed, while IHL requires an investigation only when there is reason to believe a war crime has been committed.[137]

Given these differences, it is not surprising that the U.S. has tried to expand the number of individuals who can be targeted in NIAC by analogizing to IAC. Although IHRL continues to apply during armed conflict, it is generally accepted that targeting is the one area in which IHL does, in fact, generally function as the *lex specialis* – either displacing competing rules of IHL or, as held by the ICJ in the *Nuclear Weapons* case,[138] providing the test for when a killing in armed conflict should be considered "arbitrary." The wider the application of IHL in NIAC, therefore, the easier it is for the U.S. to justify using lethal force against members of "al-Qaeda and its associated forces."

1. Membership in Organized Armed Groups

As noted, IHL defines a "civilian" in NIAC negatively, as someone who is neither a member of the state's armed forces nor a member of an organized armed group. The distinction is critical, because non-civilians – normally referred to as combatants, even though that term does not appear in CA3 or AP II – may be attacked at any time, whereas civilians may only be targeted "for such time as" they directly participate in hostilities.

There is little controversy over who qualifies as a member of the State's armed forces in NIAC: "membership" is generally[139] a formal criterion determined by domestic law.[140] It is much less clear, however, who should be considered a member of an organized armed group, because AP II does not provide a definition of membership. The ICRC takes a functional approach to that question, according to which "the decisive

Conflicts and Situations of Occupation, University Centre for International Humanitarian Law, Geneva, at 8 (September 1–2, 2005), available at www.geneva-academy.ch/docs/expert-meetings/2005/3rapport_droit_vie.pdf.

137 Kretzmer, *Rethinking*, *supra* note 29, at 26; Doswald-Beck, *supra* note 49, at 887.

138 *Nuclear Weapons*, *supra* note 48, at ¶ 25.

139 AP II includes functional criteria as well. As the ICRC Commentary notes, AP II refers to "armed forces" instead of to "regular armed forces" because the drafters wanted to include armed forces "not included in the definition of the army in national legislation of some countries," such as "national guard, customs, police forces, or any other similar force." COMMENTARY ON THE ADDITIONAL PROTOCOLS, *supra* note 125, § 4462.

140 *See* MELZER, *supra* note 84, at 844–45.

criterion for individual membership in an organized armed group is whether a person assumes a continuous function for the group involving his or her direct participation in hostilities."[141] The ICRC thus excludes from membership – and thus from ongoing targetability – a variety of individuals "who continuously accompany or support an organized armed group, but whose function does not involve direct participation in hostilities,"[142] most notably those who "assume exclusively political, administrative or other non-combat functions" in the group[143] or assume "support functions" such as recruitment, training, financing, and propagandizing.[144] According to the ICRC, the "continuous combat function" (CCF) definition of membership reflects customary international law.[145]

The U.S., by contrast, targets and detains on the basis of a much broader definition of membership in an organized armed group. Specifically, as Judge Walton acknowledged (with approval) in *Gherebi*, the USG takes the position that membership in an organized armed group should be determined by analogy to the definition of membership in a state's armed forces in IAC – thus relying on both formal and functional criteria:

> As for the criteria used to determine membership in the "armed forces" of the enemy, the Court agrees with the government that the criteria set forth in Article 4 of the Third Geneva Convention and Article 43 of Additional Protocol I should inform the Court's assessment as to whether an individual qualifies as a member of the "armed forces" of an enemy organization like al-Qaeda. Although these provisions obviously cannot be applied literally to the enemy organizations contemplated in the AUMF – if that were the case, the conflict at hand would not be governed by Common Article 3 in the first place – they may nevertheless serve as templates from which the Court can glean certain characteristics necessary to identify those individuals who comprise an "armed force" for purposes of Common Article 3.[146]

[141] DPH Study, supra note 123, at 33. [142] *Id.* at 34. [143] *Id.* [144] *Id.*

[145] *See Id.* at 73 ("Under customary and treaty IHL … persons assuming a continuous combat function for an organized armed group belonging to a party to the conflict, lose their entitlement to protection against direct attack.").

[146] Gherebi v. Obama, 609 F. Supp. 2d 43, 68 (D.D.C. 2009); *see also* Respondents' Memorandum, *supra* note 9, at 5 (arguing that "standing U.S. jurisprudence, as well as law-of-war principles, recognize that members of enemy forces can be detained even if they have not actually committed or attempted to commit any act of depredation or entered the theatre or zone of active military operations."); Harold H. Koh, *The Obama Administration and International Law*, Speech to the American Society of International Law (March 25, 2010), available at www.state.gov/s/l/releases/remarks/139119.htm (arguing that membership "includes, but is not limited to, whether an individual joined with or became part of al-Qaeda or Taliban forces or associated forces, which can be demonstrated by relevant evidence of formal or functional membership").

This is a distinction with a difference, because the U.S. definition of membership brings within IHL's continuous targeting regime a category of individuals who could not lawfully be targeted under the ICRC definition: namely, anyone who qualifies as a member of an organized armed group under the U.S.'s dual formal/functional approach but does not assume a continuous combat function in the group. That is likely a sizable category, given the variety of "characteristics" the USG and courts believe qualify an individual as a member of organized armed group by analogy to GC III and AP I. Harold Koh, for example, publicly claimed while the State Department's Legal Adviser that taking an "oath of loyalty" to al-Qaeda qualifies as membership.[147] Similarly, the DC Circuit has held that an individual can be considered a "facilitator" of al-Qaeda – and thus "part of" the organization – if he stays at an al-Qaeda guest-house, travels along a route that leads toward hostilities, and is captured with a large amount of unexplained cash.[148] Needless to say, none of these actions even qualify as direct participation in hostilities.

It is important to note that, unlike the other analogies discussed in this chapter, the membership analogy does not use an IAC-based rule of IHL to fill a gap in the conventional and customary IHL of NIAC. There *is* a basis in conventional IHL for the concept of membership in an organized armed group; the question is simply how membership should be defined. Defining membership by analogy to state armed forces in IAC should thus probably be called "soft" analogy.

Nevertheless, the U.S. definition of membership in an organized armed group is still problematic. As discussed in Section I, analogized rules of IHL represent domestic humanitarian law, not international humanitarian law, and thus cannot be applied either territorially or extraterritorially in the face of contrary prohibitive rules of international law. Here there are such contrary prohibitive rules: namely, the rules of IHRL governing the use of lethal force. Those much more limiting IHRL rules can be displaced or modified by customary rules of IHL that apply in NIAC – such as the rule that says a civilian can be targeted for such time as he or she directly participates in hostilities – but they cannot be displaced or

147 *Id.*

148 Almerfedi v. Obama, 654 F.3d 1, 14–15 (D.C. Cir. 2011); *cf.* Uthman v. Obama, 637 F.3d 400, 405 (D.C. Cir. 2011) ("Being captured in the company of a Taliban fighter and two al Qaeda members and Osama bin Laden bodyguards 12 miles from Tora Bora in December 2001 might not be precisely the same as being captured in a German uniform 12 miles from the Normandy beaches in June 1944. But it is still, at a minimum, highly significant.").

modified by an IAC-based rule that is applied to NIAC solely by analogy. As result, insofar as the U.S. definition of membership in an organized armed group goes beyond the customary definition of membership, the targeting of individuals who qualify as members under the former definition but not the latter is governed by IHRL, not by IHL. And there is little question that IHRL does not permit the use of lethal force at all – much less the use of force at any time – against individuals who have sworn loyalty to al-Qaeda or who have "facilitated" terrorism by carrying cash and staying in al-Qaeda guesthouses.

Numerous scholars, primarily but not exclusively American, have criticized the ICRC's "continuous combat function" definition of membership.[149] Interestingly, though, it is difficult to find a scholar who has challenged the ICRC's assertion that the definition reflects customary international law.[150] Instead, criticism has focused almost exclusively on the fact that the CCF definition treats state armed forces and organized armed groups *asymmetrically*: because non-combat personnel in NIAC qualify as members of state armed forces but not as members of organized armed groups, state personnel can be targeted at any time, but non-state personnel can only be targeted while directly participating.[151] Watkin's criticism of that asymmetry is typical:

> The choice made in the Interpretive Guidance to treat organized armed groups in a completely different fashion than regular State armed forces in both international and non-international armed conflict is novel and problematic. It does not reflect either the nature of warfare or the historical and contemporary scope of armed conflict. In effectively creating a third category of participant in armed conflict, it represents a dramatic shift from the approach taken by the ICRC to date.[152]

149 *See, e.g.*, Kenneth Watkin, *Opportunity Lost: Organized Armed Groups and the ICRC "Direct Participation in the Hostilities" Interpretive Guidance*, 42 N.Y.U. J. Int'l L. & Pol. 641, 693–95 (2010); Bill Boothby, *"And For Such Time As": The Time Dimension to Direct Participation in Hostilities*, 42 N.Y.U. J. Int'l L. & Pol. 741, 757 (2010); Michael N. Schmitt, *The Interpretive Guidance on the Notion of Direct Participation in Hostilities: A Critical Analysis*, 1 Harv. Nat. Sec. J. 5, 21–24 (2010); Sivakumaran, *supra* note 29, at 361–62,

150 To the contrary, one scholar has noted that, despite the controversy, the continuous combat function definition "has substantial support among a wide cross section of states." *See* Jens Ohlin, The Assault on International Law 169–70 (2014).

151 Sivakumaran, *supra* note 29, at 361–62.

152 Watkin, *Opportunity Lost*, *supra* note 149, at 693; *see also* Boothby, *supra* note 149, at 757 (criticizing CCF for "creat[ing] legal inequality between the opposing parties, thus eroding the international law assumption that the law applies equally to each party to the conflict"); Schmitt, *supra* note 149, at 23 (criticizing the fact that, under the CCF test, "a

This is an unpersuasive criticism. There is no question that conventional IHL is generally predicated on symmetry, even in NIAC: the rules of CA3 and AP II apply to both state armed forces and organized armed groups equally.[153] From a positivist perspective, though, such symmetry is not an *inherent requirement* of IHL; no rule of international law prohibits states from adopting conventional or customary law that treats states and organized armed groups differently.[154] Indeed, there is at least one asymmetry between states and organized armed groups in conventional IHL: the Protocol on the Involvement of Children in Armed Conflict (Children in Armed Conflict Protocol),[155] ratified by 159 states, requires organized armed groups to avoid recruiting children under the age of eighteen, but permits States Parties to recruit children of any age as long as it is voluntary.[156] As long as the ICRC is correct that conventional and customary IHL dictate the asymmetry between state armed forces and organized armed groups in terms of membership, therefore, it is difficult to see how that asymmetry could be *legally* problematic.[157]

Moreover, one of the primary critics of the membership asymmetry – Watkin – has argued that members of the states armed forces are entitled to the combatant's privilege, but members of organized armed groups are not.[158] He does not explain why, as a matter of law, asymmetry in

cook in the regular armed forces may be lawfully attacked at any time; his or her counterpart in an organized armed group may be attacked only if he or she directly participates and then only for such time as the participation occurs").

153 Sassoli, *Internment*, *supra* note 54, at 602; Sivakumaran, *supra* note 29, at 303.

154 *See* Watts, *supra* note 56, at 150 (noting that "no 'equal application' principle operates in the present law of NIAC"); *cf.* Jonathan Somer, *Jungle Justice: Passing Sentence on the Equality of Belligerents in Non-International Armed Conflict*, 89 Int'l Rev. Red Cross 655, 659 (2007) ("Yet while the principle [of equality] is undoubtedly established in the law of international armed conflict, there is good reason to question its status in the law of non-international armed conflict.").

155 A/RES/54/263 of 25 May 2000. 156 *Id.*, §§ 3(3) & 4(1).

157 It may, of course, be normatively problematic. *See, e.g.*, Sivakumaran, *supra* note 29, at 361–62.

158 Kenneth Watkin, *Warriors Without Rights? Combatants, Unprivileged Belligerents, and the Struggle over Legitimacy*, Harvard Program on Humanitarian Policy and Conflict Research, at 65 (2005), available at www.hpcrresearch.org/sites/default/files/publications/OccasionalPaper2.pdf. *But cf.* Lawrence Hill-Cawthorne & Dapo Akande, *Does IHL Provide a Legal Basis for Detention in Non-International Armed Conflicts?*, EJIL: Talk! (May 17, 2014), available at www.ejiltalk.org/does-ihl-provide-a-legal-basis-for-detention-in-non-international-armed-conflicts/ ("If IHL did indeed provide a legal basis for killing in a NIAC, it would have to do so on the basis of equality and would provide a privilege to kill (and a corresponding immunity from prosecution. It does not do this).").

membership is "novel and problematic," but asymmetry in the combatant's privilege is completely acceptable. Instead, he simply claims that extending the combatant's privilege to members of the state's armed forces but not organized armed groups is "logical."[159]

By contrast, another scholar who believes the combatant's privilege applies asymmetrically in NIAC, Ian Henderson, does try to provide a legal defense of that asymmetry. Henderson's argument is straightforward: state armed forces are entitled to the combatant's privilege because states have always insisted that "it is lawful for a government to engage in a non-international armed conflict with a non-state actor," while organized armed groups are not entitled to the privilege because states have equally insisted that "there is no legal right under international law for a non-state actor to engage in a non-international armed conflict."[160] It is an open question whether Henderson's view of the combatant's privilege is correct; he and Watkin are in the (extreme) minority.[161] But his underlying point is correct: if states want to asymmetrically apply the combatant's privilege to NIAC, whether as a matter of convention or custom, there is nothing stopping them from doing so. Henderson's position thus actually *supports* the idea that nothing in international law prohibits states from defining membership asymmetrically.

Finally, it is important to note that relying on the membership analogy makes it very likely the U.S. will engage in extraterritorial targeting that violates the *jus ad bellum*. The U.S., of course, takes a maximalist view of self-defense under Art. 51 – most famously declaring, in its 2002 National Security Strategy, that it is willing to act "even if uncertainty remains as to the time and place of the enemy's attack."[162] This endorsement of preventive self-defense has been widely criticized, both by states[163] and by scholars.[164] But even accepting that there is still a great deal of uncertainty about the current state of self-defense under customary

[159] Watkin, *Warriors*, *supra* note 158, at 65.

[160] Ian Henderson, *Civilian Intelligence Agencies and the Use of Armed Drones*, 13 Y.B. Int'l Hum. L. 133, 150 (2010).

[161] *See, e.g.*, Kretzmer, *Rethinking*, *supra* note 29, at 35; Hill-Cawthorne & Akande, *supra* note 158; Rona, *supra* note 40, at 114; Watts, *supra* note 56, at 149.

[162] National Security Strategy of the United States 2002, at 15, available at www.state.gov/documents/organization/63562.pdf.

[163] *See* Kretzmer, *Inherent*, *supra* note 104, at 248 (noting that not even the United Kingdom, the U.S.'s closest ally, accepts the USG's view of self-defense).

[164] *See* Ruys, *supra* note 93, at 322 (noting that "[o]n the whole, legal scholars have almost *unisono* denounced the doctrine of preventive self-defence").

international law,[165] it is clear that the U.S.'s analogical expansion of membership in an organized armed group beyond the customary CCF standard is problematic, because it permits the U.S. to extraterritorially target a variety of individuals who cannot be legitimately attacked under *any* conception of self-defense. Assume, for example, that al-Qaeda has engaged in such a "chain of successive attacks" against the U.S. that the USG is entitled to use force not just to repel attacks as they happen, but also to prevent future attacks from taking place.[166] In such a situation, it may well be possible to argue that the U.S. can legitimately use force against any member of al-Qaeda who assumes a continuous combat function in the group – the individuals who have taken part in the previous attacks and will take part in future ones. But it is difficult to see how self-defense could justify targeting "members" of the group who do *not* take part in combat – the cooks, the clerks, etc. Targeting them would appear to represent precisely the kind of "punitive" attack that is categorically impermissible under Art. 51.[167] Such individuals, however, are lawful targets in NIAC if membership is defined by analogy to GC III and AP I.[168]

2. Co-Belligerency

According to the USG, the AUMF entitles it to use force not only against al-Qaeda, but also against its "associated forces."[169] To define the concept of an "associated force" of al-Qaeda, the USG has consistently analogized

[165] *See generally* Christian J. Tams, *The Use of Force Against Terrorists*, 20 EUR. J. INT'L L. 359–97 (2009) (discussing the contested areas).

[166] On the legal issues raised by this type of preventive self-defense, *see Id.* at 390; RUYS, *supra* note 84, at 116; Kretzmer, *Inherent*, *supra* note 104, at 271–72.

[167] *See* Kretzmer, *Inherent*, *supra* note 104, at 254 (noting that using force "to punish for the harm done, either out of a feeling of justice or outrage," is "entirely foreign to self-defence").

[168] A skeptic might ask why, if this argument is correct, the *jus ad bellum* doesn't prohibit states from targeting cooks and clerks in an IAC. The answer is straightforward: in IAC, *all* members of a state's armed forces have the right to participate in hostilities. *See* GARY SOLIS, LAW OF ARMED CONFLICT 188 (2010). In other words, cooks and clerks can lawfully participate in armed attacks, even if they usually don't. They are thus included in the category of individuals self-defense can justify attacking under the *jus ad bellum*.

[169] *See, e.g.*, White Paper, *supra* note 85, at 1; Congressional Research Service, Al Qaeda-Affiliated Groups: Middle East and Africa, at 5 (October 10, 2014), available at http://fpc.state.gov/documents/organization/233708.pdf (noting that "associated forces are considered legal targets of U.S. military force per the laws of armed conflict"); *cf.* National Defense Authorization Act for Fiscal Year 2012, Pub. L. No. 112–81, § 1021 (2011) (arguing same with regard to detention).

to the concept of co-belligerency in IAC – the idea that a "fully fledged belligerent fighting in association with one or more belligerent powers"[170] is not entitled to invoke the protections of the law of neutrality.[171] In a speech at the Oxford Union, Jeh Johnson, then General Counsel to the Department of Defense (DoD), stated that an "associated force" is "a co-belligerent with al Qaeda in hostilities against the United States or its coalition partners."[172] In its notorious al-Aulaqi memo, the Department of Justice (DoJ) approved targeting "a leader of AQAP, an organized enemy force that is either a component of al-Qaida or that is a co-belligerent of that central party to the conflict."[173] And even more specifically, in the *Hamlily* litigation, the DoJ argued that the AUMF provides the USG "authority to detain individuals who, in analogous circumstances in a traditional international armed conflict between the armed forces of opposing governments, would be detainable under principles of co-belligerency."[174]

Scholars have also argued that the concept of "associated forces" should be defined by analogy to co-belligerency. Bradley and Goldsmith have argued, for example, that because "[d]ictionary definitions" of "organization" are not useful, "[t]he international law concepts of neutrality and co-belligerency provide better guidance, and confirm that the 'enemy' in an armed conflict can include the enemy's affiliates":

> These principles provide a guide for determining which terrorist organizations are included within the AUMF. Terrorist organizations that act as agents of al Qaeda, participate with al Qaeda in acts of war against the United States, systematically provide military resources to al Qaeda, or serve as fundamental communication links in the war against the United States, and perhaps those that systematically permit their buildings and safehouses to be used by al Qaeda in the war against the United States, are analogous to co-belligerents in a traditional war. Because the laws of war at a minimum would deem "neutrals" that systematically violate the laws of neutrality by supporting or assisting other terrorist organizations to be lawful military targets, the AUMF should be consistent with its text, with presidential practice in prior wars, and with standard delegation principles

170 Morris Greenspan, The Modern Law of Land Warfare 531 (1959).

171 Rebecca Ingber, *Untangling Belligerency from Neutrality in the Conflict with Al-Qaeda*, 47 Tex. Int'l L. J. 75, 90 (2011).

172 Jeh Johnson Speech, *supra* note 17.

173 White Paper, *supra* note 85, at 27.

174 Respondents' Memorandum, *supra* note 9, at 7. Although the brief specifically addressed detention, not targeting, the USG has never indicated that it believes co-belligerency is limited to the former power.

extend to terrorist organizations that are functional co-belligerents of al Qaeda.[175]

The appeal of the co-belligerency analogy is evident: like the declaration-of-war analogy, it ensures that targeting al-Qaeda's "associated forces" is governed by the rules of IHL instead of by the far more restrictive rules of IHRL. In the absence of co-belligerency, the U.S. could avoid IHRL only by demonstrating that it was involved in a *separate* NIAC with each and every associated force it wanted to target, either directly (in terms of hostilities between the U.S. and that associated force) or with the consent of a government involved in such a separate NIAC.[176] For at least some terrorist groups outside of Afghanistan and Pakistan, such as al-Shabaab in Somalia and AQAP in Yemen, that could be difficult.

It is impossible to argue, though, that the concept of co-belligerency applies in NIAC. Co-belligerency is an aspect of the law of neutrality, as Bradley and Goldsmith openly acknowledge, and there is widespread scholarly agreement that the law of neutrality applies only in IAC.[177] Indeed, *the very idea* that co-belligerency can be applied to NIAC by analogy is inconsistent with the law of neutrality; numerous scholars have pointed out that a state could traditionally invoke neutral rights and duties with regard to an insurgency only by recognizing the insurgents as belligerents, thereby – in modern terms – transforming the NIAC into an IAC. As Tucker says, "operation of the international law of neutrality presupposes, and is dependent upon, the recognition of insurgents in a civil war as belligerents. Prior to such recognition – whether by the parent state or by third states – there can be no condition of belligerency,

[175] Bradley & Goldsmith, *supra* note 22, at 2112–13; *see also* Robert Chesney, *Thoughts on the Brennan Speech: Scope of the AUMF, CCF, JSOC, and Other Issues*, Lawfare (May 2, 2012), available at www.lawfareblog.com/2012/05/thoughts-on-the-brennan-speech-scope-of-the-aumf-ccf-jsoc-and-other-issues/ (arguing that the AUMF must reach the Haqqani Network, because they "are the NIAC equivalent to a classic 'co-belligerent' state"); Christopher Greenwood, *International Law and the 'War Against Terrorism'*, 78 Int'l Aff. 301, 313 (2002) ("The Taliban – and thus Afghanistan – . . . at the very least, its position was analogous to that of a neutral state which allows a belligerent to mount military operations from its territory.").

[176] *See* Noam Lubell & Nathan Derejko, *A Global Battlefield? Drones and the Geographical Scope of Armed Conflict*, 11 J. Int'l Crim. Just. 65, 83 (2013).

[177] *See, e.g.*, Robert W. Tucker, The Law of War and Neutrality at Sea 200 n. 8 (1955); Oppenheim, *supra* note 30, at 532; Quincy Wright, *The Present Status of Neutrality*, 34 Am. J. Int'l L, 391, 393 (1940); Stephen C. Neff, War and the Law of Nations: A General History 260 (2005); Kress, *supra* note 50, at 266–67.

hence no neutrality in the sense of international law."[178] Finally, and perhaps most importantly, there is no evidence that any state other than the U.S. has *ever* invoked the law of neutrality – much less co-belligerency – in a NIAC.[179]

Because co-belligerency does not apply in NIAC as a matter of conventional or customary international law, the USG's adoption of that concept by analogy to IAC represents nothing more than "domestic humanitarian law." But that means the ostensible advantages of the analogy for the U.S. are illusory: in the absence of a separate NIAC with those groups, targeting members of al-Qaeda's "associated forces" remains subject to the prohibitive rules of IHRL, not IHL.

Indeed, the U.S.'s co-belligerency analogy is flawed in another respect. As discussed earlier, Goodman's argument that the U.S. is entitled to asymmetrically analogize between IAC and NIAC – applying the permissive IHL rules but not the prohibitive ones – depends on the idea, adopted by the PCIJ in the *Lotus* case, that "[r]estrictions upon the independence of States" concerning their domestic law "cannot . . . be presumed." We have seen that, because of the rise of competing prohibitive rules of IHRL, the U.S.'s traditional freedom no longer exists in the realm of targeting and detention; unless the analogized IHL rule has a basis in customary international law, it cannot displace or modify a competing rule of IHRL. But even such a customary basis would not necessarily be enough to justify the co-belligerency analogy. As noted earlier, although symmetric rule application is not a necessary feature of IHL – states are always free to adopt asymmetrical rules via convention or custom – the "default" position is that IHL rules do, in fact, apply symmetrically in both IAC and NIAC. If that's the case, the U.S. could

[178] Tucker, *supra* note 177, at 200 n. 8; *see also* Neff, supra note 177, at 260 ("[T]his general legal bias in favor of governments against insurgents—in the absence of recognition of belligerency—was already widely accepted in state practice in the nineteenth century. If, on the other hand, the conflict was a civil war in the strict sense of the term, then the law of neutrality would apply."); Oppenheim, *supra* note 30, at 532 ("[R] ecognition of belligerency alone brings about the operation of rules of neutrality as between the parties to the civil war and foreign States."); Wright, *supra* note 177, at 393 (noting, with regard to third states that assist the government to quell an insurgency, that "the word neutrality is hardly appropriate"); *Note, International Law and Military Operations Against Insurgents in Neutral Territory*, 68 Colum. L. Rev. 1127, 1128 n. 4 (1968) ("Strictly speaking, neutrality is a concept which applies only to international warfare, and its status in a civil war in which the rebels have not been recognized as belligerents is highly doubtful.").

[179] *See* Kress, *supra* note 50, at 267.

not justify using co-belligerency to target al-Qaeda's "associated forces" simply by showing that there is a customary basis for applying the law of neutrality in NIAC; it would also need to show that customary international law permits the law of neutrality to be applied *asymmetrically* in NIAC. The U.S. is not applying neutrality law *in general* to its NIAC with al-Qaeda. On the contrary: it is appropriating only those aspects of neutrality law that maximize its power to target and detain. And that is not a coincidence: for reasons I have discussed elsewhere,[180] the U.S. would never apply the entire body of the law of neutrality to NIAC by analogy, because doing so would cripple its ability to fight al-Qaeda. Applied symmetrically, for example, the law of neutrality would entitle members of al-Qaeda to both the combatant's privilege and POW status upon capture.[181] It would also prohibit the U.S. from establishing or maintaining military bases on the territory of any state that wanted to remain neutral in the U.S.'s NIAC with al-Qaeda.[182]

Finally, as with GC III/AP I membership, applying co-belligerency to NIAC by analogy is likely to lead to significant violations of the *jus ad bellum* – at least insofar as the U.S. follows Bradley and Goldsmith's approach, which at least one U.S. court has already done.[183] As Bothe notes, in the post-Charter era, "[a]rmed reprisals are generally unlawful. As a consequence, a reaction against violations of neutrality which would involve the use of force against another state is permissible only where the violation of the law triggering that reaction itself constitutes an illegal armed attack."[184] Bradley and Goldsmith, however, do not limit al-Qaeda's "associated forces" to organized armed groups that have attacked the U.S., either singly or alongside al-Qaeda; in their view, a group qualifies as an associated force as long as it "systematically violate[s] the laws of neutrality" by "provid[ing] military resources to al Qaeda or serv[ing] as fundamental communication links in the war against the United States." That is deeply problematic from a *jus ad bellum* standpoint, because

180 Kevin Jon Heller, *The Law of Neutrality Does Not Apply to the Conflict with Al-Qaeda, and It's a Good Thing, Too: A Response to Chang*, 47 Tex. Int'l L. J. 115–41 (2011).

181 *See* Hersch Lauterpacht, *supra* note 34, at 175 ("Given the required conditions of belligerency as laid down by international law, the contesting parties are legally entitled to be treated as if they are engaged in a war waged by two sovereign States.").

182 *See* Oppenheim, *supra* note 30, at 559 (noting that the duty of impartiality prohibits a neutral state from allowing a belligerent to "occupy a neutral fortress").

183 *See* Hamlily Memorandum Opinion, *supra* note 19, at 16.

184 Michael Bothe, *The Law of Neutrality*, *in* The Handbook of International Humanitarian Law 571, 581 (Dieter Fleck ed., 2nd ed. 2009).

although such "unneutral service" by an organized armed group would entitle the U.S. to respond by imposing countermeasures, it would *not* entitle the U.S. to respond with military force:

> A state not originally party to an armed conflict will only commit an act of war, and thus risk making itself a party to the conflict, by giving direct support to the military operations of one of the belligerents. Financial, political, and intelligence support will not have such an effect.[185]

The (invalid) co-belligerency analogy, in short, permits the U.S. to extraterritorially target individuals against whom it cannot lawfully use force in self-defense – namely, members of organized armed groups that become an "associated force" by providing al-Qaeda with non-military support. (The Nusra Front may be an example.[186]) After all, the point of the analogy is to allow the U.S. to target members of al-Qaeda's associated forces as if they were members of al-Qaeda itself.

3. "Belonging to" and Associated Forces

Ryan Goodman provides an alternative interpretation of "associated forces" – but one that is no less based on analogy to IAC. In his view, an organized armed group qualifies as an "associated force" in the U.S./Al-Qaeda NIAC if it can be said to "belong to" al-Qaeda under Art. 4(a)(2) of GC III:

> [T]he law of armed conflict stipulates that members of armed groups (e.g., AQAP) with a particular relationship to a party to a conflict (e.g., al-Qaeda) are legitimate targets. Specifically, Article 50(1) of Additional Protocol I states that a person cannot be considered a civilian (e.g., for the purpose of lethal targeting) if he is a member of an organized armed group with such an association. That association is defined in Article 4(a)(2) of the POW Convention: "members of other militias and members of other volunteer corps, including those of organized resistance movements, belonging to a Party to the conflict." In short, "belonging to" a

[185] Christopher Greenwood, *Scope of Application of Humanitarian Law*, *in Id.* at 58; *see also* Michael Bothe, *Neutrality in Naval Warfare: What Is Left of Traditional International Law*, *in* Humanitarian Law of Armed Conflict: Challenges Ahead 387, 396 (Astrid J.M. Delissen & Gerard J. Tanja et al. eds., 1991) ("An unneutral service is not an armed attack, and it thus does not trigger a right of self-defence against the neutral State. Hence, the *ius contra bellum* excludes a reaction which would be legal under the traditional law of neutrality."); Wolf Heintschel von Heinegg, *Visit, Search, Diversion and Capture in Naval Warfare*, 30 Canadian Y.B. Int'l L. 89, 131 (1992) ("[U]nneutral service performed by a non-belligerent state would not be sufficient to justify the use of force against that state, since unneutral service is not an armed attack.").

[186] *See* CRS Report, *supra* note 169, at 43.

> party to the conflict is a form of an associated group, which renders its members subject to lethal force and detention.[187]

The "belonging to" analogy is just as problematic as the co-belligerency analogy – and for the same reasons. First, there is simply no evidence that Art. 4(a)(2) applies in NIAC. In terms of conventional law, neither CA3 nor AP II mention "belonging to," even though the former refers to "armed forces" and the latter (in Art. 1) refers to "organized armed groups." Moreover, Goodman cites no state practice – not even by the U.S., which takes a wider view of the material field of NIAC than any other state – in support of the idea that "belonging to" applies in NIAC as a matter of customary international law.[188] The "belonging to" analogy thus represents the kind of domestic humanitarian law that is not capable of displacing or modifying the more restrictive targeting rules of IHL.

Second, although Art. 4(a)(2) of GC III permits members of resistance organizations who belong to a party to an IAC to be targeted, it also entitles them to the combatant's privilege and POW status upon capture.[189] It would thus not be enough for Goodman to establish a customary basis for applying "belonging to" in NIAC. Because the default position in IHL is that rules apply to all parties equally, he would have to show that custom applies "belonging to" to NIAC *asymmetrically* – permitting the U.S. to take advantage of its permissions without being bound by its prohibitions.

Third, and finally, apply the "belonging to" analogy to the U.S./al-Qaeda NIAC would create even more serious *jus ad bellum* problems than co-belligerency. As Goodman notes, "belonging to" is an easily satisfied standard in IAC; according to the ICRC Commentary to GC III, the necessary "de facto" relationship between the resistance organization and the party to the conflict "may find expression merely by tacit agreement, if the operations are such as to indicate clearly for which side the resistance organization is fighting."[190] Needless to say, if the U.S. would violate the *jus ad bellum* by targeting organized armed groups that

[187] Ryan Goodman, *Al-Qaeda, the Law on Associated Forces and "Belonging To" a Party*, JUST SECURITY (October 18, 2003), available at http://justsecurity.org/2191/al-qaeda-law-forces-belonging-to-party-drones-reports/.

[188] Notably, the ICRC study of custom does not indicate that "belonging to" applies in NIAC. *See* CUSTOMARY IHL STUDY, *supra* note 4, at Rule 4.

[189] Assuming, of course, they satisfy the four criteria mentioned in the provision.

[190] ICRC, COMMENTARY ON THE GENEVA CONVENTION (III) RELATIVE TO THE TREATMENT OF PRISONERS OF WAR 57 (Jean S. Pictet ed., 1960).

become an "associated force" by providing al-Qaeda with non-military support, it would violate the *jus ad bellum* by targeting organized armed groups that become an "associated force" simply by tacitly agreeing to support al-Qaeda.[191]

D. Detention

In IAC, conventional IHL both authorizes and regulates detention. Art. 21 of GC III provides that a state "may subject prisoners of war" – generally members of the enemy's armed forces – "to internment." Because POWs are presumed to pose a security threat simply by virtue of their right to participate in hostilities,[192] they can be detained without any kind of review until "the cessation of active hostilities."[193] The detention of civilians, in turn, is governed by the Fourth Geneva Convention (GC IV). Art. 42(1) permits a state to detain a civilian on its own territory if its security "makes it absolutely necessary," while Art. 78(1) permits a state to detain a civilian in occupied territory if it "considers it necessary, for imperative reasons of security" – although it is generally agreed that there is little, if any, substantive difference between the two standards.[194] Civilian detention must end "as soon as the reasons which necessitated his internment no longer exist"[195] and cannot extend beyond the "cessation of hostilities."[196] GC IV thus requires the detaining state to continually review whether detention is warranted. For civilians detained on state territory, the initial decision to detain must be "reconsidered as soon as possible by an appropriate court or administrative board designated by the Detaining Power for that purpose" and must be reviewed by the same court or administrative board at least twice per year thereafter.[197] Civilians detained in occupied territory have the right to

[191] To be sure, insofar as a "tacit agreement" led an organized armed group to launch its own armed attack against the U.S., the U.S. could lawfully target members of the group. In such situations, however, the group's targetability under the *jus ad bellum* would in no way depend on its status as an "associated force."

[192] See ICRC Position Paper, Internment in Armed Conflict: Basic Rules and Challenges, at 4 (Nov. 2014), available at www.icrc.org/en/document/internment-armed-conflict-basic-rules-and-challenges#.VKvETIqsUmc.

[193] GC III, *supra* note 10, Art. 118(1).

[194] *See* ICRC, Commentary on the Geneva Convention (IV) Relative to the Protection of Civilian Persons in Time of War 367 (Jean S. Pictet ed., 1958).

[195] Convention Relative to the Treatment of Prisoners of War, August 12, 1949, Art. 132(1), 6 U.S.T. 3316, 75 U.N.T.S. 135, 136.

[196] *Id.*, art. 133(1). [197] *Id.*, art. 43(1).

appeal their detention and, if their detention is upheld, the right to "periodical review, if possible every six months, by a competent body set up by the said Power."[198]

In NIAC, by contrast, conventional IHL is largely silent concerning detention. Unlike GC III and GC IV, neither CA3 nor AP II contain a provision that authorizes a party to a NIAC to detain anyone – member of the state's armed forces, member of an organized armed group, or civilian.[199] The authorization for detention is left to domestic law.[200] Moreover, neither CA3 nor AP II specifies any "procedural safeguards for persons interned in NIAC," even though they each recognize that such detention will take place.[201] Instead, their purpose "is simply to guarantee a minimum level of humanitarian treatment for people who are in fact detained."[202]

Because IHL authorizes and regulates detention in IAC but not in NIAC, the relationship between IHL and IHRL is very different in the two kinds of armed conflict. In IAC, the rules of IHL predominate; as the ICRC notes, "[a]s the *lex specialis* crafted specifically for situations of armed conflict, IHL applicable in IAC is the interpretive tool by means of which the interplay between this body of norms and HR law may be determined.[203] By contrast, the absence of detention-related rules of IHL in NIAC means that IHRL predominates under *either* possible version of the *lex specialis* principle – as partial displacement or as norm-conflict resolution. If there is no IHL *lex*, IHL cannot be *lex specialis*.[204]

[198] *Id.*, art. 78(2).

[199] *See, e.g.*, Expert Meeting on the Supervision of the Lawfulness of Detention During Armed Conflict, University Centre for International Humanitarian Law, Geneva, at 3 (July 24–25, 2004), available at www.geneva-academy.ch/docs/expert-meetings/2004/4rapport_detention.pdf; Rona, *supra* note 40, at 114; Hill-Cawthorne & Akande, *supra* note 158; Serdar Mohammed v. Ministry of Defence [2014] EWHC 1369 (QB), ¶ 251.

[200] *See, e.g.*, Expert Meeting on Supervision of Detention, *supra* note 199, at 3; Hill-Cawthorne & Akande, *supra* note 158.

[201] ICRC Position Paper, *supra* note 192, at 6; *see also* Sassoli, Internment, *supra* note 54, at 623; Hill-Cawthorne & Akande, *supra* note 158.

[202] Mohammed, *supra* note 199, ¶ 251.

[203] ICRC Position Paper, *supra* note 192, at 3; Kress, *supra* note 50, at 262.

[204] *See, e.g.*, Sassoli, *Internment*, *supra* note 54, at 621 ("As humanitarian law applicable to non-international armed conflict is silent on the procedural regulation of internment, it would seem clear that in accordance with the *lex specialis* principle as a maxim of logic, human rights should step in to fill the gap."); Expert Meeting on Supervision of Detention, *supra* note 199, at 3 (noting that because "the grounds and procedure of detention" are not regulated by IHL in NIAC, "only national law is relevant, as well as international human rights law"); Rona, *supra* note 40, at 114 ("NIAC fighters are mere

IHRL significantly limits the ability of states to detain in NIAC. IHRL does not categorically prohibit detention; a state is entitled to detain individuals who commit a criminal offense or pose a legitimate threat to its security.[205] But there is little question that IHRL imposes much greater procedural restrictions on detention than conventional IHL in IAC, as the Human Rights Committee made clear in its recent General Comment No. 35 (Liberty and Security of the Person):

> To the extent that States parties impose security detention (sometimes known as administrative detention or internment), not in contemplation of prosecution on a criminal charge, the Committee considers that such detention presents severe risks of arbitrary deprivation of liberty. Such detention would normally amount to arbitrary detention as other effective measures addressing the threat, including the criminal justice system, would be available. If under the most exceptional circumstances, a present, direct and imperative threat is invoked to justify detention of persons considered to present such a threat, the burden of proof lies on States parties to show that the individual poses such a threat and that it cannot be addressed by alternative measures, and this burden increases with the length of the detention. States parties also need to show that detention does not last longer than absolutely necessary, that the overall length of possible detention is limited, and that they fully respect the guarantees provided for by Article 9 in all cases. Prompt and regular review by a court or other tribunal possessing the same attributes of independence and impartiality as the judiciary is a necessary guarantee for these conditions, as is access to independent legal advice, preferably selected by the detainee, and disclosure to the detainee of, at least, the essence of the evidence on which the decision is taken.[206]

Three procedural differences between IHRL and IHL in IAC are particularly critical. First, and most obviously, IHRL security detention does not distinguish between POWs and civilians; the same protections apply to both. It is thus not possible under IHRL to detain anyone without periodic review.[207] Second, IHRL entitles all detained individuals to periodic review of their detention by a court or quasi-judicial

criminals under domestic law, and so, rules concerning their detention fall under domestic law, tempered by international human rights obligations.").

[205] *Id.*, ¶ 15; *see also* Lawrence Hill-Cawthorne, *The Copenhagen Principles on the Handling of Detainees: Implications for the Procedural Regulation of Internment*, 18 J. CONFLICT & SEC. L. 481, 485 (2013). Under the ECHR, security detention likely requires derogation. But that requirement is not germane to this discussion.

[206] HRC General Comment 35, *supra* note 65, ¶ 15.

[207] *Id.* The right to review is also non-derogable. *Id.*, ¶ 67.

tribunal, whereas IHL only requires periodic review by a court or "administrative body." Although the difference between IHRL's "other tribunal" and IHL's "administrative body" is not completely clear, most scholars agree that the former must be more independent than the latter.[208] Third, and finally, IHRL makes it difficult, if not impossible, to justify detaining someone until the end of an armed conflict[209] – particularly in a transnational NIAC involving terrorist groups, where "[n]ot only can we not envision an end to the hostilities, but more problematic, we have absolutely no way of identifying what that end might look like."[210]

These differences almost certainly explain why the U.S. has consistently relied on analogy to apply IAC-based IHL detention rules in NIAC.[211] They also explain why certain scholars have relied on analogy to argue that organized armed groups have the right to detain. None of those analogies, however, withstand critical scrutiny.

1. General Detention Power

The first two analogies, which can be addressed together, are unsurprising: analogizing to IAC to define the general detention power in NIAC with regard to organized armed groups and civilians. The U.S. considers members of organized armed groups to be "unprivileged belligerents" who "may lawfully be detained until a competent authority determines that the conflict has ended or that active hostilities have ceased"[212] – language that precisely mirrors Art. 118(1) of GC III. Similarly, the U.S. takes the position that civilians may be interned "for imperative reasons of security" and must be "released when the reasons that necessitated

208 *See, e.g.*, Hill-Cawthorne, *supra* note 205, at 208.

209 *See, e.g.*, Fiona de Londras, Detention in the 'War on Terror': Can Human Rights Fight Back? 192 (2011).

210 Laurie R. Blank, *A Square Peg in a Round Hole: Stretching Law of War Detention Too Far*, 63 Rutgers L. Rev. 1169, 1181 (2011).

211 *Cf.* Marco Sassoli, *Transnational Armed Groups and International Humanitarian Law*, Harvard Program on Humanitarian Policy and Conflict Research, at 27 (2005), available at www.hpcrresearch.org/sites/default/files/publications/OccasionalPaper6.pdf (noting that "[o]ne of the reasons why the United States administration so obstinately wants to apply the laws of war to its struggle against international terrorism is, arguably, that it considers it necessary in that struggle to have recourse to war-like internment which goes beyond what the human rights supervisory bodies admit outside declared situations of emergency").

212 DoD Directive, *supra* note 11, ¶ 3(f).

internment no longer exist and a safe and orderly transfer or release is practicable"[213] – the GC IV standard for interning civilians in occupied territory. Both categories are entitled to period review of their detention by a "competent authority"[214] – another GC IV reference – which must be a military judge for "unprivileged belligerents held in long-term detention."[215]

Scholars also support the analogies to GC III and GC IV. In Goodman's view, for example, because "the Fourth Geneva Convention does generally contain the most closely analogous rules concerning the detention of civilians," it "constitutes the best approximation of IHL rules when interpretive gaps arise."[216] Similarly, Kress suggests that "[i]n line with the most recent practice of the USA, in particular," states are increasingly likely to adopt an "an 'armed conflict model' for preventive detention" in NIAC "through 'translation' or analogizing principles from the laws of war governing traditional" IACs.[217]

There is, however, an important methodological difference between Goodman and Kress: while Goodman claims that nothing prevents the U.S. from applying GC IV's detention standards in NIAC, Kress argues – or at least strongly implies – that those standards could only be applied in NIAC if a sufficient number of states adopted the U.S.'s analogy to GC IV. In other words, while Goodman believes that the U.S. analogy is already *lex lata*, Kress believes that it is currently *lex ferenda* that could become *lex lata* as a matter of customary international law.

Kress is absolutely right. Nothing in international law would prohibit states from applying GC IV's detention regime to NIAC through convention or custom. Indeed, through convention or custom, states could apply GC III's much more detention-friendly regime to members of organized armed groups, civilians who DPH, and even ordinary civilians. As discussed earlier, no matter how we understand the *lex specialis* principle, a clear and specific conventional or customary rule of IHL will have priority in an armed conflict – IAC or NIAC – over a competing conventional or customary rule of IHRL.

[213] *Id.*, ¶ 3(m)(5). [214] *Id.*, ¶ 3(m)(1). [215] *Id.*, ¶ 3(i).

[216] Goodman, *Detention of Civilians*, *supra* note 24, at 50. Interestingly, Goodman does not explain why the U.S. could not maximize its detention authority by analogizing to GC III instead of to GC IV. He simply says that GC IV "constitutes the best approximation of IHL rules when interpretive gaps arise." If analogy is a legitimate source of IHL, however, an analogy's ostensible substantive fit would seem to be irrelevant.

[217] Kress, *supra* note 50, at 264.

The problem with the U.S. position is that, as Kress implies, the available state practice is insufficient to conclude that customary IHL authorizes detention in NIAC[218] – much less that it authorizes detention by reference to GC III and/or GC IV. The U.S. analogies to IAC thus fail for the same reason they fail in the context of targeting: an analogized rule represents domestic humanitarian law, which is not capable of displacing or even modifying IHRL.[219] Detention in NIAC is simply not an area of international law in which "every State remains free to adopt the principles which it regards as best and most suitable." On the contrary, there are now prohibitive rules of IHRL that, via *lex specialis*, define the limits of NIAC detention. And as we have seen, those prohibitive rules simply do not permit detention on par with GC III or GC IV – particularly the kind of indefinite detention that GC III contemplates.

It is also worth highlighting another problem with the U.S.'s analogy to GC III: its asymmetry. Although Art. 4 of GC III permits a state to detain combatants until the end of hostilities, such detainees are entitled to POW status.[220] As we saw in the context of targeting, therefore, it would not be enough for the U.S. to establish a customary rule extending GC III's detention power to NIAC. Because the default position is that IHL applies symmetrically, it would have to show that custom permits it to apply the permissive rules of IHL (detention) while ignoring its prohibitive rules (POW status).

218 *See, e.g.*, Mohammed, *supra* note 199, ¶ 257 ("I have been shown no evidence of any recognition by states involved in noninternational armed conflicts of IHL as providing a legal basis for detention. . . . Nor has the MOD pointed to any official statement by the UK government (or any other government) which suggests that IHL does, or could, provide a legal basis for detention in any non-international armed conflict."); Hill-Cawthorne & Akande, *supra* note 158 ("That the legal basis for detention in NIACs does not lie in IHL, whether as an implied right or a customary right, is supported by state practice. . . . If either the applicable treaty provisions or customary international law could be said to provide a legal basis for detention in NIACs, one would expect practice generally to confirm this. This does not, however, seem to be the case.").

219 *See* Hill-Cawthorne & Akande, *Locating the Legal Basis for Detention in Non-International Armed Conflicts: A Rejoinder to Aurel Sari*, EJIL: Talk! (June 2, 2014), available at www.ejiltalk.org/locating-the-legal-basis-for-detention-in-non-international-armed-conflicts-a-rejoinder-to-aurel-sari/ ("That IHL should provide such a basis [for detention in NIAC] as a matter of logic (with which one may or may not agree) cannot make up for this lack of supporting practice.").

220 *See* GC III, *supra* note 10, Art. 4(A) (defining POWs as "persons belonging to one of the following categories, who have fallen into the power of the enemy").

2. Substantial Support

The U.S. does not believe that it is limited to detaining individuals who are members of al-Qaeda or one of its associated forces. It also takes the position that it can detain anyone who "substantially supports" any such group. The USG thus defines "unprivileged belligerents" – who may be detained until "the conflict has ended or … active hostilities have ceased" – as "[i]ndividuals who have forfeited the protections of civilian status by joining or substantially supporting an enemy non-state armed group in the conduct of hostilities."[221] That position, as the USG openly acknowledges, is based on analogy to IAC – in particular, to the "persons accompanying" provision of GC III:

> The term "substantial support" covers support that, in analogous circumstances in a traditional international armed conflict, is sufficient to justify detention. The term thus encompasses individuals who, even if not considered part of the irregular enemy forces at issue in the current conflict, bear sufficiently close ties to those forces and provide them support that warrants their detention in prosecution of the conflict. See, e.g., Geneva Convention III, Art. 4.A(4).[222]

Courts have consistently upheld the U.S.'s right to detain individuals who substantially support al-Qaeda or its associated forces,[223] and at least one has implicitly adopted the analogy to GC III's "persons accompanying" provision. In *al-Bihani*, the appellant argued that he could not be lawfully detained because he was nothing more than a "civilian 'contractor' rendering services" to one of al-Qaeda's associated forces.[224] The DC Circuit rejected that argument – but held that he would be detainable even if he was not a member of that associated force, because substantial support "clearly include[s] traditional food operations essential to a fighting force and the carrying of arms."[225]

Applying the "persons accompanying" provision in Art. 4(A)(4) of GC III to NIAC by analogy, however, is no less problematic than applying by

[221] DoD Directive, *supra* note 11, at 14; *see also* 2012 NDAA, *supra* note 171, § 1021 (providing that the AUMF's detention power extends to individuals who provide substantial support).

[222] Quoted in Ryan Vogel, *The DoD Detainee Directive and Its Definition of "Unprivileged Belligerency,"* Just Security (September 22, 2014), available at http://justsecurity.org/15312/dod-detainee-directive-definition-unprivileged-belligerency/; *see also* Lederman & Vladeck, *supra* note 23 ("[P]erhaps substantial supporters of enemy forces who are apprehended while accompanying such forces can be detained on roughly the same terms as the forces themselves, just as they can be in an international conflict.").

[223] *See, e.g.*, Al-Bihani, *supra* note 20, at 872. [224] *Id.* at 873. [225] *Id.*

analogy Art. 21 of GC III and Arts. 42(1) and 78(1) of GC IV. Conventional IHL limits the detention of "persons accompanying" to IAC, and there is no evidence that the rule applies in NIAC as a matter of customary international law. Indeed, as Danner notes, the idea that individuals who support organized armed groups are detainable in the same way as members of organized armed groups comes not from IHL, but from "the domestic law of complicity, which targets those who aid and abet the principal perpetrators of crimes."[226] The "persons accompanying" analogy is thus precisely the kind of domestic humanitarian law that cannot supplant a competing prohibitive rule of IHRL.

To be sure, IHRL does not necessarily prohibit the U.S. from detaining individuals who substantially support al-Qaeda or one of its associated forces. IHRL's priority simply means that the U.S. must determine the detainability of a substantial supporter by reference to IHRL – the "present, direct and imperative threat" standard, in particular – and must afford anyone thereby detained all of IHRL's procedural guarantees. Many actions the USG considers "substantial support" likely satisfy the IHRL standard, such as financing or recruiting for al-Qaeda. Cooking for an associated force of al-Qaeda, however, clearly does not.

3. Detention by Organized Armed Groups

All of the analogized rules of IHL discussed thus far reflect the U.S.'s desire to maximize its targeting and detention power in NIAC. A few scholars, by contrast, have relied on analogy expand the power of organized armed groups – in particular, by contending that GC III entitles such groups to detain members of the state's armed forces. Casalin argues, for example, that because CA3 and AP II do not prohibit detention by organized armed groups and even seem to contemplate it, the circumstances in which such detention is acceptable should be defined "using the analogous IHL of international armed conflict (i.e., the standards of Geneva Convention III)":

> Detention by armed opposition groups in a situation analogous to those prescribed by the law of international armed conflict would therefore not be considered arbitrary for want of a legal basis, since Common Article 3 (and, in certain cases, Article 5 of Additional Protocol II) serves

226 Allison M. Danner, *Defining Unlawful Enemy Combatants: A Centripetal Story*, 43 Tex. Int'l L. J. 1, 12 (2007).

> as the preexisting legal grounds for detention.... In such a case, Geneva Convention III would then be used for guidance in interpretation of what it means to detain in connection with hostilities. This could be considered a type of "quasi-POW" detention (i.e., imprisonment of enemy fighters for the purpose of placing them hors de combat).[227]

The problem with this analogy is a familiar one: a permissive rule applied to NIAC from solely by analogy to IAC cannot supplant a competing prohibitive rule of IHRL under any conception of *lex specialis*. Here such an IHRL rule clearly exists: namely, that detention in NIAC is permissible only insofar as it is authorized by law.[228] Only such authorization ensures that detention in NIAC is neither arbitrary nor unlawful.[229] In IAC, IHL itself provides the necessary authority to detain; domestic authorization is not necessary.[230] IHL does not, however, authorize detention in NIAC; the necessary authorization is left to domestic law. Any attempt to rely on analogy to argue that organized armed groups can detain members of the state's armed forces is thus doomed to fail. As Casalin herself notes, "the domestic law of all states prohibits detention by armed opposition groups."[231] IHRL thus does not permit organized armed groups to detain anyone.[232]

[227] Casalin, *supra* note 54, at 754; *see also Sassoli*, Internment, *supra* note 54, at 623 ("Applied by analogy, the humanitarian law of international armed conflict allows for internment and provides for review procedures ... Given the organizational criteria a non-state actor must meet to be considered a party to an armed conflict, any non-state actor should be able to fulfill these obligations.").

[228] *See, e.g.*, HRC General Comment 35, *supra* note 65, ¶ 44; Hill-Cawthorne, *supra* note 205, at 485.

[229] *See* HRC General Comment 35, *supra* note 65, ¶ 11.

[230] ICRC Position Paper, *supra* note 192, at 4 (noting that this position is "generally uncontroversial").

[231] Casalin, *supra* note 54, at 744; *see also* LIESBETH ZEGVELD, ACCOUNTABILITY OF ARMED OPPOSITION GROUPS IN INTERNATIONAL LAW 66 (2002) ("Human rights treaties presume the state to be the only authority within the state territory, and under this law the state, represented by a government, is the only authority entitled to arrest and detain persons on such grounds and in accordance with the law.").

[232] It is worth noting that Casalin's reliance on analogy is oddly selective. Although she believes that IHL permits organized armed groups to detain members of the state's armed forces in NIAC, she insists that the detention of civilians continues to be determined by IHRL. Casalin, *supra* note 54, at 755. She also argues that analogy to IAC provides only the authorization to detain members of the state's armed forces; the procedural limits on their detention must still be determined by IHRL. *Id.* Casalin never explains why, if analogy is permissible, organized armed groups must appropriate only those aspects of IHL that she finds normatively desirable.

Conclusion

Karl Rove once famously accused Democrats who opposed the Bush Administration's counterterrorism policies of having a "pre-9/11 mindset."[233] As it turns out, the USG as a whole has a "pre-1949" mindset – its consistent reliance on analogy to maximize its ability to target and detain harkens back to an age before World War II, when non-international conflicts were actually non-international and universal human rights were nothing more than a gleam in Eleanor Roosevelt's eyes. In that *Lotus*-dominated era, no prohibitive rules of international law prevented a state from adopting whatever targeting and detention rules it considered "best and most suitable" for quelling an insurgency; if it wanted to look to international armed conflict for inspiration, it was free to do so.

The legal landscape, however, has changed dramatically since World War II. In a NIAC, IHL is no longer the only game in town; both targeting and detention are also subject – at least potentially – to IHRL's prohibitive rules. And NIAC is no longer predominantly non-international; transnational NIACs are now the norm, not the exception. Prohibitive rules that protect a state's sovereignty – the principle of non-intervention and the prohibition on the use of force – thus also affect how a state fights a NIAC.

In our legally overdetermined era of transnational armed conflict, there is simply no room in IHL for analogy between IAC and NIAC. First and foremost, there is the IHRL problem. IHRL prevents analogy because analogized rules have no basis in either conventional or customary IHL; they are simply rules of domestic humanitarian law that cannot supplant contrary rules of IHRL under any conception of *lex specialis*. And then there is the sovereignty problem. Analogized rules may not necessarily violate the principle of non-intervention and the prohibition on the use of force; it is always possible to imagine situations in which self-defense would permit the U.S. to extraterritorially target or detain individuals who have become targetable or detainable because of a rule analogized from IAC to NIAC. But there are far more scenarios in which analogized rules will permit – even encourage – the U.S. to use force extraterritorially in a manner that is inconsistent with the principle of non-intervention and the prohibition on the use of force. Analogy thus makes it exceptionally likely, if not actually certain, that the U.S. will routinely use extraterritorial force unlawfully.

[233] Branden Crocker, *Over the Top*, American Spectator (February 15, 2006).

The Permanent Court of International Justice held in 1927 that "[r]estrictions upon the independence of States cannot ... be presumed." That principle was sound in the era in which it was written. But that is not our era. In the Age of Rights, the U.N. Charter, and transnational armed conflict, such restrictions no longer have to be presumed – they exist throughout positive international law.

PART III

New Frameworks for Regulating Armed Violence

8

Forcible Alternatives to War

Legitimate Violence in 21st Century International Relations

JANINA DILL

Introduction

The legal and moral principles we draw on to determine the permissibility of resort to force and of legitimate conduct in war are fundamentally at odds with widely shared normative beliefs about proper behavior in international relations. This chapter shows that in the twenty-first century war is therefore irredeemably illegitimate.[1] As a result, armed conflict,[2] even if it accords with the principles of just war theory and the strictures of international law, is increasingly politically costly. At the same time, no social system can survive without a mechanism for the legitimate use of force. It follows that we require what I refer to as "forcible alternatives to war."

If those were readily available, states would have stopped waging war already, given the high material and reputational costs of engaging in armed struggles with other states.[3] Rather, envisaging mechanisms for the legitimate use of violence in the international system other than war – meaning a violent,[4] large-scale, formally symmetrical confrontation between individuals on behalf of states – requires the contemplation of

[1] For a detailed elaboration of this argument see Janina Dill, Legitimate Targets? International Law, Social Construction and US Bombing, chapter 9 (2015).

[2] I use the terms "war" and "armed conflict" interchangeably. Throughout this chapter they refer to confrontations between states. Intra-state or civil wars, even those that are regionalized and cut across state boundaries, pose different regulative challenges and therefore warrant a separate discussion.

[3] The prevalence of armed conflict between states has in fact decreased significantly since 1945, without, however, showing signs of disappearing altogether.

[4] The terms "armed," "violent," and "forcible" are used interchangeably. They all designate coercive political interactions that involve the use of kinetic force.

institutional structures that radically diverge from the current reality of international relations. As a result, this chapter may be vulnerable to the charge of utopianism. While the ultimate goal of research into forcible alternatives to war must be the proposal of *practicable* changes to international institutions and international law, this chapter serves only as a first step on the way to a transcendence of war in international relations.

The modest aim of the chapter is twofold: first, to pinpoint the problem of why war and its legal regulation are at odds with contemporary normative expectations of legitimate state conduct and effective international law. In fact, I argue that armed conflict and international law *cannot* easily be changed to meet those expectations. The chapter thus makes the case for the urgency of the search for forcible alternatives to war. The second aim is to explore what kind of rules and institutions could potentially avoid which of the regulative problems and normative challenges posed by the use of violence in interstate relations that the chapter has identified. The chapter hence strives to move beyond the general argument that, given the "advent of a general distaste for the waste of human life"[5] and "a long-term trend toward humanizing the 'other,'"[6] warfare is decreasingly politically acceptable. It provides an understanding of the specific normative implications of these trends for the international order.

The argument proceeds in four steps. The first section defines war by identifying four constitutive features that have to cumulatively obtain for an instance of interstate violence to count as war or international armed conflict. The second section links one of those features – collectivity – to the challenge that international humanitarian law (hereinafter IHL) faces in the regulation of conduct in war. It thereby explains why one of the oldest regimes of international law, the laws of war or IHL, no longer provides a source of political legitimacy sufficient to ward off reputational costs: the rise of individual rights in international relations. Another constitutive feature of war, what I refer to as formal symmetry, is linked in section three to the impossibility of making the protection of

[5] Theodor Meron, The Humanization of International Law 6 (2006).

[6] Margaret Keck and Kathryn Sikkink, Activists Beyond Borders: Advocacy Networks in International Politics (1998); similar Neta C. Crawford, *Decolonization as an International Norm: The Evolution of Practices Norms and Beliefs*, *in* Emerging Norms of Justified Intervention (Laura W. Reed and Carl Kaysen eds., 1993); Martha Finnemore and Kathryn Sikkink, International Norm Dynamics and Political Change, 52 IO 887 (1998); James L. Ray, The Abolition of Slavery and the End of International War, 43 IO 405 (1989); Kathryn Sikkink, The Justice Cascade: How Human Rights Prosecutions are Changing World Politics (2011).

individual rights the touchstone for legitimate resort to force. The final section is a tentative exploration of ways to alter or mitigate the implications of these two features that make war an illegitimate means of solving conflict or enforcing international law.

What I suggest here as alternative mechanisms for the use of violence in international relations is not new. Many, in my terminology, forcible alternatives to war have been dismissed as impracticable by scholars of law and international relations and occasionally as morally undesirable by scholars concerned with international ethics. Rather than evaluating their potential to be implemented, the chapter assesses them in light of their ability to circumvent the legitimacy problem of war by minimizing the implications or even the prevalence of war's major two problematic features, collectivity and symmetry. This is meant to be a contribution to the debate about their normative desirability, without being a definitive answer to the question whether they are, all things considered, morally justified forcible alternatives to war.

I. The Problem with War

In order to grasp the fundamental disconnect between, on the one hand, the reality of interstate warfare, and on the other hand, widely shared beliefs about legitimate state conduct and indeed expectations of effective international law, it is first necessary to define war. What exactly do I argue is no longer an acceptable way of conducting international relations even if it accords with international law and a traditional understanding of just state conduct?[7] The introduction used the definition of war as a 1) violent, 2) large-scale 3) confrontation between individuals (natural persons) on behalf of states (collective agents), 4) in which the latter are formally in a symmetrical relationship. In the following I clarify what I understand by these four elements and discuss their contestability as constitutive features of war. I also touch on the ways in which they may render war normatively problematic, which I elaborate on in the sections that follow.

Instances of cross border violence whose designation as war is debatable, due to the absence or contestability of one of the four mentioned elements, are useful starting points for the search for forcible alternatives to war. The exception to this is the first element of the aforementioned

[7] This is a reference to conventional just war theory. I will differentiate between conventional and revisionist just war theory below. Here I mean the former and its long standing assumption that there is such a thing as a fully just war both in conduct and resort.

definition: violence. Recent allegations of cyber-attacks by states have sparked a debate about whether they could ever "on their own" constitute a violation of the prohibition on the use of force or an armed attack. A similar, older controversy concerns the imposition of economic sanctions and their status as violations of Article 4(2) U.N. Charter. Even though both cyber-attacks and economic sanctions can create significant material damage and harm, the means of damage infliction is non-kinetic, or "non-forcible." This chapter assumes that social relations require for their maintenance and prosperity a means to forcibly reign in "spoilers," i.e., solve conflicts among members and enforce the rules of the game.[8] As it is this physical, kinetic kind of coercion that specifically challenges contemporary normative expectations of appropriateness, the chapter brackets the potential role of coercion in cyber space as well as sanctions in international dispute settlement or law enforcement.

Out of the four, the element of scale is the most contestable as a constitutive feature of war. Not every instance of cross border violence presumably amounts to a full-fledged war. Yet, the minimum intensity and the required spatial and temporal extension of violence for it to count as an international armed conflict are subject to debate. It is beyond the scope of this chapter to retrace or add to the debate about what distinguishes a "mere" skirmish from a "proper" war and what separates a "mere" violation of the prohibition on the use of force from a full-fledged armed attack. For the purpose of finding a legitimate means of using violence in international relations scale is only indirectly relevant: the scale of violence is related to the possibility of controlling and delimiting its effects. Element number two is hence closely tied to element number three – collectivity – which, it turns out, is crucial for the normative acceptability of the use of force.

That wars are fought by collections of individuals on behalf of states is the constitutive feature of international armed conflict that most immediately challenges twenty-first century norms on proper state conduct and effective international law. International relations used to mean relations among sovereign states. International law hence centered on regulating states' coexistence and securing their rights, such as territorial integrity and non-intervention, vis-à-vis each other.[9] How states treated the populations on the territory under their control was for the most part

[8] It is beyond the scope of the chapter to properly argue rather than merely state that point.

[9] For this argument see Bruno Simma, *From Bilateralism to Community Interest in International Law*, 250 Collected Courses of The Hague Academy of Int'l L. 217 (1994).

not a matter of concern in states' relations with each other. Yet, in the second half of the twentieth century the understanding increasingly gained ground that states do not hold independent moral value, but are worthy of preservation and bear rights at least primarily on behalf of the populations they represent. On that view, the individual should be the beneficiary of legal regulation where domestic as well as international law is concerned.[10] This idea animated the creation, elaboration, and increased justiciability of a global human rights regime under international law.[11]

Yet, from the point of view of conventional just war theory as well as international law, war is a struggle between collective agents (states). During that struggle natural persons are granted rights and incur obligations not in virtue of their individual moral agency or legal subjectivity, but in virtue of their membership in the collective at war. Conventional just war theory like IHL divides individuals belonging to the collectives at war into two groups, civilians and combatants. Both normative frameworks then posit the relative immunity for one group (civilians) at the expense of the other group (combatants), which is exposed to permissible lethal attack.[12] Killing combatants, regardless of their individual moral status, is a legally privileged course of action conventionally overriding their individually held legal right to life.[13] Moreover, international law and conventional just war theory permit the incidental harming of civilians irrespective of the rights they enjoy qua being human, as long as that harm is proportionate to an

[10] This change is observed by scholars of international law, such as Armin von Bogdandy, *Constitutionalism in International Law*, 47 Harv. Int'l L.J. 223 (2006); Jean Cohen, *Sovereignty in the Context of Globalization: A Constitutionalist Pluralist Perspective*, *in* The Philosophy of International Law (Samantha Besson and John Tasioulas eds., 2010); Neil McCormick, *Beyond the Sovereign State?* 56 The Modern L. Rev. 1 (1993); Kate Parlett, The Individual in International Law (2011); Theodor Schilling, On the Constitutionalization of General International Law (2005); Bruno Simma and Andreas L. Paulus, *The 'International Community'. Facing the Challenge of Globalization*, 9 EJIL 266 (1998). It is also observed by scholars of international relations; most famously, Barry Buzan, From International to World Society (2004); Anne-Marie Slaughter, A New World Order (2004).

[11] I use the terms "individual rights" and "human rights" interchangeably. The former is preferred by just war theorists, while the legal regime in question is referred to by the latter.

[12] In turn, combatants acquire a "right" to participate in hostilities, which civilians lack.

[13] I return later to the relationship between international humanitarian and human rights law and the impossibility of truly reconciling them with each other.

independently legal/justified military gain sought by the belligerent.[14] In other words, the principles we rely on to guide and assess the conduct of war, both moral and legal, do not even strive to give the individual her moral or (peacetime) legal due.

The fourth constitutive feature of war is formal symmetry among state belligerents. That, of course, cannot mean factual, even just rough, equality of belligerents in manpower, technology, or resources devoted to strategy development. Wars are very rarely balanced in such a material sense. Neither of course are wars *prima facie* legally or morally symmetrical. To the contrary, the prohibition on the use of force[15] with its two acknowledged exceptions presupposes that any legal resort to force is preceded by a violation of international law in the form of either a "threat to the peace, breach of the peace or act of aggression"[16] or an "armed attack" in the meaning of Article 51 U.N. Charter. Just war theory leaves room for debate about what exactly constitutes a just cause for the resort to force, but it likewise acknowledges that logically only one side, if any, can avail itself of this justification.

Yet, once states are belligerents they are treated as if they were legal and moral equals. IHL prescribes conduct without reference to the reasons "espoused by or attributed to the Parties to the conflict."[17] Whether a state is an aggressor or pursues legally permissible self-defence is immaterial for the courses of action that the state may take in hostilities. Conventional just war theory likewise guides conduct in combat operations based on an assumption of belligerent symmetry, bracketing the justness of and the reasons why a state has resorted to force, in the first place.[18]

This normative equalization of states once they have assumed the role of belligerents accounts for the fact that it is asymmetries between belligerents in material power, numbers of men, or technology that in fact decide the outcome of wars, not asymmetries in legality or justness of

[14] Article 51(5)(b) Protocol Additional to the Geneva Conventions of August 12, 1949, and relating to the Protection of Victims of International Armed Conflicts (Protocol I), June 8, 1977, 1125 UNTS 3 [herein API or the Protocol].

[15] Article 2(4) Charter of the United Nations (San Francisco, June 26, 1945), 3 Bevans 1153, 59 Stat. 1031, T.S. No. 993, *entered into force* October 24, 1945 [herein U.N. Charter].

[16] Article 39 U.N. Charter. [17] Preamble AP I

[18] For the most influential elaboration of conventional just war theory, see MICHAEL WALZER, JUST AND UNJUST WARS: A MORAL ARGUMENT WITH HISTORICAL ILLUSTRATIONS (4th ed., 2006); also *Id.*, ARGUING ABOUT WAR (2004).

cause, culpability, or desert. The normative equalization of belligerents also expresses that international armed conflict is symmetrical in a more fundamental sense. Neither side in a war between states is formally acting on behalf of a higher authority. Contrary to domestic law enforcement, international armed conflict is a belligerent's fight primarily on its own behalf. No higher authority is necessarily involved in the resolution of a conflict among states once it has descended into the use of force.[19]

This symmetry challenges recently solidified and now widely shared normative beliefs about the appropriate role of violence in international relations. An early and crucial manifestation of these changing normative beliefs was the formal legal prohibition on the use of force in 1945. Armed conflict has not been an acceptable means of conducting international relations or a normal tool of sovereign statecraft since. The prescription of peaceful "friendly" relations among states is arguably the key-stone of the contemporary international legal order. All that separates a pariah of the international society from a member exercising legitimate self-defence or even carrying out a mandate by the Security Council is the reason behind the resort to force. It is counterintuitive that this strong, some would say constitutional legal norm, should abdicate as soon as it is violated in order to make way for an assumption of legal symmetry.

To sum up this first enquiry into the problem with war, violence is constitutive of wars. It is also constitutive of the kind of alternatives to it that this chapter is exploring. The scale of violence is indirectly relevant for its normative acceptability. The collective nature of war and the constructed normative symmetry among belligerents together ground war's decreasing acceptability. These two constitutive features of war mirror the two major dimensions of contestation befalling the legitimacy of the use of force in international relations. They are therefore crucial for the conceptual search for alternative mechanisms for the legitimate use of violence for the purposes of conflict resolution and law enforcement. I will discuss these dimensions of contestation in turn in the following two sections.

[19] The use of force mandated by the Security Council may seem to be an exception. Yet, majority opinion maintains that IHL applies and belligerent symmetry holds even between a state identified as having threatened or breached the peace and a state or group of states carrying out a U.N. mandate.

II. International Humanitarian Law's Deal with the Devil is Off

IHL is varyingly described as resting on "an uneasy compromise"[20] or drawing a "delicate balance."[21] These images express that the regulative purpose of this branch of international law is split: in order to have the opportunity to render war as humane as militarily feasible IHL ensures that warfare remains not only practically possible but also as militarily expeditious as can be in light of humanitarian concerns. To that end, international law permits what in terms of human rights law are clear infringements of individual rights and what often amount to morally reprehensible courses of action. IHL is a product of a Faustian Pact of law with military necessity: IHL endorses an "evil" as legal in order to be able to effectively prohibit another considered even worse: unrestrained warfare. In turn, belligerents following IHL may, as we generally do when complying with law, expect that their behavior is perceived as legitimate even if it involves "killing people and breaking things."

This expectation is increasingly often disappointed. Since 1945, public outrage about the harmful consequences of combat operations conducted by state belligerents has steadily increased. The victimization of civilians during the U.S. engagement in Korea mattered little to the international or indeed the American public.[22] The humanitarian implications of the war in Vietnam eventually attracted public attention and stirred opposition to the war.[23] In 1991, the global public followed the conduct of

[20] Henry Shue and David Wippman, *Limiting Attacks on Dual-Use Facilities Performing Indispensable Functions*, 35 Cornell Int'l L.J. 559 (2002).

[21] Michael N. Schmitt, *Military Necessity and Humanity in International Humanitarian Law: Preserving the Delicate Balance*, 50 Va. J. Int'l L. 795, *passim* (2010); similar Yoram Dinstein, The Conduct of Hostilities under the Law of International Armed Conflict 5 (2010); Jens David Ohlin, *The Duty to Capture*, 97 Minn. L. Rev. 1268, 1315 (2013).

[22] For detailed accounts of changing attitudes toward collateral damage, see Sahr Conway-Lanz, Collateral Damage: Americans, Non-Combatant Immunity and Atrocity after World War Two (2006); Ward Thomas, The Ethics of Destruction: Norms and Force in International Relations (2001). For a discussion of the changing role of civilians in armed conflict, see Andreas Wenger and Simon L. A. Mason, *The Civilianization of Armed Conflict: Trends and Implications*, 90 Int'l Rev. Red Cross 872 (2008).

[23] David M. Barrett ed., Lyndon B. Johnson's Vietnam Papers: A Documentary Collection 159 & 289 (1997); see also George McT. Kahin, Intervention: How America Became Involved in Vietnam 284 (1987); John T. Smith, The Strategic Bombing Campaign in North Vietnam 1965–1968 287 (1994). For more general accounts of the role of public perception in military operations against Vietnam, see Mark Clodfelter, The Limits of Air Power. The American Bombing of North Vietnam (2006); Jeffrey Record, The Wrong War: Why We Lost in Vietnam (1998); *Id.* and W. Andrew Terrill, Iraq and Vietnam: Differences, Similarities and Insights (2004).

Operation Desert Storm even more closely. The bombing of a shelter, which caused more than 400 civilian casualties, engendered such discontent that the incident ended "the strategic air campaign against targets in Baghdad."[24] Nowadays in warzones that attract popular attention, such as Afghanistan, political leaders make the minimization of civilian casualties a priority to the point of allegedly making war all but impossible to wage. In 2008, General Stanley McChrystal famously tightened the rules on air strikes in Afghanistan imposing in effect a policy of zero expected collateral damage in certain circumstances. These drastic changes to the rules of engagement exceeded the U.S.' legal obligations and attracted vociferous criticism from McChrystal's subordinates as well as from military peers. At the same time, they failed to quell public protests and criticism from the Afghan government.

As adumbrated, in war civilians are protected from intentional direct attack, but may permissibly be harmed and killed as a side effect of military operations, if that is necessary and proportionate. Proportionality is a highly indeterminate concept and military practitioners as well as legal commentators may reasonably disagree on many air strikes' qualification as proportionate or excessive. What is remarkable is that *public* discontent decreasingly centers on the alleged excessiveness of warfare. Rather, any killing of individuals not otherwise perceived as culpable is worthy of criticism. This is particularly striking as public and academic attention has shifted from U.S. air strikes in Afghanistan to targeted killings with unmanned aerial vehicles (UAVs) primarily in Pakistan. A number of third-party reports have largely debunked the myth of UAV's surgical precision to show that, contrary to a narrative carefully crafted by the Obama administration, targeted killings do cause incidental harm to civilians.[25] The criticism implied by or explicitly based on these findings does often not focus on the question of whether or not what we colloquially refer to as drone strikes is a proportionate means of inflicting damage. The killing of civilians as such imposes ever higher

[24] 2 U.S. Department of Defense, Conduct of the Persian Gulf War: Final Report to Congress 206 (1992); similar Rick Atkinson, Crusade: The Untold Story of the Persian Gulf War 286 (1993).

[25] See, for instance, Human Rights Watch, *Between a Drone and Al Qaida: The Civilian Cost of US Targeted Killings in Yemen* (2013); International Human Rights and Conflict Resolution Clinic Stanford Law School and Global Justice Clinic NYU Law School, *Living under Drones: Death, Injury, and Trauma to Civilians for US Drone Practices in Pakistan* (2012).

reputational costs on the U.S.[26] – costs that the current administration sought to avoid by replacing, wherever possible, conventional military employments abroad with remote air power.

The notorious casualty aversion specifically of Western societies is by no means focused singularly on civilians. Primarily in their countries of origin, combatants' deaths are no longer deemed an inevitable acceptable evil, even if they are, and they mostly are, legal.[27] The so-called Highway of Death incident during which the U.S. attacked Iraqi forces on the road leading from Kuwait City to Basra in the final days of Operation Desert Storm, brought into sharp relief that the international public no longer perceives combatants' lives as simply dispensable.[28] The legally sanctioned interest of belligerents in killing as many individuals designated as combatants on the other side as deemed militarily useful offends the cross-culturally internalized understanding that combatants like other individuals have rights qua being human – rights which transcend a status given to them by sovereign prerogative. Complying with the strictures of IHL therefore no longer vouchsafes the acceptability of belligerent conduct. International law's deal with the devil is off.

Could belligerents wage war in such a way as not to commit individual rights violations? Two suggestions to do justice to the understanding that combatants as human beings carry a right to life have recently attracted attention. I will refer to them as the necessity and the threat condition respectively. Niels Melzer introduced the norm that civilians directly participating in hostilities and combatants should only be subject to lethal attack if that was in fact necessary to disable them.[29] Gabriella Blum has added to this suggestion the proposal that combatants should only be legitimate targets for as long as they actually pose a threat to the enemy.[30] To be sure, these attempts at reinterpreting IHL with a view to coming closer to meeting human rights standards have attracted reproof for allegedly

[26] Eric V. Larson and Bogdan Savych, Misfortunes of War: Press and Public Reactions to Civilian Deaths in Wartime (2007).

[27] *Ibid.*

[28] Seymour Hersh, Overwhelming Force: What Happened in the Final Days of the Gulf War, The New Yorker, May 22, 2000.

[29] Nils Melzer, Interpretive Guidance on the Notion of Direct Participation in Hostilities under International Humanitarian Law (2009); see also *Id.*, *Bolstering the Protection of Civilians in Armed Conflict*, *in* Realizing Utopia: The Future of International Law 508 (Antonio Cassese ed., 2012).

[30] Gabriella Blum, *The Dispensable Life of Soldiers*, 2 J. Legal Analysis 1, 6 (2010).

being impracticable.[31] The following paragraphs discuss some practical and normative implications of the threat and the necessity conditions.

Under *lex lata* an attacker has to establish that a person is a combatant or directly participating in hostilities before deliberate and direct attack is legal. In case of doubt a person is to be considered civilian. In modern warfare, specifically warfare from the air, it is often not at all obvious whether an individual is indeed a combatant or directly participating in hostilities. It may be even less obvious whether a person encountered on the 'battlefield' is threatening. The first objection to the threat condition is hence that it would add to the considerable epistemic burden placed on the conscientious attacker. One reported challenge in determining whether a person is directly participating in hostilities is the requirement to infer hostile intent from actions. A threat-condition would in fact demand that every lethal attack is preceded by such an inference of hostile intent. In addition, an attacker would need to determine whether an individual encountered in a combat theater has the ability to inflict harm. A combatant that lacks either the intent to cause harm or the ability to do so could not be deemed threatening.

Much turns on whether doubts about the threatening nature of a combatant would mean she may be presumed a legitimate target of attack or not. As mentioned, the, as it were, default status of an individual is civilian. This prior in-case-of-doubt rule is regularly broken, particularly in contemporary air warfare and in military operations involving non-state armed groups, simply because most fighters cannot be identified as combatants beyond doubt. It is unlikely that an added rule granting even combatants that are positively identified as such by default immunity from attack would gain much traction. If, on the other hand, a combatant may be considered threatening in case of doubt, any restraining force of the rule hinges on whether or not reasonable observers agree on when doubt is appropriate.

A second possible objection to the treat condition is the argument that wars might end up much prolonged if belligerents may only disable combatants on the opposing side that in any given situation present a threat. After all, combatants who could easily be disabled while not posing a threat might, once out of reach of the enemy, change their mind or acquire the ability to be threatening. The underlying concern is that drawn-out wars are ultimately more destructive and harmful to

[31] For instance, Michael N. Schmitt, *The Interpretive Guidance on the Notion of Direct Participation in Hostilities: A Critical Analysis*, 1 Harv. Nat. Sec. J. 5 (2012); also *Id.*, *supra* note 21.

civilians than briefer, more efficient military operations. Whether sharp wars are indeed brief enough to warrant their increased sharpness is an empirical question that is virtually impossible to answer. Nonetheless, this objection draws attention to the risk that a rule meant to further humanitarianism in war may well have perverse consequences. Specifically a potential trade-off between the protection of combatants and civilians needs to be taken into account.

The necessity condition raises an even more fundamental epistemic question than the threat condition. While it may in practice be difficult for one combatant to determine whether another is threatening, in theory, we know what it means that an individual poses a threat in war: She has the ability and the intent to inflict harm on the adversary. But what does it mean that it is necessary to kill a combatant on the battlefield? First, we need to clarify with regard to which goal indispensability of lethal attack has to obtain. Is it necessary to kill a combatant if that is the only way to avoid harm to friendly forces? In this understanding of the condition as "necessary to kill in order to avoid being killed," the necessity and the threat condition overlap.

If an attack has to be indispensable not with regard to the goal of staying alive, but the broader aim of winning a war, the necessity condition might imply an obligation to capture rather than kill a combatant, if possible. After all, in theory, overcoming an enemy military can be accomplished by taking prisoner a sufficient number of persons in arms. Capture or kill, of course do not exhaust the ways in which a belligerent can remove a combatant's ability to contribute to the enemy's military operations. It might be sufficient to disable and therefore unnecessary to kill a combatant. Moreover, the impossibility of apprehending a combatant on the battlefield does not even establish the necessity of inflicting any, even only disabling rather than lethal violence, in order to deny the enemy that combatant's contribution to the war effort. What about psychological warfare, or crudely put, the possibility of convincing a combatant not to contribute to the adversary's military effort? What is necessary, in order to deny the enemy a combatant's contribution to the war effort is not only situationally contingent. It also depends on that individual. For kinetic attacks to be necessary, do belligerents have to exhaust non-kinetic means of information warfare?

Of course, the deeper question is whether a belligerent can ever know which combatants contribute enough or at all to the war effort for it to be necessary to disable them in order to win. Again, this would require the determination of whether an individual has both the intention and the ability to stand in the way of their enemy's victory. Two questions arise in this context. First, what does it mean to win? Second, can we reasonably assume that combatants have the ability and the intention to stand in the way of the adversary achieving victory? If winning a war means something other than military victory, it may, depending on the political goal of a war, be entirely unnecessary to attack most combatants. In turn, and more problematically, it may be necessary to disable a group of people that is not at all or only partly made up of combatants. Here it would need to be clear that necessity of attack to may not be an independent grounds for attacking a person, but a condition for rendering a person a legitimate target of attack in addition to the condition of combatant status.

Combatants compared to civilians may have enhanced abilities to stand in the way of *military* victory. After all, the status of combatant denotes a reasonable connection between a person and military operations based on the right to participate in hostilities. Civilians that lack this right are therefore unnecessary to engage, unless they chose to directly participate in hostilities, which effectively means "stand in the way of military victory." Beyond that reasonable connection between attacking combatants and achieving military victory, we cannot make any assumptions about individuals' training, motivation, or talents, in other words their true contribution to the war effort and the necessity to disable them. It is beyond the scope of this chapter to further discuss the problem that it may never be necessary to attack any one specific individual given alternative courses of action.

Not least due to these open questions IHL has resisted pressures to change and make necessity or threat conditions of legitimate attacks against combatants. Human rights law, which does require a threat and the necessity of a defensive response to allow one person to kill another, has nonetheless started to penetrate IHL's regulative purview. Adjudicative bodies, such as the Inter-American Commission and Court on Human Rights, have deemed situations of internal and even interstate armed conflict within their jurisdiction, using IHL to elucidate the meaning of the American Convention on Human Rights in the context of war.[32] The European Court of Human Rights has assessed the legality

[32] American Convention on Human Rights (San Jose, Costa Rica, November 22, 1969), 9 I.L.M. 673 (1970), *entered into force* July 18, 1978. Landmark cases are, among others, I/A Court H.R., Bámaca Velásquez v. Guatemala, Judgment on the Merits of November 25, 2000, Series C, No.70, para. 209.; I/A Court H.R., Las Palmeras v. Colombia, Preliminary Objections of February 4, 2000, Series C, No. 67, para. 33; I/A Court H.R., Serrano de la

of belligerents' conduct during armed conflict in light of the European Convention on Human Rights,[33] raising the question to what extent the human right to life that even combatants *prima facie* enjoy can be protected in war. Article 2 of the European Convention on Human Rights (ECHR) stipulates: "Everyone's right to life shall be protected by law. No one shall be deprived of his life intentionally save in the execution of a sentence of a court following his conviction of a crime for which this penalty is provided by law."[34] Similarly, Article 6 of the International Covenant on Civil and Political Rights (ICCPR) provides that "[e]very human being has the inherent right to life. This right shall be protected by law. No one shall be arbitrarily deprived of his life."[35]

The International Court of Justice argues that international humanitarian law as *lex specialis* sets the parameters within which Article 6 is to be interpreted.[36] This argument glosses over the fact that no morally or legally relevant connection exists between a person dying as incidental damage of an otherwise legitimate attack and that very fate. Common usage of the term "arbitrary" suggests that losing one's life as a means to an extraneous military end without that even being intended by the agent seeking that end is a case par excellence of losing one's life arbitrarily. A contextual interpretation similarly suggests that compliance with IHL does not ensure that the inevitable rights deprivations that the conduct of hostilities involves meet the criteria of exceptions to Article 2 ECHR or Article 6 ICCPR. After all, the right to life in human rights law is bound

Cruz Sisters v. El Salvador, Preliminary Objections of 23 November, 2004, Series C, No. 120, para. 112.

[33] Important cases include Ergi v. Turkey (just satisfaction), no. 23818/94, July 28, 1998, ECHR 1998-IV; Güleç v. Turkey (just satisfaction), no. 21593/93, July 27, 1998, §§63–64, ECHR 1998-IV; Loizidou v. Turkey (merits), no. 15318/89, December 18, 1996, ECHR 1996-VI; Loizidou v. Turkey (preliminary objections), no. 310, March 23, 1995, ECHR 1995, Özkan v. Turkey (merits), no. 21689/93, 6 April 2004, ECHR 2004.

[34] European Convention for the Protection of Human Rights and Fundamental Freedoms (Rome, November 4, 1950), 312 E.T.S. 5, *as amended by* Protocol No. 3, E.T.S. 45; Protocol No. 5, E.T.S. 55; Protocol No. 8, E.T.S. 118; and Protocol No. 11, E.T.S. 155; *entered into force* September 3, 1953 (Protocol No. 3 *on* September 21, 1970, Protocol No. 5 *on* December 20 1971, Protocol No. 8 *on* January 1, 1990, Protocol 11 *on* January 11, 1998).

[35] International Covenant on Civil and Political Rights, adopted and opened for signature, ratification, and accession by General Assembly resolution 2200A (XXI) of December 16, 1966, entry into force March 23, 1976, in accordance with Article 49.

[36] *Legality of the Threat or Use of Nuclear Weapons*, ICJ Reports 1996, 5, 240, §25; see also Magdalena Forowicz, The Reception of International Law in the European Court of Human Rights 314 (2010); Christian Tomuschat, *Human Rights and International Humanitarian Law*, 21 EJIL 15 (2010).

up with the guarantee to be subject to due process before receiving the death penalty. Due process entails an enquiry into conduct and state of mind of an individual that determination of combatant status or a collateral damage estimate cannot replace.

Another way to render a deprivation of life non-arbitrary in the meaning of human rights law is demonstrating its necessity. However, necessity in this context needs to meet a much higher threshold, both in terms of the urgency of the threat to be averted as well as the importance of the public interest to be protected, than necessity of an attack in the belligerent's struggle for military victory.[37] As mentioned earlier, a reasonable connection exists between killing combatants and the goal of military victory, making killing combatants on the whole necessary for the achievement of military victory. That is not the same as saying that killing any one combatant was literally "the only way" to achieve military victory. The latter only is necessary in the meaning of human rights law.

The controversy about whether human rights law can meaningfully be applied to the conduct of hostilities and how individual rights interact with IHL, mirrors a debate in ethics between conventional and so-called revisionist just war theorists. The latter challenge the permission to kill combatants regardless of their individual moral status that just war theory traditionally grants. Scholars like Jeff McMahan maintain that waging war justly means harming individuals only to the extent that they are morally responsible for contributing to an unjustified threat and are therefore liable to being attacked. Of course, the epistemic and practical obstacles to allocating harm in war in accordance with individuals' personal liability are significant.[38] I have argued elsewhere that what revisionist just war theorists demand is impracticable.[39] By the same token, it is unclear how international law could better attune protection in war to individual moral status.[40]

[37] Ohlin, *supra* note 21, at 1298ff.

[38] For this argument, see Seth Lazar, *The Responsibility Dilemma for Killing in War: A Review Essay*, 38 Phil & P. Aff. 180 (2010); *Id.*, *Responsibility, Risk, and Killing in Self-Defense*, 119 Ethics 699 (2009); Henry Shue, *Do We Need 'A Morality of War'? in* Just and Unjust Warriors: The Moral and legal status of Soldiers (David Rodin and Henry Shue eds., 2008).

[39] Janina Dill, The Twenty-First Century Belligerent's Trilemma, 26 EJIL 1 (2015) 83–108

[40] Combatant status is not entirely divorced from individual moral status as combatants tend on the whole to contribute more directly to a war than civilians and are often less

The reality that many combatants will not in an individual rights sense be liable to being killed, should of course not therefore be ignored. Impracticability does not automatically invalidate a moral imperative. This explains the urgency and intuitive appeal of the proposal discussed earlier, which is to add threat and necessity conditions to the legal permissibility of deliberate lethal attack. Of course, even a higher threshold for the permissible killing of combatants leaves untouched a considerable disconnect between individual rights that natural persons enjoy in peacetime and the protection that international law affords them in war. Similarly an alternative "more optimistic" view on the possibility of implementing the logic of liability elaborated by Bradley Strawser indicates the possibility of a small step in the direction of connecting individuals' moral to their legal status in war, while implicitly underlining the impossibility of ever truly bringing the two into congruence. Strawser proposes to further subdivide the groups of combatants in line with individuals' moral status and proximity to the war effort into combatants 1, 2, and 3.[41] Of course, no matter how many times we subdivide combatants we end up with groups that are less differentiated than the moral liability of their respective members. In addition, an individual's moral status is not static, but may change with every causal intervention into the world.

Strawser's argument is nonetheless extremely important because he convincingly shows that modern militaries are actually capable of and to some extent committed to more differentiation than the simple distinction between civilians and combatants. They do not, in fact, treat all combatants as equally liable to lethal attack, or so Strawser argues. This claim of feasibility is crucial as an undue complication of the principle of non-combatant immunity may jeopardize the ability of IHL to elicit belligerents' compliance and to guide even a conscientious belligerent's actions. Both the subdivision of combatants and the addition of threat and necessity conditions to the permissibility of direct attack under IHL carry that risk. What exactly it looks like when IHL protects individual rights as much as possible, while not losing its ability to make any difference in war at all, may depend on the war and the belligerent with

vulnerable. Neither of these two features, even together, however, justifies a presumption of legitimate infringement of an individual's right to life.

[41] Bradley Jay Strawser, *Revisionist Just War Theory and the Real World: A Cautiously Optimistic Proposal*, *in* Routledge Handbook of Ethics and War: Just War Theory in the 21st Century 76 (Fritz Alhoff, Nicholas G. Evans and Adam Henschke eds., 2014).

the strategic offensive in question. This, in turn, is problematic for international law, which needs to be predictable, accessible, and perceived as fair. Nonetheless, the case for the impracticability of a subdivision of the combatant category or indeed for additional conditions to direct lethal attack has not yet been made. Strawser's practically informed account casts doubt over the claim that *any* complication of the principle of non-combatant immunity will undermine belligerents' commitment to IHL thus carrying the risk of a reverse to unrestrained warfare.

Yet, the claim that is decreasingly subject to doubt is that a regime of international law which, like IHL, systematically privileges individual rights violations by states on a large scale loses the ability to vouchsafe the perceived legitimacy of compliant behavior, which is so crucial for international law's compliance pull. At the same time, the conclusion is inescapable that, as long as war is a conflict between collective agents fought out in a violent struggle among individuals, it will be impossible to provide, whether through moral principle, IHL, or even belligerents' commitment, that individuals retain the rights they enjoy qua being human. To wage war *without* denying individuals their rights on a significant scale is impossible.

III. International Law's Dilemma with Resort to Force

The view that war can be morally justified, even though it inevitably infringes individual rights – in other words a reluctance to embrace pacifism even among revisionist just war theorists – is widespread. The reason is that in the international system as it is currently constituted war may sometimes be the only means to prevent or halt the large-scale violation of individual rights. Humanitarian intervention to halt ethnic cleansing or a defensive war against a tyrannical aggressor will almost certainly involve the infringement of individuals' rights, but that may turn out to be the lesser evil compared to not waging war. Consequentialist justifications for so-called *mala in se*, one of the most important examples of which is certainly the otherwise unjustified taking of human life, tend to be viewed with suspicion. However, as I argued elsewhere, if we accept that war is only justified as the lesser evil when it preserves many individuals' rights while violating some, individual rights remain the touchstone of the justification.[42] I propose that the infringement of individual rights

[42] Janina Dill, *Should International Law Ensure the Moral Acceptability of War?* 26 The Leiden J. Int'l L. 2 (2013).

during war can be justified as the lesser evil if the greater evil would consist of more violations of individual rights.

Yet, as mentioned earlier, IHL as it currently stands cannot ensure that killing in war is justified as the overall lesser evil in terms of individual rights infringements. The legal and moral symmetry accorded to states once they assume the role of belligerents means that who wins a war is entirely unrelated to who is on the side of justice, international law, or indeed the defense of individual rights. Of course, that symmetry could be revisited so that permissibility of conduct in war would be connected to the legal or moral value of the goals a belligerent pursues. In fact, if the aim of a legal or moral code for waging war was to distribute harm in a way even remotely connected to individual moral status we would *have* to give up belligerent symmetry anyway. After all individuals who contribute to a justified threat – for instance by participating in their state's war of self-defense against a tyrannical aggressor – are not in virtue of their contribution to that war liable to attack. However, just as the distribution of harm in war in accordance with individual liability is impracticable, IHL cannot afford to be asymmetrical. After all, *not* privileging one belligerent and thus prejudging the outcome of an armed struggle is part of IHL's mentioned pact with military necessity. Only international law that does not up front tip the scales against one belligerent can be expected to be applied also by that belligerent.

If not of conduct, can we make asymmetry a matter of resort? Legally, of course, it already is. Although IHL treats belligerents equally, the violation of law that a belligerent commits by illegally resorting to force is not redeemed by conduct that complies with IHL in war. Yet, the legality of resort to force is not currently tied to the protection of individual rights, but to the two mentioned exceptions to the prohibition on the use of force, self-defense, and a Security Council mandate. How would international law have to change if legality of resort to force depended on whether or not it served the overall better preservation of individual rights?

The main reason why a social system requires a mechanism for the legitimate use of violence is to enforce law or, as I put it earlier, to reign in spoilers who flout the rules of the game. Many a defiance of international law primarily violates another *state's* right. For instance, defaults on treaty obligations in the realms of commerce, diplomatic relations, or even defense will often first and foremost damage other state parties without necessarily having implications for the preservation of individual rights. If legality of resort to force was attached to a lesser evil justification for the protection of human rights, such violations of international law could never be met with a forcible response. Because no infringement of individual rights in the course of the use of force could be justified as the lesser evil, if no individual rights were threatened in the first place. However, this does not seem to imply a departure from international law. With the appearance and solidification of a customary prohibition on forcible reprisals, states may not currently use force to counter treaty violations anyway. Only an armed attack triggering a right to self-defense provides a state with legal access to unilateral force. Can we imagine an armed attack that does not threaten individual rights? In other words, is a case possible in which states have a legal right to resort to force under current international law, but they would not have such a right, if the overall preservation of individual rights were made the touchstone of legitimate resort to force?

The recent crisis in Eastern Ukraine at first seemed to transform the so-called "bloodless invasion" from a pure hypothetical into a realistic scenario. With the question of whether to attribute separatist activities in Eastern Ukraine to Russia still contested and with now many lives on both sides lost, the crisis does not in fact present an instance of an international armed conflict, i.e., the deployment of military units attributable to a state outside that state's borders, without individual rights violations. Yet, the case brings into sharp relief that whether an armed attack has occurred and whether individual rights have been and are being violated are separate questions. In a legal regime that consistently privileges individual rights over states' rights, the controversial case in which a state in the face of an armed attack has no right to self-defense, which Article 51 U.N. Charter marks out as inherent, is a possibility.

The hypothetical of a bloodless invasion also draws attention to the fact that the singular focus on individual rights to life and bodily integrity may be misguided.[43] The right to cultural or political self-determination may well be valuable enough for some individuals to risk their right to life in a defensive struggle against a bloodless invader. The consistent and unquestioned privileging of individual rights to life and bodily integrity over other rights, such as political self-determination, might not actually mean that this hypothetical international law succeeds in its stated

[43] This chapter cannot exhaustively discuss the legal and moral challenges posed by bloodless invasions. For a recent and detailed discussion see Helen Frowe and Seth Lazar, The Morality of Defensive War (2014).

mission of regulating international relations so as to give the individual her moral due. Nonetheless, we can conclude that states' right to unilaterally use force for the purpose of responding to violations of international law is already so narrow that, except for the discussed case of the bloodless armed attack, connecting legality of resort to force to the preservation of individual rights, would not significantly curtail states' access to the use of force under *lex lata*.

But what about the Security Council's legal power to mandate force? It is currently triggered by Article 39 and the establishment of "a threat to the peace, breach of the peace or aggression." The interpretation of what constitutes such a state has changed over the years, specifically to include situations that involve the large-scale infringement of individual rights *without* cross-border implications. Can we imagine an Article 39 case in which the threat to the peace, breach of the peace, or aggression does not infringe individual rights? It is extremely unlikely that a breach of international law serious enough to trigger Article 39 has no implications for individual rights. Nonetheless, in theory, a legal regime that makes the overall better preservation of individual rights to life and bodily integrity the condition for legal resort to force would reduce the Council's freedom of action. Article 39 is open to interpretation and the Security Council has used the open-endedness of concepts such as threat to the peace to adapt the provision's application to changing shared normative beliefs. In comparison, the criterion of large-scale infringement of individual rights as a trigger for the Council's right to mandate force may leave some, though considerably less, room for interpretation.

However, I have so far neglected that a lesser evil justification for war is not available as soon as individual rights are threatened or violated on a large scale. In addition, a determination is necessary whether forcible intervention would in fact be the lesser evil in terms of the infringement of individual rights. Let us then turn to violations of international law that *do* involve the denial of individual rights to life and bodily integrity. Such violations may occur within the violating state's jurisdiction or on another state's territory. A conventional armed attack would be an instance of the latter. Examples of individual rights violations on a state's own territory that also violate international law include ethnic cleansing and genocide. If the premise of this hypothetical international legal order was that individual rights systematically override states' rights, then jurisdiction and territory would be morally and legally irrelevant. The breach of a state's sovereignty that would be inevitable in the attempt to stop rights violations on a violator's territory would not count in the lesser evil calculus. Yet, such a calculus would be necessary if the overall better preservation of individual rights was the only legitimate grounds for legal resort to force. This calculus can have three different outcomes. While violations of international law without individual rights violations, discussed earlier, present case one, I will refer to the three possible scenarios of legal violations which involve the denial of individual rights as cases two to four.

In case two a state or a coalition of states has a reasonable chance of being successful in defeating the rights violator without causing more harm in the process. In this case a legal right to resort to force would exist – either for the Security Council to bestow or for states to exercise unilaterally, depending on the precise institutional make-up of this hypothetical international legal order. In this case, both self-defense against cross-border violations of international law as well as "humanitarian intervention" into another state's territory would be legal means to counter violations of international law. However, all it takes for no such reasonable chance of preventing more rights infringements than committing to exist is a militarily stronger and/or determined aggressor. Case three are violations of international law that are so fierce or so serious as not to be easily remedied. They will remain unaddressed. Contrary to case one discussed earlier, in which violations of states' rights remain unaddressed because they do not have implications for individual rights, in this greater evil scenario of case three individual states as well as the Security Council may not be forcibly redress violations of *individual* rights for lack of a reasonable chance of success, meaning doing so without infringing even more individual rights.

This obligation to make a lesser evil calculation before forcibly intervening in or defending one-self against an individual rights-denying violation of international law creates a moral hazard: A potential aggressor should appear as vindictive and promise to be as brutal as possible in the face of a possible intervention or self-defense in order to render the latter the greater evil. Of course, the privileging of individual over states' rights could also provide a would-be aggressor with the incentive to keep an aggression bloodless and a violation of the aggressed state's rights only. After all this would mean an aggressor could avoid creating legal grounds for a forcible intervention by other states or the Security Council, in the first place.

The likeliest scenario that members of the international society face when making a lesser evil calculation is case four: It is impossible or at least extremely difficult to establish whether a forcible intervention to redress a violation of international law would not create more individual rights violations than it would prevent. I have called this an epistemically cloaked forced choice for the state or for the Security Council faced with a scenario in which standing by involves allowing the large-scale violation of individual rights to proceed, but so does intervening, and it is genuinely unclear which is the overall preferable course of action with a view to preserving as many individual rights as possible.[44] I have argued that in such cases the moral difference between killing (in a forcible intervention) and letting die (while standing by) is not a satisfactory basis for adjudicating legitimate resort to force in an international order which is primarily concerned with upholding individual rights rather than with states' rights not to get their hands dirty.

If the international society in one form or another, one of which might be the Security Council, were committed to intervene on behalf of states whose rights under international law (those that involve the infringement of individual rights) were violated, then due to the increased strength of the coalition standing up to the initial violator of international law, the likelihood of a response being an epistemically cloaked forced choice or a greater evil would be reduced. That does not mean that it could ever be ruled out that no forcible redress is available under international law against the large-scale violation of individual rights.

The argument of this section is that even the full acceptance of the preservation of individual rights to life and bodily integrity as the sole legal grounds for the legitimate resort to force does not solve the problem with war. In fact, the rationale behind this enquiry into forcible alternatives to war is the premise that social systems need a kinetic means to enforce rules and reign in spoilers. One benefit of such law enforcement is that social relations become more predictable and agents can develop security of expectations. Yet, this section has shown that making the preservation of individual rights the touchstone of legal resort to war deprives the international community of the option to "enforce" international law vis-à-vis spoiler states in three out of four possible cases. In the first and two final cases described here, the resort to force to redress an initial violation of international law would not be available even to the Security Council if it had the executive strength of the international society to enforce international law at its disposal.

[44] Dill, *supra* note 42.

IV. De-Collectivizing Conduct and Adjudicating Asymmetry in Resort

If we accept, first, that safeguarding individual rights is the correct moral standard in international relations and the touchstone of successful international law; second, that it is impossible to avoid significant violations of individual rights in war; and third, that the international order requires a mechanism for the legitimate use of violence in order to be sustainable, we need to find forcible alternatives to war. What changes to the way in which violence is used in international relations do the two developments described demand? In the following section of the chapter I argue that two imperatives simultaneously need to guide our search for forcible alternatives to war: de-collectivization of conduct and adjudication of asymmetrical resort.

The previous section suggested that reaffirming asymmetry of resort to force, but adjusting it to cater to the preservation of individual rights only, without also addressing the collectivity of war, does not mean war becomes an available and acceptable means of using force in the twenty-first century. Merely making war an instrument of law enforcement for the purpose of the overall best preservation of individual rights paradoxically deprives states as well as the Security Council of a mechanism for the legitimate use of violence in three out of four cases of spoilers flouting the rules of the game. Two of the three cases involve the violation of individual rights and hence present instances in which an international legal order geared toward the preservation of individual rights should offer an effective response that is also legal.

Targeted killings present an opposing scenario in which the collectivity of war is mitigated and violence directed toward, not a collective agent, but an individual framed as liable to the infliction of harm. The second section suggested that this de-collectivization is insufficient because even targeted killings create collateral damage. Moreover, and this is crucial in the search for forcible alternatives to war, replacing all-out war with targeted killings not only leaves unaddressed, it also adds urgency to the question of how to adjudicate legal resort to force if the goal is to preserve individual rights as best as possible. That the question is unaddressed is brought into sharp relief by the fact that the only (reluctantly) acknowledged state sponsored program of targeted killing shrouds in secrecy the criteria for how an individual can end up on the kill-list. Targeted killings add urgency to the question because their availability arguably lowers the threshold to the resort to force. After all, what we colloquially refer to as drone strikes are much less costly in blood and treasure than collective military operations.

What we need is to simultaneously overcome the two features that render war normatively unacceptable in the twenty-first century and find means of using force that lack them both. The following paragraphs discuss a three-step forcible alternative to war in light of the imperative to simultaneously de-collectivize violence and adjudicate asymmetry of legal resort to it. The proposal is a graduation from an international arrest warrant to a targeted abduction and finally to targeted lethal attack by Special Forces.

The twofold use of the attribute "targeted" highlights that this forcible alternative to war strives to funnel violence to individuals rather than collective agents in order to delimit to the intended target as much as possible its harmful effects. The extent to which that is possible depends on at least three variables: first, the scale of the violence used, second, the superiority in material power of the state, institution, or coalition that forcibly responds to the identified "spoiler," and third, the technological means and strategies employed. As mentioned, an increased resort to targeted killings often with unmanned aerial vehicles is a reaction to the problem of collectivized violence. The de-collectivization of violence it provides, however, is insufficient in so far as the means used do avoid, but regularly cause, collateral damage. As technologically speaking there is no means to guarantee zero collateral damage in air-to-ground deployment of force, whether with manned or unmanned vehicles, air power is as of now an unsuitable means of conducting forcible alternatives to war. Of course, collateral damage may likewise be unavoidable in ground operations. Yet, compare the most precise and skilled means of delivering air power from a vantage point of maximum superiority, arguably the U.S.' drone program, to the best equipped and trained ground unit operating from a vantage point of maximum superiority. Depending on what exactly maximum superiority in ground operations can mean, I venture the latter has a better collateral damage record than the former. Of course, whether this is true also chiefly depends on the risk those ground troops are prepared to take themselves. In the mitigation of collateral damage caused by ground troops force protection tends to be the limiting factor.

Given the need to establish individual liability beyond a reasonable doubt to safe-guard the right to due process, the first enforcement measure against an individual suspected of being a spoiler, i.e., having authorized or committed a violation of international law, should be an international arrest warrant to be enforced by local authorities. As most violations of international law will be committed or authorized by individuals in positions of power, a second step is very likely to be necessary for the international community to take over once state authorities have proven unwilling or unable to cooperate with an international warrant. Rather than killing the person this second step should be a trial *in absentia* combined with an attempt at abduction by Special Forces, either volunteered by a state or, ideally at the disposition of the institution adjudicating "legitimate resort," to arrest warrants and abductions. If abduction fails due to local resistance or the inevitability of causing too much collateral damage in the process, a targeted assassination as a last resort could be authorized after the completion of a trial *in absentia* and a guilty verdict. As mentioned, it should be carried out with the most precise means available and from a vantage point of maximum superiority of strength to avoid collateral damage at all costs.

Conclusion

This chapter concludes by raising three kinds of open questions posed by the three-step forcible alternative to war proposed: legal, moral, and institutional. In the process I touch on the extent to which the chapter has established or leaves open to contestation the feasibility and desirability of transcending war in international relations.

Existing international criminal law provides a ready blueprint to answer some regulative questions this three-step forcible alternative to war raises. What is the evidentiary threshold to start an international process of enquiry and issue a warrant? What is the threshold of gravity of a violation of international law for this proposed mechanism to get triggered? In what ways can an individual be implicated in a violation of international law? It is the *ratione materiae* of international criminal law that needs extending for the proposed forcible alternative to war to become a reality. Here a crucial question is beyond the scope of the chapter and remains unanswered. How many and what kind of violations of international law can reasonably, feasibly, and fairly be attributed to individual decision-makers? What about inherently collective violations of international law, such as cabinet or even parliamentary decisions sanctioning aggression or ethnic cleansing?

I cautioned at the outset that this discussion proposes a forcible alternative to war that addresses what I refer to as "the problem with war." The chapter does not definitively establish that changing international law and institutions in order to implement the three-step proposal would be morally justified. After all, whether a forcible alternative to war is all things considered morally justified also depends on its consequences. If those were shown to be systematically undesirable so would be the proposed alternative to war. What if removing an individual spoiler from power is unlikely to result in a cessation in the defiance of international law?[45] What if such a removal makes ongoing violations of individual rights worse?

Besides its *ratione materiae* the institutional structures now upholding international criminal law would have to be significantly amended for this proposal to be implemented. The chapter did not set out to answer the question whether replacing war with forcible alternatives is feasible. It is, however, crucial to highlight the question to which we require an answer in order to determine the feasibility of forcible alternatives to war. How can an international mechanism for the adjudication and control of resort to force attract the cross-cultural confidence, operate at the necessary speed, and muster the material power to be effective? It is crucial that a proposal of forcible alternatives to war does not depend on a quasi-world government. Yet ultimately we will not get around to answering the hard question of whether we can have a rule of international law directly over individuals in a legal order that also continues to attribute rights to states. Are the limitations of forcible alternatives to war a function of how far away we want the international order to stay from world government?

[45] For a discussion of this issue see Andrew Altman and Christopher Heath Wellman, *From Humanitarian Intervention to Assassination: Human Rights and Political Violence*, 118 Ethics 228 (2008).

9

Whither International Martial Law?

Human Rights as Sword and Shield in Ineffectively Governed Territory

JOHN C. DEHN*

Introduction

Transnational terrorism challenges the global geopolitical order and the international law that attempts to preserve it, particularly notions of absolute territorial sovereignty and universal human rights. Clandestine non-state actors in remote locations exploiting ever-advancing technology threaten the safety and security of even the most powerful states and their populations. Gaps in *de facto* governing capacity over the activities of such groups at national, international, and supranational levels create governance vacuums from which terrorists may undermine sovereign authority and deprive others of their basic human rights. Either individually or collectively, states must deter and eliminate these threats to ensure the basic human rights of their populations.

Counter-terrorism operations by the U.S. government outside active theaters of armed conflict or beyond active battlefields have generated significant criticism and legal debate.[1] The key aspect of disagreement is

* Assistant Professor, Loyola University Chicago School of Law and Senior Fellow, West Point Center for the Rule of Law. The views presented are the author's personal views. The author thanks Pooja Shah for her excellent editorial work. Any errors are the author's sole responsibility.

[1] *See e.g.*, "Report of the U.N. Special Rapporteur on Extrajudicial, Summary, or Arbitrary Executions," Christopher Heyns, U.N. Doc. A/68/382 (September 13, 2013) (transmitted by Note of the Secretary General at 68th session of the U.N. General Assembly) [hereinafter Heyns Report]; Special Rapporteur on extrajudicial, summary or arbitrary executions, *Study on targeted killings*, Philip Alston, U.N. Doc. A/HRC/14/24/Add.6 (May 26, 2010) (delivered at 14th Session of the Human Rights Council) [hereinafter Emmerson Report]; Chris Jenks, *Law from Above: Unmanned Aerial Systems, Use of Force, and the Law of Armed Conflict*, 85 N.D. L. Rev 649 (2009); Mary Ellen O'Connell, *Unlawful Killing with Combat Drones: A Case Study of Pakistan, 2004–2009, in* Shooting to Kill:

fundamentally a choice of law question. With regard to the bare right to resort to force against these threats, there is disagreement concerning whether, or the circumstances under which, a state may exercise its inherent right of self-defense against non-state actors.[2] Regarding the actual use of force against terrorists, some claim international human rights law ("HRL") governs these operations, limiting their permissible scope to routine law enforcement measures.[3] Others claim that the law of war, now commonly referred to as international humanitarian law ("IHL"), is the applicable or analogous legal framework for at least some counterterrorism operations, allowing use of war-like targeting and detention measures.[4]

The United States has not articulated its precise understanding of how relevant international law permits or limits its counterterrorism efforts. Available statements indicate that its executive branch believes that these operations are either acts of national self-defense or part of an armed

Socio-Legal Perspectives on the Use of Lethal Force 263 (Simon Bronitt, Miriam Gani, Saskia Hufnagel, eds., 2013). *See also Will I be Next?: U.S. Drone Strikes in Pakistan*, Amnesty International (October 22, 2013), www.amnestyusa.org/research/reports/will-i-be-next-us-drone-strikes-in-pakistan; *Between a Drone and Al-Qaeda: The Civilian Cost of U.S. Targeted Killings in Yemen*, Human Rights Watch (October 22, 2013), www.hrw.org/reports/2013/10/22/between-drone-and-al-qaeda.

2 *See e.g.*, Sean D. Murphy, *The International Legality of Cross-Border Operations from Afghanistan into Pakistan*, 85 Int'l L. Stud. 109, 126 (2008) ("[I]f the [International Court of Justice] still views Article 51 as restricted to self-defense only against an attack by another State, then the Court is out of step with both the Security Council and State practice." (citation omitted)).

3 *See* Mary Ellen O'Connell, *Unlawful Killing with Combat Drones: A Case Study of Pakistan, 2004–2009, in* Shooting to Kill: Socio-Legal Perspectives on the Use of Lethal Force (Simon Bronitt, Miriam Gani, Saskia Hufnagel, eds., 2013).

4 *See e.g.*, Michael N. Schmitt, *Charting the Legal Geography of Non-International Armed Conflict*, 90 Int'l L. Stud. 1 (2014) (concluding that IHL applies throughout the territory of a state party to a non-international armed conflict, border areas of neighboring states, and in states where violence reaches the intensity level of armed conflict) [hereinafter *NIAC Geography*]; Geoffrey S. Corn, *Self-Defense Targeting: Blurring the Line between the Jus ad Bellum and Jus in Bello*, 88 Int'l L. Stud. 57, 64 (Kenneth Watkin and Andrew J. Norris, eds., 2012) ("employing combat power in self-defense against transnational non-State operatives must be characterized as armed conflict"); Jordan J. Paust, *Self-Defense Targetings of Non-State Actors and Permissibility of U.S. Use of Drones in Pakistan*, 19 J. of Transnat'l L. & Pol'y. 237 (2010) (asserting existence of customary law of self-defense against non-state actors with war-like powers of targeting and detention, unless actual armed conflict results, at which point customary and conventional IHL of international armed conflict applies); Brian Finucane, *Fictitious States, Effective Control, and the Use of Force Against Non-State Actors*, 30 Berkley J. Int'l L. 35 (2012) (asserting longstanding customary international legal right to use necessary and proportionate force in response to armed attacks by non-state actors).

conflict, both of which are regulated by IHL, though various constraints are allegedly observed beyond active battlefields.[5] But what if there are *no* relevant active battlefields for a given terrorist group? Are intermittent acts of cross-border self-defense against violent non-state actors subject to the same norms that regulate the resort to force between states? Is the use of force in cross-border self-defense regulated by IHL, HRL, or something else? These are quite relevant questions, but publicly available U.S. policy statements only suggest rather than provide clear answers to them.[6]

Disputes regarding the applicable legal framework stem largely from disagreements regarding: (1) the circumstances under which a state may exercise its inherent right of self-defense against a non-state actor in the territory of another state, (2) the circumstances that establish a non-international armed conflict to which IHL applies between a state and extraterritorial non-state actor,[7] (3) the territorial and functional

[5] President Barack Obama, Remarks by the President at National Defense University (May 23, 2013) (transcript available at www.whitehouse.gov/the-press-office/2013/05/23/remarks-president-national-defense-university); The White House Office of the Press Secretary, *Fact Sheet: U.S. Policy Standards and Procedures for the Use of Force in Counterterrorism Operations Outside the United States and Areas of Active Hostilities* (May 23, 2013) *available at* www.whitehouse.gov/the-press-office/2013/05/23/fact-sheet-us-policy-standards-and-procedures-use-force-counterterrorism. For analysis of these policies, *see infra* part I.C.

[6] For an insightful analysis of the post-battlefield legal environment, primarily from the U.S. perspective, *see generally* Robert M. Chesney, *Beyond the Battlefield, Beyond Al Qaeda: The Destabilizing Legal Architecture of Counterterrorism*, 112 Mich. L. Rev. 163, 167 (2013) ("[T]he second post-9/11 decade will be increasingly characterized by a kind of "shadow war," taking place on an episodic basis in locations far removed from zones of conventional combat operations and involving opponents not readily described as members of al Qaeda as such. The legal architecture that developed to a point of seeming stability over the past decade is not well adapted to this environment, and ... will become increasingly apparent and problematic.").

[7] *See* Int'l Comm. of the Red Cross, *International Humanitarian Law and the Challenges of Contemporary Conflicts*, 31IC/11/5.1.2, 10 (October 2011) (prepared for the 31st International Conference of the Red Cross and Red Crescent (regarding transnational acts of terrorism and counterterrorism, it states, "the ICRC has taken a case by case approach ... [s]ome situations have been classified as an IAC [international armed conflict], other contexts have been deemed to be NIACs [non-international armed conflicts], while various acts of terrorism taking place in the world have been assessed as being outside any armed conflict.") [hereinafter 31st Conference Report]; *NIAC Geography, supra* note 4 at 18–19. For an interesting proposal that states should declare war against non-state actors, *see* Richard V. Meyer, *The Privilege of Belligerency and Formal Declarations of War, in* Targeted Killings: Law and Morality in an Asymmetrical World 183 (Claire Finkelstein, Jens David Ohlin, and Andrew Altman, eds. 2012).

applicability of IHL once a non-international armed conflict exists,[8] and (4) the legal regime(s) regulating the use of force in self-defense against extraterritorial non-state actors. No matter how destructive, it is generally accepted that singular or sporadic armed attacks by non-state actors do not establish an armed conflict.[9] Yet it is not difficult to imagine planned, developing, or imminent "spectacular" attacks for which standard law enforcement measures, which are primarily reactive rather than proactive, seem inadequate. Experts in IHL and HRL often disagree regarding the exact point at which non-state actor violence rises to the level of "hostilities" in an armed conflict regulated by IHL.[10] In this fuzzy middle, there are competing interpretations of IHL and HRL that seek to extend their temporal, territorial, and functional scope based upon their exceptionally broad humanitarian objectives, an approach known as teleological interpretation.[11]

This chapter probes the bases and boundaries of IHL, HRL, state sovereignty, and self-defense to propose how contemporary international law might regulate responses to transnational armed attacks emanating from ineffectively governed territory. It offers and briefly outlines two concepts. The first is "transnational self-defense" by states against non-state actors, a concept distinct from and in some ways more permissive than the concept of self-defense that has developed between states. Specifically, it argues that a right of transnational self-defense must allow a potential victim state to counter a reasonably certain threat of a mass casualty terrorist attack, at least when that state is also reasonably certain that the territorial state cannot or will not effectively do so. The second is somewhat of a hybrid IHL/HRL legal framework, here termed "international martial law." The term "martial law" is not intended to evoke

[8] 31st Conference Report, *supra* note 7 at 9–11 (describing typologies of non-international armed conflicts, including those that cross borders, and need for case-by-case analysis).

[9] *See e.g.*, Michael N. Schmitt, *Extraterritorial Lethal Targeting: Deconstructing the Logic of International Law*, 52 Colum. J. Transnat'l L. 77, 98 (2013) ("Although the threshold lacks exactitude, it is clear that extraterritorial operations directed against groups that engage in only a single (and last) act of violence, no matter how destructive, or that engage in violence on an infrequent basis, are not subject to international humanitarian law norms.") [hereinafter *Extraterritorial Lethal Targeting*].

[10] Int'l Comm. of the Red Cross, *The Use of Force in Armed Conflicts: Interplay Between the Conduct of Hostilities and Law Enforcement Paradigms* 32–33 (February 11, 2013) (by Gloria Gaggioli) [hereinafter *ICRC, IHL-IHRL Interplay Report*] (noting disagreement among experts regarding proper legal paradigm for government response to "powerful criminal groups, such as drug cartels, resorting to armed violence").

[11] *See infra* parts II.B, II.C.

images of harsh military rule and perfunctory punishment, but rather of militarized law enforcement operations rendered necessary by the nature, gravity, and location of a threat. It allows limited collective targeting based solely upon conduct and limited incommunicado investigatory detention, but prohibits collateral deaths of innocent civilians that are not strictly unavoidable under the circumstances. It shuns extraordinary courts and indefinite preventive detention as unnecessary departures from generally applicable human rights norms.

Both of the preceding concepts represent a contextual balancing of obligations to protect and respect human rights and state sovereignty. A proper understanding of the traditional scope of customary and conventional IHL and HRL – and a proper situating transnational armed attacks and responsive acts of self-defense in contemporary international law regulating the use of force – not only allow for but arguably support these concepts. Alternatively, these concepts could be based in HRL, including states' affirmative human rights obligations and a broader understanding of permissible deprivations of life or liberty.[12]

At bottom, when a state's alleged obligations to perfectly respect formal state sovereignty and the human rights of extraterritorial non-state actors are in tension with its acknowledged obligation and fundamental purpose to protect its territory and the basic human rights of its population,[13] states will err toward fulfilling the latter. The obligation to protect and ensure human rights becomes a sword that requires affirmative action to eliminate transnational threats – the imperative to respect human rights a shield for those believed to be posing them and the innocent civilians among whom they often hide. If the only available options are a traditional, inter-state concept of self-defense and a narrow view of permissible force under HRL, states will doubtless seek to expand the scope of self-defense and IHL to create more permissive resort to force and use of force regimes.[14] However, a contextual balancing of competing rights and obligations related to transnational terrorism emanating from

[12] *See infra* part 3.

[13] Durand v. Hollins, 8 F.Cas. 111, 112 (C.C.S.D.N.Y. 1860) ("The great object and duty of government is the protection of the lives, liberty, and property of the people composing it, whether abroad or at home; and any government failing in the accomplishment of the object, or the performance of the duty, is not worth preserving.").

[14] *NIAC Geography*, *supra* note 4 at 18 (detailing many factors that "will likely motivate States involved in [conflicts with non-state actors] to adopt expansive interpretations in IHL's scope"); Corn, *supra* note 4 at 64.

ineffectively governed territory would arguably result in a net increase in the protection of human rights. Though it may at first seem anachronistic, carefully constructed concepts of transnational self-defense and international martial law, whether considered independent parts of customary international law or situated within HRL, better balance the rights and obligations of states and individuals.

I. The Uncertain International Law of "Transnational Self-Defense"

Armed attacks by non-state actors across international borders and responsive uses of force by states in self-defense are hardly new phenomena in the Westphalian global system. From the oft-cited 1837 *Caroline* incident, in which Britain sank an American-flagged ship being used by Canadian rebels, to the 1916 U.S. military expedition against Poncho Villa and his henchmen in Mexico,[15] to the 2006 Israeli conflict with Hezbollah in Lebanon, states have frequently used extraterritorial armed force to prevent or stop non-state actor attacks against their territory and population.[16] Examples before and after the attacks of September 11, 2001 are too numerous to catalogue here.

This chapter adopts the term "transnational" for non-state actor armed attacks and acts of self-defense against non-state actors when either cross international borders. In other words, although transnational attacks and transnational self-defense involve the territory of two (or more) states, they occur only between states and non-state actors. Some argue that a state's use of force ("attacking state") against a non-state actor located in another state's territory ("territorial state") without the latter's consent creates an international armed conflict between the states concerned.[17] This chapter rejects that historically

[15] For an interesting account of this event at the tactical, day-to-day level with strategic insights, *see* Carlo D'Este, Patton: A Genius for War 156–184 (1995).

[16] For a more extensive but incomplete list of incidents, *see* Noam Lubell, The Extraterritorial Use of Force Against Non-State Actors 3–4 (2010); Finucane, *supra* note 4 at 61–82 (briefly recounting and analyzing numerous incidents).

[17] *See e.g.*, Craig Martin, *Going Medieval: Targeted Killing, Self-Defense and the Jus Ad Bellum Regime, in* Targeted Killings: Law and Morality in an Asymmetrical World 223, 235 (Claire Finkelstein, Jens David Ohlin, Andrew Altman, eds., 2012) (targeted killing "undertaken without consent of the target state … constitute[s] a use of force in *Jus ad bellum* terms giving rise to aspects of international armed conflict"). *See also* Paust, *supra* note 4 at 258–261 (asserting that although international armed conflict [IAC] does not necessarily result from attack of non-state actor in a state by another, IAC does result if the attacked non-state actor qualifies "as an insurgent force").

and theoretically questionable view, at least when: (1) an attacking state's response is directed against only a non-state actor; (2) the attacking state does not seize and only minimally enters and remains upon foreign territory without territorial state consent; (3) the attacking state directs no force against the armed forces, general population, or government of the territorial state; and (4) the territorial state does not respond with military force to the attacking state's use of force within its territory.[18]

Whatever has been the international law regulating these issues in the past, developments in international law over the last century, such as the development of customary and conventional HRL, must be taken into account. International law only broadly regulated the U.S. expedition against Poncho Villa's group in Mexico.[19] Contemporary international law, particularly HRL, has more to say about the rights and obligations of states exercising transnational self-defense. Commentary that does not examine the potential affect of these developments on an alleged longstanding and customary right to engage in transnational self-defense is simply incomplete.[20] This section briefly introduces the international law affecting transnational uses of force, drawing out substantive legal asymmetries and ambiguities that result in this context. "Substantive legal asymmetries" refer to substantive differences in the scope of application of a body of international law, meaning the circumstances under which a body of law, such as HRL or IHL, regulates similar parties, conduct, or situations similarly. Substantive legal asymmetries also refer to differences in the content of the law, meaning in the precise way a body of law regulates similarly situated actions and actors. The section then briefly dissects recent U.S. policy statements to demonstrate how they are not fully consistent with commonly asserted understandings of relevant international norms.

[18] Dapo Akande, *Classification of Armed Conflicts: Relevant Legal Concepts*, *in* International Law and the Classification of Conflicts 32, 72 (Elizabeth Wilmshurst ed., 2012) ("[C]onflicts involving the use of force by a State against a non-State group on the territory of another State are non-international armed conflicts where the force is directed solely at that non-State group.").

[19] *See* Finucane, *supra* note 4 at 61–82 (briefly recounting and analyzing numerous incidents); see also D'Este, *supra* note 15 (recounting political and practical considerations affecting the operation).

[20] *See e.g.* Finucane, *supra* note 4; Paust, *supra* note 4.

A. *A Brief Introduction to Legal Frameworks*

There are primarily three bodies of international law implicated by transnational uses of force by states and non-state actors.[21] The first regulates the resort to armed force against or in the territory of another state, known as the *jus ad bellum*.[22] The two other pertinent frameworks, IHL and HRL, regulate: (1) the precise circumstances under which force may be used, (2) permissible means and methods of force, and (3) rights or protections to be afforded groups and/or individuals. Within the context of an armed conflict, the exact relationship between IHL and HRL is uncertain.[23] Because this chapter addresses transnational armed attacks and transnational self-defense unrelated to an existing international or non-international armed conflict, this issue is not engaged.

1. *Jus ad Bellum*. Stated succinctly, the resort to force "against the territorial integrity or political independence of any state" is prohibited by Article 2(4) of the U.N. Charter.[24] It is only permissible: (1) when authorized by the Security Council in the exercise of its powers under Chapter VII of the U.N. Charter; or (2) when it is a lawful act of individual or collective self-defense.[25] It is generally understood that *jus ad bellum* addresses only the bare right to resort to armed force. It does not intrinsically speak to the means or methods of force authorized,[26] except in the

[21] Other international law, such as the Convention for the Prevention and Punishment of Genocide, may also be relevant depending upon the particular facts surrounding a use of force.

[22] Because it involves a Latin term for war, *bellum*, the use of this term seems inappropriate unless the use of force is necessarily considered to initiate an armed conflict. As earlier explained, this point is contested. *Compare* Craig Martin, *Going Medieval: Targeted Killing, Self-Defense and the Jus Ad Bellum Regime, in* Targeted Killings: Law and Morality in an Asymmetrical World 235 with Paust, *supra* note 4 at 258 ("a defensive use of force [against non-state actors] will not create a state of war or an armed conflict of any duration between the state engaged in self-defense and the state on whose territory the self-defense targetings take place").

[23] *See generally, ICRC, IHL-IHRL Interplay Report, supra* note 10.

[24] U.N. Charter, Art. 2, para. 4.

[25] *Id.* at Arts. 42, 51; *See e.g.*, Yoram Dinstein, War, Aggression and Self-Defence, 88 (4th ed. 2005)[hereinafter Dinstein, WASD].

[26] On the importance of differentiating between the resort to force and the means and methods employed in its use, *see* Robert D. Sloane, *The Cost of Conflation: Preserving the Dualism of Jus ad Bellum and Jus in Bello in the Contemporary Law of War*, 34 Yale J. Int'l L. 47 (2009). Of course, a Security Council resolution may identify the permissible purposes of any force authorized by it, and sometimes also place limitations on the means authorized. *See e.g.*, S.C. Res. 1973, ¶ 4, U.N. Doc. S/RES/1973 (March 17, 2011) (authorizing Member States "to take all necessary measures ... to protect civilians and civilian populated areas under threat of attack in the Libyan Arab Jamahiriya, including

context of inter-state uses of armed force, which should generally be understood to create an international armed conflict regulated by IHL.[27] As a general matter, the quantum or extent of force permitted in self-defense is limited to actions necessary and proportionate to the threat confronted.[28]

A state may also resort to force in another state's territory with the consent of that state. Consent permits the resort of force but does necessarily determine whether IHL or HRL regulates the parameters of its use. At least theoretically, a state might limit its consent to something less than what international law allows under the circumstances, for example, the use of only law enforcement measures in the context of an armed conflict.[29] Logically, however, a state may only consent to uses of force permitted by relevant international and domestic law under the circumstances.[30] It is unclear precisely which body of international law applies, IHL or HRL, when a territorial state consenting to a use of force

Benghazi, while excluding a foreign occupation force of any form on any part of Libyan territory").

[27] True inter-State uses of armed force generally establish an armed conflict regulated by IHL. *See Extraterritorial Legal Targeting, supra* note 9 at 93 (Suffice it to say that if the organs of one state, such as the military or intelligence agencies, are using armed force against another state, an international armed conflict is almost certainly underway and international humanitarian law applies); Laurie Blank, *The Continuing Importance of a Low Threshold for LOAC Application in International Armed Conflict*, Just Security, http://justsecurity.org/2014/03/19/guest-post-continuing-importance-threshold-loac-application-international-armed-conflict/ ("No matter how short-lived or minor, any hostilities between the armed forces of two or more states constitute an international armed conflict, even if one or both states deny the existence of an armed conflict."). *But see* The 74th Conference of the International Law Association, The Hague, The Netherlands, August 15–20, 2010, *Final Report on the Meaning of Armed Conflict in International Law* 29, *available at* www.ila-hq.org/en/committees/index.cfm/cid/1022 ("The assessment here of state practice and *opinio juris*, judicial opinion, and the majority of commentators support the position that hostilities must reach a certain level of intensity to qualify as an armed conflict.") [hereinafter ILA Armed Conflict Report]; Paust, *supra* note 4 at 260 (arguing that the concept of self-defense against non-state actor includes the right to use necessary and proportionate force that is, in substance, analogous to that of armed conflict); Finucane, *supra* note 4 at 155.

[28] *See e.g.*, Legality of the Threat or Use of Nuclear Weapons, Advisory Opinion, 1996 I.C.J. 226, para. 41 (July 8); Oil Platforms (Iran v. U.S.), 2003 I.C.J. 161, para. 43, 73–74, 76 (November 6).

[29] *See* Terry D. Gill, Military Intervention at the Invitation of a Government, *in The Handbook of the International Law of Military Operations* 229 (Terry D. Gill & Dieter Fleck eds., 2010).

[30] *See* Ashley S. Deeks, *Consent to the Use of Force and International Law Supremacy*, 54 Harvard Int'l L. J. 1, 5 (2013) ("[P]urported consent by a host state to a different type of force than that which it lawfully may use cannot serve as a basis for the acting state to use

is not a party to an armed conflict with a resident non-state actor, but an attacking state is,[31] or when an attacking state engages in acts of transnational self-defense that are below the threshold for non-international armed conflict, discussed shortly.

2. International Humanitarian Law (IHL). International humanitarian law regulates the means and methods of permissible actions, or "hostilities," between or among parties to an international or non-international armed conflict. It regulates the permissible means, methods, and objects of an armed attack, and provides specific protections to individuals depending upon their status. The key to IHL's applicability is the existence of an armed conflict. Put differently, the forming or ripening of a situation into an armed conflict triggers the application of IHL to the actions of all parties to the conflict.

Under IHL, attacking an enemy is generally permitted but must be limited to military objectives, meaning combatant members of an armed force of a party to the conflict,[32] civilians taking a direct part in hostilities,[33] or "objects which by their nature, location, purpose or use make an effective contribution to military action and whose total or partial destruction, capture or neutralization, in the circumstances ruling at the time, offers a definite military advantage."[34] IHL also permits indefinite detention of members of an enemy armed force[35] and sometimes of

force. The acting state should bear a 'duty to inquire' to determine whether the host state's consent exceeds the scope of the host state's legal authority.").

[31] *See* John C. Dehn, *Targeted Killing, Human Rights and Ungoverned Spaces: Considering Territorial State Human Rights Obligations*, 54 Harvard Int'l L. J. Online 84, 87 (2012) ("A territorial state may . . . violate its human rights obligations by consenting to an attacking state's targeted killing operation").

[32] An armed force may consist of combatant or fighting and non-combatant or non-fighting members. Non-combatant members include medical and religious personnel who may not attack and are protected from attack. *See* Protocol Additional to the Geneva Conventions of August 12, 1949, and relating to the Protection of Victims of International Armed Conflicts Art. 43(2), June 8, 1977, 1125 U.N.T.S. 3 [hereinafter AP I] ("Members of the armed forces of a Party to a conflict (other than medical personnel and chaplains covered by Article 33 of the Third Convention) are combatants, that is to say, they have the right to participate directly in hostilities.").

[33] Int'l Comm. of the Red Cross, *Interpretive Guidance on the Notion of Participation in Hostilities Under International Humanitarian Law* 21–22 (Nils Melzer ed., 2009) [hereinafter *DPH Interpretive Guidance*]; AP I, *supra* note 32, art. 51(3); Protocol Additional to the Geneva Conventions of August 12, 1949, and relating to the Protection of Victims of Non-International Armed Conflicts Art. 13(3), June 8, 1977, 1125 U.N.T.S. 609 [hereinafter AP II].

[34] AP I, *supra* note 32 at Art. 52(2).

[35] *Id.* at art. 45, 75.

civilians posing a threat to the security of an armed force.[36] The extent to which IHL authorizes indefinite detention of fighters or civilians in non-international armed conflict is unclear and contested.[37] In any event, as the preceding discussion makes clear, within IHL permissible uses of force and detention depend upon the status of the individual to be targeted or detained, which is sometimes determined by an individual's conduct.[38]

3. International Human Rights Law (HRL). International human rights law regulates states in their interactions with individuals. Although there are many sources of HRL,[39] the International Covenant on Civil and Political Rights ("ICCPR") is the most broadly applicable treaty that regulates the use of lethal force against and detention of individuals.[40] It prohibits "arbitrary" deprivations of life[41] and liberty[42] without further definition. It places specific procedural and substantive constraints upon some deprivations of life and virtually all detentions.[43]

The European Convention on Human Rights ("ECHR") is even more detailed. Permissible legal bases for detention are prescribed, not quite

[36] Geneva Convention (IV) Relative to the Protection of Civilian Persons in Time of War, Arts. 41–43, August 12, 1949, 75 U.N.T.S. 287 (providing for internment of civilians).

[37] *Compare* Marco Sassòli and Laura Olson, *The relationship between international humanitarian and human rights law where it matters: admissible killing and internment of fighters in non-international armed conflicts*, 90 INT'L REV. OF RED CROSS 599, 618–626 (2008) (Noting lack of express authority to detain in law of non-international armed conflict and proposing complementary application of detention rules of international armed conflict and human rights law to non-international armed conflict) *with* Jelena Pejic, *Procedural principles and safeguards for internment/administrative detention in armed conflict and other situations of violence*, 87 INT'L REV. OF RED CROSS 375 (2005) ("Deprivation of liberty for security reasons is an exceptional measure of control that may be taken in armed conflict, whether international or non-international.").

[38] *See e.g.*, COLONEL MARK *"Max" Maxwell, Rebutting the Civilian Presumption: Playing Whack-A-Mole Without a Mallet? in* TARGETED KILLINGS: LAW AND MORALITY IN AN ASYMMETRICAL WORLD 32 (Claire Finkelstein, Jens David Ohlin, and Andrew Altman, eds. 2012) (explaining status based targeting in armed conflict, including conduct-based status determinations); *DPH Interpretive Guidance, supra* note 33.

[39] For a "rough picture of the landscape," *see* Eric A. *Posner, Human Welfare, not Human Rights*, 108 COLUM. L. REV. 1758, 1763 (2008); see also *Chapter IV: Human Rights*, UNITED NATIONS TREATY COLLECTION *available at* http://treaties.un.org/Pages/Treaties.aspx?id=4&subid=A&lang=en.

[40] International Covenant on Civil and Political Rights, G.A. Res. 2200A (XXI), U.N. Doc. A/6316 (1966) [hereinafter ICCPR].

[41] *Id.* at Art. 6(1). [42] *Id.* at Art. 9(1).

[43] *See Id.* at Arts. 7 (regulating capital punishment), 9 (providing for judicial review of detention).

exhaustively,[44] as are minimal procedural rights for those arrested or detained.[45] Regarding the right to life, the ECHR first mandates that member states must protect it,[46] and then provides,

> Deprivation of life shall not be regarded as inflicted in contravention of this Article when it results from the use of force which is no more than absolutely necessary: (a) in defence of any person from unlawful violence; (b) in order to effect a lawful arrest or to prevent the escape of a person lawfully detained; (c) in action lawfully taken for the purpose of quelling a riot or insurrection.[47]

From this regional treaty and its case law,[48] as well as other documents of limited functional scope,[49] it is often asserted that HRL permits a state to use lethal force only when strictly necessary to prevent imminent loss of life.[50] But even in the ECHR, two of three permissible textual justifications for lethal force include purposes other than the protection of life. Thus, neither the non-binding opinions of HRL bodies, special rapporteurs and commentators, nor even the binding opinions of *regional* HRL tribunals, may delineate the entire range of non-arbitrary deprivations of life or liberty for purposes of the ICCPR.[51] To use a well-worn

[44] Convention for the Protection of Human Rights and Fundamental Freedoms, November 4, 1950, 213 U.N.T.S. 222, art. 5(1) [hereinafter ECHR].

[45] *Id.* at Art. 5(2)-(5). [46] *Id.* at Art. 2(1). [47] *Id.* at Art. 2(2).

[48] *See e.g.* Stewart v. United Kingdom, (Application No 10044/82), Decision of July 10, 1984.

[49] *See e.g.* Eighth United Nations Congress on the Prevention of Crime and the Treatment of Offenders, Havana, Cuba, August 27–September 7, 1990, *Basic Principles on the Use of Force and Fire-arms by Law Enforcement Officials*, U.N. Doc. A/CONF.144/28/Rev.1, 112, 114 (1990) [hereinafter *Basic Use of Force Principles*]. This document was clearly drafted for law enforcement measures, not as guidance for extraterritorial operations against violent non-state actors. Even then, it is not clear that the document supports the weight being assigned to it. *See infra* part III.B.3.

[50] "Report of the U.N. Special Rapporteur on the promotion and protection of human rights and fundamental freedoms while countering terrorism," U.N. Doc. A/68/389, at 17 (September 18, 2013) (transmitted by Note of the Secretary General at 68th session of the U.N. General Assembly) ("Outside situations of armed conflict, the use of deadly force is lawful only if strictly necessary and proportionate, if aimed at preventing an immediate threat to life and if there are no other means of preventing the threat from materializing."); Heyns Report, *supra* note 1 at 8 ("The use of force is . . . a matter of last resort under international human rights law. . . . Any force must be necessary and proportionate, and intentional force can be used only where strictly necessary to protect against an imminent threat to life.").

[51] *But see* Beth van Schaack, The United States' Position on the Extraterritorial Application of Human Rights Obligations: Now is the Time for Change, 90 INT'L L. STUD. 20, 31 (2014) ("When [treaty] language is indefinite, either inadvertently or by design, State representatives, in effect, delegate interpretive authority to courts and other enforcement

current term of art in international law, HRL is "fractionalized" in both content and application.[52] Universal HRL norms beyond the vague language of the ICCPR are much more ambiguous than many commentators and advocacy groups admit.[53]

B. *Legal Asymmetry and Ambiguity*

Uncertainty in the precise application of these legal frameworks is the result of legal asymmetries that arise in the context of transnational non-state actor armed attacks and transnational self-defense. For example, international legal prohibitions on the use of force between states inherently apply only to states, not to entirely autonomous non-state actors.[54] Transnational armed attacks by non-state actors outside the context of an armed conflict and lacking actual or constructive state control are typically violations of a state's municipal (domestic) rather than international law.[55] While victim states have prescriptive jurisdiction to adopt laws criminalizing violent acts originating extraterritorially and directed toward or occurring within their territory,[56] they lack inherent

bodies.") Van Schaack's imprecise proposition includes no citation in support of it. It certainly may be true insofar as a state expressly and affirmatively cedes legally binding adjudicative and/or enforcement authority to any such bodies, but is not accurate absent such circumstances. For a view similar to Van Schaack's, *see ICRC, IHL-HRL Interplay Report, supra* note 10 at 70 (Written Statement of Françoise Hampson: "When considering human rights law, the meeting [of experts] needs to take account not only of the binding legal judgments of regional human rights courts and the authoritative decisions of the Human Rights Committee under the first Optional Protocol to the International Covenant on Civil and Political Rights (ICCPR). Attention should also be paid to Advisory Opinions, Concluding Observations on State reports and General Comments of those bodies and to the work of Special Procedures and holders of analogous mandates (e.g., Commissioner for Human Rights of the Council of Europe.)").

52 *See* IHL-HRL Interplay Report *supra* note 10 at 71 (Written Statement of Françoise Hampson: "The relevant ECHR provisions are unlike the equivalent provisions in other treaties.").

53 *See infra* part I.B.

54 *See e.g.*, U.N. Charter, Art. 2, para. 4; Military and Paramilitary Activities in and Against Nicaragua (Nicar. v. U.S.), 1986 I.C.J. 14 (June 27).

55 ILA Armed Conflict Report, *supra* note 27 at 9. *But see* Dinstein, WASD *supra* note 25 at 206 ("[I]t is indisputable that toleration by a State of activities by terrorists or armed bands, is unlawful ... [and] even constitutes a crime under international law." (citation omitted)).

56 *See e.g.*, Ian Brownlie, Principles of Public International Law 299 (6th ed. 2003) (discussing the objective territorial principle); Antonio Cassese, International Criminal Law 278 (2003).

enforcement powers of investigation, arrest, or detention in the territory of other states from which they emanate.[57]

This complicates the right of self-defense applicable to armed attacks by non-state actors. Generally speaking, a state may respond in kind to armed attacks by states. For some, however, the necessity principle of self-defense requires an attacking state to first ask a territorial state to address an actual or impending transnational terrorist attack before resorting to self-help.[58] Others suggest that the requirement for coordination with a territorial state before taking a defensive action is conditional and contextual.[59] Thus, there is much legal ambiguity in this area when a territorial state in no way supports or tolerates the attacks and may even be unable to prevent them. In any event, at least at first blush, any right of transnational self-defense is potentially more constrained than inter-state self-defense, but to an uncertain extent.

Transnational non-state actor armed attacks expose asymmetries in IHL as well, the most important of which are the conditions that establish an armed conflict regulated by it. In a statement widely accepted as accurate, the International Criminal Tribunal for the former Yugoslavia ("ICTY") concluded that international armed conflict exists "whenever there is a resort to armed force between States," but that non-international armed conflict arises only "whenever there is [...] protracted armed violence between governmental authorities and organised armed groups or between such groups."[60] The requirement for protracted armed violence is often referred to as an "intensity" requirement.[61] Although some commentators and courts assert that protracted

[57] Anthony Aust, Handbook of International Law 44 (2005) ("Officials of a foreign state cannot take evidence or exercise other jurisdiction without the consent of the territorial state.").

[58] *See* Lubell, *supra* note 16 at 46 ("So long as [the] option [to demand the territorial state take measures to end the hostile activities of the non-state actor] exists and has not been tried, then it can be said the [self-defense] requirement of necessity has not been fulfilled.").

[59] *Extraterritorial Lethal Targeting, supra* note 9 at 86 ("In light of both [its duty to prevent the use of its territory to harm another state] and its right of sovereignty, the [territorial state] must be afforded a reasonable opportunity to put an end to harmful actions emanating from its territory. The duration of such an opportunity depends on how pressing the need to conduct defensive operations is for the victim State." (citations omitted)).

[60] Prosecutor v. Tadic, Case Np. IT-94-1-T, Decision on the Defence Motion for Interlocutory Appeal on Jurisdiction, ¶ 70 (Int'l Crim. Trib. for the Former Yugosalvia Oct. 2, 1995).

[61] *See* ILA Armed Conflict Report, *supra* note 27 at 14.

violence is a condition precedent to the existence of international as well as non-international armed conflict,[62] the better view is that IHL applies to any hostile engagement between the armed forces of states.[63] This view aligns with the language of applicable treaties and their commentary,[64] as well as the views of the International Committee for the Red Cross ("ICRC").[65] Thus, while armed conflict arises from any armed attacks between states, the point at which transnational armed attacks coupled

[62] *See generally* ILA Armed Conflict Report, *supra* note 27.

[63] There are limited incidents of armed hostilities that end quickly and do not create an indefinite state of armed conflict resulting in more formal termination. Professor Dinstein refers to such matters as "closed incidents." DINSTEIN, WASD, *supra* note 25 at 11. Others refer to them as "incidents," "border clashes," or "skirmishes." ILA Armed Conflict Report, *supra* note 27 at 13. These incidents involve acts of armed violence waged on behalf of states in their corporate or collective capacities. Whether the states involved choose to continue the conflict indefinitely, the reciprocal acts of armed violence between government forces should be considered hostilities regulated by IHL rather than potentially criminal acts committed by and against the members of opposing armed forces. *See DPH Interpretive Guidance supra* note 33 at 43 ("the concept of 'hostilities' refers to the (collective) resort by the parties to the conflict to means and methods of injuring the enemy") and *infra* note 64.

[64] Article 2 of all four 1949 Geneva Conventions provides "the present Convention shall apply to all cases of declared war or of any other armed conflict which may arise between two or more of the High Contracting Parties, even if the state of war is not recognized by one of them." Geneva Convention (I) for the Amelioration of the Condition of the Wounded and Sick in Armed Forces in the Field Art. 2, August 12, 1949, 75 U.N.T.S. 31 [hereinafter GC I]; Geneva Convention (II) for the Amelioration of the Condition of Wounded, Sick and Shipwrecked Members of Armed Forces at Sea Art. 2, August 12, 1949, 75 U.N.T.S. 85 [hereinafter GC II]; Geneva Convention (III) Relative to the Treatment of Prisoners of War Art. 2, August 12, 1949, 75 U.N.T.S. 135 [hereinafter GC III]; Geneva Convention (IV) Relative to the Protection of Civilian Persons in Time of War Art. 2, August 12, 1949, 75 U.N.T.S. 287 [hereinafter GC IV]; *See also* Commentary on the Geneva Conventions of August 12, 1949, *Vol. I Geneva Convention for the Amelioration of the Condition of the Wounded and Sick in Armed Forces in the Field* 32 (Jean Pictet ed., 1952) ("Any difference arising between two States and leading to the intervention of armed forces is an armed conflict within the meaning of Article 2, even if one of the Parties denies the existence of a state of war. It makes no difference how long the conflict lasts, or how much slaughter takes place. ... Nor, incidentally, does the application of the Convention necessarily involve the intervention of cumbrous machinery. It all depends on circumstances. If there is only a single wounded person as a result of the conflict, the Convention will have been applied as soon as he has been collected and tended ...").

[65] *Opinion Paper: How is the Term Armed Conflict Defined in International Humanitarian Law*, INTERNATIONAL COMMITTEE OF THE RED CROSS, 1 (March 2008) ("An IAC occurs when one or more States have recourse to armed force against another State, regardless of the reasons or the intensity of this confrontation. ... The existence of an IAC, and as a consequence, the possibility to apply International Humanitarian Law to this situation, depends on what actually happens on the ground.) *available at*

with responsive uses of defensive force become a non-international armed conflict differs from identical inter-state behavior.[66] Non-international armed conflict requires some level of intensity that relates to the nature of the violence: its duration, its frequency, its destructiveness, or some combination of these,[67] all of which may have a "dynamic relationship to one another."[68]

Another IHL asymmetry in this context might be its territorial or functional applicability once a transnational non-international armed conflict exists. In international armed conflict, IHL applies in the territory of all states party to the conflict, as well as to their hostile actions *inter se* on the high seas or in international airspace,[69] what some scholars referred to as the "belligerent intercourse" of the parties to the conflict.[70] In other words, IHL applies both functionally and territorially to the actions of the parties. In non-international armed conflict, IHL unquestionably applies between the parties to the conflict in the territory of any state where the intensity and organization elements are satisfied.[71] Beyond such territory, however, its applicability is contested and unclear.[72] It is also unclear whether the intensity requirement for non-international armed conflict can be satisfied by exchanging transnational armed attacks only, or whether mutual hostilities within a given state or

www.icrc.org/eng/assets/files/other/opinion-paper-armed-conflict.pdf [hereinafter *ICRC Armed Conflict Definition*].

66 *Compare Extraterritorial Lethal Targeting, supra* note 9 at 109 (asserting "most defensive acts, combined with the armed attack to which they respond, will comprise either an international or non-international armed conflict") with ILA Armed Conflict Report, *supra* note 27 at 29 ("The assessment here of state practice and *opinio juris*, judicial opinion, and the majority of commentators support the position that hostilities must reach a certain level of intensity to qualify as an armed conflict.").

67 SANDESH SIVAKUMARAN, THE LAW OF NON-INTERNATIONAL ARMED CONFLICT 167 (2012).

68 Robert Chesney, *Transatlantic Dialogue on International Law and Armed Conflict: When Does LOAC Cease to Apply?*, LAWFARE, (September 3, 2014), www.lawfareblog.com/2014/09/transatlantic-dialogue-on-international-law-and-armed-conflict-when-does-loac-cease-to-apply/.

69 *See NIAC Geography, supra* note 4 at 5; DINSTEIN, WASD *supra* note 25 at 19–24.

70 *See e.g.*, HENRY W. HALLECK, ELEMENTS OF INTERNATIONAL LAW AND LAWS OF WAR 153 (1866); WILLIAM WINTHROP, MILITARY LAW AND PRECEDENTS 742 (2nd ed. 1920) (defining "customs of war" as unwritten rules and principles "which regulate the intercourse and acts of individuals during the carrying on of war between hostile nations or peoples.").

71 *ICRC Armed Conflict Definition, supra* note 65.

72 *See* 31st Conference Report, *supra* note 7; *NIAC Geography, supra* note 4 at 11–12 (discussing "spillover" and "geographically unfocused" conflicts).

location must reach a certain intensity level to establish a non-international armed conflict regulated by IHL.[73] Thus, the territorial and functional applicability of IHL in non-international armed conflict may differ.

The primary asymmetry in HRL lies in the fact that it formally binds only states. When non-state actors violate individual human rights, it is typically a compensable injury or crime under municipal rather than international law.[74] Additional asymmetry arises from contested claims regarding the extent to which HRL binds states when acting extraterritorially. The ICCPR's general requirement that each state undertake "to respect and to ensure to all individuals within its territory and subject to its jurisdiction the rights recognized in the present Covenant" is susceptible of at least three interpretations: first, that its positive ("ensure") and negative ("respect") obligations apply between states and individuals only within a state's territory *and* jurisdiction; second, that states must "respect" these rights everywhere, but must "ensure" them only within their territory and jurisdiction; and third, that the obligations apply fully within state territory and attach to the fullest extent consistent with a state's decision to exercise its "jurisdiction," or "power and effective control," abroad.[75] The last interpretation is the position taken by the U.N. Human Rights Committee.[76]

The United States has consistently taken the position that the ICCPR applies only within a state's territory and jurisdiction.[77] Although the

[73] *See e.g.*, *NIAC Geography, supra* note 4 at 17 ("[T]hose who support the possibility of non-geographically focused [non-international armed conflicts] . . . typically evaluate conflicts with transnational organized armed groups on a case-by-case basis by applying the intensity and organization criteria. In this approach, the activities of organized armed groups may only be combined to satisfy the intensity criterion when the groups concerned can reasonably be characterized as a single coherent organization operating collaboratively." (citations omitted)).

[74] This is certainly not meant to assert that non-state actors may never commit international crimes. Non-state actors may commit genocide, war crimes, and crimes against humanity. *See e.g.*, Rome Statute of the International Criminal Court, arts. 5–8, July 17, 1998, 2187 U.N.T.S. 90 [hereinafter Rome Statute].

[75] *See e.g.*, Van Schaack, *supra* note 51 at 28 (surveying range of possible ICCPR interpretations).

[76] Human Rights Comm., General Comment 31, Nature of the General Legal Obligation on States Parties to the Covenant, U.N. Doc. CCPR/C/21/Rev.1/Add.13 (2004).

[77] *See e.g.*, Fourth Periodic Report of the United States of America to the United Nations Committee on Human Rights Concerning the International Covenant on Civil and Political Rights, ¶¶ 504–505 (December 30, 2011).

U.S. position is a fair reading of the ICCPR's text, this chapter takes a middle course. It accepts that states must "respect" individual human rights outlined in the ICCPR everywhere, but must "ensure" human rights only within their territory and jurisdiction, where they clearly possess the prescriptive, enforcement, and adjudicatory powers necessary to do so. A state must therefore observe the ICCPR prohibitions of arbitrary arrest, arbitrary detention, and arbitrary deprivation of life both territorially and extraterritorially – though we have yet to discern what is fairly considered "arbitrary" in this context.

C. *Current U.S. Policy: Exploiting Ambiguity or Forcing Symmetry?*

These asymmetries and ambiguities are evident in a close examination of recent U.S. policy statements about its use of force outside areas of active hostilities. Several elements of these policies are vague and likely in violation of restrictive interpretations of HRL. At the same time, they appear to expand the concept of non-international armed conflict and the application of related IHL without fully leveraging IHL authorities. These policies include:

> *First*, there must be a legal basis for using lethal force, whether it is against a senior operational leader of a terrorist organization or the forces that organization is using or intends to use to conduct terrorist attacks.
>
> *Second*, the United States will use lethal force only against a target that poses a continuing, imminent threat to U.S. persons. It is simply not the case that all terrorists pose a continuing, imminent threat to U.S. persons; if a terrorist does not pose such a threat, the United States will not use lethal force.
>
> *Third*, the following criteria must be met before lethal action may be taken:
>
> 1) Near certainty that the terrorist target is present;
> 2) Near certainty that non-combatants will not be injured or killed;
> 3) An assessment that capture is not feasible at the time of the operation;
> 4) An assessment that the relevant governmental authorities in the country where action is contemplated cannot or will not effectively address the threat to U.S. persons;
> 5) An assessment that no other reasonable alternatives exist to effectively address the threat to U.S. persons.
>
> *Finally*, whenever the United States uses force in foreign territories, international legal principles, including respect for sovereignty and the law of armed conflict, impose important constraints on the ability of the

> United States to act unilaterally – and on the way in which the United States can use force. The United States respects national sovereignty and international law.[78]

There are several important points of analysis.

First, the idea that there must be a "legal basis" for using force seems both obvious and unnecessarily vague. In HRL, there is only one *asserted* basis for an intentional, extrajudicial use of force in self-defense: that the targeted individual(s) poses an immediate threat to someone. Moreover, the policy strongly implies collective targeting is appropriate rather than individualized threat assessment by its reference to terrorist "organizations" and the "forces" that non-state actors "are using or intend to use." Such collective or status-based targeting is an IHL concept logically inconsistent with the individualized approach to the defensive use of force under HRL.[79]

Additionally, the requirement that a terrorist pose a "*continuing*, imminent threat to U.S. persons"[80] indicates a flexible concept of imminence that likely includes those who are more or less continuously planning attacks to be carried out at some indefinite point in the future. This is not the concept of imminence typically associated with HRL or inter-state (*jus ad bellum*) self-defense, both of which are understood to require an immediately imminent or in-progress attack rather than an indefinite future attack.[81] To firmly believe or perhaps even to know that a non-state actor plans an armed attack at some indefinite point in the future does not, under restrictive understandings of self-defense and HRL, permit an attack to prevent that threat from materializing. It is commonly asserted that a state must use non-lethal measures unless or until responsive lethal force becomes absolutely necessary to counter an imminent or immediate grave threat.[82]

[78] *Fact Sheet: U.S. Policy Standards and Procedures for the Use of Force in Counterterrorism Operations Outside the United States and Areas of Active Hostilities*, THE WHITE HOUSE (May 23, 2013) *available at* www.whitehouse.gov/the-press-office/2013/05/23/fact-sheet-us-policy-standards-and-procedures-use-force-counterterrorism.

[79] *See e.g., ICRC, IHL-HRL Interplay Report, supra* note 10 at iv ("The conduct of hostilities does not prohibit the killing of legitimate targets, provided that, among others, the IHL principles of proportionality and precautions are fulfilled. Instead, under law enforcement, lethal force may be used only as a last resort in order to protect life, when other available means remain ineffective or without any promise of achieving the intended result.").

[80] *Id.* (emphasis added)

[81] *See infra* part III.A.3.

[82] *See NIAC Geography, supra* note 4; DINSTEIN-WASD, *supra* note 25.

It may seem a welcome sign of respect for the right to life for the administration to require "near certainty that non-combatants will not be injured or killed." The terminology used, however, suggests reliance on an IHL legal model. This is demonstrated by a footnote defining "non-combatants."

> Non-combatants are individuals who may not be made the object of attack under applicable international law. The term "non-combatant" does not include an individual who is part of a belligerent party to an armed conflict, an individual who is taking a direct part in hostilities, *or an individual who is targetable in the exercise of national self-defense.*[83]

The first two categories of targetable individuals are clearly based in IHL,[84] not HRL. The third category is not defined in either body of law. As earlier noted, not every non-state actor armed attack creates an armed conflict permitting status- or membership-based targeting of "combatants" or "fighters." The exact conduct or characteristics of groups or individuals the U.S. considers "targetable in the exercise of national self-defense" is unclear.[85] Thus, "near certainty that non-combatants will not be injured or killed" is either too broad or too narrow. It would be too broad under HRL because *anticipated* "collateral damage" is almost always unacceptable and arbitrary outside of armed conflict and IHL. It would be too narrow under IHL because in an actual armed conflict, incidental loss of life, and destruction of property is permitted when not excessive in relation to the military advantage anticipated from an attack.

Additionally, it is not clear if the feasibility of capture assessment required by the policy is based solely on the present physical location and situation of the individual(s) to be captured or killed or whether it takes into account extrinsic factors. Available information suggests that it may also reflect political or diplomatic considerations involved with using force in the territory of another state and the risk to U.S. forces of attempting capture. Indeed, the policy's emphasis on "respect for sovereignty" could very well indicate that conditional territorial state consent may impose limitations on the presence of U.S. troops such that

[83] *Id.* (emphasis added).

[84] *See supra* notes 32–33 and related text.

[85] *See* Paust, *supra* note 4 at 264. Professor Paust asserts that under customary international law individuals "actively participating in and taking a direct part in armed attacks (including a person who is planning or directing such attacks)" may be targeted or captured, which suggests participation-based group or collective targeting.

capture is not feasible, but a drone attack is. For example, if a state consents to a counterterrorism operation within its territory only if there are no U.S. "boots on the ground," then capture may not be politically or legally feasible (in that exceeding the scope of consent would violate the territorial state's sovereignty) even though it may be objectively achievable in the actual circumstances on the ground. However, a use of lethal force not strictly necessary as a factual matter would violate commonly-held understandings of HRL.

For those who assert that an armed conflict model and IHL provide the appropriate or analogous legal framework, there are also inconsistencies between U.S. policy and IHL. For example, the requirement to capture a targetable individual whenever feasible is inconsistent with the fact that a member of an armed force of a party to an armed conflict may generally be targeted at any time based solely on their status.[86] There is no general duty to capture an enemy when feasible in armed conflict.[87] Likewise, requiring "near certainty that noncombatants will not be injured or killed" is a much stricter standard than the IHL prohibitions on attacking civilians or civilian objects[88] or indiscriminate or disproportionate attacks, primarily meaning those "which may be expected to cause incidental loss of civilian life, injury to civilians, damage to civilian objects, or a combination thereof, which would be *excessive* in relation to the concrete and direct military advantage anticipated"[89] (emphasis added). Finally, if IHL applies, no imminence is required before enemy armed forces/groups and their leaders may be attacked, making this an

[86] *See e.g., ICRC, IHL-IHRL Interplay Report, supra* note 10 at iv ("The conduct of hostilities does not prohibit the killing of legitimate targets, provided that, among others, the IHL principles of proportionality and precautions are fulfilled.").

[87] Jens David Ohlin, *The Duty to Capture*, 97 Minn. L Rev 1268, 1271(2013) ("If IHL – and IHL alone – applies, then . . . there is no implied duty to capture."); Geoffrey S. Corn, et. al., *Belligerent Targeting and the Invalidity of a Least Harmful Means Rule*, 89 Int'l L Stud. 536 (2013); Marco Sassòli and Laura M. Olson, *The Relationship Between International Humanitarian and Human Rights Law Where It Matters: Admissible Killing and Internment of Fighters in Non-International Armed Conflicts*, 90 Int'l Rev. Red Cross 599, 606 (2008) ("The traditional understanding is that no rule restricts the use of force against combatants only to those circumstances in which they cannot be captured." (citations omitted)); *but see* Ryan Goodman, *The Power to Kill or Capture Enemy Combatants*, 24 European J. of Int'l Law 819, (forthcoming 2013) ("In the final analysis, [restraints on the use of force]—and the least restrictive means approach in particular—fit well within the law of modern warfare.").

[88] AP I, *supra* note 34 at Art. 51(1)&(2).

[89] *Id.* at Art. 51(5)(b). Indiscriminate attacks are more broadly defined in Art. 51(4) and (5).

unnecessary restriction on the use of force. Although it is certainly possible that the imminence requirement refers to the bare, jus ad bellum *resort* to force in self-defense rather than to the specific use of force being considered, recall that the policy applies to uses of force "outside areas of active hostilities." Thus, a relevant armed conflict justifying status-based targeting may exist somewhere. The policy's blending of the resort to force and use of force issues, however, creates confusion.

On the whole, it seems the U.S. is fundamentally relying on an IHL framework in lethal extraterritorial counterterrorism operations, adopting what it believes to be wise policy constraints on permissible measures. The relaxed concept of imminence, the clear inclusion of collective or status-based rather than individualized, conduct-based targeting, and a malleable concept of feasibility to capture rather than kill all violate widely asserted understandings of HRL norms. At the same time, the policy constrains counterterrorism operations in ways that IHL would permit. While these limits may be viewed as "rules of engagement," restrictions imposed for various policy rather than legal reasons, U.S. opacity masks their law or policy basis and increases confusion regarding the U.S. view of applicable law.[90]

Perhaps more troubling still, the policy is silent regarding whether it will continue to apply if active battlefields in which the U.S. is directly involved no longer exist, or if a specific terrorist threat is unrelated to an existing armed conflict. Its exclusion of those "targetable in the exercise of national self-defense" from the definition of "non-combatant" portends reliance on IHL's collective or status-based targeting that does not depend upon the existence of a non-international armed conflict as currently defined by IHL. It therefore seems that the U.S. is either exploiting ambiguities in international law or attempting to force symmetry upon the international law of self-defense and armed conflict. In other words, it appears to be seeking to eliminate any duration or intensity requirement for non-international armed conflict when

[90] *See* Geoffrey S. Corn, *The Military Component of Counter-Terror Operations*, JUST SECURITY *available at* http://justsecurity.org/2013/09/30/military-component-counter-terror-operations ("Some argue that recent administration statements regarding operations conducted beyond the geography of the ongoing hostilities in Afghanistan indicate a transition from conduct of hostilities to law enforcement norms. . . . However, these arguments misconstrue statements of policy restraint for declarations of a shift in legal interpretation. . . . the President and his administration have not always been clear on the basis for the self-imposed limitations on attack authority.").

exercising transnational self-defense. This allows application of IHL to all actual, imminent, or future transnational armed attacks and responsive uses of force.[91]

II. Efforts to Create Legal Symmetry

Asymmetry in international law regulating transnational armed attacks and transnational self-defense exposed potential lacunae in the use of force regime. While it seems states and most commentators accept that a state's right of self-defense extends to transnational armed attacks, it is not immediately clear whether this right is necessarily the same as that preserved between states by Article 51 of the U.N. Charter,[92] or whether IHL, HRL, or merely general principles of necessity and proportionality govern its exercise.[93] Historical examples of nations exercising transnational self-defense do not fit neatly into the U.N. Charter framework. Additionally, it is well known that the Bush administration exploited what it interpreted to be a gap in IHL and HRL to justify the use of war measures without observing fundamental protections required by both bodies of law, including the prohibition of torture and the requirement for humane treatment of those detained. The quest to fill that asserted gap has produced competing teleological interpretations of the scope of IHL and HRL. Contenders on both sides rely on the broad underlying humanitarian purposes of both bodies of law to argue for their extension to transnational counterterrorism operations. This section briefly introduces and critiques these efforts and justifies an alternative approach.

91 *E.g.*, Professor Corn, a former U.S. Army senior law of war expert, has suggested that the Martens Clause, incorporated in various forms in IHL treaties from The Hague to Geneva Conventions, "supports the assertion of a category of armed conflict that is beyond the scope of a textual analysis of the Geneva law triggering articles." *Id.* This view certainly supports a broader application of IHL to all situations involving the use of armed force between states and non-state actors.

92 U.N. Charter Art. 51 ("Nothing in the present Charter shall impair the inherent right of individual or collective self-defence if an armed attack occurs against a Member of the United Nations, until the Security Council has taken measures necessary to maintain international peace and security.").

93 *See e.g.*, Nils Melzer, Targeted Killing in International Law 55 (2008) ("[T]here can be no doubt that the law of interstate force as it stands today requires clarification, particularly with regard to operations that are directed exclusively against non-State actors...").

A. *Identical Concepts of Inter-State and Transnational Self-Defense?*

Many commentators assert or assume that the inherent right of self-defense preserved by Article 51 is identical whether exercised in response to inter-state or transnational armed attacks.[94] Former U.S. Secretary of State Daniel Webster's letter in response to the 1837 *Caroline* incident, an exercise of transnational self-defense as herein defined, is often cited as a longstanding, uniform standard for the exercise of self-defense, requiring that the "necessity of that self-defense is instant, overwhelming, and leaving no choice of means, and no moment for deliberation."[95] The U.S. Constitution adopted a similar standard for when its member states could engage in war without a declaration by the national government,[96] further supporting the idea of a universal standard of self-defense for inter-state and transnational attacks. After adoption of the U.N. Charter, however, the International Court of Justice strongly implied that a state has no right of self-defense against transnational armed attacks unless it may also exercise that right against the territorial state from which they emanate.[97] Both the United Nations Security Council[98] and the North Atlantic Treaty Organization,[99] however, considered the inherent right of self-defense to be triggered by al-Qaeda attacks in the United States on September 11, 2001. Thus, that there is a right of self-defense against transnational non-state actor attacks seems to be well accepted by states, if not well understood by the International Court of Justice.

Controversy remains, however, regarding the precise scope and content of this right, specifically the point at which it is triggered. Under the Charter language, a right of self-defense may be exercised when an "armed attack occurs."[100] While some suggest that the Charter language requires a completed attack, a majority of scholars and states also accept

[94] *See e.g.*, *Id.* at 75 ("Many authors interpret the right of self-defence in light of the Caroline Case (1837), concluding that it justifies military action not only against States, but also against non-State actors in the territory of a different State. . ."); Dinstein, WASD, *supra* note 25 at 204–211 (analyzing right of self-defense against non-state actors with reference to Articles 2(4) and 51 of the U.N. Charter, and customary inter-state requirements of necessity, proportionality, and immediacy).

[95] *See e.g.*, Paust, *supra* note 4 at 242.

[96] U.S. Const. art. 1, § 10, cl. 3 ("No State shall . . . engage in War, unless actually invaded, or in such imminent Danger as will not admit of delay.").

[97] Legal Consequences of the Construction of a Wall in the Occupied Palestinian Territory, Advisory Opinion, 2004 I.C.J. 136, ¶ 139 (July 9); Armed Activities on the Territory of the Congo (Dem. Rep. of the Congo v. Uganda), 2005 I.C.J. 168, ¶¶ 146–147 (December 19).

[98] S.C. Res. 1368, ¶ 1, U.N. Doc. S/RES/1368 (September 12, 2001).

[99] Dinstein-WASD, *supra* note 25 at 207–208.

[100] U.N. Charter Art. 51.

what *Caroline* suggests, an imminence standard,[101] one that might require that an attack be underway in some respect, such that a responsive attack "intercepts" it.[102] Although many agree that a purely preventive use of force to counter a gathering threat is impermissible between states,[103] there is disagreement over what counts as preventive. A restrictive view of the imminence requirement requires a state to respond to each attack as it is launched. A more permissive view would allow a continuous right of self-defense against a non-state actor that has attacked or attempted an attack and appears likely to continue doing so.[104] An even more permissive view would permit interdicting a threat believed to be absolutely certain but indefinite as to its future timing and/or location. At least one commentator asserts that states have begun to accept a broader concept of self-defense in response to the threat posed by transnational terrorism.[105] It is thus important to remember that adopting a different standard of self-defense for actual or impending transnational, non-state actor attacks would not require parallel changes in the law of inter-state self-defense. In other words, the concept of transnational self-defense may, by custom, be separated and differentiated from that of inter-state self-defense.

B. *Teleological Interpretation of HRL*

Another approach has been to posit that restrictive views of HRL apply to all uses of force not governed by IHL, thereby assuming uniform application of a state's human rights obligations extraterritorially. As earlier mentioned, notwithstanding the text of the ICCPR, the U.N. Human Rights Committee has adopted an elastic concept of "jurisdiction" that

[101] *Extraterritorial Lethal Targeting*, *supra* note 9 at 88.

[102] Dinstein-WASD, *supra* note 25 at 190–192. Professor Dinstein asserts a concept of "interceptive self-defense" that ripens when an attack is launched even though there may be substantial time before it reaches its intended destination. For example, if the U.S. had detected the impending attack on Pearl Harbor after the Japanese fleet left port to conduct it, it could have attacked in self-defense even though the actual attack had not begun. Needless to say, this approach is broader than an imminence standard.

[103] Tallinn Manual on the International Law Applicable to Cyber Warfare 63–66 (Michael Schmitt ed., 2013) (discussing views of group of experts).

[104] *Extraterritorial Lethal Targeting*, *supra* note 9 at 90.

[105] Christian J. Tams, *The Use of Force Against Terrorists*, 20 Eur. J. Int'l L. 359, 361 (2009) (arguing "in the course of two decades the legal rules governing the use of force have been re-adjusted so as to permit forcible responses against terrorism under more lenient conditions.").

purports to extend human rights obligations extraterritorially whenever and wherever states exert "power and effective control" over individuals.[106] Some propose flexible concepts of "jurisdiction" that effectively extend HRL to virtually any state assertion of official power over or against an individual wherever it occurs.[107] While an "idealized vision of human rights as universal attributes that we all enjoy simply by virtue of our shared humanity . . . [and the] . . . indeterminacy [of human rights treaties] invites teleological interpretation,"[108] it seems unlikely that states ever intended or will readily accept such wide-ranging obligations. Though it may seem "untenable and perverse" to think that a state may lawfully treat those outside its territory differently than those within it,[109] the options for addressing transnational armed attacks are often limited by a lack of local governing capacity needed to effectively deter or constrain terrorist groups, a lack of capacity that terrorists often exploit.

Moreover, states have long understood that there is an interdependent relationship between effective governance and human rights. Although basic human rights are said to "derive from the inherent dignity of the human person,"[110] humans have long understood the need for and endeavored to create societies with just and capable governments to protect those rights. The U.S. Declaration of Independence affirmed that "Governments are instituted among men" to secure their "inalienable" human rights. According to the French Declaration on the Rights of Man, "[t]he aim of all political association is the preservation of the natural and imprescriptible rights of man. The rights are liberty, property, *security* and resistance to oppression." (emphasis added)

The origins and sources of contemporary HRL also recognize that states are essential to and primarily responsible for securing individual human rights. The 1949 U.N. Declaration on Human Rights made it the responsibility of "every individual and every organ of society . . . to promote respect for these rights and freedoms and . . . to secure their universal and effective recognition and observance. . . ." More recently the ICCPR noted, "the ideal of free human beings enjoying civil and political freedom and freedom from fear and want can only be achieved if conditions are created whereby everyone may enjoy his civil and political

[106] *See* Human Rights Comm., *supra* note 75.

[107] For a discussion of the range of elastic interpretations, *see* Van Schaack, *supra* note 51 at 28–29; Lubell, *supra* note 16 at 195–207.

[108] Van Schaack, *supra* note 51 at 24. [109] *Id.*

[110] ICCPR, *supra* note 40 at Preamble.

rights, as well as his economic, social and cultural rights."[111] To advocate for observing the full measure of human rights without recognizing the concomitant need for governments capable of securing and protecting them seems blindly aspirational.

Creating conditions that ensure individual human rights requires states to establish and sustain stable and capable national, international, and supranational governance. Human rights have only an abstract and tenuous existence without societal structures in which they are recognized and protected.[112] Governments must possess both authority and capacity to prevent or remediate unwarranted public *and private* derogations or deprivations of them. The current system of global governance lacks sufficiently functional structures and governing capacity to perfectly maintain universal human rights, particularly in the context of transnational attacks emanating from ineffectively governed territory. Although universal uniformity is and should be the ultimate goal of the HRL project, context is critical in HRL's current application. While total or partial forfeiture of individual rights should never be lightly presumed, states must also possess power to restore a peaceful equilibrium when violent non-state actors subvert sovereignty and exploit weak governance to purposefully deprive others of their basic human rights.

As for the powers needed to restore a peaceful civil society from violent tumult that is at least temporarily beyond the government's ability to control through standard measures of law enforcement, it is somewhat clear that states have long retained some measure of autonomy and flexibility. For example, states purposefully limited the scope of the Protocol Additional to the Geneva Conventions of August 12, 1949, and Relating to the Protection of Victims of Non-International Armed Conflicts ("Protocol II"), adopted over a decade *after* the ICCPR, to avoid "undertak[ing] international legal obligations with regard to the conduct of hostilities in all kinds of internal armed conflicts."[113] Doing so was entirely nonsensical if states believed a much narrower regulation of

[111] *Id.* (emphasis added)

[112] Admittedly, this assertion implicitly adopts H.L.A. Hart's concept of law, in which states necessarily provide what Hart called "secondary rules" of recognition, change, and adjudication that are necessary to the practical existence or enforcement of primary rules of law. *See generally*, H.L.A. Hart, The Concept of Law (Joseph Raz and Penelope Bullock eds., 2nd ed. 1994).

[113] Laura Perna, The Formation of the Treaty Law of Non-International Armed Conflicts 101 (2006). *See also* ILA Armed Conflict Report, *supra* note 27 at 12 ("Additional Protocol II sets a higher threshold for application than Common Article 3.

the use of force under the ICCPR or customary HRL would fill the void.[114] Given this implicit rejection of such an understanding of the ICCPR for *internal* violence, it is highly unlikely that states broadly interpret the ICCPR to regulate extraterritorial uses of force in self-defense. Alternatively, if states truly understood the ICCPR would apply to internal violence or conflict not regulated by Protocol II or Common Article 3, this history raises significant questions about how states actually understand or interpret the non-derogable ICCPR prohibitions on arbitrary deprivation of life and liberty, a point to be taken up later. Regardless, any attempt to interpret HRL to regulate all uses of force as if they occurred within a state's peaceful, well-governed territory seems untenable, particularly when non-state actors exploit ineffectively governed territory to deprive others of their most basic human rights.

C. *Teleological Interpretation of IHL*

The prevalent understanding that limiting the scope of IHL treaties *increased* a state's flexibility in internal situations of violence also undermines arguments for expanding the concept of non-international armed conflict to encompass all transnational uses of force in self-defense. Although the object and purpose of IHL certainly support a territorially "unrestricted approach [to applying IHL, which] tracks the traditional emphasis on party status as the decisive determinant to IHL applicability,"[115] the traditional approaches to identifying the intensity of armed violence and the nature of the putative parties to a non-international armed conflict do not. Put differently, the requirement to observe IHL in non-international armed conflict has always been restricted by the nature of the violence and the nature of the non-state party or parties involved. The purposes underlying these restrictions counsel against expanding IHL's scope to loosely organized terrorist groups.

When identifying the nature of permissible non-state parties to non-international armed conflict, states have required a non-state armed group to have the capacity to adhere to applicable IHL. Logically,

This was done in order to make its more detailed and demanding rules acceptable to states." (citations omitted)).

114 Moreover, if states then believed that the ICCPR or HRL writ large continue to apply during armed conflict, it is difficult to understand why the basic human rights protections adopted in AP I, Art. 75 and AP II, Art. 6 were necessary.

115 *NIAC Geography*, *supra* note 4 at 18–19.

observing constraints on violence should be mutual to ensure that the humanitarian aims of IHL are fully advanced. One-sided voluntary compliance is certainly helpful but not sufficient and will put the compliant party at a comparative disadvantage in battle. While there is much that might be discussed, such as the belligerency/insurgency distinction under the law of war,[116] for brevity let us begin with the first international regulation of non-international armed conflict by treaty, which came in the form of Common Article 3 of the 1949 Geneva Conventions.[117] Still in force today, Common Article 3 requires that in "armed conflict not of an international character occurring in the territory of one of the High Contracting Parties ... each Party to the conflict" must observe certain minimal restrictions and protections.[118] Excluding from its intended scope "any form of anarchy, rebellion, or even plain banditry" while asserting "that the scope of application of the Article must be as wide as possible,"[119] the commentary to Common Article 3 provide non-exclusive criteria for the existence of an armed conflict subject to its requirements. These requirements emphasize that the non-state group must possess an organized military force under responsible command.[120]

[116] On this distinction and various considerations informing its use, both legal and political, *see e.g.*, Henry Wheaton, Elements of International Law 34–36 (Richard H. Dana, ed., 2nd ed. 1866).

[117] GC I, Art. 3; GC II, Art. 3; GC III, Art. 3; GC IV, Art. 3, *supra* note 63. *See also* ILA Armed Conflict Report, *supra* note 29 at 11 ("Common Article 3 is a revolutionary provision in that it was the first international treaty provision to attempt to regulate non-international armed conflict.").

[118] ILA Armed Conflict Report, *supra* note 27 at 11.

[119] Commentary on Geneva Convention Relative to the Treatment of Prisoners of War 35–36, August 12, 1949 (J S Pictet ed, 1960).

[120] More completely, the criteria are

(1) That the Party in revolt against the de jure Government possesses an organized military force, an authority responsible for its acts, acting within a determinate territory and having the means of respecting and ensuring respect for the Convention.

(2) That the legal Government is obliged to have recourse to the regular military forces against insurgents organized as military and in possession of a part of the national territory.

(a) That the de jure Government has recognized the insurgents as belligerents; or

(b) That it has claimed for itself the rights of a belligerent; or

(c) That it has accorded the insurgents recognition as belligerents for the purposes only of the present Convention; or

(d) That the dispute has been admitted to the agenda of the Security Council or the General Assembly of the United Nations as being a threat to international peace, a breach of the peace, or an act of aggression.

The general tenor of this commentary and much pre-September 11, 2001 state practice is reasonably clear. Governments retained discretion to deal with "banditry, unorganised and short-lived insurrections, or terrorist activities" free from Common Article 3 requirements both before and after formally accepting relevant HRL obligations.[121] By 1977, when the additional protocols to the 1949 Geneva Conventions were adopted, states steadfastly refused conventional IHL protections to non-state armed groups unless "under responsible command" and able to "carry out sustained and concerted military operations and to implement [Protocol II]."[122] The requirement for a qualifying non-state armed group to be both an organized and reasonably disciplined armed force able to follow applicable IHL is clear. Clandestine, relatively small, and diffuse non-state actors committing acts of transnational terrorism simply do not meet these requirements. Indeed, the 2015 Paris and other attacks show that these groups often intentionally and successfully inspire independent and uncontrolled acts of violence by anyone ideologically aligned with their views and goals.

The heightened nature of the violence necessary to establish non-international armed conflict has also been an important distinguishing feature for the application of IHL. As just noted, a significant factor to the existence of a non-international armed conflict under Common Article 3 is a concerted and sustained nature of organized dissident military operations that forces a state to have "recourse to the regular military forces." Protocol II distinguishes such violence from "situations of internal disturbances and tensions, such as riots, isolated and sporadic acts of violence and other acts of a similar nature, as not being armed conflicts,"[123] a distinction maintained in the Rome Statute of the

(e) That the insurgents have an organization purporting to have the characteristics of a State.
(f) That the insurgent civil authority exercises de facto authority over the population within a determinate portion of the national territory.
(g) That the armed forces act under the direction of an organized authority and are prepared to observe the ordinary laws of war.
(h) That the insurgent civil authority agrees to be bound by the provisions of the Convention.

Commentary on the Geneva Convention for the Amelioration of the Condition of the Wounded and Sick in Armed Forces in the Field August 12, 1949 (J S Pictet ed., 1952).

[121] ILA Armed Conflict Report, *supra* note 27 at 11 (citing Prosecutor v. Boskoski and Tarculovski, Case No. IT-04–82-T, Trial Judgment at ¶¶ 175,176 (Int'l Crim. Trib. for the Former Yugoslavia July 10, 2008).

[122] AP II, *supra* note 33 at Art. 1(1).

[123] *Id.* at Art. 1(2).

International Criminal Court.[124] Thus, in relevant treaties, states repeatedly set a higher threshold for the level of armed violence that would establish a non-international armed conflict and require the application of IHL. The sporadic nature of actual and attempted transnational terrorist attacks both before and after September 11, 2001 do not likely meet this threshold.

There is certainly evidence that some advocate a broader definition of armed conflict and a resulting broader application of IHL. The ICRC often encourages opposing parties to acknowledge fighting as armed conflict and to apply IHL.[125] This may simply reflect a belief that agreeing to observe some rules is better than following no rules at all. Because HRL does not regulate the violent activities non-state armed group(s), little *international* law does in the absence of an armed conflict and IHL. Thus, expanding the application of IHL is perhaps seen as the best way to advance humanitarian concerns and constrain the activities of non-state parties to protracted and systemic armed violence.

Common Article 1 of the 1949 Geneva Conventions promotes this broader obligation to observe IHL, requiring that states "undertake to respect and to ensure respect for the present Convention in all circumstances."[126] Of course, this hortatory provision did not change the treaties' terms regarding the point of inception or "triggering" of international armed conflict. In the decisions of the International Criminal Tribunal for the former Yugoslavia, there has been a general trend toward relaxing the requirements of Common Article 3, Protocol II, and their commentaries to find that an armed conflict existed, and hence, that there is jurisdiction to adjudicate war crimes.[127] While this inclination is understandable given the context, it is contrary to what has been the clear intent of states when adopting conventional IHL regulating non-international armed conflict.

124 Rome Statute, *supra* note 74 at Art. 8(2)(d) (excluding from non-international armed conflict "situations of internal disturbances and tensions, such as riots, isolated and sporadic acts of violence or other acts of a similar nature").

125 ILA Armed Conflict Report, *supra* note 27 at 4 (citations omitted).

126 ICCPR, *supra* note 40 at Art. 1.

127 *See* ILA Armed Conflict Report, *supra* note 27 at 19–22 (discussing cases, including the standards adopted and factors considered to determine whether the nature of the violence and of the parties qualified as armed conflict regulated by IHL). *See e.g.*, Prosecutor v. Milošević, Case No. IT-02-54-T, Decision on Motion for Judgment of Acquittal, ¶¶14–40 (Int'l Crim. Trib. for the Former Yugoslavia June 16, 2004) (applying Tadic criteria and dismissing ICRC Commentary as "neither definitive nor exhaustive").

D. *The "Normative Space" for an Alternate Approach*

Rather than attempt to create legal symmetry through uniform interpretation of the right of self-defense in both inter-state and transnational contexts, or through teleological interpretation and application of IHL or HRL, a better course might embrace what seems a traditionally more limited understanding regarding the scope of these bodies of law. States may then clarify the international law governing the resort to and use of transnational force to counter armed attacks by non-state actors from ineffectively governed territory. This is not law by analogy[128] or "folk" international law.[129] Rather, this approach accepts the ambiguity in international law's current content and scope rather than adopting or promoting preferred international legal norms. An unduly static or fixed view of the law is inconsistent with the very nature of international law, particularly customary international law.

With that said, it is important to recognize that circumscribing IHL and HRL within their proper limits does not result in a normative void. Doing so merely creates normative space in which competing international rights and obligations may be balanced. States must take affirmative measures to protect the human rights of their populations from known threats;[130] they have a general responsibility to protect their populations from harm.[131] Under the ICCPR interpretation accepted here, states must also respect the human rights of all people wherever located to the greatest extent possible. A proper approach must balance these rights and obligations, as well as the sovereign rights and obligations of territorial states.[132]

[128] See Chapter 7. [129] See Chapter 6.

[130] *See e.g.*, Ergi v. Turkey, App. No. 23818/94, Eur. Comm'n H.R. Dec. & Rep. ¶ 79, Judgment of 28 July, 1998 (concluding a state "may be required to take certain measures in order to "secure" an effective enjoyment of the right to life.").

[131] Int'l Comm. on Intervention and State Sovereignty, The Responsibility to Protect 13 (2001) ("Thinking of sovereignty as responsibility, in a way that is being increasingly recognized in state practice, has a threefold significance. First, it implies that the state authorities are responsible for the functions of protecting the safety and lives of citizens and promotion of their welfare. Secondly, it suggests that the national political authorities are responsible to the citizens internally and to the international community through the U.N. And thirdly, it means that the agents of state are responsible for their actions; that is to say, they are accountable for their acts of commission and omission.").

[132] *See e.g.*, *Extraterritorial Lethal Targeting, supra* note 9 at 86 ("A different, . . . normatively sounder, approach balances competing rights. . . . This approach contends that when the rights of states conflict in international law, the appropriate methodology is to seek the accommodation that best balances the object and purposes of those rights.").

III. Embracing Legal Asymmetry and Balancing Conflicting Obligations

The present ability of non-state actors to clandestinely coordinate and perpetrate mass-casualty attacks across borders amplifies the need for a state's formal legal (*de jure*) sovereignty to translate into actual (*de facto*) territorial control. Of course, states will never be perfectly capable of detecting and preventing all harms that may originate within or pass through their territories. Their ability to exercise reasonably effective control of that territory, however, is essential to fulfilling their internal and external sovereign and human rights obligations. When *de facto* sovereignty is substantially absent, the resort to and use of force regimes must be adapted to this reality.[133]

Accepting that neither IHL nor restrictive interpretations of HRL apply to the use of force in transnational self-defense moves us beyond static and dichotomous "armed conflict or law enforcement" debates. Embracing the fundamentally different nature and context of transnational armed attacks short of armed conflict offers a sounder approach. Complete HRL symmetry in the law of self-defense and transnational uses of force short of armed conflict in some cases may sacrifice the sovereignty and human rights of potential victim states and peoples to advance the human rights of terrorists and the sovereignty of territorial states unable to control them. Such an approach seems far more untenable and perverse than urging legal adaptations to the international law regulating self-defense for threats emanating from ineffectively governed territory.

This section offers a pragmatic balancing of relevant rights and interests. Regarding the resort to force, it considers various factors that affect the necessity analysis and argues for a more permissive right of transnational self-defense than exists between states. Specifically, it argues that the right of transnational self-defense must allow a potential victim state to counter a reasonably certain threat of an attack that will result in mass casualties when that state is also reasonably certain that the territorial state cannot or will not effectively do so. Regarding the use of force in transnational self-defense, it considers a range of international legal rules

[133] *See* Kenneth Watkin, *The President's Speech, Al Qaeda and the Legal Challenge of the Future*, Just Security (June 4, 2014), http://justsecurity.org/11197/guest-post-presidents-speech-al-qaeda-legal-challenge-future (Exclusionary approaches, which favor either human rights law or the law governing armed conflict do not match either the complexity of the threat, or the required sophistication of the response.)

that account for a lack of governing capacity to inform the proper norms to be adopted. These norms include collective targeting of those participating in collective violence, a requirement to capture rather than kill under certain circumstances, a prohibition upon collateral deaths unless strictly unavoidable, and temporary incommunicado investigatory detention. They do not allow for extraordinary courts or indefinite detention without trial.

A. *"Transnational Self-Defense" – The Resort to Force*

As earlier discussed, a state's inherent right of self-defense has traditionally been limited by the principles of necessity and proportionality and is often believed to be the same whether exercised in response to an actual or imminent attack by a state or non-state actor. However, some argue that the necessity principle of transnational self-defense is further limited by an alleged need to seek redress by a territorial state before resorting to self-help. This section explains why the necessity principle applicable to the exercise of transnational self-defense in ineffectively governed territory should be more permissive rather than less, given systemic differences in the context of transnational threats and the lack of state control over the instruments of non-state violence. It also posits how the proportionality principle of self-defense operates in this context.

1. Systemic Differences Regarding Inter-State and Transnational Threats

The law governing inter-state self-defense appears to be premised on the notion of a somewhat functional legal and political framework for interstate relations and the peaceful resolution of international disputes. States first adopted constraints on the resort to force in the Kellogg-Briand Pact, in which they condemned "recourse to war for the solution of *international controversies*" and "renounced war as an instrument of *national policy* in their relations with one another."[134] They also agreed to resolve their differences by peaceful means.[135] Later, states adopted a broad prohibition on the use of force but preserved their inherent right of self-defense[136] as part of a larger U.N. Charter framework for addressing and peacefully resolving threats to international peace and security.[137]

[134] General Treaty for the Renunciation of War (Kellogg-Briand Pact), Art. 1, August 27, 1928. (emphasis added)

[135] *Id.* at Art. 2. [136] U.N. Charter, Arts. 2(4), 51. [137] *Id.* at Arts. 23–54.

While the Charter system never has been and never will be entirely effective, states have the capacity to conduct bilateral and multilateral diplomatic exchanges outside the Charter system, through regional and other multilateral treaty organizations as well as presidents, prime ministers, foreign ministers, ambassadors, and others. In short, states may address and resolve their differences and disputes in myriad ways and forums. These formal and informal diplomatic channels facilitate the airing of grievances, including those involving military activities that generate insecurity. In any number of ways, assurances may be sought, activities explained, demands made, or sanctions imposed, all in an effort to clarify intentions and deter aggression. In this complicated, multidimensional environment with several potential coercive or non-binding enforcement mechanisms, states reserved their right of self-defense whenever an armed attack occurs, including when such an attack is truly immediate or imminent.

Contrast this multifaceted, albeit imperfect, system with the dearth of peaceful means to address violent non-state groups. Terrorist organizations choose force over peaceful dispute resolution and strike unexpectedly. The international legal and political system that encourages peaceful resolution of disputes between or among states has the opposite effect for non-state terrorist groups. Although such groups often have political goals, they are outsiders in the international system, largely limited to indirect communication channels to make demands and issue threats in order to bring attention to their grievances and agenda. There are no systemic disincentives to violence, particularly when the prospect of capture or prosecution is limited by a lack of local governing capacity.

2. Government Control over Instruments of Violence

These systemic differences are magnified by another factor, government control over the potential instruments of violence. Governments are typically in control of their militaries, although there have certainly been exceptions. Therefore, a state's explanations and assurances regarding military activities have added weight. Although governments are certainly not always honest regarding their intentions, deception will typically be discovered, as most traditional government military operations, particularly those that would inflict a large number of casualties, are difficult to hide from international view.

On the other hand, governments that lack governing capacity often lack the ability to detect or suppress the activities of violent non-state groups. Whether due to a lack of adequate law enforcement, military power, or some combination thereof, territorial states may simply be unable to apply measures necessary to prevent or suppress transnational armed attacks, even if they can detect or be notified of those attacks before they are launched. This lack of state control over the instruments of violence further amplifies the need for adapting the law of international peace and security to the new reality.

3. Balancing Sovereign Responsibilities in Context

As earlier mentioned, the resort to force in transnational self-defense implicates the sovereign rights and obligations of both attacking and territorial states. For potential attacking states, their affirmative obligation to ensure the human rights of their populations compels them to act to avert a reasonably certain threat. While states can usually delay action between their militaries to exhaust peaceful avenues of redress when possible, failing to prevent a reasonably certain transnational terrorist attack against their civilian population violates their internal HRL obligation to ensure human rights.

Attacking states must show due respect to the sovereignty of territorial states and the human rights of those states' populations. This includes the rights of those suspected of planning and conducting transnational armed attacks as well as the innocent civilians among whom such individuals hide. These obligations are as weighty as an attacking state's responsibility to protect its population, and must necessarily limit the discretion of attacking states to respond.

It is tempting to argue that existing inter-state self-defense law already balances these competing sovereign and human rights obligations. But as shown earlier, inter-state self-defense law developed with disputes between or among states in mind, and assumes a state's ability to control the instruments of violence. Thus, the right of transnational self-defense must allow a potential victim state to counter a reasonably certain threat of an attack that will result in mass casualties when that state is also reasonably certain that the territorial state cannot or will not effectively do so. This suggestion is not entirely new,[138] and is not without criticism,[139] but is justified when the entire range of relevant sovereign rights and obligations are considered.

[138] *See e.g.*, Daniel Bethlehem, *Self-Defense Against Imminent or Actual Armed Attack by Non-State Actors*, 106 AM. J. INT'L L. 770, 776 (2012).

[139] *See e.g.*, Elizabeth Wilmshurst, & Michael Wood, *Self-Defense Against Non-State: Reflections on the Bethlehem Principles*, 107 AM. J. INT'L L. 390 (2013); Dapo Akande &

A reasonably certain threat is one that available, reliable information strongly indicates will occur at some point in the future, even if the time and place are uncertain. A reasonable certainty of mass casualties is necessary for three reasons: first, to justify the infringement of sovereignty occasioned by resort to force in the territorial state; second, to justify the risk of harm created by the resort to force against suspected terrorists and any innocent bystanders; and third, to distinguish transnational armed attacks from routine transnational crime. For example, competing international drug traffickers involved in lethal duels across borders should not be understood to rise to the level of a transnational armed attack.

Reasonable certainty that a territorial state is unable or unwilling to effectively address a threatened transnational attack is necessary to justify the infringement of its sovereignty. This precondition to an exercise of transnational self-defense is met in at least three ways. First, it exists when there is substantial and reliable information that a territorial state has no effective control over a relevant portion of its territory and does not possess the capacity to gain effective control. Second, it exists when there is substantial and reliable information that there is insufficient time for a territorial state to marshal its available resources to counter a threat before it is likely to materialize. This necessarily requires some level of knowledge regarding the relative imminence of the threat. Third, it exists when there is substantial and reliable information that the territorial state will not take effective measures to counter the threat, even though it possesses the means to do so. In any of these circumstances, the attacking state is left with no choice but to resort to force in order to ensure the human rights of its population.

Proportionality in the resort to force context generally implies that the defensive act(s) must end when the circumstances that gave rise to it no longer exist. This is a difficult and contested issue in every context. Obviously, reasonable minds may certainly differ regarding whether a state may invade and destroy a perpetually hostile government or group that has attacked it or whether it may only counter any immediate threats posed.[140] Nevertheless, in the context of transnational self-defense, the

Thomas Liefländer, *Clarifying Necessity, Imminence and Proportionality in the Law of Self-Defense*, 107 AM. J. INT'L L. 563 (2013); Dire Tladi, *The Non-Consenting Innocent State: The Problem with Bethlehem's Principle 12*, 107 AM. J. INT'L L. 570 (2013).

140 *See e.g.*, DINSTEIN-WASD, *supra* note 25 at 219–244 (distinguishing defensive armed reprisals from defensive wars in timing, scope, duration, and ultimate potential result).

outer boundaries of proportionality seem to be a bit clearer because the territorial state is not a party to the violence. Therefore, proportionality requires that counterterrorism operations in transnational self-defense not infringe upon a territorial state's sovereignty any more than is absolutely necessary to address specific and known aspects of a reasonably certain threat. Otherwise, without consent to its continued presence, the attacking state would infringe too significantly on the territorial state's sovereignty. It is also necessary because an attacking state should "not seize or meaningfully occupy (temporally or geographically) foreign territory without sovereign consent," lest it create an international armed conflict.[141]

B. *"International Martial Law" – The Use of Force in Transnational Self-Defense*

Before presenting the rules regulating the specific uses of force in transnational self-defense, it is helpful to consider how international law has traditionally dealt with individuals engaging in unlawful violence in effectively ungoverned territory or spaces, such as trade routes (on land and sea), war zones, and in situations of riots or short-lived insurrections. Doing so yields consistent themes regarding the use of force in ungoverned spaces that inform what should be permissible in the context of transnational self-defense.

1. Trade Routes

States have long recognized that practical limitations of state sovereignty and governing capacity create ungoverned spaces, such as trade routes through remote lands or on the high seas. These areas have therefore traditionally had different norms for the use of force. Pirates and so-called highway robbers exploited gaps in governing capacity along these routes to violate the rights of states and their citizens.[142] Those engaging in such acts presented a threat not only to the geopolitical and

[141] *See* Akande, *supra* note 18. Recall that international armed conflict results from the used of armed force between states, and "to all cases of partial or total occupation of the territory of a High Contracting Party, even if the said occupation meets with no armed resistance." *Supra* note 64.

[142] Instructions for the Government of Armies of the United States in the Field (1863), Art. 83, *reprinted in* The Laws of Armed Conflicts: A Collection of Conventions, Resolutions and Other Documents 3 (Dietrich Schindler & Jirí Toman eds., 1988) [hereinafter Lieber Code] (irregular forces fighting without state

international legal order, such as it was, but also to individual rights. The law of nations denominated these acts "crimes against mankind" and sought to deter them by permitting any state to capture and summarily punish those who perpetrated them.[143]

2. War Zones

In the law of war, an analogous approach developed with respect to governance vacuums created by armed conflict. Under the Lieber Code of 1863 – widely recognized as the first codification of the law of war – armies that successfully displaced hostile forces and their government exercised martial law in the area of their operations.[144] Individuals who engaged in hostilities without affirmative state sanction, such as irregular forces and fighters, could be summarily punished.[145] Others who engaged in surreptitious means and methods of warfare, such as spies and saboteurs, were similarly treated.[146] And, civilians who used the fog of war to engage in acts hostile to their country or to a party to the conflict could also be punished.[147] Consistent with the Anglo-American common law approach to felonies, most offenses against the law of war were punishable by death.[148] And the law of war did not prescribe any specific procedural or evidentiary requirements for punishment.[149]

commission "are not entitled to the privileges of prisoners of war, but shall be treated summarily as highway robbers or pirates").

143 *See* Antonio Cassese & Paola Gaeta, Cassese's International Criminal Law 19 (3rd. ed. 2013); William Blackstone, Commentaries of the Laws of England 71 (1803).

144 Lieber Code, *supra* note 142 at Arts. 1–10.

145 *Id.* at Art. 82.

146 *Id.* at Arts. 83–85, 88.

147 *Id.* at Arts. 90–104, 157.

148 *Id.* at Arts. 44 (wanton violence, pillage, rape, maiming of inhabitants of invaded country), 58 (enslavement of captured enemy), 66 (member of unit granting no quarter), 77 (conspiracy among prisoners of war to escape or rebel), 82 (irregular fighters), 83 (scouts dressed as civilian or in uniform of his enemy), 83 ("war-rebels," meaning persons in occupied territory who take arms against occupier), 88 (spies to be hanged by the neck), 89 (citizen providing information to the enemy), 91 ("war-traitors," meaning those who betray to the enemy "anything concerning the condition, safety, operations, or plans of the troops holding or occupying the place or district"), 95 (voluntarily serving as enemy guide), 97 (providing false information as guide), 124 (breaking parole granted to prisoner of war), 127 (granting parole without proper authority).

149 U.S. commentary expanding upon the Lieber Code noted that a fair hearing was required. *See* Winthrop, *supra* note 70 at 841 ("In the absence of any statute or regulation governing the proceedings of military commissions, the same are commonly conducted according to the rules and forms governing courts-martial . . . are indeed more summary in their action than are the courts held under the Articles of war . . . their

It is against this historical background that we should consider human rights in the governance vacuums created by armed conflict. Early IHL treaties addressing the law of war on land, such as The Hague Conventions of 1899 and 1907, sought primarily to regulate the means and methods of warfare. They were "intended to serve as a general rule of conduct for the belligerents in their mutual relations and in their relations with the inhabitants."[150] Both included what is known as the Martens Clause, declaring that "in cases not included in the Regulations adopted by them, populations and belligerents remain under the protection and empire of the principles of international law, as they result from the usages established between civilized nations, from the laws of humanity, and the requirements of the public conscience."[151] Nevertheless, the relatively summary justice regime for irregular fighters and other hostile civilians articulated by Lieber remained largely intact. Prior to the Second World War, reprisals against a hostile civilian population as well as group and summary punishment of irregular fighters were neither uncommon nor considered intrinsically unlawful.[152]

It wasn't until the Geneva Conventions of 1949 that states sought to constrain the power of their battlefield commanders when punishing unlawful participants in war. Protections introduced by the 1949 Geneva Conventions were both very basic and incomplete, including a prohibition of "the passing of sentences and the carrying out of executions without previous judgment pronounced by a regularly constituted court, affording all the judicial guarantees which are recognized as indispensable by civilized peoples" in non-international armed conflict.[153] Although collective punishments were prohibited,[154] individual civilians

proceedings ... will not be rendered *illegal* by the omission of details required upon trials by courts-martial. . . ." (emphasis in original) (citations omitted)).

150 Hague Convention (IV) Laws and Customs of War on Land, October 18, 1907, 36 Stat. 2277.

151 *Id.* at preamble.

152 *See generally*, Frits Kalshoven, Belligerent Reprisals (2005); *see also* Sir Thomas Erskine Holland, The Laws of War on Land 60–61 (1908) (clarifying exceptional circumstances under which reprisals against the civilian population were then lawful); William Winthrop, Military Law and Precedent 798 (2nd ed. 1920) (similar); Ottfried Nippold, The Development of International Law After the World War 78–79 (1923) (calling for clarification of the law of reprisal after First World War); *see also* Judgement of the Nuremberg International Military Tribunal, United States of America vs. Otto Ohlendorf, et. al. ("Einsatzgruppen trial") (containing numerous charges for killing of hostages and *excessive* reprisals against civilian populations).

153 GC IV, *supra* note 64 at Art. 3(1)(d).

154 GC IV, *supra* note 64 at Art. 33.

could be punished for violations of the laws and customs of war committed before occupation by a hostile army.[155] At this point, though, there were still very few substantive and procedural protections prescribed by IHL. Most of what we would now consider a robust "due process" component of HRL did not materialize in conventional IHL until 1977, in the Additional Protocols to the 1949 Geneva Conventions. Both contained articles that preserved basic human and due process rights for those who did not clearly merit a protected status specifically defined and regulated by those treaties or other customary and conventional IHL.[156] Therefore, even within armed conflict, certain basic rights are now clearly protected for all who fall under a state's *actual* power and control.

Equally important, though, is the significantly reduced protection afforded the right to life of those who take a direct part in the hostilities of an armed conflict. As earlier mentioned, members of opposing armed forces may generally be attacked at any time.[157] Civilians are protected against direct attack by the armed forces of parties to an armed conflict. Civilians who take a direct part or role in those hostilities lose this protection for such time as they do so. They may even be attacked if their conduct does not directly threaten harm. The commentary to Additional Protocol I notes, "[d]irect participation in hostilities implies a direct causal relationship between the activity engaged in and the harm done to the enemy at the time and the place where the activity takes place."[158] Recent ICRC guidance on direct participation in hostilities clarifies, "where a specific act does not on its own directly cause the required threshold of harm, the requirement of direct causation would still be fulfilled where the act constitutes an integral part of a concrete and coordinated tactical operation that directly causes such harm."[159] Thus, those who participate in the collective violence of armed conflict may be attacked even if their actions standing alone do not pose a direct and immediate threat of harm. The recent ICRC guidance further notes, "[t]he causal relationship between the ... means [of participation] and the ensuing harm remains direct regardless of temporal or geographical proximity."[160] In other words, in the relatively ungoverned spaces

155 GC IV, *supra* note 64 at Art. 70.
156 *See* AP I, *supra* note 32 at Art. 75; AP II, *supra* note 33 at Art. 6.
157 *See* ILA Armed Conflict Report *supra* note 27.
158 Commentary on the Additional Protocols of June 8, 1977 to the Geneva Conventions of August 12, 1949 (Yves Sandoz et al. eds.) [hereinafter AP Commentary].
159 *DPH Interpretive Guidance*, *supra* note 33 at 54–55. 160 *Id.* at 55.

created by armed conflict, civilians who directly contribute to group or collective violence may be lawfully targeted and killed even if they do not individually pose an immediate threat of harm. If captured, civilian security threats may be indefinitely detained, including a period of incommunicado detention,[161] although they must eventually receive a fair trial before any punishment is imposed or inflicted.

3. Riots and Short-Lived Insurrections

A particularly difficult issue is whether or the extent to which a state can use lethal force or temporary security detention to restore order when there is violent resistance to state authority such that the state has substantially lost control of some portion of its territory. Recall that the ICCPR prohibits only arbitrary deprivations of life or liberty. The ECHR permits the deprivation of the right to life "in action lawfully taken for the purpose of quelling a riot or insurrection."[162] The ECHR therefore begs the question regarding the precise actions considered lawful. Neither, therefore, clearly addresses what is permitted in such circumstances.

It is often asserted that the U.N.'s *Basic Principles on the Use of Force and Firearms by Law Enforcement Officials* supports the idea that lawful uses of lethal force outside of armed conflict include only that which is absolutely necessary to counter an immediate threat.[163] However, a close reading of this document does not unequivocally support that assertion. The principles first require that law enforcement officials escalate the use of force, going from non-violent to violent means *when possible*.[164] It next clarifies that "[w]henever the lawful use of force and firearms is unavoidable," law enforcement officials should show "restraint in such use and act in proportion to the seriousness of the offence and the legitimate objective to be achieved" while minimizing "damage and injury" and respecting and preserving human life.[165] It continues, "[l]aw enforcement officials shall not use firearms against persons except in self-defence or defence of others against the imminent threat of death or serious injury," *or* "to *prevent* the perpetration of a particularly serious

[161] GC IV, *supra* note 64 at Art. 5. The commentary to Articles 5 and 136 suggest a period of two weeks. Commentary on the Geneva Convention of August 12, 1949 relative to the Protection of Civilian Persons in Time of War 53, 525 (J S Pictet ed., Geneva: ICRC, 1958).

[162] ECHR, *supra* note 44 at Art. 2(2).

[163] *Basic Use of Force Principles*, *supra* note 49.

[164] *Id.*

[165] *Id.*

crime involving grave *threat* to life," *or* "to arrest a person presenting such a danger and resisting their authority, or to prevent his or her escape."[166] Lethal force in any of these situations may be used "only when less extreme means are insufficient to achieve these objectives," and intentional lethal force must be "strictly unavoidable in order to protect life."[167]

While it is certainly reasonable to interpret "strictly unavoidable in order to protect life" as meaning only immediate threats to life, that is not the only fair reading of this phrase in the context of the document. If preventing truly imminent loss of life were absolutely required, the only ground for the use of lethal force would be in defense of self or others. The presence of other grounds permitting the intentional use of firearms and lethal force, including the *prevention* of crimes involving grave threats to life and *prevention of escapes* by those posing such dangers imply a degree of discretion in determining the point at which "other available means remain ineffective or without any promise of achieving the intended result."[168] Thus, "strictly unavoidable in order to protect life" seems to include the prevention of future harm that is serious and relatively certain but not necessarily imminent.

Given the violent and lawless nature of a riot or insurrection, both situations would seem to permit the use of firearms to *prevent* crimes involving grave threats to life regardless of whether such crimes are truly imminent, at least until the government can establish a superior force and effective control over the affected area. Depending upon the size and nature of rioting or rebelling groups, it may be difficult or impossible to make individualized determinations regarding the threats posed. If a violent group is advancing upon an isolated police officer or group of innocent civilians, for example, other officers need not wait until one or more individuals clearly initiate an imminent act of violence before responding with potentially deadly force. If mob violence posing a threat to life is reasonably certain, the use of deadly force may become absolutely necessary to prevent it unless clearly superior force can first be generated.

166 *Id.* 167 *Id.*

168 *ICRC, IHL-HRL Interplay Report, supra* note 10 at 7 (asserting that under these principles a "strict or 'absolute' necessity standard is attached to any use of force, meaning that force may not exceed what is strictly or absolutely necessary to protect life. Specifically, this implies that where possible, an arrest must be effected by using non-lethal means.").

Additionally, in this case, as with the case of a civilian taking a direct part in hostilities, the contributions of an individual to impending group violence need not be such as to directly inflict the harm to be prevented. It need only be more or less directly causal to that harm. Those who advocate for an individualized imminence determination in every case assume a degree of factual clarity that is simply inconsistent with dynamic situations like these. A group of experts considering the international law relevant to a violent riot occurring within the context of an armed conflict could not provide clarity regarding the applicable law, suggesting a situation could evolve from a law enforcement to war fighting event depending upon events and circumstances that would be extremely difficult for any one individual involved in the situation to gather and measure before using force.[169]

4. Balancing Obligations and the Norms Governing the Use of Force

The earlier discussion clarifies that when states are unable to monopolize and control violence, they have relaxed the international rules regarding who may be the subject of lethal force and under what circumstances. Although it is common to oversimplify the law enforcement paradigm, states facing the difficult task of maintaining order in dynamic situations attempt to balance the rights of peaceful individuals with those who engage in armed violence. Nowhere is that task more difficult than within the territory of an ineffectively governed state. Those who project unlawful violence across borders to deprive others of their most basic human rights should not be protected by overly restrictive interpretations of HRL, or by the rights of the sovereign whose territory they exploit. These should not be a complete or substantial shield to effective suppression and prevention of their unlawful activities. On the other hand, the rights of those suspected of involvement in transnational terrorist attacks and the innocent civilians among whom they are often found requires a careful balancing of the power to take life in order to preserve others. Moreover, basing a state's right to take defensive action in its affirmative

[169] *Id.* at 26–27 ("[S]ituations of civilian unrest in the context of an armed conflict can be highly volatile and can turn into actual armed clashes amounting to hostilities. Thus, a situation . . . could become mainly governed by the conduct of hostilities paradigm if fighters or civilians directly participating in hostilities actually outnumber peaceful and rioting civilians (whose acts do not amount to direct participation in hostilities). In other words, a situation can change in nature and the predominant paradigm may not always be the same.").

HRL obligations requires considering each life that may be lost in more absolute terms.

Accounting for these many variables related to transnational terrorism and self-defense supports adopting of the following norms regulating the use of force:

(1) Terrorist organizations or individuals may be targeted (for capture or with lethal force, discussed next) if a state is reasonably certain, based upon available and reliable information, that they are preparing to conduct an attack causing mass casualties, even if the time and location of the attack is uncertain. The specific actions of individuals to be targeted must indicate that they will directly inflict the harm or be within one causal step of inflicting harm. This form of collective targeting substitutes conduct for status as the sole basis for targeting, but does not require imminent harm as a precondition to the resort to force. It is justified by the risk of substantial harm that such individuals pose, which is more than a routine criminal act, and the substantial risk that a clandestine transnational attack may not be detected at the point it becomes imminent. A state's obligation to ensure the basic human rights of its population requires it to prevent acts involving a grave threat to many lives.

(2) Suspected terrorists must be captured if feasible. Feasibility does not depend upon whether an attacking state can, solely as a factual matter, capture a terrorist. It is a lesser harm analysis in which the anticipated casualties of a capture operation should not be greater than those that would result from lethal targeting. This approach accounts for the reduced human rights protections to be afforded transnational terrorists. It also recognizes that capturing some terrorists may risk substantial casualties for an attacking state, and that such casualties need not be accepted if they can be avoided by lethal targeting. This approach, however, also ensures that the state will respect the lives of those in the territorial state and may not subordinate the lives of anticipated innocent victims of a counter-terrorism operation to the lives of its operatives or agents. Doubt regarding anticipated casualties should be resolved in favor of capture.

(3) Respect for the human rights of a territorial state's population, including suspected terrorists, requires that if the basis of a resort to force is consent, and a territorial state limits its consent to stand-off targeting only, the attacking state must nevertheless comply with this lesser harm requirement. It must either seek expanded consent

for a capture operation if fewer casualties would result, or determine that such consent is not reasonably forthcoming. If such consent is not provided or forthcoming, the attacking state must consider the territorial state ineffectively governed for the purpose of each operation for which capture is feasible, and must violate the conditions of consent and conduct a capture operation.

(4) Lethal counterterrorism operations should not cause *anticipated* harm to individuals not targetable under these standards unless absolutely unavoidable. This requirement is in addition to the feasibility of capture analysis required earlier. In other words, not only must an attacking state determine that fewer total casualties are reasonably likely to result from its operation, but also that any anticipated harm to those not subject to targeting must be avoided if at all possible. This limitation is also required by the obligation to respect the human rights of the territorial state's population, and is much, much narrower than the proportionality standard applicable to armed conflict.

(5) Captured suspected terrorists are subject to temporary investigatory incommunicado detention. Such detention should be no longer than necessary to elicit relevant information regarding an impending attack or a period of two weeks, whichever is shorter. After this period expires, captured individuals must be transferred for regular civilian criminal proceedings or released. This approach is obviously adapted from the provisions regulating security threats in armed conflict. However, it eschews indefinite preventive detention in favor of the substantive and procedural protections of the criminal justice system. Although uncertainty surrounding transnational armed attacks justifies a period of incommunicado detention to elicit relevant information regarding impending threats, it does not justify prolonged internment, prolonged inability to access legal counsel or family, or extraordinary courts.[170]

IV. Conclusion

States and scholars have been groping for legal arguments to justify entirely sensible and appropriate acts of transnational self-defense because standard legal regimes are thought to be unsatisfactory. The

[170] In an early instance of what could properly be called martial law in the U.S., military forces, led by Alexander Hamilton, used force as a last resort, used incommunicado detention and interrogation but also required punishment to be imposed by the local civilian courts. See RON CHERNOW, ALEXANDER HAMILTON 468–478 (2005).

standards regulating the resort to and use of force in self-defense applicable between states are simply not designed to deal with the contemporary ability of non-state actors to commit transnational violence resulting in mass casualties. Regarding the resort to force, attacking states will never and should never place the sovereignty of territorial states and the human rights of terrorists above their obligation to ensure the human rights of their population. Likewise, when a territorial state can prevent transnational threats in order to respect the sovereign rights of other states and the human rights of their populations, it should. When it cannot or will not, potential victim states and peoples must not be left without effective recourse. The right to resort to force must be separated from the right of self-defense existing between states and modified to meet the threat and circumstances.

This chapter attempts to refocus the current debate by recognizing that the resort to and use of force legal standards have historically been and continue to be less clear or fixed than is often asserted, particularly in ineffectively governed or ungoverned territory. It also attempts to more responsibly balance competing rights and obligations than would be achieved by extending law enforcement or armed conflict paradigms to this context.

A potential objection to this approach is that it favors states with advanced militaries able to project lethal force across borders without physically occupying foreign territory. The standards proposed, however, are broad enough to permit "conventional" military force to engage in limited transnational self-defense operations. The acceptable risks and necessary methods might differ, but the relevant considerations should not.

Another potential objection is that these standards do not require external or judicial review to prevent abuse or error. As has been made clear in the earlier analysis, however, no standards governing the use of force in IHL or HRL have been defined, explained, or interpreted with the precision necessary to prevent abuse or error. The rule of law depends as much for its existence upon voluntary, good faith interpretation and compliance as it does the existence of external checks and balances. It is not the purpose of this chapter to address the latter, but to propose the standards that should govern the former.

Ultimately, the attacks of September 11, 2001 and those that have followed it did not and should not change everything about the law regulating the resort to and use of force in self-defense. Those attacks did demonstrate, however, a need to reassess permissible responses to transitional terrorist attacks. In the present patchwork of global governance, well-developed concepts of the resort to and use of force in transnational self-defense – concepts that view human rights as both sword and shield – are essential and unavoidable. Whither international martial law? Yes, if we wish to better protect human rights by avoiding the greater evil of the lives to be lost by applying inter-state standards regulating the resort to or use of force to transnational terrorist violence.

10

The Next Geneva Convention

Filling a Law-of-War Gap with Human Rights Values

BRIAN OREND

In general, this chapter is a case study for how, and in what ways, international human rights law (IHRL) and humanitarian values more broadly can help the laws of armed conflict (LOAC). There is evidence in favor of a kind of convergence and mutual support between the two bodies of law, especially since the mid-twentieth century.[1] Perhaps it is more a reflection of the overall moral and political mindset of our times, but it is quite hard – when contemplating issues of armed conflict, the behavior of belligerents, and the treatment of nations and peoples – not to view the one at least partly through the prism of the other. This may reflect the hegemony which human rights has come to exert over our thinking about the most fundamental ways in which institutional structures, and political practices (including international ones), ought to be shaped. As John Rawls has declared, human rights form the bedrock of political legitimacy in our time.[2]

In particular, this chapter alleges that *there is a big, bad gap in the LOAC, which ought to be remedied by filling it in with values and principles gleaned from the IHRL*. Specifically, it is argued that – in stark contrast to the immense detail and sophistication of the LOAC in connection with the outbreak of war (*jus ad bellum*) and with conduct during war (*jus in bello*) – there is next-to-no clear and effective attempt, in the LOAC, to regulate the termination phase of war (or "*jus post bellum*"). Reasons will be given for why this is, at least, sub-optimal – and, at most

[1] Please note the supportive, and the contrasting, understandings of this "mutual support thesis" between IHRL and LOAC displayed by the other contributors throughout this volume. See, too: United Nations, International Legal Protection of Human Rights in Armed Conflict (New York: United Nations, 2012); C.L. Sriram, *et al.*, War, Conflict, and Human Rights: Theory and Practice (London: Routledge, 2nd edition, 2014); and G. Oberleitner, Human Rights in Armed Conflict: Law, Practice, Policy (Cambridge: Cambridge University Press, 2015).

[2] J. Rawls, The Law of Peoples (Cambridge: Harvard University Press, 1999), 8–9.

(and quite probably), disappointing and even dangerous. In my view (and for the sake of tapping into prior, prominent name recognition), the international community should negotiate and ratify a brand new Geneva Convention; and it ought to be exclusively devoted to articulating principles to guide belligerents in the aftermath of armed conflict. But where should such principles come from? The IHRL – or, more precisely, from a combination of principles contained within the IHRL and the LOAC, drawing insight along the way from historical best practices. Effort will then be expended to develop and explain such principles, or at least to argue in favor of a coherent and reasonable set of proposed post-war rules and regulations.

1. A Gap in the LOAC

Historically, it was assumed that, as the old saying goes, "to the victor go the spoils of war." As a result of this widespread belief, there is next-to-no clear international law regulating the termination phase of war. "Next-to-no," because admittedly there *are* a handful of fragments of law regarding war termination. For instance, there are Articles 32–41 of The Hague Convention IV (1907). But such laws are: 1) very dated, over 100 years old now; 2) quaint, even; and 3) radically thin and lacking in action-guiding substance. Consider, e.g., Article 32:

> A person is regarded as bearing a flag of truce who has been authorized by one of the belligerents to enter into communication with the other, and who advances bearing a white flag. He has a right to inviolability, as well as the trumpeter, bugler or drummer, the flag-bearer and interpreter who may accompany him.

And Article 37:

> An armistice may be general or local. The first suspends the military operations of the belligerent States everywhere; the second only between certain fractions of the belligerent armies and within a fixed radius.[3]

Contrast such quaint banality with the manifold laws and treaties which regulate the outbreak of war (*jus ad bellum*) and emphatically conduct within war (*jus in bello*). For instance, in terms of the *jus ad bellum*, the

[3] In War and International Justice: A Kantian Perspective (Waterloo, ON: Wilfrid Laurier University Press, 2000), pp. 218–20, I go through all these articles systematically, and contrast their datedness, quaintness, and vagueness with the modernity and substantiality of the rules designed to govern the outbreak of, and conduct within, war.

following are just a sample of relevant laws, resolutions, judgments, and treaties directly addressing the subject of the outbreak of hostilities:

- Hague Convention I & III (1907)
- The Kellogg-Briand Pact (1928)
- Charter of the United Nations (1945), especially Articles 1, 2, 5, 6, 23–7 and 33–54
- United Nations General Assembly Definition of Aggression (1974)
- Decision of the International Court of Justice on *Nicaragua vs. United States of America* (1986)
- Any one of a range of United Nations Security Council (UNSC) resolutions authorizing the use of force in such recent armed conflicts as: the Persian Gulf War (1991); the Bosnian civil war (1992–95); Somalia (1993); Kosovo (1999); Afghanistan (2001); and Libya (2011)

And these various pieces of *jus ad bellum* law explain and expound four strong legal principles (and perhaps two further norms of customary expectation) regarding the question of when, if ever, states may resort to armed force. The answer (in list form) is that states may fight *only if* they satisfy *all* of the following legal rules: Just Cause; Proportionality; Public Declaration of War by a Proper Authority; and Last Resort. (The two further, softer norms of expectation, include: Right Intention [in terms of being motivated mainly – or only – by the just cause]; and Probability of Success).[4]

To quickly illustrate the much greater effort and clarity on *jus ad bellum*,[5] compared to *jus post bellum*, consider how almost all international lawyers endorse the following framework understanding of the seminal Just Cause rule, especially for instance as codified in Article 51 of the U.N. Charter:

Step 1: All countries have the inherent, or "natural," right to go to war in self-defence from aggression. (Aggression is defined, initially, as the first use of force against another country. Any armed attack which

[4] For much more on the content and complexities of these *jus ad bellum* principles, alongside case studies, consult: M. Walzer, Just and Unjust Wars (New York: Basic Books, 1977), 3–33 and 51–126; & B. Orend, The Morality of War (Peterborough, Canada: Broadview, 2nd edition, 2013), 33–110.

[5] Please note the "much greater clarity and effort" language: not that there isn't residual vagueness (and many subjects for dispute) within the *jus ad bellum*. But, for all that, it is still *so much more* developed – and full of helpful content – in contrast to the *jus post bellum*. Ditto, as we'll see, for the *jus in bello vs. post bellum*.

crosses an international border constitutes aggression and is a *casus belli*, i.e., "a cause for war." Put otherwise, aggression is the unjustified use of armed force to violate the two core rights which any legitimate, recognized country enjoys under international law: i.e., political sovereignty and territorial integrity.)

Step 2: All countries have the further "natural," or inherent, right of other-defense – otherwise known as "collective security" – to go to war as an act of aid, or assistance, to *any* country victimized by aggression; and

Step 3: *Any other* use of force – e.g., pre-emptive strike, or armed humanitarian intervention (AHI) – is *not* an inherent, or natural, right of states. Any country wishing to engage in such is supposed to get *the prior approval* of the UNSC. Failing to receive such prior authorization renders any such use of force illegal, itself an act of aggression.[6]

Suffice it to say that there is no such analogous consensus regarding substantive *jus post bellum* principles. We see this, too, when we quickly examine the general structure of the *jus in bello*. Consider the following small sample of relevant laws, resolutions, judgments, and treaties directly addressing the subject of the proper methods (tactics) and means (especially weapons) used during fighting:

- United States' Field Army Manual (or "Lieber's Code") (1863)
- Hague Conventions (1899–1907)
- Convention Regulating Poisonous Gases (1925)
- Convention Regulating Genocide (1948)
- Geneva Conventions (1949)
  - Additional Protocols to the Geneva Conventions (1977 and 1996)
- Convention Regulating Cultural Property and Sites during Wartime (1954)

[6] With the LOAC, I prefer, and have used extensively: W. Reisman and C. Antoniou, eds. The Laws of War: A Comprehensive Collection of Primary Documents Governing Armed Conflict (New York: Vintage, 1994). But see also: G. Best, War and Law Since 1945 (Oxford: Clarendon, 1994); M. Byers, War Law (Washington, DC: Atlantic, 2009); A. Gillespie, History of The Laws of War (New York: Hart, 3rd edition, 2011); M. Howard, The Laws of War: Constraints on Warfare in The Western World (New Haven: Yale University Press, 1994); D. Kennedy, Of War and Law (Princeton, Princeton University Press, 2006); S. Neff, War and The Law of Nations (Cambridge: Cambridge University Press, 2008); A. Roberts & R. Guelff, eds. Documents on the Laws of War (Oxford: Oxford University Press, 3rd edition, 2000); G. Simpson, Law, War and Crime (Oxford: Polity, 2007); & G. Solis, The Law of Armed Conflict (Cambridge: Cambridge University Press, 2010).

- United Nations General Assembly Resolutions Prohibiting Nuclear Weapons (1961) and (1973)
- Convention Regulating Aircraft Offenses (1963), including Aircraft Seizure (1970) and Civil Aviation Safety (1971)
- Convention Regulating Biological Weapons (1972)
- Convention Regulating Diplomatic Agents during Wartime (1973)
- Convention Regulating Weapons Which Modify the Environment (1976)
- Convention Regulating Hostages during Wartime (1979)
- Convention Regulating Excessively Injurious or Indiscriminate Weapons (1980)
- Convention on the Prohibition of the Use, Stockpiling, Production, and Transfer of Anti-Personnel Mines, and On Their Destruction (1999)

Any one of these treaties stipulates dozens – and often hundreds – of very detailed rules regarding what counts as a banned weapon, and/or what counts as the kind of tactic which it seeks to prohibit. For instance, Article 6 of the Convention on Excessively Injurious Weapons defines what a "booby trap" is, and goes on to list ten specific things to which it is prohibited to attach a booby trap, such as: items for food and drink; children's toys; any kind of medical equipment; items of religious significance; dead or wounded human bodies, or the bodies of animals. Again, suffice it to say that such (just one tiny *jus in bello* rule) is a long way – in detail, sophistication, and stringent binding-ness – from the earlier quoted *post bellum* Hague Article on waving a white flag of truce and being accompanied by a trumpeter as one moves to surrender.[7]

Just as with *jus ad bellum*, there has emerged over the centuries quite stable expert consensus on the general framework of *jus in bello* principles (even if not always of how exactly they apply in concrete cases). In list form they are: Discrimination / Non-Combatant Immunity; Benevolent Quarantine for Prisoners-of-War (POWs); Follow the Doctrine of Double Effect (DDE); Proportionality; No Illegal Weapons (especially Weapons of Mass Destruction [WMD]); No Means "*Mala in Se*"

[7] Please see note 6 for sources on the laws. For very valuable and thorough online sourcing of the LOAC, see:

The Avalon Project at Yale Law School: www.yale.edu/lawweb/avalon/lawofwar/lawwar.htm

University of Minnesota Law of Armed Conflict: www1.umn.edu/humanrts/instree/auoy.htm

Air War College: www.au.af.mil/au/awc/awcgate/awc-law.htm.

(or "evil-in-themselves," like torture); and No Reprisals (which are tit-for-tat violations of the rules).[8] Once more: there is nothing approaching such consensus, or such content-ful principles, when we turn to consider the termination phase of war. Suffice it then to conclude that it has now been shown – perhaps not in absolute terms, but certainly in relative terms – that the endings of war are woefully under-regulated compared to both the outbreak of war and conduct within war.[9]

2. Why the Post-War LOAC Gap is Bad, and Should be Filled

There are many reasons why this substantial under-development of proper war-termination is harmful, and ought to be remedied with a new Geneva Convention devoted exclusively to post-war justice. They include:

- ***Completion.*** As shown earlier, there are many international laws regulating both the start of war and the middle of war. Moreover, many of these laws make sound strategic, and good moral, sense.[10] Thus, to complete our analysis of war's many impacts on international life, we need to consider the ending phase of war. Bottom line: if it's important to guide both *the start* and *the middle*, it's just as important to guide *the end.*
- ***Focus.*** The practical task of drafting, and then ratifying, a binding legal document on this issue – or even just achieving more consensus on the ethical principles – would focus international attention on doing something constructive and improving about war in general, and take *jus*

[8] For much more on the content and complexities of these *jus in bello* principles, alongside case studies, consult: WALZER, WARS, 34–50 and 127–224; & OREND, MORALITY, 11–184.

[9] The earlier section has been my reply to those at the conference who challenged my assertion whether there is such a gap at all. This was a helpful challenge, requiring a substantial reply. Lawyers, obviously, are taught to abhor a legal vacuum – and to be suspicious about whether there ever are such. Strictly, as stated, I'm not saying there's a total vacuum but, obviously, a relative one. And two further points: there *is* an aspect of post-war justice which has, post-1945, come to enjoy some clear and substantial international legal regulation, and this concerns war crimes trials. Mention will be made of this below (see also Note 49). And there is something else called "Occupation Law," also to be mentioned at the proper time (see also Notes 78–79).

[10] D. LACKEY, THE ETHICS OF WAR AND PEACE (Englewood Cliffs, NJ: Prentice Hall, 1989). Consider, e.g., how the rule of proportionality makes both good moral sense (precluding needless killing and violence) and sound strategic advice (consistent with "economy of force" principles, and the effective marshalling of one's finite resources).

post bellum out of abstract theory and into the concrete reality of global politics.

- ***Guidance.*** The function of any kind of law is to guide behavior, hopefully in a way useful, advantageous, and improving for all.[11] The laws of *jus ad bellum* and *jus in bello* are designed to guide the behavior of all belligerents. The rules of *jus post bellum* could likewise guide both the winner and the loser in the aftermath of armed conflict. (This is assuming there even *is* a clear-cut winner and loser, which sometimes *isn't* the case, such as with the Iran-Iraq War of 1979–89, when the belligerents just stopped fighting after – eventually – realizing that neither of them could prevail.)[12] *Both winners and losers would gain by there being clear post-war rules.* The losers, of course, could be assured that they would not be subjected to cruel, vindictive treatment at the hands of a gloating, arrogant winner. And the winners could get a clear understanding of their rights and obligations during the aftermath of war. In particular, winners would appreciate being able to point to such rules and say: "Look, we've done what we're duty-bound to do, and now we are out of here." Rules provide assurances and expectations for everyone, plus clear ways of proceeding, and all parties benefit from such clarity and can put greater confidence in the process moving forward.[13]
- ***Ending the Fighting.*** Failure to regulate war termination probably prolongs fighting on the ground. Since they have few assurances, or firm expectations, regarding the nature of the settlement, belligerents will be sorely tempted to keep using force to jockey for position. Since international law imposes very few constraints upon the winners of war, losers can conclude it is reasonable for them to refuse to surrender and, instead, to continue to fight. Perhaps, they think: "We might get lucky and the military tide will turn. Better that than just throw ourselves at the mercy of our enemy." Many observers felt this reality plagued the Bosnian civil war (1992–95), which had many failed

[11] R. Wacks, Understanding Jurisprudence (Oxford: Oxford University Press, 3rd edition, 2012).

[12] W. Murray & K. Woods, The Iran-Iraq War (Cambridge: Cambridge University Press, 2014).

[13] This is my reply to those conference participants who said that winners would never accept restrictions on their conduct in the post-war moment. See also: A. Cassese, International Law (Oxford: Oxford University Press, 2nd edition, 2005) & M. Shaw, International Law (Cambridge: Cambridge University Press, 2008).

negotiations and a three-year "slow burn" of continuous violence as the very negotiations took place.[14]

- ***Restraining the Winner.*** Failure to construct principles of *jus post bellum* is to allow unconstrained war termination. And to allow unconstrained war termination is, indeed, to allow the winner to enjoy the spoils of war. This is dangerously permissive, since winners have been known to exact peace terms which are draconian and vengeful. The Treaty of Versailles, terminating World War I in 1918–19, is often mentioned in this connection. It is commonly suggested that the sizable territorial concessions, and steep compensations payments, forced upon Germany created hatred and economic distress, opening a space for Hitler to capitalize on, saying in effect: "Let's vent our rage by recapturing our lost lands, and let's rebuild our economy by refusing to pay compensation, and by ramping up war-related manufacturing."[15]
- ***Preventing Future Wars.*** When wars are wrapped up badly, they sow the seeds for future bloodshed. Some people, e.g., think that America's failure to remove Saddam Hussein from power after they first beat him in 1991 prolonged a serious struggle and eventually necessitated the second war, of regime change, in 2003. *Would the second war have happened at all had the first been ended differently* – i.e., more properly and thoroughly, with a longer-range vision in mind? Many historians ask the exact same question of the two World Wars and the recent, related Serb wars, first in Bosnia and then over Kosovo (1999).[16]

Peace treaties should still, of course, remain tightly tailored to the historical realities of the particular conflict in question. There is much nitty-gritty detail which is integral to each peace treaty. But admitting this is *not* to concede that the search for general guidelines, or universal standards, is futile or naïve. There is no inconsistency, or mystery, in holding particular actors, in complex local conflicts, up to more general, even universal, standards of conduct. Judges and juries do that on a daily basis, evaluating the factual complexities of a given case in light of general

[14] D. Reiff, Slaughterhouse: Bosnia and The Failure of the *West* (New York: Simon and Schuster, 1995). Such a (severe) problem of lack of mutual trust and expectation leading to interminable fighting plagues efforts to settle the protracted and complicated Arab-Israeli conflict. See, e.g.: J. Gelvin, The Modern Middle East (Oxford: Oxford University Press, 3rd edition, 2011) & K. Schulze, The Arab-Israeli Conflict (London: Longman, 2nd edition, 2008).

[15] M. Boemeke, ed. The Treaty of Versailles (Cambridge: Cambridge University Press, 1998) & M. Macmillian, Paris 1919 (New York: Macmillan, 2003).

[16] William Martel, Victory in War (Cambridge: Cambridge University Press, 2011).

moral and legal principles. We should do the same regarding war termination.[17]

3. Overcoming Important Challenges Regarding the Starting Assumptions behind *Jus Post Bellum*

3.1. When Does War End?

Now, some have argued that the "termination phase" of war often does not have a clear starting point, and/or that the notion of victory itself can be quite vague.[18] This is important, as: when will the norms of *jus post bellum* kick in? And out, as it were? Locating the exact "end" of war may well, at times, be quite difficult; and it may turn out, as already noted, that victory is only one possible outcome (alongside defeat, indeterminacy, military victory but political loss, vice-versa, etc.). Thus, *we should think of the war termination phase, crucially, as a kind of process* – along a continuum – wherein there aren't razor-sharp distinctions between the *jus in bello* phase and the *jus post bellum* phase; and the end result may be a number of things, with victory for one side being only one – albeit important – option.[19]

That said, the LOAC is confronted with a similar issue elsewhere, notably at the beginning of war when the question arises: when has a war truly begun? This can strike some people as simple and obvious: "well, when the shooting starts, no?" But the answer actually is not so clear and both international lawyers and social scientists have grappled with the issue of when a war can truly said to have begun, such that the principles of *jus ad bellum* have kicked in – or, rather (depending on the timing), those of *jus in bello* and other humanitarian law principles.[20] Social scientists, e.g., have long argued that a war doesn't count as a war until there are 1,000

[17] S.J. Cimbala, Strategic War Termination (New York: Praeger, 1986); S. Albert and E. Luck, eds. On the Endings of Wars (London: Kennikat Press, 1980); F.O. Hampson, Nurturing Peace: Why Peace Settlements Succeed or Fail (Washington, DC: U.S. Institute of Peace, 1996).

[18] I'm indebted to Michael Walzer, of Princeton University, for pushing me on this. See also: G. Blum, "*The Fog of Victory*", European Journal of International Law (2013), 391–421.

[19] P.R. Pillar, Negotiating Peace: War Termination as a Bargaining Process (Princeton: Princeton University Press, 1983).

[20] D. Fleck, The Handbook of Humanitarian Law in Armed Conflicts (Oxford: Oxford University Press, 1995).

battlefield casualties.[21] Some such threshold is thought needed to distinguish between a genuine war and, say, a large-scale domestic police action (e.g., against heavily-armed drug dealers, or inner-city rioters). And international lawyers have long insisted that the use of force in question, to count as a war, must not only meet a kind of *quantum threshold of violence or killing*, but also that it must be to some considerable degree *widespread* (not merely, e.g., a skirmish between rival border patrols) and to *express the deliberate will of the belligerents* in question.[22] This question was recently wrestled with, prominently, in The Tadic decision of the International Criminal Tribunal for the former Yugoslavia. "The Tadic criteria," as they have come to be called, specify a set of criteria which must be met for an armed conflict truly to exist in a legally relevant sense: fighting below such a threshold – while still fighting – is nevertheless not thought to count as an armed conflict or war because it is not widespread enough, and/or there is not sufficient quantum of killing force being deployed, and/or there is an issue about whether one or more of the belligerents truly intends the violence (as opposed to, say, a rogue group within the organization which doesn't truly represent it).[23] By analogy with these *jus ad bellum* issues, one could say: a similar thing happens toward the end of armed conflict. Even though there may still be sporadic fighting, once that fighting has dropped below a threshold we expect of warfare, then for our purposes the war has stopped, or at least has truly begun a war termination process, and we can now meaningfully speak of new norms being needed – such as those of *jus post bellum*.[24]

3.2. *The Vagueness of Victory*

The reason why most conceptions of post-war justice focus on (or even assume) victory is not simple-mindedness, or a failure to realize that wars

[21] K.J. Holsti, Peace and War (Cambridge: Cambridge University Press, 1991); C. Gelpi, *et al.*, Paying the Human Costs of War (Princeton: Princeton University Press, 2009). And note how such a standard raises interesting issues of what a "battlefield casualty" might be, especially for instance in the case of such recent dense urban fighting environments as those in Mogadishu during the intervention in Somalia in 1993, or else of course in the Gaza Strip.

[22] Orend, Morality, 2–4.

[23] ICTY, The Prosecutor v Dusko Tadic, Judgment, IT-94-1-T, May 7, 1997. See also S. Vite, "*Typology of Armed Conflicts in International Humanitarian Law*", International Review of The Red Cross (2009), 69–84.

[24] I'm grateful to Jens Ohlin, of Cornell University Law School, for help on this point.

can end in truly messy and muddled ways.[25] Rather, the focus is methodological: it is just easier to start with more ideal cases, and then move to messier ones. Thus, when we talk about *jus post bellum*, it is just easier to take the ideal case where the just side (in terms of *jus ad bellum*, e.g., the Victim of an aggressive invasion) has achieved a clear victory (e.g., over the prior Aggressor whose actions triggered the war), and then ask about rights and duties in those situations. This turns out to be surprisingly hard in itself, and laden with controversy (as we will see later). *But it needs to be done before moving on to the more complex cases.* Think of it as directly analogous to the *jus ad bellum*: in the ideal case there, you have the vital, foundational concepts of: a) aggression; and b) defense from aggression. These two binary concepts are absolutely central in both the morality and law of the *jus ad bellum*.[26] One thinks through the rights and duties in such an ideal case, and then uses them to wade into such trickier, more advanced concepts as: preventive war and anticipatory attack; civil war; AHI; asymmetrical war against non-state actors; and so on.[27] We are here firmly in the realm of the ideal, trying to make sense of the best concepts and principles, and then to apply them to more muddled and difficult cases. Hence some simplifying starting assumptions (*already embedded in the existing LOAC*)[28] about Aggressor and Victim, loss and victory, and – as we'll see later – retribution versus rehabilitation as post-war policy.

(As a helpful initial claim, I'd say that victory has been achieved when the goal for which the war was started has been achieved: e.g., if the goal was to repulse an Aggressor and kick it out of the Victim country which it had invaded, then the *post bellum* phase begins when that has been achieved. There may still be some actual fighting going on at that time, but clearly the victorious country will then move to shut down the violence after that point. This would be a grey area between the *jus in bello* and the *jus post bellum*. Once the violence has subsided [usually accompanied by a cease-fire or surrender] – and emphatically if the regime in Aggressor has collapsed – then it becomes progressively clearer that we've entered an importantly new and different phase of war termination and possibly

[25] I appreciate Cian O'Driscoll, of the University of Glasgow, for pushing me on this.

[26] As noted earlier, and consult, Notes 4, 6, & 7.

[27] For more on non-traditional forms of armed conflict, see, e.g., Orend, Morality, 71–110.

[28] W. Reisman and C. Antoniou, eds. The Laws of War: A Comprehensive Collection of Primary Documents Governing Armed Conflict (New York: Vintage, 1994).

post-war occupation and regime transformation. Not to pretend that such is a complete definition of victory: merely a useful, *prima facie* one for the purposes of moving our discussion onward.)[29]

4. With What Rules and Values Should the Post-War LOAC Gap Be Filled?

As stated earlier, there seem to be two plausible legal sources for filling in this harmful gap in the LOAC: they are the general principles already contained within the existing LOAC (i.e., the rules of *jus ad bellum* and *jus in bello*), plus the general principles contained in IHRL. And there's probably a third: namely, the major policies at play – historically – in post-war situations. More about these policies next section.[30] Here, we comment on human rights. Assertion is here made that, *where there are gaps in the LOAC, human rights laws and principles exist to help provide the proper standards and guidance for all relevant actors in armed conflict.* IHRL – especially as enshrined in "big picture" terms by the triad of the Universal Declaration of Human Rights (UDHR), and the two International Covenants (the International Covenant on Civil and Political Rights [ICCPR] and the International Covenant on Economic, Social and Cultural Rights [ICESCR]) – functions as *the normative net we need* to catch the relevant actors, and to prevent them from falling below a minimal standard of acceptable conduct in these fraught situations.[31]

More will be said, throughout the remainder of this chapter, on the conception of human rights here being proffered and endorsed. As a helpful quick orientation, though, consider this. Human rights are core entitlements we all have to those things we *both* vitally need as human beings *and* which we can reasonably demand from other people and the social institutions we share. Which things are these? As I have argued elsewhere,[32] the most important set of human rights objects are "the

[29] See also MARTEL, VICTORY, *passim*.

[30] And we'll see how deeply such policies are shot-through with principles derived from existing LOAC.

[31] A. MCBETH, *ET AL.*, THE INTERNATIONAL LAW OF HUMAN RIGHTS (Oxford: Oxford University Press, 2012); *Twenty-Five Human Rights Documents* (New York: Columbia University Center for the Study of Human Rights, 1995); and the superb www.bayefsky.com.

[32] B. OREND, HUMAN RIGHTS: CONCEPT AND CONTEXT (Peterborough, ON: Broadview Press, 2002); B. OREND, INTRODUCTION TO INTERNATIONAL STUDIES (Oxford: Oxford University Press, 2012), 248–76.

foundational five": 1) physical security (i.e., your very life and freedom from violent threats to it); 2) material subsistence; 3) personal freedom; 4) elemental equality (i.e., non-discrimination); and 5) social recognition as a person and rights-holder. These are the essential elements we all require to live minimally decent lives in the modern world – which is the very point of human rights themselves. Though the plethora of international human rights treaties enumerates dozens, scores, maybe even hundreds of specific rights objects, my own view is they all reduce to one, or some combination, of these foundational five.[33]

Human rights are, as James Nickel has said, "what we want, no matter what we want." Whatever else we want out of life – whatever goals we wish to pursue – we truly need what Alan Gewirth has labelled *the all-purpose means* of security, subsistence, freedom, etc., which are required to pursue any such goals in the first place. (Try becoming a software billionaire without your life; try becoming head of state without subsistence; indeed, try pursuing anything without the very freedom needed to do so.)[34] We each, therefore, have the most powerful reasons of self-interest to claim these foundational five objects *as* our most basic rights (to use Henry Shue's renowned term). Finally, and perhaps most famously, John Rawls – in his landmark *A Theory of Justice* – showed how even actors trapped in an "original," pre-social, condition behind "a veil of ignorance" radically stripping them of knowledge about their own endowments, preferences, and social position, would still (as a matter of bare, self-interested rational prudence) insist on having such all-purpose means of effective human action as are denoted by human rights.[35]

Though the idea of human rights originates in Western civilization, it is thought – by its supporters – to have *genuinely universal* appeal and application.[36] After all, who doesn't have goals and desires? And who doesn't want the objects needed to pursue such? And so we all want to

[33] Orend, Human Rights, 101–55; J. Donnelly, Universal Human Rights in Theory and Practice (Ithaca, NY: Cornell University Press, 2nd edition, 2002).

[34] J. Nickel, Making Sense of Human Rights (Berkeley, CA: University of California Press, 1987); A. Gewirth, Human Rights: Essays on Justification and Application (Chicago: University of Chicago Press, 1982).

[35] H. Shue, Basic Rights: Subsistence, Affluence and U.S. Foreign Policy (Princeton: Princeton University Press, 2nd edition, 1996); J. Rawls, A Theory of Justice (Cambridge, MA: Harvard University Press, 1971).

[36] Orend, Human Rights, 155–88. But see, too: A. Pollis & P. Schwab, Human Rights: Cultural and Ideological Perspectives (New York: Praeger, 1979); and R.P. Calude & B.H. Weston, eds. Human Rights in the World Community (Philadelphia, PA: Penn State University Press, 3rd edition, 2006).

claim security, subsistence, liberty, etc., for ourselves. But, why should we acknowledge and respect the human rights claims *of others*? Several strong reasons:

- Generally, as Jan Narveson says, *it's the prudent thing to do*, as one wants others to respect one's own rights claims (and, as they say, "what goes around comes around").[37]
- Also, as Rawls says, *it's the fair thing to do*: it's only fair that, if you get your human rights, others should get theirs, too.[38]
- There's an emerging, global, overwhelming social consensus in favor of human rights, as Michael Walzer has noted, and arguably as revealed in the huge number, and worldwide spread, of national, regional, and even global human rights treaties.[39]
- Since human rights are designed to protect what everyone vitally needs for a minimally good life, it follows that, to disrespect or violate someone's human rights is to do them serious harm. And every major civilization has it, as a foundational duty, not to inflict serious harm on other human beings. As Thomas Pogge concludes: *there's a powerful negative duty not to harm.*[40]
- Human rights aren't just about avoiding the bad but also about achieving the good. John Stuart Mill argued, long ago, that *respecting and realizing human rights will create a better world.*[41] And modern studies show, time and again, that both *objective* quality of life (e.g., life-span, income, health, educational attainment, etc.) and *subjective* quality of life satisfaction (i.e., personal happiness) are much higher, on average, in human rights–respecting societies versus that in those where human rights are not respected.[42]

[37] J. Narveson, Respecting Persons in Theory and Practice (New York: Rowman & Littlefield, 2002). See also D. Gauthier, Morals by Agreement (Oxford: Clarendon, 1986).

[38] Rawls, Theory of Justice, *passim*; Orend, International, 248–76; A. Iriye, *et al*, The Human Rights Revolution (Oxford: Oxford University Press, 2012).

[39] M. Walzer, Thick and Thin (Notre Dame, IN: Notre Dame University Press, 1994); D. Moeckli, International Human Rights Law (Oxford: Oxford University Press, 2nd edition, 2014); O. DeSchutter, International Human Rights Law (Cambridge: Cambridge University Press, 2010); D. Shelton, The Oxford Handbook of International Human Rights Law (Oxford: Oxford University Press, 2013).

[40] T. Pogge, Realizing Rawls (Ithaca, NY: Cornell University Press, 1989).

[41] John Stuart Mill, On Liberty (Indianapolis, IN: Hackett, 1978). *First published* 1859.

[42] C. Graham, Happiness Around the World (Oxford: Oxford University Press, 2009); M. Seligman, Authentic Happiness (New York: The Free Press, 2002).

This is the general vision of human rights values, drawing especially on the two core Covenants and the Universal Declaration, which ought to inform our construction of a *jus post bellum* doctrine, to be used as the basis for a new and needed Geneva Convention. Let's now consider the remaining element to draw upon in this regard: post-war policies which have had historical predominance.

5. The Two Traditional Models of Post-War Justice: Retribution vs. Rehabilitation

5.1. *Retribution*

According to the older retribution model, the basic aspects of a decent post-war peace are these (and, again, as an ideal theory it assumes that "the good side" won, and that the aggressive side lost)[43]:

- ***Public Peace Treaty.*** While it does not need to be nit-picky in detail, the basic elements of a peace agreement should be written down, and publicly proclaimed, so that: everyone's expectations are clear; everyone knows the war is over; and everyone has an idea of what the general framework of the new post-war era will be. (Sometimes, by contrast, back in medieval Europe, the most crucial parts of a peace treaty were often kept secret from the public.)[44]
- ***Exchange of Prisoners of War (POWs).*** At war's end, all sides need to exchange all the POWs from the armed conflict.[45]
- ***Apology from the Aggressor.*** The Aggressor in war, like the criminal in domestic society, needs to admit fault and guilt for causing the war by committing aggression. This may seem quaint and elemental yet it can be quite controversial. For example, Germany has offered many, and profuse, official apologies for WWII, and especially for The Holocaust. (Germany to this day still pays an annual reparations fee to Israel for the latter.) By contrast, Japan has been nowhere near as forthcoming with a meaningful, official apology for WWII (perhaps as a result of

[43] Because, indeed, justice would fail to be done otherwise; and we would thus no longer be speaking of post-war justice but, rather, of some version of "degrees of less bad." See Orend, Morality, 185–214.

[44] Perhaps no one insisted on this publicity requirement more than I. Kant, in his landmark On Perpetual Peace, first published in 1795. Kant may well have been the very first theorist of *jus post bellum*. See: I. Kant, On Perpetual Peace, edited by B. Orend and translated by I. Johnston (Peterborough, ON: Broadview Press, 2015).

[45] S. Scheipers, ed. Prisoner in War (Oxford: Oxford University Press, 2010).

suffering the atomic bombings of Hiroshima and Nagasaki?). This reticence enrages China, in particular, which suffered mightily from Japanese aggression and expansion in the 1930s.[46]

- ***Aggressor to give up any war gains.*** The thinking here is that the Aggressor, as the wrong-doer, cannot be rewarded for its aggression and be allowed to keep any gains it may have won for itself during its aggression. For instance, during its initial campaign in 1992–94, the Serb side of the Bosnian Civil War initially conquered 70% of Bosnia: way beyond the area traditionally occupied by ethnic Serbs. More dramatically, during the Blitzkrieg of 1939–40, Hitler's Germany conquered Austria, Czechoslovakia, France, Poland, and the Scandinavian countries. This principle requires that, at war's end, the Aggressor give back all such unjust gains.[47]
- ***Aggressor must be demilitarized to avoid a repeat.*** Since the Aggressor broke international trust, so to speak, by committing aggression, it *cannot* be trusted *not* to commit aggression again (at least in the short-term, and in the absence of regime change there). The international community is entitled to some added security. The tools the Aggressor has to commit aggression must thus be taken away from it, in a process known as demilitarization. This is to say that, often, defeated aggressors lose many of their military assets and weapons capabilities, and have "caps" placed on their ability to re-build their armed forces over time.[48]
- ***War Crimes Trials for those Responsible.*** The world's first post-war international war crimes trials were held after WWII, in 1945–46, in both Nuremberg and Tokyo. The vast majority of those tried were soldiers and officers charged with *jus in bello* violations, like torturing POWs and deliberately targeting civilians. But a handful of senior Nazis were also charged with the *jus ad bellum* violation of "committing crimes against peace," i.e., of launching an aggressive war. In 1998, the international community passed the Treaty of Rome, creating the

[46] J. Keegan, The Second World War (New York: Vintage, 1990). See also: A. MacLachlan, "*Government Apologies to Indigenous Peoples*" *in* A. MacLachlan & A. Speight, eds. Justice, Responsibility and Reconciliation in the Wake of Conflict (Dordrecht: Springer, 2013), 183–204; L. Radzik, Making Amends (Oxford: Oxford University Press, 2009).

[47] Orend, International, 186–212. See also: R. Chambers, *et al.*, eds., Philosophical Foundations of the Law of Unjust Enrichment (Oxford: Oxford University Press, 2009).

[48] D. Cummings, Demilitarization (London: Biblioscholar, 2012).

world's first *permanent* international war crimes tribunal. Situated mainly at The Hague, in Holland, its ambitious mandate is to prosecute *all* war crimes, committed by *all* sides in *all* wars, and to do so using lawyers and judges from countries which were *not* part of the war in question. Recently, this new court has heard many cases from the Bosnian civil war and from various African wars. It has even put on trial former heads-of-state, and not just ordinary soldiers: Slobodan Milosevic of Serbia (until his death while in custody in 2006); and Jean Kambanda, the former prime minister of Rwanda during the 1994 genocide.[49]

Most post-war experts, including rehabilitation theorists, endorse the aforementioned six principles.[50] *They might even be said to form a minimal, thin, or overlapping consensus between the two historically dominant theories.* (This important point will be re-examined later, in the chapter's conclusion.) But beyond this point, consensus breaks down, and a truly sharp division emerges between the models of retribution and rehabilitation. The core intuition behind retribution theory is that *the defeated Aggressor must be rendered worse-off than prior to the start of the war.* This is thought to be required for proper punishment, and the elemental demands of justice. Why must there be punishment at all? Why can't we just cancel Aggressor's unjust war gains, and then "live and let live"? Three reasons are articulated by retribution theorists, such as Robert Nozick. First, there's the obvious – yet powerful – reason of *deterrence*. Punishing past aggression deters future aggression, or at least does so more than if we had no punishment at all. No punishment seems a lax policy which actually invites future aggression. Secondly, it's thought that proper punishment can be *an effective spur to atonement and change* on the part of Aggressor (since presumably it doesn't want to suffer through such punitive measures again). Finally, and most powerfully, *failing to punish the Aggressor degrades and disrespects the worth,*

[49] J. Persico, Nuremburg (New York: Penguin, 1995); T. Maya, Judgment at Tokyo (Lexington, KY: University of Kentucky Press, 2001); W. Schabas, An Introduction to the International Criminal Court (Cambridge: Cambridge University Press, 2011); V. Peskin, International Justice in Rwanda and The Balkans (Cambridge: Cambridge University Press, 2008); R. Steinberg, Assessing the Legacy of the ICTY (London: Brill Academic, 2011); G. Gahima, Transitional Justice in Rwanda (London: Routledge, 2012).

[50] L. May & A. Forcehimes, eds. Morality, Jus Post Bellum and International Law (Cambridge: Cambridge University Press, 2012); L. May, After War Ends: A Philosophical Perspective (Cambridge: Cambridge University Press, 2012).

status, and suffering of the victim. Thus, it's not enough merely to take away the unjust gains of Aggressor, and force it to apologize publicly. It must suffer some retribution as a matter of balance and fairness. This is the same reasoning which explains and articulates criminal punishment in domestic society: if someone, e.g., has stolen something, we don't just make him give it back, and apologize to his victim: we make him suffer further – make him worse-off than prior to his deed – for instance by making him pay a fine, or spending some time in jail.[51]

So, how do retribution theorists recommend that we should make the defeated Aggressor worse-off than prior to the war? Demilitarization, as discussed earlier: yes. War crimes trials for those individuals complicit in aggression: absolutely. But two further things get advocated by retribution theorists: 1) a backward-looking system of compensation payments, from Aggressor to Victim(s); and 2) a forward-looking system of sanctions, placed by Victim and the international community on Aggressor. The goal of the first is to offer some amendment to Victim, to help it pay for its costs incurred during the fight for its rights. The second is to hamper, deliberately, the economic growth of Aggressor moving forward, as a kind of fine for, and lesson about, the commission of aggression.

The final distinctive aspect of the model of retribution – which may or may not be an expression of this desire to render the defeated Aggressor worse-off – is a refusal to aid or assist the defeated country with regime change. The defeated regime is left in place, and the winning country, and/or allies, exit the defeated Aggressor as soon as they have firmly set into place the measures of post-war punishment.[52]

5.1.2: Two Historical Examples of Retribution, Leading to Its Pros and Cons

The two clearest examples of the retribution model in action, in modern times, are the end of World War I (1918–19), and the end of the Persian Gulf War of 1991. The Treaty of Versailles ended World War I (1914–18), and is widely deemed to be a controversial failure which in a clear sense contributed to the conditions sparking World War II. The First World War had been a disaster for perhaps all belligerents except the USA. It cost way more, and lasted so much longer, than anyone had predicted and,

[51] R. Nozick, Anarchy, State and Utopia (Cambridge, MA: Harvard University Press, 1974). See also: H. Wallace & C. Robertson, Principles of Criminal Law (Englewood Cliffs, NJ: Prentice Hall, 5th ed, 2011).

[52] Orend, Morality, 185–214.

indeed, it only came to an end, and with victory for the Allied side, when America intervened in 1917. Because of all the cost and misery, the European powers were determined to punish Germany for invading Belgium and sparking the war to begin with. So Germany was extensively demilitarized, had all its war gains taken away and, furthermore, lost some valuable territory of its own as one aspect of punishment. Crushing reparations payments were levied upon Germany, and they would have lasted into the 1980s (!) had the peace terms stuck. But they didn't, because essentially these fines bankrupted Germany within only a few years, causing massive economic dislocation, hardship and, eventually, civil unrest. The victorious powers also tried to force elections upon Germany, but the only result was that the people there came to associate democracy with the huge economic problems, and they began to turn to radical, non-democratic parties promising simple solutions in a time of complex crisis. Hitler was thus able to come to power; he stopped all reparations payments; he cancelled all elections and named himself the dictator; and he re-built the German war machine - growing the economy - and promised to get all the lost lands back. He did, or tried to, thus sparking World War II.[53]

The 1991 Treaty ending the Persian Gulf War - triggered by Iraq's aggressive invasion of Kuwait in 1990 - was similarly punitive and also paved the way for a second war. The treaty called upon Saddam's Iraq to give up any claims on Kuwait, officially apologize for the aggression, and surrender all POWs. Saddam was left in power, though, and no attempt was made either to change the regime or to bring anyone to trial on war crimes charges. But Iraq *was* to be extensively demilitarized. It lost many weapons, and had strict caps put on any re-building. Iraq had No-Fly-Zones (NFZs) imposed on it, both in the north (to protect the Kurds in Iraq from Saddam) and in the south (to protect the Shi'ites). Saddam also had to agree to a rigorous, and U.N.-sponsored, weapons inspections process. This process lasted from 1991–98, and it found and destroyed literally tons of illegal weapons, including chemical and biological agents. After Saddam kicked out the inspectors in 1998, this issue grew into a major factor in favor of war in 2003, as the Americans suspected Saddam still had WMDs and, moreover, was plotting to give some to al-Qaeda to enable another 9/11-style terrorist strike on America. Finally, and financially, Iraq had to pay reparations to Kuwait for the aggressive invasion in

[53] MACMILLAN, PARIS 1919; J. KEEGAN, THE FIRST WORLD WAR (New York: Vintage, 1994); KEEGAN, SECOND, *passim*.

1990 and, moreover, had to suffer continuing sweeping sanctions on its economy, especially on its ability to sell oil. These sanctions devastated Iraqi civilians and did very little to hurt Saddam. There is, in fact, evidence that the sanctions only cemented Saddam's grip on Iraq, as increasingly impoverished citizens grew more and more dependent on favors from Saddam's government in order to survive.[54]

Considering these illustrative historical examples, and reflecting on both the human rights, and other LOAC principles described previously, one can arrive at the following meaningful comparison of the retributive policy's general pros and cons:

Pros: It's simple and straightforward; it's the historical norm (and there may be some value in long-standing habitual practice); there's no messing around with complex, costly, and controversial regime change and post-war reconstruction; and, if one believes that justice requires retribution as a matter of principle, then one is going to be deeply moved by retribution's claims.

Cons: It can seem like angry revenge and not balanced justice; the reparations and sanctions very often wind up hurting innocent civilians, and thus violate the established *jus in bello* principle of discrimination/non-combatant immunity; and, in historical cases where retribution has been employed, there often has been imperfect – or even quite shoddy – results (i.e., the revenge creates bad feelings and new generations of enemies, and the aggressive regime is left in place, combining together over time to produce – rather regularly – a second war). This negates any supposed "savings" of not trying to rehabilitate the decrepit regime.[55]

Thus, there are strong grounds for concluding that the retribution model – beyond the most basic six tenets mentioned first earlier, such as publicity and war crimes trials for criminals – is *not consistent* with the background norms of existing LOAC or IHRL, in particular the principles of discrimination/non-combatant immunity and then the threats to subsistence and security which have been produced, causally, by practices integral to the retribution model, namely the compensations and sanctions regimes. Indeed, by intentionally leaving in place an

[54] L. Freeman and E. Karsh, eds. The Gulf Conflict, 1990–91 (Princeton: Princeton University Press, 1993); G. Simons, The Scourging of Iraq (New York: Macmillan, 2nd edition, 1996).

[55] For more, see Orend, Morality, 185–248.

aggressive regime – regimes very often as complicit in domestic rights-violation as they are in international aggression[56] – the retribution policy reveals itself to be, very broadly and to say the least, *insensitive to all the human rights claims* of the ordinary civilians left in the defeated country.

5.2. *Rehabilitation*

If the overall goal of the model of retribution is to make the defeated Aggressor *worse-off* than prior to the war, the overall goal of rehabilitation is to make the defeated Aggressor *better-off* than prior to the war. Where the models differ specifically is over three major issues. First, the rehabilitation model *generally rejects sanctions*, especially on grounds that they have been shown, historically, to harm civilians and thus to violate discrimination/non-combatant immunity.[57] Second, the rehabilitation model *rejects compensation payments*, for the same reason. In fact, the model favors *investing in* a defeated Aggressor, to help it re-build and to help smooth over the wounds of war.[58] Finally, the rehabilitation model *favors forcing regime change* in the defeated Aggressor whereas the retribution model views that as too risky and costly. That it may be, but those who favor the rehabilitative model suggest that it can be worth it over the long-term, leading to the creation of a new, better, non-aggressive – even progressive – member of the international community.[59] To those who scoff that such deep-rooted transformation simply can't be done, supporters of the rehabilitative model reply that, not only *can* it be done, it *has* been done. The two leading examples are West Germany and Japan after World War II.

5.2.1. Two Historical Cases

The Allies, genuinely working with nationals in both countries – more so in Germany than Japan, perhaps – first undertook a purging process, which in Germany came to be known as "de-nazi-fication." All signs,

[56] Orend, Morality, 215–50; J. Glover, Humanity: A Moral History of the 20th Century (New Haven, CT: Yale University Press, 2001).

[57] G.C. Hufbauer, *et al.*, Economic Sanctions Reconsidered (Washington, DC: The Petersen Institute, 3rd edition, 2009).

[58] J. Miller and R. Kumar, Reparations: Interdisciplinary Inquiries (Oxford: Oxford University Press, 2007).

[59] J. Mertus and J. Helsing, eds. Human Rights and Conflict: Exploring the Links between Rights, Law and Peacebuilding (Washington, DC: United States Institute of Peace, 2006).

symbols, buildings, literature, and things directly associated with the Nazis were destroyed utterly. The Nazi party itself was abolished and declared illegal. Surviving ex-Nazis – but not all of them[60] – were put on trial, put in jail, or otherwise punished and prohibited from political participation. The militaries of both Germany and Japan were utterly disbanded, and for years the Allied military became *the* military, and the direct ruler, of both Germany and Japan.

After the negative purging process, the Allies in both countries established written constitutions or "Basic Law." These constitutions, after the period of direct military rule ended, provided for bills and charters of human rights, eventual democratic elections, and – above all – the checks and balances so prominently featured in the American system. Since government had grown so huge and tyrannical in both Germany and Japan in the 1930s, it had to be shrunk down, and then broken into pieces, with each piece only authorized to handle its own business. Independent judiciaries and completely reconstituted police forces were an important part of this – and they went a long way to re-establishing the *impersonal* rule of law over the *personal* whims of former fascists. The executive branches, much more so than in the American system, were made more accountable to, and closely tied to, the legislative branch. The goal, of course, was to ensure that the executive couldn't grow into another dictator. By design, there were to be no strong presidents. So Germany and Japan became true *parliamentary* democracies, more in the European than American style.

Western-style liberal democracy was not the only change forcibly implemented. The education systems of both Germany and Japan were overhauled, since they played huge propaganda roles for both regimes and the content of their curricula had been filled with racism, ultra-nationalism, and distorted ignorance of the outside world. Western experts re-designed these systems to impart concrete skills needed to participate in reconstruction, as well as to stress a more objective content favoring the basic cognitive functions ("the three Rs") as well as critical thinking and especially science and technology. The curricula were radically stripped of political content (though, of course, some lessons on the new social institutions and their principles were required).

The Americans quickly saw that their sweeping legal, constitutional, social, and educational reforms would lack stability unless they could

[60] Some especially useful ex-Nazis were provided safe havens in the West, particularly those who were working on Hitler's rocket program.

stimulate the German and Japanese economies. The people needed their vital needs met, as well as a sense of hope that, concretely, the future would get better. Otherwise, they might revolt, and the reforms fail. Instead of making the (World War I) mistake of *sucking money out* of these ruined countries through mandatory reparations payments, the Americans were the ones *who poured money into* Germany and Japan. America shunned the retribution paradigm and embraced the rehabilitative one. It was a staggering sum of money, too, channeled through the so-called "Marshall Plan." Money was needed to buy essentials, as well as to clear away all the rubble and ruined infrastructure. It was also just needed to circulate, to get the Germans and Japanese used to free market trading. Jobs were plentiful, as entire systems of infrastructure – transportation, water, sewage, electricity, agriculture, finance – had to be rebuilt. Since jobs paid wages, thanks to the Marshall Plan, the people's lives improved and the free market system deepened. But it wasn't just the money. American management experts poured into Germany and Japan, showing them the very latest, and most efficient, means of production. By the 1980s, (West) Germany and Japan had not only rebounded economically, they had the two strongest economies in the world after America itself, based especially on quality high-tech manufacturing, for instance of automobiles. These economic strengths endure today (though other economies, e.g., China, are now thought to be larger).

The post-war reconstructions of Germany and Japan easily count as the most impressive post-war rehabilitations in modern history; rivaled perhaps only by America's re-building of its own South after The Civil War (1861–65). Germany and Japan, today, have massive free market economies, and politically remain peaceful, stable, and decent democracies. They are both very good citizens on the global stage. In addition, these countries are by no means "clones" (much less colonies) of America: they each have gone their own way, adding local color, and pursuing political paths quite distinct from those that most interest the United States – consider especially Germany's formative role in the European Union. So we have clear evidence that even massive and forcible post-war changes need *not* threaten "a nation's character," or what makes it unique and special to its people. But such success *did* come at a huge cost in terms of time and treasure: it cost trillions of dollars; took trillions of "man-hours" in work and expertise; it took decades of real time; it took the co-operation of most of the German and Japanese people; and, above all, it took the will of the United States to see it through. It was American money, American security, American know-how, American patience, and American generosity which brought it all into being. Such is the magnitude of commitment needed by any party bent on successfully implementing substantial post-war rehabilitation.[61]

Now, these are not the only historical cases of forcible post-war reconstruction. Nor are they the most recent: Afghanistan, post-2001, and Iraq, post-2003, also readily leap to mind. And these two more recent cases do *not* leap to mind in such a successful way as do the reconstructions of Germany and Japan over fifty years ago. The imperfections of, and difficulties with, these more recent cases do indeed need to be addressed, and will be in the forthcoming sections. For now, a reminder that what we are most centrally looking for is lessons from: a) historical best practices; about b) what has worked as a post-war policy respectful of the background norms of the LOAC and the IHRL; and c) which has been shown to be capable, when successful, of generating substantial and happy consequences for those societies. Thus, the emphasis here on the earlier, rather than those later, cases – as the former are more helpful guides to the ideal principles than the latter.

5.2.2. Ends and Means

The ideal goal of justified post-war regime change is the timely construction of a minimally just political community. Drawing on the IHRL, and the LOAC (and international law more broadly), it seems reasonable to contend that such a community makes every reasonable effort to: 1) avoid violating the rights of other minimally just communities (especially by not aggressing against them); 2) gain recognition as being legitimate in the eyes of the international community and its own people; and 3) realize the human rights of all its individual members.[62] The ideal

[61] L.V. Segal, Fighting to the Finish: The Politics of War Termination in America and Japan (Ithaca: Cornell University Press, 1989); H. Schonberger, Aftermath of War: Americans and The Remaking of Japan (Ohio: Kent State University Press, 1989); M. Schaller, The American Occupation of Japan (Oxford: Oxford University Press, 1987); and E. Davidson, The Death and Life of Germany: An Account of the American Occupation (St. Louis: University of Missouri Press, 1999).

[62] Orend, Human Rights, 15–36; Orend, Morality, 37–43; B. Roth, Governmental Illegitimacy in International Law (Oxford: Oxford University Press, 2001); A. Buchanan, Human Rights, Legitimacy and The Use of Force (Oxford: Oxford University Press, 2010); T. Buergenthal & H. Maier, Public International Law (St. Paul, MN: West Legal Press, 1990); S. Besson & J. Tasioulas, The Philosophy of International Law (Oxford: Oxford University Press, 2010).

of a human rights-respecting, minimally just political community is a justified one to pursue because, as suggested earlier in Section 4:

- It is in every individual's self-interest;
- It respects everyone's potential for autonomy and self-direction;
- It thus has universal appeal;
- It already enjoys very strong international consensus, both morally and legally;
- It is based on thin, reasonable, and accessible values like living a minimally good life;
- It generates good consequences, especially in terms of average quality of life; and
- It promotes long-term international peace and stability.[63]

It is these values – their strength and moral resonance – which ground, for rehabilitators, regime-changing measures in a post-war environment. These are not extreme, narrow, "Crusading," or "imperialistic" values; they are modest, secular, widely accepted, and based on appeal *to the first principle* of respecting individual human rights as well as *to after-the-fact considerations* of generating concrete beneficial consequences for everyone. But how to achieve this goal?

According to sound empirical research analyzing the majority of historical cases since 1865,[64] the core blueprint for transforming defeated, rights-violating aggressor regimes into minimally just societies is something like what follows. (And comparative references will here be made to contemporary Afghanistan and Iraq, showing where, perhaps, some of the difficulties may have originated.)

- ***Adhere diligently to the LOAC during the regime take-down and occupation.*** This is morally vital for its own sake, as well as to help win the hearts and minds of the locals. (America, of course, ran afoul

[63] M. Doyle, Liberal Peace (New York: Routledge, 2011); M. Brown, ed., Debating the Democratic Peace (Cambridge, MA: MIT Press, 1996).

[64] J. Dobbins, *et al.*, America's Role in Nation-Building: From Germany to Iraq (Santa Monica, CA; RAND, 2003); J. Dobbins, *et al.*, The United Nations' Role in Nation-Building: From Congo to Iraq (Santa Monica, CA: RAND, 2005); J. Dobbins, *et al.*, Europe's Role in Nation-Building: From The Balkans to Congo (Santa Monica, CA: RAND, 2008); J. Dobbins, *et al.*, The Beginner's Guide to Nation-Building (Santa Monica, CA; RAND, 2009); R.S. Jennings, The Road Ahead (Washington, DC: United States Institute of Peace, 2003); & A. Donini, ed. Nation-Building Unravelled? (New York: International Peace Academy, 2004).

of this principle in Iraq, owing to the prisoner abuse scandal at the Abu-Ghraib prison.[65])

- ***Purge much of the old regime, and prosecute its war criminals.*** Much, but not necessarily all. Clearly, anyone materially connected to aggression, tyranny, or atrocity cannot be permitted a substantial role in the new order. They've lost the right to govern. But others – say, middle-ranking civil servants – might be kept on for their local knowledge and bureaucratic expertise. There always needs to be some continuity, even in the face of a sea-change in institutions.[66]
- ***Disarm and demilitarize the society.*** The target military does need to be disarmed and demobilized – but then something needs to be done with them. (Many critics of the American occupation of Iraq from 2003–2011 argue that a key decision which helped spark the insurgency was the U.S. choice in mid-2003 to promptly disband the 400,000 strong Iraqi army… and then leave them to their own devices. Plans for employing these potentially dangerous men, providing them opportunity, should have been developed.[67] A related problem, in Afghanistan, is that it has always been a highly weaponized society, with most adult males having their own guns. Many groups – some organized into drug cartels, others into radical religious and political factions – thus have always retained formidable weaponry which has posed serious and on-going challenges to securing peace and stability in post-2001 Afghanistan.[68])
- ***Provide effective military and police security for the whole country.*** Most experts suggest a two-stage approach here: the successful "attack and overthrow" war divisions be replaced by other divisions *specifically trained* in post-combat peace-keeping and nation-building.

[65] M. Danner, Torture and Truth: America, Abu Ghraib and The War on Terror (New York: New York Review of Books, 2004).

[66] F. Fukuyama, State-building: Governance and World Order in the 21st Century (Ithaca: Cornell University Press, 2004).

[67] R. Scarborough, Rumsfeld's War (New York: Regnery, 2004); U.S. Special Inspector General, Hard Lessons: The Iraq Reconstruction Experience (Washington, DC: US Independent Agencies and Commissions, 2009); M. Lamani & B. Momani, From Desolation to Reconstruction: Iraq's Troubled Journey (Waterloo, ON: CIGI, 2010).

[68] U.S. Government, Afghanistan Reconstruction (Washington, DC: Bibliogov, 2011); M. Tondini, Statebuilding and Justice Reform: Post-Conflict Reconstruction in Afghanistan (New York: Routledge, 2010); D. Zakheim, A Vulcan's Tale: How the Bush Administration Mismanaged the Reconstruction of Afghanistan (Washington, DC: Brookings Institute, 2011).

The transition should be as seamless as possible, and the ratios are crucial. *The nation-building research shows you need about 20 soldiers per 1,000 residents to stabilize and secure post-war populations.* (Incidentally, both the Afghanistan and Iraq occupation forces were always well short of this ratio.) The moral is to go in big, with plenty of "boots on the ground," boots tutored in what The Pentagon labels "stability operations." Show the locals strong – not hesitant – intentions to protect them and to provide a secure back-drop for the development of law and legitimacy.[69]

- ***Work with a cross-section of locals on a new, rights-respecting constitution which features checks and balances.*** Limited government is required to prevent re-growth of tyranny; legitimate government is needed both for moral fitness and for stability. The picture here is of a genuine political partnership between the war-winner and the local civilian population. The facts show that *the meaningful participation and support of both is absolutely necessary*, and usually more extensive international participation is desirable as well. Constitution-making is a process, and so we can't rationally expect perfection or closure the first time out. Even the most developed societies occasionally change their constitutions and/or take several tries before creating a workable one in the first place. So while the post-war atmosphere is pressured, and there's a desire to rapidly end foreign occupation, some patience is required on the part of everyone. Good things often take time. In terms of inclusion in the constitution-building process, Andrew Arato reminds us that every group must be included: 1) whose non-participation could ruin any subsequent arrangement; and 2) who is committed to the creation of a minimally just state. If these two conditions are met, all relevant groups – as guided by the war-winner – are to develop an inclusive framework for limited, accountable, and rights-respecting government.[70]

In this regard, and to their credit, the Americans and other allies did struggle mightily during both recent occupations to engage in constitution-making, including the holding of several democratic elections to

[69] J. Traub, "*Making Sense of the Mission*", New York Times Magazine (April 11, 2004), 36; R. Paris, The Dilemmas of Statebuilding (New York: Routledge, 2009); A. Ghani and C. Lockhart, Fixing Failed States (Oxford: Oxford University Press, 2009).

[70] A. Arato, "*Constitution-Making in Iraq*", Dissent (Spring, 2004) 32–6; A. Arato, Civil Society, Constitution and Legitimacy (Lanham, MD: Rowman Littlefield, 2000); C. Zelizer, Integrated Peacebuilding (Boulder, CO: Westview, 2013).

ratify such changes. It's unclear, however, whether such changes will "stick," or rather have already become unglued: particularly in Iraq, where recent local governments have failed to include crucial ethnic and religious groups, and where outsiders – such as the radical Islamic State group ISIS – have carved out huge chunks of northern Iraqi territory for themselves and, as of writing, both seem to have effective power in such lands and also seem to have the potential to draw the United States back into Iraq, in some fashion (if only to weaken ISIS via air-bombing).[71]

- ***Allow other, non-state associations, or "civil society," to flourish.*** Civil society associations refer to all groupings which don't involve the state. They range from chambers of commerce to little league sports associations, and from volunteer charities to online social media groups. Research stresses how important such associations are, not only to enjoyment of life but also to people's commitment to their society. These groupings connect people to each other, provide satisfaction, and promote non-political aspects of life. They serve to take pressure off the state (by providing diverse outlets for energy), they help to legitimize the society (by increasing participation and happiness), and they also indirectly limit state power (by showing there's more to life than politics). It's always the mark of a tyrannical government when there is little activity within civil society. Robust civil societies are thus an important ingredient in creating mature, legitimate social conditions. (There's no denying that, in both Afghanistan and Iraq, there has been some success in this regard in the past twelve years, compared to the next-to-no civil society allowed at all, by either The Taliban, or Saddam, in those two countries prior to that.)[72]
- ***Forego compensation and sanctions in favor of investing in and rebuilding the economy.*** Many modern peace arrangements – notably the Treaty of Versailles and the terms ending the Persian Gulf War, discussed earlier—unraveled, or created perverse consequences, when they included hefty compensation terms and sweeping sanctions. Punitive settlements do not seem to work, in that sense. The goal of proper regime change is the creation of a stable, minimally just social

[71] See Notes 67 and 68 for more on the attempts at constitutional re-making in Iraq and Afghanistan.

[72] M. Edwards, Civil Society (London: Polity, 2nd edition, 2009); R. Putnam, Bowling Alone (New York: Simon Schuster, 2000).

condition. This is difficult enough as it is; trying to achieve it while sucking resources *out* of the target country becomes nigh impossible. (Thankfully, in Iraq in 2003, the old punitive sanctions were dropped, and investment started to flow in. This need for funds is a strong argument for including international partners in reconstruction. Realistically speaking, though, such partners will probably volunteer their resources only if they believe the war was justified to begin with. There has been a similar attempt to invest in Afghanistan, but in both cases the political instability, and long-term challenges with creating good pro-business infrastructure, have prevented such investment from being what it could have been – and certainly, in neither case, anything anywhere near approaching something like the Marshall Plan.)[73]

- ***If necessary, re-vamp educational curricula to purge past propaganda and cement new values.*** The fascists in the 1930s used school systems to warp future citizens so that they would subscribe to highly destructive doctrines of racial and national supremacy, with the flip-side being hatred and aggression against "Others." In Afghanistan under the Taliban, and elsewhere still in the Middle East, great controversy attaches to the teaching of Islamic extremism and its attitudes toward violence, Israel, the West, and women in particular. Much development research powerfully shows the beneficial effects of massive commitment to the education of girls and women. Indeed, some have even pronounced this one of the few "silver bullets" in development, which correlates very strongly with such other desirable social outcomes as economic growth, higher life expectancy, lower crime rates, and internal political stability. (There has been some progress on this in Afghanistan, at least relative to what education existed for females under The Taliban.)[74]
- ***Ensure that the benefits of the new order will be: 1) concrete; and 2) widely, not narrowly, distributed.*** As Michael Walzer says, you've got to increase *everyone's* stake in the new, developing order. In particular, you must avoid a situation where it seems that the foreign occupier is favoring one group above the rest, giving that group most of the power. That group will soon be marked as traitors and foreign agents, and will lose legitimacy and popular support. This was frequently the case during

[73] See Notes 67 & 68.

[74] M. Nussbaum, Women and Human Development: The Capabilities Approach (Chicago: University of Chicago Press, 2001); P. Haslam, *et al.*, eds., Introduction to International Development (Oxford: Oxford University Press, 2008).

the European colonial era – particularly with France and Belgium – when the colonizer would select an elite group to rule, creating bitter ethnic and communal rivalries which persist today. The reconstructions of Germany and Japan showed, by contrast, that there must be widespread concrete benefits distributed throughout the population to make reconstruction work. Political things like getting to vote and run for office where you couldn't before; civic things like having your daughter go to school where before she couldn't, social things like starting up reading clubs where they used to be banned; and, above all, economic things like an average rise in living standards within a reasonable time.[75]

- ***Follow an orderly, not-too-hasty exit strategy when the new regime can stand on its own two feet.*** This requires walking a fine line. On the one hand, the foreign occupier can't stay forever – for that's conquest, not reconstruction. The locals must see that occupation will come to an end and they will return to full sovereignty. This knowledge should diffuse some tension. On the other hand, if you're going to do something as important as post-war rehabilitation, you should try to do it well. Plus *there's a moral responsibility not to "cut and run."* A botched reconstruction benefits no one, including impatient locals.

This ten-point recipe for reconstruction is only a general blueprint; clearly, in particular cases, some things will need to be emphasized over others. The best recipes always allow for individual variance and input, depending on time and the ingredients at hand. We should also note the heavy interconnectedness of many of these elements. U.S. Major-General William Nash is probably only exaggerating a bit when he declares: "The first rule of nation-building is that everything is related to everything, and it's all political."[76] We also have noted, throughout this section, the degree of difference between what the ideal recipe, employed during the German and Japanese cases, would call for – compared to what was sought after, and/or what has actually been achieved, in contemporary Afghanistan and Iraq. *It might thus be worth stressing how the sub-optimal results in the two current cases need not be thought to have critical implications for the rehabilitative approach in general, given this very real degree of difference.*[77] Yet it admittedly may, as we'll re-visit

[75] M. Walzer, Arguing About War (New Haven: Yale University Press, 2004), 164–5.
[76] W. Nash, quoted in Traub, "*Making Sense*," 35.
[77] J. Bridoux, American Foreign Policy and Post-War Reconstruction: Comparing Japan and Iraq (New York: Routledge, 2012).

below, have practical political implications for what state governments and general publics have appetites for, regarding the legislating of post-war requirements.

5.2.3. Completing the Rehabilitation vs. Retribution Comparison

This leads naturally into a summary of the pros and cons of the rehabilitation model, especially as contrasted with its main rival, retribution. The two main cons of rehabilitation are these: 1) it takes a ton of time, effort, and resources; and 2) there's controversy attaching to the imposition of values. (And, perhaps it should be noted how the more recent cases show that the ideal results aren't always achieved.) But the main pros of rehabilitation are as follows:

1) In historical cases where it has worked well, the rehabilitation model has been an amazing success, well beyond what the retribution model could ever have dreamed of achieving. (Indeed, in some historical cases, such as Germany, the rehabilitation model has been employed *to clean up the messes left behind* by the retribution model.)
2) The rehabilitation model does not leave behind rights-violating regimes which often serve as the causal agents of a second, and worse, war. The rehabilitation model does not leave the aggressive regime in place, nor does it trust that measures of punishment and/or containment will suffice to handle the issue of the bad regime. It views the bad, rights-violating regime as itself the main problem, and thus as needing tackling, through such rehabilitative measures as political therapy, defined previously.
3) Rehabilitation cannot be accused of creating a new generation of enemies, nor can it plausibly be seen as sowing the seeds of a second war. Clearly, this model is trying to help the people in the defeated Aggressor and, though complex emotions might be created by such actions, the desire for revenge is not typically one of them.
4) Against the accusation that rehabilitation involves the infliction of narrow or parochial values, contention has already been made that rehabilitation ought to be limited to the construction only of a minimally just state, one characterized by values which are neither parochial nor narrow nor harmful: the values underlying the structure of a minimally just society and otherwise endorsed by both the IHRL and the LOAC.

Altogether, this adds up to a compelling case, suggesting strongly that rehabilitation is a superior model of post-war justice, as compared with retribution.

6. Occupation Law?

Now, there is a body of international law referred to as "occupation law." It is quite dated, and experts on it, such as Simon Chesterman, Yoram Dinstein, and Eyal Benvenisti, disagree both about its utility and about whether – and/or to what extent – it is still actually in force.[78] But it does seem fair to say: a) given the resurgence of interest in the subject (no doubt owing to the cases of Iraq and Afghanistan, and perhaps related to the Arab-Israeli conflict, too); and b) the growing number of recent important publications on it,[79] that we ought at least briefly consider what occupation law has to share in this regard.

There is strong suggestion that the bulk of occupation law, if it is still in force, is not inconsistent with the previous argument – with perhaps the one exception of the issue of regime change. Occupation law, in summary terms for our purposes here, stipulates that

- Any foreign occupation be temporary
- The occupier may not engage in collective punishment (which would seem to rule out, or be at tension with, retribution – but not with war crimes trials)
- The principle of discrimination and non-combatant immunity must be respected by occupation forces (but. . .)
- The occupation forces do have the right to defend themselves from armed attack
- Occupation forces cannot engage in looting, and must respect the property of civilians
- The occupier has a duty to provide for basic civilian well-being, especially in connection with: a) public order and safety; and b) such

[78] S. Chesterman, "*Occupation as Liberation: International Humanitarian Law and Regime Change,*" Ethics and International Affairs (2004), 51–64; Y. Dinstein, The International Law of Belligerent Occupation (Leiden: Brill, 2009); E. Benvenisti, The International Law of Occupation (Oxford: Oxford University Press, 2nd edition, 2012).

[79] See also: M. Schmidtt and W. Von Heinegg, Detention and Occupation in International Humanitarian Law (London: Ashgate, 2012); and S. Talmon, Occupation of Iraq: The Governance of Occupied Territory in Contemporary International Law (Oxford: Hart, 2015).

vital needs as food and water, and such elemental infrastructure as water sanitation and sewage treatment. (This last, obviously, seems to mandate a general concern with the most basic aspects of rehabilitation.)

Now, there are many strident references in occupation law forbidding forcible regime change (and, indeed, even changing the law at all in a defeated society). And so, Chesterman observes, occupation law "provides little support for regime change" of the sort endorsed by the rehabilitation earlier theory.[80] These passages are undeniable. Yet it is unclear whether such passages get to speak for all of international law on this issue. After all, the U.N. Security Council has authorized recent regime-changing actions in Afghanistan, Cambodia, East Timor, Kosovo, and Libya. And these authorizations are much more recent than the dated passages of occupation law in question. Additionally, and importantly, what if the war causes the existing state structure to collapse? It seems irrational to suggest that the occupying power may not change such a condition of destroyed rubble: such change could only be for the better, would it not? And what about those cases of truly abhorrent regimes, like the Nazis or Khmer Rouge? The old ban on changing regimes seems predicated on a belief that the existing state structures don't have anything severely and irredeemably wrong with them. But we now know that's not always true. Cases like this have led some scholars to wonder aloud about the continued relevance of occupation law.[81]

So, for the purposes of this chapter, assertion is here made that *the bulk of occupation law is supportive of the general previous argument*: that retribution is a worse policy than rehabilitation; that occupation should be temporary and must respect civilians; and that there is even some kind of norm to help restore and secure such vitals of civilian well-being as security and subsistence.[82] Beyond that, occupation law should be seen

[80] Chesterman, "*Liberation*", 54.

[81] THE INTERNATIONAL COMMISSION ON INTERVENTION AND STATE SOVEREIGNTY, REPORT: THE RESPONSIBILITY TO PROTECT (Ottawa: International Development Research Centre, 2002); G. EVANS, THE RESPONSIBILITY TO PROTECT: ENDING MASS ATROCITY CRIMES ONCE AND FOR ALL (Washington, DC: Brookings Institute, 2009) A. BELLAMY, RESPONSIBILITY TO PROTECT (London: Polity, 2009); N. GVOSDEV, R2P: SOVEREIGNTY AND INTERVENTION AFTER LIBYA (London: World Politics Review, 2011).

[82] Though Jens Ohlin has pointed out that such norms, as stated within occupation law, seem "radically thin" and thus as only scratching the surface of what we now know about nation-building needs and post-war reconstruction requirements in today's world. And thus the other aspects of rehabilitation theory sketched in Section 5 – involving, say,

as – in the helpful phrase of Jens Ohlin – "under-broad" when it comes to legislating requirements for belligerents in post-war situations. In the first instance, not all wars end in belligerent occupation, and so we can see how the general principles of the IHRL, and broad mandates of rehabilitation policy, can speak to a much wider range of scenario than can occupation law. Further, there is this clear deficiency when it comes to the issue of regime change. On the one hand, we can see the conservative, national sovereignty-respecting intentions of the framers of occupation law, and support that as far as it goes. On the other, we can see how such strictures can just: a) fail to meet the factual requirements of the post-war situation (in cases where the state has, as matter of fact, fallen over the course of the war); and/or b) run afoul of deep human rights-based concerns about the nature of aggressive, illegitimate, and rights-violating regimes being allowed to remain in place when the post-war moment provides an effective opportunity for doing something constructive about them.

7. Summary and Conclusion

There is an important, big, and at least relative gap in the LOAC, and it deals with war termination. Relative to the outbreak of war, and conduct within war, the aftermath of war is substantially unregulated, and this is bad and ought to be remedied for a range of reasons. Filling in this gap is most plausibly done by drawing upon three established sources: the existing LOAC; the background principles of IHRL; and the historically dominant models of post-war policy. Sustained argument was made that, ideally, some version of the policy of rehabilitation should form the core of any new Geneva Convention, designed to fill in this gap and help to legislate proper endings of armed conflict. The goal of post-war rehabilitation should be the construction of a minimally just, human-rights respecting society; and historically proven means ("the rehabilitation recipe") for achieving such were mentioned and commended.

Realizing that recent cases, such as Afghanistan and Iraq, may have dampened short-term political appetites for imposing big legislative requirements of rehabilitation on war winners, we can nevertheless advocate that the overlapping consensus between retribution and rehabilitation might nevertheless still be a plausible and principled

education, financial investment, and support for civil society – must be considered, as well.

starting point for codifying post-war principles, and then leave the more bold and demanding aspects of rehabilitation for the best future time. Thus, a two-pronged summary:

1) At the least, and for reasons given, there should be a new Geneva Convention devoted exclusively to the proper endings of wars. It should include the following general principles, which over the centuries have attracted an over-lapping consensus:
   - Public terms of settlement
   - Mutual exchange of POWs
   - Aggressor to apologize
   - Aggressor to give up unjust gains
   - Aggressor to demilitarize
   - War crimes trials (*Jus ad Bellum* trials for Aggressor; *Jus in Bello* trials for all sides)
2) Once political appetites change, regarding willingness to require bolder aspects of rehabilitation, such a Geneva Convention should debate and consider the wisdom of requiring war-winners to aid in the reconstruction of a minimally just society, as defined earlier, and using the ten measures contained in "the rehabilitation recipe" as reliable means to get there.

Steps 1 and 2, together, draw upon plausible, principled, and well-established norms of conduct, and a conservative, and legally familiar, methodology of inferring from prior legislation, widely accepted background principles, and historical best practices. They would, if implemented, constitute clear progress toward remedying a harmful gap in international law.[83]

[83] Thanks to Jens Ohlin, and all the conference participants, for very helpful feedback on these ideas.

Index